The Pay Board's Progress

STUDIES IN WAGE-PRICE POLICY

The Pay Board's Progress
Wage Controls in Phase II

ARNOLD R. WEBER
DANIEL J. B. MITCHELL

THE BROOKINGS INSTITUTION
Washington, D.C.

Copyright © 1978 by
THE BROOKINGS INSTITUTION
1775 Massachusetts Avenue, N.W., Washington, D.C. 20036

Library of Congress Cataloging in Publication Data:

Weber, Arnold Robert.
  The Pay Board's progress.

  (Studies in wage-price policy)
  Includes bibliographical references and index.
  1. United States Pay Board.   I. Mitchell, Daniel
J. B., joint author.   II. Title.   III. Series.
HD4975.W38   339.5   77-91820
ISBN 0-8157-9266-2
ISBN 0-8157-9265-4 pbk.

9 8 7 6 5 4 3 2 1

Foreword

SINCE THE END of World War II most Western industrialized nations have engaged in intermittent experiments with wage-price policy, ranging from exhortations to abide by loosely defined guidelines to direct wage and price controls enforced by elaborate administrative mechanisms. The continuing interest in wage-price policy reflects the persistence of inflation as a national and international problem. To the extent that fiscal and monetary policies have been unable to contain inflation—for whatever reasons—governments have been increasingly disposed to set standards for, or to intervene directly in, private wage and price decisions.

U.S. wage-price policy has been articulated in one form or another since 1946. The broad historical record of this experience presented in an earlier (1975) Brookings book, *Exhortation and Controls: The Search for a Wage-Price Policy, 1945–1971*, edited by Craufurd D. Goodwin, confirms that the most extensive peacetime experiment in wage-price policy in the United States took place in the period 1971–74. In four different phases, the Nixon administration imposed a series of wage-price freezes, direct controls with explicit wage and price standards, and a less drastic program of voluntary compliance. The second phase was of special interest because it involved direct comprehensive control of prices and wages by two regulatory agencies: the Price Commission and the Pay Board. The work of the former has been evaluated by Robert F. Lanzillotti, Mary T. Hamilton, and R. Blaine Roberts in *Phase II in Review: The Price Commission Experience* (Brookings, 1975).

This volume is devoted to a summary and analysis of the activities of the Pay Board. As a tripartite agency consisting of representatives of business, labor, and the public, the board was the focus of controversy from its inception in October 1971 until its formal dissolution in early 1973. An examination of its record sheds light on both the efficacy of wage controls in themselves and the special problem of maintaining organizational arrangements that will support a system of wage regulation.

Arnold R. Weber and Daniel J. B. Mitchell wrote this study from the perspective not only of academic researchers but also of participant ob-

vii

servers. Weber, who is provost of Carnegie-Mellon University and dean of the Graduate School of Industrial Administration, was a public member of the Pay Board. Mitchell, now a senior fellow in the Brookings Economic Studies program on leave from the University of California at Los Angeles where he is professor of economics in the Graduate School of Management, served the board as chief economist. Thus their assessment of this particular stage of the experiment with U.S. wage-price policy reflects the pragmatism of those who had to apply theory to practice.

The authors dedicate this book to the memory of Kermit Gordon, who served as a public member of the Pay Board while he was also president of the Brookings Institution. His appointment to the board was his last major public service assignment before his untimely death in June 1976. During his distinguished career he was closely associated with efforts to develop what he called "social inventions" to resolve the dilemma of achieving price stability and full employment. Kermit Gordon would undoubtedly cast a skeptical eye on some of the judgments offered in this study, but it is equally certain that he relished the Pay Board's effort to define and promote the public interest.

Among former members of the staffs of the Pay Board and the Cost of Living Council whose assistance the authors acknowledge with gratitude are Millard Cass, Ross Azevedo, Jerome M. Staller, and Robert Kopp. Victor J. Sheifer and Joseph Talbot of the Bureau of Labor Statistics also aided in the collection and analysis of statistical data.

This volume is the fifth in the Brookings series of Studies in Wage-Price Policy. The manuscript was edited by Tadd Fisher and was checked for accuracy by Evelyn P. Fisher and Kathleen Kane. The index was prepared by Florence Robinson.

The views expressed here are those of the authors and should not be ascribed to the officers, trustees, or other staff members of the Brookings Institution.

BRUCE K. MAC LAURY
President

January 1978
Washington, D.C.

Contents

Text Tables

Appendix Tables

Abbreviations

AFL	American Federation of Labor
AFT	American Federation of Teachers
ARIMA	Autoregressive integrated moving average
BCOA	Bituminous Coal Operators Association
BCW	Bakery and Confectionery Workers' International Union of America
BLS	Bureau of Labor Statistics
BNA	Bureau of National Affairs, Inc.
BRS, Signalmen	Brotherhood of Railroad Signalmen
Carmen	Brotherhood of Railway Carmen of the United States and Canada
CIO	Congress of Industrial Organizations
CISC	Construction Industry Stabilization Committee
CLC	Cost of Living Council
Clothing Workers	Amalgamated Clothing Workers of America
CMA	Case Management and Analysis Office
COLA	Cost of living adjustment
CONASA	Council of North Atlantic Shipping Associations
CPI	Consumer price index
CWA, Communications Workers	Communications Workers of America
FMCS	Federal Mediation and Conciliation Service
GAI	Guaranteed annual income
Hotel and Restaurant Employees	Hotel and Restaurant Employees and Bartenders International Union
IAM, Machinists	International Association of Machinists and Aerospace Workers
IBEW	International Brotherhood of Electrical Workers
ILA	International Longshoremen's Association
ILWU	International Longshoremen's and Warehousemen's Union
IRS	Internal Revenue Service
IUE	International Union of Electrical, Radio, and Machine Workers
Ladies Garment Workers	International Ladies' Garment Workers' Union
LASH	Lighter aboard ship
Locomotive Engineers	Brotherhood of Locomotive Engineers

Maintenance of Way Employees	Brotherhood of Maintenance of Way Employees
MCBW	Amalgamated Meat Cutters and Butcher Workmen of North America
M&M	Mechanization and modernization
NLRB	National Labor Relations Board
NMB	National Mediation Board
NOSSA	New Orleans Steamship Association
Oil, Chemical, and Atomic Workers	Oil, Chemical and Atomic Workers International Union
OMB	Office of Management and Budget
PCOMP	Percentage change in private nonfarm compensation per man-hour (excluding required employer contributions for social insurance)
PMA	Pacific Maritime Association
PSTMAN	Percentage change in average hourly earnings in manufacturing (excluding overtime)
QBs	Qualified benefits
Railway Clerks	Brotherhood of Railway, Airline and Steamship Clerks, Freight Handlers, Express and Station Employees
Rubber Workers	United Rubber, Cork, Linoleum and Plastic Workers of America
SCME	American Federation of State, County and Municipal Employees
Steelworkers	United Steelworkers of America
Teamsters	International Brotherhood of Teamsters, Chauffeurs, Warehousemen and Helpers of America
Textile Workers	Textile Workers' Union of America
UAW, Auto Workers	International Union, United Automobile, Aerospace and Agricultural Implement Workers of America
UMW	United Mine Workers
UTU	United Transportation Union
WGMA	West Gulf Maritime Association

The Pay Board's Progress

And Phase I Begat Phase II

The imposition of a wage-price freeze on August 15, 1971, was the first step—Phase I—of an extended experiment with direct economic controls under peacetime conditions in the United States. From the outset the top policymakers in the Nixon administration knew that the freeze could be only a temporary measure. Its primary objective was to dampen expectations of rising prices by providing dramatic evidence of the government's resolve to vanquish inflation. This goal was to be achieved by the immediate, almost mechanical, suppression of all wage and price increases for a ninety-day period.[1] But the overriding operational objective of the freeze was to provide time to construct a durable system of economic controls that would permit adjustments in wages and prices that were consistent with considerations of equity and economic stability. Although the ninety-day freeze could be sustained by the public euphoria and support it engendered, detailed planning and widespread consultation with major interest groups were necessary before what was to be called Phase II could be launched. When the thaw commenced, the administration ardently hoped that it would enrich rather than engulf the economy.

Official concern about the rate of wage increases had been a significant consideration in the initial decision to impose direct controls. Throughout the summer of 1971 Congress had subjected the Nixon administration to a steady drumbeat of criticism for failing to contain inflation while the economy also endured a 6 percent unemployment rate. This slack in the labor market, however, did not appear to restrain union demands at the bargaining table. By the end of 1970 the average first-year increase in collective bargaining agreements exceeded 8 percent. In the first six months of 1971 the average first-year increase in wages and benefits in major bargaining settlements was 10.4 percent.[2] The settlement in the steel industry in mid-1971 called for an estimated 16 percent hike in total compensation during the first year.

1. For a description of the policies and administrative procedures used in the wage-price freeze of 1971, see Arnold R. Weber, *In Pursuit of Price Stability: The Wage-Price Freeze of 1971* (Brookings Institution, 1973), chaps. 3 and 7.
2. U.S. Department of Labor press release 71-416, July 29, 1971.

The general concern about collective bargaining developments rose to a high level of anxiety because of union wage movements in the construction industry. Beginning in late 1967 construction wages had experienced a sharp upsurge that was subsequently characterized as an "explosion." During 1970 the median first-year wage increase for collective bargaining agreements in construction was approximately 17 percent. For many observers, particularly in the business sector, construction wages were the fuse on an already unstable labor market situation that posed the threat of a classic wage-push inflationary spiral.

The perceived crisis in construction wages had precipitated the Nixon administration's first direct intervention in the process of wage determination. In March 1971 the administration issued an executive order establishing the Construction Industry Stabilization Committee (CISC) and giving it authority to modify collective bargaining agreements in that sector. The CISC was set up under the terms of the Economic Stabilization Act,[3] the same statute that was invoked to impose the freeze and the subsequent three phases of the controls program. Once this first step was taken, it was not surprising that wages were included in the comprehensive freeze of August 15. Although a variety of domestic and international factors prompted the decision to impose controls, wage pressure was also viewed as one of the culprits on the economic scene.

The procedural link between Phase I and Phase II of the economic stabilization program was created by the presidential executive order that imposed the freeze. Some attention was given to the shape of the post-freeze program on the weekend of August 13, 1971, when the freeze and the other measures designated as the New Economic Policy were planned. In fact, the specifications for a Phase II controls system had been incorporated in the original memorandum prepared by the Office of Management and Budget (OMB) at the direction of George P. Shultz. This blueprint was never given serious consideration, however, on the grounds that any plan for an ongoing system of controls was premature. Instead, public reaction to the freeze was to be determined before developing a fixed position. The ninety-day period would be used to formulate a set of detailed options and to canvass opinion both within and outside government.

3. Enacted August 15, 1970, as an amendment to the Defense Production Act (84 Stat. 799).

This commitment to prior consultation was included in the executive order that officially imposed the freeze.

The [Cost of Living] Council shall consult with representatives of agriculture, industry, labor, and the public concerning the development of policies, mechanisms, and procedures to maintain economic growth without inflationary increases in prices, rents, wages, and salaries.[4]

President Nixon reaffirmed this commitment to a public discussion of the economic stabilization program in his address to a joint session of Congress on September 9, 1971. At that time he also stated that the freeze would end as scheduled on November 13, 1971, and would be supplanted by a more refined system of controls.[5] The announcement that the freeze would be terminated on schedule was unequivocal—the freeze had been viewed as short-term shock therapy from the start—and it established a public deadline for the initiation of Phase II. Thus planning for Phase I went forward almost as soon as the basic regulations governing the wage-price freeze were dry.

Wages and Phase I: Setting the Mold

The design of a durable system of wage controls was conditioned by the policies enunciated during the freeze and by experience with these policies as the stabilization program evolved. In addition, administration officials recognized that relations with organized labor posed delicate questions of political strategy that might override otherwise meritorious economic and administrative considerations.

The freeze curtailed wage increases broadly and rigidly. Under the regulations promulgated by the Cost of Living Council (CLC), wages and salaries were defined to include virtually all forms of compensation that could be identified by the most compulsive personnel administrator.

"Wages and salaries" includes all forms of remuneration or inducement to employees by their employers, including but not limited to: vacation and holiday payments; bonuses; lay-off and supplemental unemployment insurance benefits; night shift, overtime, and other premiums; employer contributions to insurance, savings, or other welfare benefits; employer contributions to pension

4. Executive Order 11615, August 15, 1971, sec. 3(c).
5. "The President's Address to the Congress Delivered before a Joint Session of Congress, September 9, 1971," *Weekly Compilation of Presidential Documents,* vol. 7 (Government Printing Office, September 13, 1971), p. 1253.

or annuity funds, payments in kind, job perquisites, cost-of-living allowances,
. . . payments for deferred compensation, and all other fringe benefits.

In addition, there may be no changes in working conditions which result in
more pay per hour worked (for example, a schedule which shortens the work
week without a proportionate decrease in pay).[6]

The implementation of this provision was as stringent as the language
implied. As the freeze progressed, additional elements of compensation
that were not specifically included in the regulation, such as longevity
increases that provided for periodic wage increments based on length of
service, were proscribed. Similarly, when an employer offered to provide
his employees with interest-free loans during the freeze, this arrangement
was determined to be an "inducement" and therefore was prohibited.

This comprehensive ban on increases in wages and salaries was virtually absolute for the duration of the freeze. The CLC permitted price and
wage adjustments only under narrowly defined circumstances, and these
exceptions probably afforded greater flexibility to prices than to wages.
Under the terms of the "seasonality rule"—which was probably the most
significant relaxation of Phase I controls—wages and prices could increase if they paralleled upward fluctuations that had occurred at identifiable time periods during each of the previous three years. This rule
afforded relief to hotels and resorts during the Labor Day weekend, to
automobile manufacturers when they introduced the new models for
1972, and to sellers of Halloween candy. But the records of the Office of
Emergency Preparedness, which was responsible for the day-to-day administration of Phase I, do not reveal that the seasonality rule was ever
applied to wages.

CLC regulations permitted increases in wages in only three highly restricted situations. Newly hired employees who had completed their pro-
bationary period could be paid the higher regular wage rate if the proba-
tionary period was three months or less. Wage increases could also be
given to workers who had completed a designated stage of a bona fide
apprenticeship or learner's program. And employer contributions to a
pension or health insurance plan might be augmented to cover unavoidable costs if there was no increase in the level of scheduled benefits.

From organized labor's point of view the most draconian policy
adopted during Phase I was the flat ban on deferred increases. Various
collective bargaining agreements entered into before August 15, 1971,
provided for wage adjustments to become effective during the ninety-day

6. Office of Emergency Preparedness, Stabilization Program Guideline 4.0814.

freeze period. For the unions involved, these deferred increases constituted payment due for concessions that had been made during the negotiation of contracts and were recognized quid pro quos for accepting multiyear contracts. In labor's view the denial of these gains would destroy the sanctity of the labor agreement and repudiate the initial accommodation between management and the unions. The Bureau of Labor Statistics estimated that during the freeze deferred increases would be payable to 1,368,000 workers under the terms of 280 major agreements.[7]

The CLC did not deal with deferred increases as a separate issue but handled them in the larger context of devising a policy to govern all types of "futures contracts"; that is, contracts binding buyers to pay a specified price for the delivery of goods or services at some future date. Rental charges might be increased with the beginning of a new lease; steel products scheduled for future delivery might command a higher price than those shipped at a prior date. Because the increases encompassed by these futures contracts could result in a substantial jump in individual wages, prices, and rents that would be difficult to explain or justify to the public, the CLC uniformly prohibited their implementation during the freeze. Consequently deferred increases under existing labor contracts were proscribed. The fact that the same policy applied to landlords who had raised rents to cover increased taxes and to businesses that had incurred higher labor costs immediately before the outset of the freeze did not mitigate organized labor's ire. Union officials attacked the ruling as a "payoff to business" and as the "theft" of labor's legitimate proceeds.[8] The controversy over the disposition of the deferred wage increases continued with great intensity into Phase II and threatened to capsize the program before it had actually gotten under way.

Despite the stringent wage controls, the freeze enjoyed widespread and enthusiastic public support. The magnitude and durability of the support for economic controls was a source of comfort, surprise, and some puzzlement to the administration. The widespread support, of course, confirmed the political attraction of controls and helped contribute to the short-term success of the freeze. The administration's puzzlement reflected the doctrinaire bias of some policymakers who held that wage and price controls constituted a significant restraint on the exercise of freedom

7. Pay Board staff memorandum, November 2, 1971.
8. Such statements were made to Weber when he served as executive director of the CLC during the wage-price freeze.

and that the public's appetite for so restrictive a program would quickly change to distaste after a full serving of bureaucratic controls. Nonetheless, both the Gallup and Harris polls continued to show broad approval of the freeze, and with few exceptions, the President's program was greeted with a chorus of acclaim.[9]

The effect of this general approbation was that it limited the administration's discretion in fashioning Phase II. As the freeze progressed through its first weeks and as attention shifted to the design of Phase II, there was anxious conjecture that the administration would initiate a major relaxation of controls resulting in a resurgence of inflation. On September 23, 1971, President Nixon moved to allay these fears in a speech before the Economic Club of Detroit. He told his audience— largely executives of major corporations—that Phase II would be comprehensive and tough and would have "teeth."[10] With this pronouncement, the President effectively set the mold for the postfreeze stabilization program.

The most vociferous criticism of the freeze came from the AFL-CIO, whose position was awkward at best. On August 9, 1971, the AFL-CIO Executive Council, meeting in San Francisco, had approved a resolution endorsing the principle of wage-price controls.[11] Clearly the council had not expected the White House to adopt a policy so contrary to the administration's stated economic philosophy within the immediate future. When controls were imposed on August 15, it was difficult for the AFL-CIO to attack the program in principle. Instead, George Meany, president of the labor federation, issued a statement affirming the AFL-CIO's willingness to cooperate with an equitable system of economic restraints but attacking Phase I on the grounds that it was "patently discriminatory"

9. The Gallup Poll for August 29, 1971, reported that 73 percent of the respondents in a national sample supported the freeze, 17 percent were opposed, and 10 percent had no opinion. See George H. Gallup, *The Gallup Poll: Public Opinion, 1935–1971* (Random House, 1972), vol. 3, pp. 2321–22. The Harris Poll also showed a response of 73 percent in support of the freeze (*New York Times,* September 8, 1971).

10. "Economic Club of Detroit," text of the President's remarks, September 23, 1971, at a question-and-answer session, *Weekly Compilation of Presidential Documents,* vol. 7 (September 27, 1971), p. 1311.

11. The AFL-CIO Executive Council stated its position as follows: "We are prepared to cooperate with mandatory government controls, if the President decides they are necessary, provided such controls are even-handed and across-the-board." (Bureau of National Affairs, Inc., *Daily Labor Report,* August 10, 1971, p. A-15.)

against workers.[12] Meany's indignation was magnified because along with the rest of the country he had been kept in the dark about the President's intentions. Early in the evening of August 15, Secretary of Labor James D. Hodgson had informed Meany that the President would deliver a television address to the nation in a few hours and had suggested that the labor leader watch. Hodgson himself had learned of the impending wage-price freeze only a short time before his call to Meany.

Meany's attitude toward the freeze became atrabilious when high-level administration officials responded to his initial salvos against the New Economic Policy. Secretary Hodgson issued a statement asserting that Meany was "sadly out of step with the needs and desires of America's working men and women."[13] Secretary of the Treasury John B. Connally, who had been appointed chairman of the Cost of Living Council, joined in the counterattack by stating that Meany was "not giving his workmen and his members credit for understanding their problems as well as they do."[14]

A more formal confrontation between the administration and organized labor came at a special meeting of the AFL-CIO Executive Council convened in Washington on August 19 to discuss labor's response to the freeze. At Meany's behest, George Shultz, then director of the OMB, attended the meeting. He was accompanied by Secretary Hodgson and two other officials. Shultz had served as secretary of labor during the first eighteen months of the administration and had won some esteem, if not favor, with Meany and the AFL-CIO. He explained the considerations that had led to the development of the New Economic Policy, outlined its objectives, and pledged that the administration would consult actively with the labor federation when drafting plans for Phase II. The reactions of the Executive Council varied between frigidity and hostility as individual council members took their turns in attacking the motives and substance of the administration's initiatives. During the course of the proceedings, Secretary Hodgson was pointedly ignored and was relegated to a bank of seats usually reserved for staff people, well-wishers, and assorted spectators.

The AFL-CIO continued to fire public broadsides at the stabilization

12. Joseph C. Goulden, *Meany* (Atheneum, 1972), p. 426. This biography of Meany presents the AFL-CIO's general views on Phase I and Phase II of the economic stabilization program.

13. Ibid., p. 427. See also *New York Times,* August 18, 1971.

14. "Unions Begin a Fight," *U.S. News and World Report,* August 30, 1971, p. 74.

program. When the Cost of Living Council handed down the ruling on deferred wage increases the attacks became more specific and intense. Speaking before the convention of the United Transportation Union, Meany remonstrated:

... because of a Presidential edict, the employer who sat at the bargaining table and reached a contract with you, now gets the money that you should get in your pay envelope as a result of deferred wage increases. . . . It means that hundreds of thousands of workers throughout the country are being robbed of millions of dollars with this money turned over to their employer. This, by an edict, by an act of the President of the United States.[15]

Labor's outrage at the denial of deferred wage increases found more constructive expression in a suit filed by the Amalgamated Meat Cutters and Butcher Workmen of North America attacking the constitutionality of the wage-price freeze in general and the illegality of the ban on deferred wage increases in particular. The prospect of immediate relief from pursuing this route was dimmed, however, when a three-man federal court upheld the government's actions.[16]

Despite these oratorical and legal attacks on the stabilization program, organized labor followed a course of tacit acceptance. Only 6 percent of the alleged violations reported during the ninety-day period related to wages, and a large share of these involved government employees. No cases were recorded in which a union struck to force an employer to institute a wage increase in violation of the CLC regulations. In addition, the total number of work stoppages declined significantly from the levels that had been experienced earlier in 1971 and in comparison with the same months in the previous five-year period.[17] While the leaders of the AFL-CIO continued to assail the program for its inequities, individual unions adopted a wait and see attitude. If the freeze had any detectable impact on collective bargaining, it was that the parties engaged in bargaining delayed reaching formal agreements until Phase II had been unveiled.[18]

As a result of the CLC's strong regulatory restraints, the acquiescence of labor, and the conventional incentives of employers to minimize labor costs, wage gains slackened sharply during the freeze. In the three-month

15. Transcript of speech delivered on August 24, 1971, released by AFL-CIO Department of Public Relations.

16. *Amalgamated Meat Cutters and Butcher Workmen of North America, AFL-CIO* v. *Connally,* 337 F. Supp. 737 (D.D.C. 1971).

17. Weber, *In Pursuit of Price Stability,* pp. 108–15.

18. Ibid., p. 115.

period August–November 1971 the rate of increase of the index of average hourly earnings for the private nonfarm economy dropped to 2.2 percent, compared with 6.7 percent in the preceding six months. In the highly unionized manufacturing sector, hourly earnings increased at an annual rate of only 0.6 percent, down from 6.2 percent during February–August 1971.[19] Whether or not organized labor's complaints concerning the inequity of the stabilization program were justified, the freeze obviously imposed a powerful brake on the upward movement of wages and the normal conduct of collective bargaining.

Planning for Phase II

Detailed planning for Phase II commenced in early September 1971, when the Cost of Living Council was still attempting to bring order to the wage-price freeze. At the direction of the CLC, a separate planning group was established under the chairmanship of Herbert Stein, a member of the Council of Economic Advisers. Stein had been present at the Camp David meeting where the freeze had been designed and was an active participant in the deliberations, even though he was not formally a member of the CLC. His group was given responsibility for developing recommendations concerning all aspects of the postfreeze program, including the policies that would govern wages, prices, and other income shares. It was also directed to draw up blueprints for the agency or agencies that would carry out the administration of Phase II. These recommendations were to be reviewed by the full council and ultimately by the President.

The planning group encompassed the bureaucratic representatives of the major interest groups that had a direct stake in the stabilization program. In addition to Stein it included Laurence H. Silberman, under secretary of labor; James T. Lynn, under secretary of commerce; and Don A. Paarlberg, director of agricultural economics at the Department of Agriculture. This trio was joined by Peter M. Flanigan, assistant to the President, who had broad responsibility for economic matters at the White House level, and Arnold R. Weber, executive director of the Cost of Living Council. Marvin H. Kosters, head of the CLC's Planning and Analysis Division, directed the staff analysis.

In accordance with the executive order that imposed the freeze, the

19. Ibid., pp. 102–03.

planning effort was accompanied by extensive consultation with representatives of the various interest groups. Initially the group considered the formation of formal advisory committees but abandoned this approach as being too unwieldy and time-consuming in view of the pressure to present the new program to the public well before the end of Phase I. Instead, it initiated a series of informal consultations between individual members of the CLC and trade union leaders, business executives, consumer-group representatives, spokesmen for the major farm organizations, and related officials. This process reached over 600 special-interest group representatives. Although many of these meetings were ceremonial, the consultations did have a significant impact on the thinking of the policy officials. For example, the decision to retain controls on rental housing units during Phase II was largely the result of arguments presented by representatives of tenant organizations and industry associations, as conveyed to the CLC by Secretary of Housing and Urban Development George W. Romney.

During the planning for Phase II five major issues were identified in defining the nature and structure of the wage stabilization program:

—Should the wage stabilization program be a government effort exclusively or should it be tripartite, including representatives of labor, business, and the public?

—Should a separate board be established to regulate wages or should wage stabilization be the responsibility of a combined wage-price board?

—Should the agency concerned with wage stabilization assume responsibility for the settlement of labor disputes or only for the determination and administration of wage standards?

—Should the President define a wage standard, either through a personal statement or a policy determination of the Cost of Living Council?

—What degree of autonomy should be exercised by the wage stabilization agency?

The Wage Stabilization Agency: Exclusively Governmental or Tripartite?

Both political and substantive factors combined to eliminate any real question concerning the organizing principle for the wage stabilization agency. As a practical matter, it was highly desirable to gain organized labor's direct involvement in the economic stabilization effort. An effective program of wage regulation required the acquiescence, if not the active cooperation, of the parties that would be most directly involved in the controls program—that is, labor and management. Without such a consensus, the durability of the program would be threatened from the outset. The experience with incomes policies in Western Europe and in the United States had revealed that wage controls are unlikely to survive in a political democracy in the face of overt labor resistance.[20] In addition, previous ventures in wage control in the United States during World War II and the Korean war had been tripartite in nature.

Circumstances surrounding the freeze and the subsequent reactions of organized labor reinforced the theoretical desirability of engaging organized labor's support for the program of wage restraint. The AFL-CIO's endorsement of wage-price controls in principle shortly before the freeze was announced had turned to harsh criticism in the first two weeks of Phase I. Thus from the administration's point of view the renewed participation of labor in the program was attractive for three reasons: it would help validate the consensus necessary to sustain the program, it would mute or channel organized labor's criticisms of the stabilization effort, and it would mean that labor had tacitly accepted partial responsibility for the outcome of the program. At the same time, the administration believed that organized labor could not easily reject an invitation to participate in the wage controls effort. Otherwise, labor's political costs would be high, considering the public's anti-inflationary fervor and enthusiasm for Phase I.

For these reasons the Stein group quickly concluded that the wage stabilization agency should be tripartite in nature and gave only pro forma consideration to alternative approaches. The AFL-CIO leadership apparently had reached the same conclusion. When a delegation from the labor federation led by George Meany met with the President, it strongly recommended a tripartite board to carry out the task of wage regulation. During the course of the discussion Meany warmly recalled labor's experiences with tripartitism during World War II and the Korean war. In this manner pragmatic and political reasons were bolstered by nostalgia.

The Stein group's recommendation for a tripartite wage board elicited only cursory discussion within the full Cost of Living Council. No mem-

20. See Murray Edelman and R. W. Fleming, *The Politics of Wage-Price Decisions: A Four-Country Analysis* (University of Illinois Press, 1965).

ber of the CLC expressed any real opposition, and the recommendation went forward to the President, who adopted it. Ultimately it was determined that tripartitism should be expressed through equal membership of representatives of organized labor, business, and the public. Although there was some concern that the number would be unwieldy, it was further decided that the board should consist of five representatives from each of these groups, for a total of fifteen. It was assumed from the beginning that the labor representatives all would be trade unionists. Even though trade union membership constituted only 21 percent of the total labor force, the union leaders represented the largest organized constituency and exercised the greatest political influence of any group within the nonagricultural labor force. Moreover, there was little doubt that the labor leaders would balk at any suggestion to share the stage with spokesmen from nonunion groups—if such spokesmen could be identified.

The designation of five labor representatives recognized the special aspects of labor movement structure and politics. The AFL-CIO was the dominant labor organization on the national scene due to its large membership and broad economic and political influence. However, two major unions, the United Automobile, Aerospace and Agricultural Implement Workers (UAW) and the International Brotherhood of Teamsters, Chauffeurs, Warehousemen and Helpers of America, remained outside the federation and were keenly sensitive to their autonomy and separate interests. Accordingly, by having five labor representatives in the wage stabilization agency, it was possible to assign three seats to the AFL-CIO and one each to the UAW and the Teamsters. Five business and public positions were then created to provide the necessary tripartite balance.

A Separate Wage Board?

The decision to administer wage controls through a tripartite agency made it apparent that separate wage- and price-regulating bodies would be established. Tripartitism never had been used in price stabilization programs in the United States (nor has yet) and has been a rare occurrence abroad. In planning for Phase II these precedents were reinforced by the preferences of the major interest groups involved. Organized labor expressed no desire to participate directly in price controls; its tactical interests called for a clear separation from decisionmaking concerning prices. If labor's representatives were involved in the process of regulating prices, they would be put in the position of giving approbation to price increases in at least some cases. By keeping a good distance between themselves and the price control components of Phase II, labor spokesmen could retain their freedom to criticize the actions of the price agency and to dramatize real or apparent inequities in the differential treatment of wages and prices. Because this element of equity was an important part of organized labor's perceptions and political rhetoric, it was vital for labor to retain formal independence from the price side.

Management groups were equally certain to strongly resist any move to extend the principle of tripartitism to price controls. Even within the context of collective bargaining, management generally has insisted that price decisions should be a matter of unilateral discretion and not a subject of joint labor-management discussions. Moreover, labor's participation in a price agency would mean that union representatives would have access to confidential cost data. Most management representatives would blanch at this prospect. Hence when it was decided that the program of wage stabilization would be administered on a tripartite basis, the issue of whether there would be one comprehensive agency for prices and wages was never seriously discussed. Separate bodies for wages and prices were predetermined.

Should the Wage Board Settle Disputes?

The decision to establish a separate wage stabilization board raised the additional question of whether the agency should have responsibility for resolving collective bargaining disputes. In past exercises in economic controls the wage board had been deeply involved in settling labor disputes that had a special significance for the stabilization effort. During World War II the wage control program had evolved from governmental efforts to deal with strikes that threatened defense production. The first wartime agency, the National War Labor Board, was extremely active on this front. The involvement of the Wage Stabilization Board during the Korean war was more informal, but its members, and particularly the chairman, often attempted to resolve labor-management conflict on a basis that would be acceptable to the parties and consistent with the objectives of the program. During the Kennedy-Johnson administration, efforts to apply wage guidelines were frequently supplemented by liberal doses of mediation or more strenuous arm-twisting. These efforts sometimes involved high government officials, such as the secretary of labor, and even the President.

The combining of wage stabilization and dispute settlement functions purports to reflect the "realities" of labor-management relations. It is argued that an exclusively economic approach to wage stabilization ignores the importance of nonpecuniary factors in collective bargaining and the political pressures that influence the behavior of union and management negotiators. Therefore it is important to preserve an element of flexibility in a system of wage controls by assigning additional dispute settlement responsibilities to the regulators. This sensitivity to the requirements of mediation would temper the purely economic approach that otherwise might lead to decisions that undermine the bargaining relationship.

The Stein group approached this issue ambivalently. The conferees recognized the desirability of building a capability for conciliation into the system of wage regulation, but the AFL-CIO's hostility toward Phase I did not create a climate that was conducive to effectively settling disputes. The planning group's enthusiasm for mixing wage controls with mediation was further dampened by a comparison of the circumstances surrounding the earlier similar efforts and those that prevailed at the end of 1971. Previous stabilization programs had been undertaken during wartime when it was necessary to maintain uninterrupted production in defense-related industries. Therefore the government had a strong interest in avoiding labor disputes that might impair the war effort. In addition, during World War II organized labor had agreed to a no-strike pledge, which put a special responsibility on the regulators to try to accommodate the union's institutional needs in the administration of the program.

These factors had no relevance to conditions in November 1971. The economy was operating under peacetime conditions, and labor retained the full arsenal of sanctions in collective bargaining. Moreover, 1972 was a relatively light year on the collective bargaining calendar, and this reduced the likelihood of a major dispute that would precipitate a confrontation with the government or throw the economy into a tailspin.

The administration ultimately adopted a narrow, if not wary, position. The wage board's formal functions would be limited to the technical task of regulating wage increases and would not include dispute settlements. The primary responsibility for resolving labor-management disputes would be retained by the parties themselves. Their efforts could be supplemented by the Federal Mediation and Conciliation Service. As it evolved, the new wage board might become informally concerned with dispute settlements, but this development would be left to the board itself. The mediation function would be the consequence of constructive relationships among the board members rather than of formal ascription by the government.

If a Numerical Wage Standard, Who Should Set It?

Once the organizational matters were resolved, the crucial substantive issues involved the nature of the wage standard and the question of who had the authority for defining this standard. In large measure the policy governing prices determined the approach taken to the wage standard. The average level of wage increases had to be linked to the goal established for price increases during Phase II. If it is assumed that real wage gains equal to national average productivity increases are consistent with price stability, then the maximum average increase in money wages should be determined by expected productivity gains plus the increase in the general price level. The generally accepted long-term productivity figure was approximately 3 percent. Hence the definition of the actual wage standard—whether publicly announced or not—awaited the specification of some price goal. The wage standard would be a crucial element in the self-fulfilling prophesy created by the system of controls.

The planning group recognized the necessity of promulgating a formal price goal to set the strategic objectives for the anti-inflation program and to establish some discipline for the stabilization agencies. Moreover, it would be difficult to maintain the credibility of the President's stricture that Phase II would be "tough" and "comprehensive" if the price goal was expressed as a vague economic cliché.

These programmatic requirements were mitigated, however, by political considerations. As everyone was aware, 1972 was a presidential election year. Although efforts to end American involvement in Vietnam continued to generate great controversy, the bread-and-butter issues of prices and employment clearly were the focus of domestic concern in the perceptions of the voters, if not in the oratory of the candidates. Because presidential prestige was inextricably related to the outcome of the battle against inflation, it was also vital for political reasons to avoid the impression as well as the fact of failure in the conduct of the stabilization program. Thus the articulation of an explicit price standard posed political perils that had to be balanced against economic and managerial requirements.

The question of defining a price goal or standard was brought to the full Cost of Living Council for discussion. The conflicting considerations were aired at some length and ultimately the CLC—like most economic policymaking bodies operating in a political context—attempted to have the best of both worlds. It agreed to recommend to the President the determination of a numerical price goal for Phase II. The goal should have three attributes: a good chance of attainment in the light of foreseeable economic trends; the ability to create downward pressure on increases in the price level; and sufficiently ambiguous terms to protect the administration from heavy political costs if the actual performance of the economy during 1972 deviated from the goal.

These magical properties were incorporated in the stated goal that the rate of increase in the general price level should be reduced to between 2 and 3 percent and that this target should be reached by the end of 1972. In this manner a putative numerical goal was determined, but with a 50 percent variance. Articulating the goal as a range rather than as a single fixed number implied that if the actual behavior of prices was marginally above 3 percent, this result would be consistent with "success" in the battle against inflation. Because prices had been increasing at an annual rate of 4.6 percent in the six months preceding the imposition of the freeze, there was considerable confidence that the actual numbers would fall in the designated range of 2 to 3 percent or would not stray too far from these boundaries.

This flexibility was augmented by the temporal ambiguity of the goal. The term "by the end of 1972" glossed over the question of whether monthly, quarterly, or annual rates would be used in gauging the effectiveness of Phase II. Presumably under this formulation price increases for all of 1972 could be above the 2 to 3 percent range as long as the rate of increase was declining and fell into the felicitous limits sometime in the fall of the year. The last government report before the 1972 election on changes in the consumer price index would be announced in October.

After defining the nature and magnitude of the price goal, the CLC agreed that the administration should remain silent on the question of a specific wage standard. First, it was believed that the specification of the price goal would determine the limits of the wage standard through the linkage of productivity, wages, and prices. Any number the wage board might settle on could not stray too far from the limits implicitly established by the price goal. Second, the prior announcement of a wage standard by the CLC would trample on the principle of autonomy associated with tripartitism in the organization of the wage board. For these reasons the administration made no formal statements concerning the wage standard other than to say that it should be generally consistent with the price goal. The wage standard was confidently expected to be about 6 percent. Meanwhile the administration's interests in the precise definition of the wage standard could be protected by hinting at a "reserve power" retained by the Cost of Living Council.

How Autonomous Should the Wage Board Be?

The most subtle—and acrimonious—issue to be resolved in building the machinery for wage controls was the degree of autonomy the wage board should have. The obverse of this question was, of course, the extent to which the Cost of Living Council would supervise or control the actions of the agency. The planners for Phase II decided that the wage board would be responsible for the regulation of wages, a price commission would be concerned with prices and rents, and a separate committee would develop guidelines governing interest and dividends. The CLC would coordinate the activities of the different agencies, provide administrative support, and supervise the overall stabilization program. The wage and price boards in particular were considered to be autonomous or quasi-independent agencies.

The notion of quasi-independence is inherently vague and lends itself to a variety of interpretations. Ordinarily the organizational metaphysics of this concept would be worked out over time as specific problems developed and as experiences accumulated. But this common law approach to defining the precise jurisdiction and authority of the wage board was not feasible. Even under the most equanimous circumstances the labor members could be expected to demand a clear delineation of the board's authority in order to determine their own sphere of influence in the system of wage controls. The need for prior agreement on the ground rules was made more compelling by labor's suspicions of the administration's motives. George Meany forthrightly stated the AFL-CIO's preferences to President Nixon, declaring that labor supported and would cooperate with "an independent voluntary agency free from government control, of a tripartite nature."[21] Without precisely defining each of the adjectives, it was clear that labor wanted the wage board to operate with complete

21. As cited in Goulden, *Meany*, p. 432.

autonomy, insulated from any intervention or second-guessing by the government.

The Stein group and the Cost of Living Council approached the problem on a more complex, functional basis. In defining the distribution of authority between the CLC and the wage board, attention centered on four categories of decisions: the determination of the *coverage* of wage controls, the formulation of general *standards* and *criteria* governing permissible wage increases, rulings in *specific cases,* and decisions to initiate *compliance activities* by the field staff or the Justice Department.

Because the determination of coverage in fact defined the scope of the stabilization program, the CLC unequivocally agreed that the council should have policymaking authority in this area. The need to retain this authority was especially important because of the complicated three-tier system of administrative categories that was developed. These categories were as follows:

	Size of firm
Category I	5,000 or more employees
Category II	1,000 to 4,999 employees
Category III	Less than 1,000 employees

Under this system the largest price- and wage-determining units (Category I) required prior approval before initiating any increases, other major units (Category II) had to report such actions to the regulatory agencies for review, and the smaller units (Category III) generally were left to self-administration and spot checks by the Internal Revenue Service (IRS). Hence the controls program could be effectively tightened or loosened by changing the size criteria for the individual administrative categories. In addition, changes in coverage could be the technical basis for the outright decontrol of specific industries or sectors of the economy. For these reasons the CLC concluded that it was necessary for a government agency, controlled directly by administration officials, to retain plenary authority over the determination of coverage.

The clarification of authority over the standards and criteria was less amenable to resolution. The CLC had placed some theoretical limits on the basic wage standard when it formulated a numerical price goal for the overall stabilization effort. Conceivably, however, if the wage board was given a completely free rein in establishing the wage standard, a yardstick could be fashioned that would make it virtually impossible to attain the price goal. On the other hand, any administration effort to determine the wage standard directly was sure to provoke strong protests from labor.

The CLC attempted to extricate itself from this dilemma by defining the distribution of authority over the wage standard in very broad terms. The wage board, on its own initiative, could determine the standards for acceptable wage behavior. But by remaining silent on the precise assignment of authority, the CLC believed it could wield reserve authority if the standards adopted by the board posed a threat to the integrity of the stabilization program.

CLC members agreed that the council should not have authority to overrule or modify the wage board's decisions in individual cases. First, each case would involve a complex set of data and relationships that would make it difficult, if not impossible, for the CLC to make informed judgments on an ad hoc basis. Second, if the CLC could overrule the board in individual cases, the council would be identified as an appellate body and would be inundated by requests for hearings from parties who, for substantive or political reasons, would not be satisfied until they had exhausted all possible channels. Nor was the CLC, with its diverse membership linked to specific interest groups, an ideal agency for dispensing economic justice.

Control over compliance activities was distributed on a more elaborate, bureaucratic basis. Because the CLC had direct authority over the IRS field staff, which serviced both the wage board and the price agency, it would retain effective control over the compliance procedures. Evidence of noncompliance in individual cases could not be gathered without the CLC's active cooperation, since neither the wage board nor the price agency would have an independent field capability. In addition, by long tradition the Justice Department had the authority to determine which complaints should be pressed in the courts. This policy had been modified during the freeze; thus the CLC had been able to insist on the litigation of cases that the Justice Department attorneys believed to be inappropriate. The department strongly opposed this arrangement for both professional and bureaucratic reasons. L. Patrick Gray III, the assistant attorney general in charge of the Civil Division, which acted on behalf of the federal government in almost all lawsuits, stated vehemently that the department would reassert its authority without compromise during Phase II. This claim was never challenged.

In this setting the wage board's direct involvement in compliance activities would be sharply limited. The board could request the CLC to direct the IRS to investigate an alleged violation. On the basis of investigative reports the board could then recommend that the Justice Department initiate legal proceedings against the violator. The Justice Department, however, would make the final decision of whether to go ahead with court action.

As the planning for Phase II progressed, most of these relationships had not been elaborated nor were their subtleties fully understood by all CLC members. It was clearly recognized that the council would not intervene in specific cases, but the other elements of authority and the implied relationships between the CLC and the wage board had not been well articulated in the planning and drafting process. This tendency to blur the jurisdictional issues reflected the dominance of other, more immediate problems and the belief that most of the operating details would be worked out once Phase II had been launched. Moreover, the first detailed description of Phase II was included in a document designed for public consumption, a format that did not lend itself to the explication of technical matters.

This schematic arrangement of authority relationships between the wage board and the CLC did not allay the union leaders' mistrust of the administration's intentions. On October 6, 1971—one day before the President announced the plans for Phase II on national television—Secretary of Labor Hodgson met with George Meany; Frank Fitzsimmons, president of the Teamsters; Leonard F. Woodcock, president of the UAW; and other labor leaders to brief them on the details of the post-freeze program. The labor leaders came away from the meeting persuaded that the wage board would be autonomous. This meant that neither individual case decisions nor the standards promulgated by the board could be set aside by the CLC. Because of Hodgson's reported assurances, Meany and the other labor leaders stated their willingness to participate in Phase II. Meany reiterated this agreement at a meeting with OMB Director George Shultz.

Meany's concern that the board would not be completely autonomous was rekindled by President Nixon's speech the next night. In Meany's perception, the brief, general speech implied that the CLC would have "supreme authority" over the wage and price agencies alike. Further questions were raised by reports of White House press briefings that hinted that the CLC could veto or modify the standards established by the wage board.

With his suspicions aroused, Meany withheld a public endorsement of Phase II and contacted Shultz to express his uneasiness. According to a labor account, Meany felt he had been double-crossed by the administration. He then issued a call for a special session of the AFL-CIO Executive Council for Tuesday, October 12. On Saturday, October 9, Shultz convened a meeting in his office in the White House that was attended by Shultz, Stein, and other members of the Stein planning group. They drafted a statement to summarize the respective roles of the CLC, the wage board, and the price agency. The statement more or less crystallized policy judgments that had been made in earlier discussions within the CLC and the Stein group. The key provision in the statement, however, did represent a significant shift in position. Rather than giving the wage board the right to develop standards and criteria while holding open the possibility of revision of the standards by the CLC, the statement ceded complete authority to the wage board.

The [CLC] will not approve, disapprove, or serve as an appeal level for case decisions made by the Pay Board and Price Commission and it will not approve, revise, veto, or revoke specific standards or criteria developed by the Pay Board and Price Commission.[22]

This memorandum was subsequently discussed with the President, who wrote on the margin "O.K. R.N. 10/11/71."

On the morning of October 12 before the scheduled meeting of the AFL-CIO Executive Council, Shultz and Hodgson personally conveyed the memo to Meany. With this assurance of autonomy, the Executive Council unanimously passed a resolution confirming labor's participation on the wage board. In a later press conference Meany brandished the memorandum, complete with presidential initials, with considerable satisfaction. Only passing attention was given to the fact that the memorandum also confirmed the CLC's authority to determine the coverage of the program and to control compliance and enforcement activities. In any case the question of the degree of autonomy of the wage board had come to a satisfactory, if noisy, conclusion.

Naming the Pay Board

As the Cost of Living Council emerged from the thicket of policy issues, one residual item remained; the name of the new wage stabilization agency. Although this question was unlikely to influence the outcome of Phase II, the CLC afforded it more than passing interest. Because the

22. "A Summary Statement of the Respective Roles of the COLC, the Pay Board and the Price Commission," in BNA, *Daily Labor Report,* October 12, 1971, pp. AA-3–AA-5.

term "Cost of Living Council" itself had been something of a public relations phenomenon, the planners believed the designation of the new agency should not be left to chance or to public relations officials. Obviously, "National War Labor Board," used during World War II, was not relevant. The term "Wage Stabilization Board," used during the Korean war, was also rejected on the grounds that it was too narrow in its reference to a particular form of compensation. Instead, an alternative name was sought that would be simple and evocative of all forms of compensation. In a casual discussion Arthur F. Burns, chairman of the Board of Governors of the Federal Reserve System, suggested that emphasis be given to the concept of "pay." This idea was greeted with general approbation and the name "Pay Board" was adopted. Even before it existed, the Pay Board had already survived the rigors of brand labeling. Its sister agency became the Price Commission.

Setting Up the Pay Board

On October 7, 1971, President Nixon went on national television to announce the broad outlines of the Phase II stabilization program. The speech was brief and low-keyed. It described the new organizational arrangements, announced the appointment of Donald Rumsfeld, a counselor to the President, as the new CLC director, and spelled out the goals of the program for the next year.[23]

The initial public reaction to Phase II was favorable, although attention was temporarily diverted by the furor over the autonomy of the Pay Board and the delivery of the presidential aide-mémoire to George Meany. With organized labor's agreement to serve on the Pay Board and participate in the Phase II program, the immediate task was to set up the new pay and price agencies. On the wage side the first step was the selection of the fifteen members of the Pay Board. The freeze was scheduled to end on November 13, so manning the board had to be carried out with some urgency. Indeed the members had to be selected and announced as soon as possible in order to permit the board to establish at least the basic policies for Phase II before November 13. The selection of nominees was the responsibility of Peter Flanigan, assistant

23. "The Continuing Fight against Inflation," text of the President's October 7, 1971, address to the nation, *Weekly Compilation of Presidential Documents,* vol. 7 (GPO, October 11, 1971), p. 1377.

to the President. In making his recommendations for the membership of the Pay Board, Flanigan relied heavily on the judgment of Secretary of Labor Hodgson and George Shultz.

The designation of the labor representatives was the easiest part of the selection process. Once it had been determined that all the labor members would be recruited from the ranks of organized labor, the nominees obviously would be drawn from the important unions, subject to the constraint that there be a distribution of representation among AFL-CIO affiliates and the major labor organizations that were outside the federation. The list of members was quickly agreed to and included George Meany, president of the AFL-CIO; I. W. Abel, president of the United Steelworkers of America; Floyd E. Smith, president of the International Association of Machinists and Aerospace Workers (IAM); Frank E. Fitzsimmons, president of the Teamsters; and Leonard F. Woodcock, president of the UAW. The Steelworkers and the IAM were AFL-CIO affiliates, while the Teamsters and the UAW maintained an independent status. All four of the international unions were large and powerful and operated in the mainstream of American industrial relations. Meany was, of course, the prima labor spokesman at the national level. He expressed some reservations "on personal grounds" about his willingness to serve, but he finally did accept the nomination.[24]

The business members also were selected with little difficulty. Some effort was made to get a broad industry representation and members who had at least a modicum of experience in labor-management relations. The five business representatives included Leonard F. McCollum, chairman of the board of the Continental Oil Company; Benjamin F. Biaggini, president of the Southern Pacific Company; Rocco C. Siciliano, president of the T. I. Corporation; Virgil Day, vice-president of the General Electric Company; and Robert C. Bassett, president of the Bassett Publishing Company in Chicago. Three of the business members had an extensive background in labor-management relations. Virgil Day was a career labor relations specialist who had been responsible for union-management relations in the General Electric Company. Rocco Siciliano had been an assistant secretary of labor under President Eisenhower and president of the Pacific Maritime Association, an employer association that dealt with the International Longshoremen and Warehousemen's Union on the West Coast. He served as under secretary of commerce

24. BNA, *Daily Labor Report,* October 12, 1971, p. AA-3.

during the Nixon administration. Robert Bassett had been a vice president for industrial relations for several large corporations and had served on a regional unit of the Wage Stabilization Board during the Korean war before starting his own publishing company. All the business representatives came from large corporations, except Bassett, who was informally considered to be the small-business representative on the Pay Board.

The most difficult aspect of constituting the board was the selection of the five public members, especially the chairman. In contrast to past wage stabilization agencies, expertise or a working background in labor-management relations was not viewed as an essential criterion for the selection of public members. It was desirable to have some public members with a background in industrial relations, but they should be balanced with other appointees who had a broader competence in economics and an appreciation of the workings of government. No political qualifications were applied. Acceptance of a position as a public member on the Pay Board was presumed to carry with it support of the general goals and operating procedures of the Phase II program. These criteria were modified somewhat when applied to the chairman. That is, it was considered important to select somebody for this position who did have acceptance and experience in labor-management relations. The chairman was designated the only full-time member of the board and was expected to provide leadership in both substantive and administrative matters.

The search for prospective public members proved to be arduous and initially unrewarding. At least seven persons with prestigious reputations as neutrals in labor-management relations were approached for the job as chairman, and each asked to be withdrawn from consideration. Personal obligations, political preferences, or a wariness of the program due to organized labor's begrudging participation entered into these decisions. Thus by the third week in October this key position remained unfilled, and the administration turned to alternatives other than industrial relations experts. One name that had been submitted from the White House was George H. Boldt. Boldt had been a federal district judge in the state of Washington for almost twenty years following his appointment by President Eisenhower. Before that he had been a practicing attorney in Tacoma, Washington, and had risen to his judgeship from a modest background. During World War II he had enlisted in the Army, even though he had been overage, and had served with the Office of Strategic Services in Burma. Boldt's formal knowledge of labor-management relations was meager and was limited to fragments of information that had been absorbed during his career as a lawyer and a federal judge. He had gained some public prominence in two major cases: as the judge who had presided at the trial leading to the conviction of Dave Beck, then president of the Teamsters, and for his role in working out the settlement between major electrical equipment producers and their customers in a landmark antitrust conspiracy case.[25] Boldt had a reputation as a man of high integrity who conducted his courtroom business in a brisk but fair manner. He was a personal friend of relatives of John D. Erlichmann, one of the chief advisers to President Nixon.

Boldt accepted the job even though he recognized that he lacked any detailed knowledge of labor-management relations. He believed that his skills as a lawyer and a judge would compensate for this deficiency and would permit him to contribute to the program. He genially admitted his deficiencies but accepted the position of chairman when it was finally offered to him, on the grounds that service to the nation was an overriding consideration. The offer was made despite the negative reactions of several members of the CLC because of Boldt's inexperience and lack of stature in labor relations. Time was running out, however, and Boldt was the best alternative available.

At his first press conference in the White House when he was publicly announced as chairman, Boldt disarmed the bemused press corps. When a skeptical reporter asked him who fingered him for the job, Boldt replied, "If I find out, he is going to be in for a bad time, especially if he needs bail in the Western District of Washington."[26]

The selection of the other public members also proceeded slowly, but by October 20 the panel was complete. The remaining public members selected were William G. Caples, president of Kenyon College; Neil H. Jacoby, professor of business, economics, and policy at the Graduate School of Management, University of California at Los Angeles; Kermit Gordon, president of the Brookings Institution; and Arnold R. Weber, professor of urban and labor economics in the Graduate School of Business at the University of Chicago. Caples had had a long career in management, rising to corporate vice-president for industrial and public relations of the Inland Steel Company in Chicago. He had also served as chairman of the Board of Education in Chicago. Jacoby, a specialist in business economics and macroeconomics, had been a member of the President's Council of Economic Advisers under Arthur Burns during the

25. *New York Times,* October 23, 1971.
26. BNA, *Daily Labor Report,* October 22, 1971, p. AA-4.

Eisenhower administration. Kermit Gordon had occupied several high posts in the Kennedy-Johnson administration, serving as a member of the Council of Economic Advisers and as director of the Bureau of the Budget. Before coming to Washington he had been a professor of economics at Williams College. He had extensive background in economic stabilization programs, had been on the staff of the Office of Price Administration during World War II and the Office of Price Stabilization during the Korean conflict, and had been closely involved in the experiment with wage guidelines during the Kennedy-Johnson years. Weber came directly to his post after three years of service in the Nixon administration as assistant secretary of labor for manpower and as associate director of the Office of Management and Budget. Shortly after announcing his intention to return to the University of Chicago, the freeze had been imposed, and he had acted as executive director of the Cost of Living Council during most of the freeze. His move to the Pay Board was coincidental with his formal return to the University of Chicago.

Thus the public members of the board represented a mix of backgrounds and skills. Caples and Weber had experience in labor-management relations. Jacoby and Gordon were broadly familiar with labor issues, particularly at the macroeconomic level, but were most accurately classified as general economists. Judge Boldt, as indicated above, lacked any real background in the field. Two of the public members, Caples and Gordon, were Democrats. Caples had worked with Mayor Richard Daley in Chicago, while Gordon had been one of the top economic advisers for Presidents Kennedy and Johnson.

Labor's reaction to the composition of the Pay Board, especially to the public members, was less than enthusiastic. Meany alleged that he had been told by Secretary Hodgson that Boldt would not be appointed as chairman because he was unqualified. The other public members were publicly and privately excoriated for their lack of either neutrality or competence. Meany's special scorn was directed at Judge Boldt and Weber because they had come to the Pay Board from federal government positions. In labor's view government service so proximate to nomination for the Pay Board disqualified Boldt and Weber as public members. In a speech and other statements made at the AFL-CIO convention in Bal Harbour, Florida, in November, Meany assailed the Pay Board as a "stacked deck" and had pungent words for each of the public members:

. . . The judge [Boldt] . . . certainly is neutral in the sense that he doesn't know a damn thing about labor and management. . . .

Mr. Weber . . . is the fellow that wrote the nice things that the Cost-of-Living Council got out. He is the hatchet man. . . .

Then we move to a gentleman, quite a nice man, by the name of Caples. His whole life has been spent in industry, executive vice-president, Inland Steel Company; entire career spent on management's side of labor-management relations, a former vice-president of the National Association of Manufacturers. . . .

Then we have Dr. Neil Jacoby, a conservative economist from the Council of Economic Advisers under Arthur Burns in the Eisenhower Administration, and he helped us to fashion those two recessions that we had in those days.[27]

Meany's displeasure with, and subsequent attacks on, the public members ensured that the Pay Board would face heavy weather when it commenced operations. Nonetheless, on October 22 the members of the Pay Board met for the first time in the White House for a briefing from the President and other administration officials. Afterwards, Judge Boldt returned to the Pay Board's cramped suite of temporary offices, a staff of one secretary on loan from the CLC, and two administrative aides conscripted from the Office of Emergency Preparedness. Phase II of the wage stabilization program was under way.

27. *Proceedings of the Ninth Constitutional Convention of the AFL-CIO, Bal Harbour, Florida, November 18–22, 1971: Daily Proceedings and Executive Council Reports* (AFL-CIO, n.d.), p. 21.

II

The Policy Trinity: The Wage Standard, Deferred Increases, and Retroactivity

As the Pay Board lurched into Phase II it was confronted with two immediate tasks. First, it had to take initial steps to build a supporting organization and to establish the operating rules and procedures of the board itself. Second, it had to formulate the basic policies governing the wage stabilization program, both for the guidance of the public and to lay the foundation for the structure of specific regulations required for a legal system of controls. Significant progress in both of these areas had to be achieved before November 13 when the ninety-day wage-price freeze was officially terminated.

The highly charged, adversary atmosphere in which the board was conceived did not facilitate the development of either an effective organization or a consensus on critical policy issues. In addition, the process of policy formulation was impaired by inadequate staff support and logistical difficulties that magnified the sensitivities of the parties. A dual concern over paper clips and policies was to characterize the deliberations of the Pay Board for the first months of its existence. But in this unstable environment the basic policies and relationships took shape that substantially conditioned the wage stabilization program for the duration of Phase II.

The Operating Rules

The basic operating rules were determined at the first business meeting of the Pay Board convened on October 27, 1971. A quorum consisted of ten of the fifteen board members. All decisions of the board required the affirmative vote of eight or more members. No verbatim record of board discussions would be kept and the minutes would consist of a statement of any decisions reached and a brief summary of the important matters that had been discussed. Somewhat innocently the members also agreed that all official announcements concerning rulings, decisions, or other actions of the board would be made exclusively by the chairman.

This preference for a sparse record and a single spokesman reflected the belief that as a tripartite body the board would function most effectively if its deliberations were shielded from close public scrutiny and if disagreements were not aired in an open forum. Although this theory had some credence if one viewed the wage stabilization program as a vehicle for collective bargaining, it proved to be difficult, if not impossible, to sustain in a restrictive, regulatory context. From the beginning the board's proceedings were marked by systematic leaks and anonymous statements to the press by members of each of the three groups. These leaks usually were designed to assail the perfidy of the other board members or to convey the "real" motives behind a particular board action.

Most of the operating principles were clear-cut and were concurred in without controversy. The major point of disagreement was the use of alternates to act for the board members. As the Pay Board was constituted, all the members except the chairman served on a part-time basis. Because many of the presidential appointees were also officials of large organizations—for example, unions, corporations, and educational institutions—it would be difficult for them to attend all board meetings while carrying out their other responsibilities. The capacity of the board to act on a regular basis would be impaired significantly if official business could be transacted only when a quorum of the appointed members was present. Even if the required quorum was present, other demands might keep members with a strong interest in the proceedings from attending key meetings. Under these circumstances important interests might not be adequately represented. This was especially true for the labor members who were deeply involved in intra-union politics or collective bargaining that kept them on the road much of the time. As a practical matter, there were persuasive reasons to permit each board member to be represented by an alternate who would have full rights of participation.

Nevertheless, some of the public members expressed misgivings about the use of alternates. These members feared that the alternates would be staff assistants of the regular members and that as such they would be unable to exercise discretion or flexibility in the board's deliberations. Rather, they would be closely instructed by the principals they represented and therefore would not be amenable to either persuasion or negotiation.

The labor members pressed the board to authorize the use of alternates with full voting rights. George Meany was especially vocal on this issue. He indicated that the use of alternates had been adopted by the tripartite wage stabilization agencies during World War II and the Korean conflict. Meany obviously had a wide range of responsibilities as president of the AFL-CIO that would prevent his regular attendance at board meetings. Moreover, the AFL-CIO convention was scheduled to begin in Bal Harbour, Florida, within the next two weeks, and Meany would have to devote a large block of time to preliminary activities and presiding at the sessions.

The board finally agreed that alternates would be permitted. Before a motion to this effect could be approved, however, a legal opinion had to be obtained clarifying the right to use alternates under the terms of the executive order that had established the Pay Board. Although an affirmative opinion was forthcoming within two days, Meany expressed his irritation about the board's apparent foot-dragging by calling President Nixon directly to apprise him of the situation and of Meany's displeasure.

Defining the Policy Issues

After the procedural issues were resolved—amicably or otherwise—the board considered the major policy issues. Staff members of the Cost of Living Council prepared a proposed list of issues. The list was long and indiscriminate. The topics ranged from the definition of a general wage standard, to the status of bonuses and fringe benefits, to the nature of reporting requirements that would be imposed on employers and unions. The board quickly discarded most of the items and agreed to give immediate priority to four issues: (1) the general standard for wage increases arising from labor agreements or unilateral employer actions initiated after November 13, 1971, when the freeze was scheduled to end; (2) the rules governing deferred wage increases agreed to before August 15, 1971, but scheduled to go into effect after November 13, 1971; (3) the disposition of claims for retroactive wage increases that were scheduled to take effect between August 15 and November 13, 1971, but that had been denied under the rules of the wage-price freeze; and (4) the policy concerning tandem wage increases for employees in units that traditionally followed the pattern set in other units. During the course of the discussions, however, the board determined the tandem issue to be the least pressing and deferred it for future consideration.

General Pay Standard

The question of the general pay standard was threefold and paralleled issues considered by the Cost of Living Council at a more general level. First, should there be a precise numerical standard or should permissible wage behavior be defined in qualitative terms? Second, if a specific numerical standard was appropriate, what should that standard be? Third, if the pay standard was expressed in qualitative terms, what criteria should be identified by the policy governing permissible wage behavior?

Although the nature and extent of the exceptions from the standard were not considered directly at this time, some broad judgment had to be made on this issue as part of the intellectual process of reaching a position on the general pay standard. That is, there was an implicit inverse relationship between the policy adopted with respect to the pay standard and the general approach to exceptions from that norm. For both substantive and administrative reasons it was necessary to formulate a general yardstick that would guide or limit employers and unions in the process of wage determination. But however artfully it was drawn, no single standard could cover all labor market situations with an equal regard for equity or efficiency. Consequently if a stringent approach was taken toward exceptions, then a tight numerical standard would be difficult to sustain in the face of pressures from the parties for relief for a variety of meritorious reasons. Conversely, if a liberal policy was adopted with respect to exceptions, then a numerical standard that was conservatively linked to the price goal would become more feasible. In formulating the general pay standard the board would have to determine whether this norm would constitute a target for average wage performance or a firm regulatory principle.

Deferred Increases

The problem of deferred increases combined considerations of equity, the stability of industrial relations practices, and the objectives of the wage stabilization program. Most major labor agreements in the United States have a duration of more than one year. Normally the contracts covering large bargaining units are negotiated for a three-year period. These multiyear contracts usually call for wage increases in all three years. The increases in the second and third years, so-called deferred increases, may be specified precisely beforehand or may be the subject of a "wage reopener" under which wage rates are negotiated further without modifying the other terms of the contract. In almost all major bargaining agreements the exact amounts of the deferred increases are spelled out at the time the contract is originally negotiated. In addition, the base adjustment may be supplemented by escalator clauses that call for automatic wage increases reflecting changes in the consumer price index that have taken place over the contract term. One consequence of the widespread negotiation of multiyear contracts is that there usually is an identifiable three-year cycle in collective bargaining in the United States.

Most academic observers and practitioners view the practice of negotiating multiyear contracts as a singular achievement of the American industrial relations system. Management generally has been favorable to this development because it provides stability in labor relations for an extended period of time and avoids the "guaranteed annual argument" and coincidental strike threats that arise when contracts are negotiated for one year. In addition, multiyear contracts afford a high degree of predictability concerning the future pattern of wage and labor costs. Labor leaders support the practice of multiyear contracts because it offers the union a significant measure of security and relieves them of the intense political pressures produced by frequent contract negotiations.

Phase II commenced at the tail end of the three-year bargaining cycle. The heaviest incidence of new agreements in the major bargaining units (including 1,000 employees or more) had taken place in 1970. The basic steel agreement covering over 300,000 workers had been signed on August 1, 1971, fifteen days before the imposition of the wage-price freeze. A new contract had been reached between the Communications Workers of America and most of the Bell Telephone system on August 14. Bargaining in the longshoring and coal industries had begun in mid-1971, although prolonged strikes had stalled negotiations. In contrast, 1972 promised to be a light year on the bargaining calendar, with negotiations scheduled for less important industries, such as garments, paper, and lumber. According to the Bureau of Labor Statistics (BLS), negotiations over the terms of *new* contracts in major bargaining units would involve only 2.8 million workers; in 1970 at the beginning of the bargaining round, approximately 4.8 million workers were affected by negotiations in large units.[1]

The relationship between the timing of Phase II and the bargaining

1. Michael E. Sparrough and Lena W. Bolton, "Calendar of Wage Increases and Negotiations for 1972," *Monthly Labor Review,* vol. 95 (January 1972), p. 4.

cycle posed conflicting considerations of equity and economics. On the one hand, the BLS estimated that during 1972, 6 million workers would receive deferred wage increases averaging about 6 percent; almost 1 million workers, many of whom were in the construction and transportation industries, were scheduled to receive deferred wage increases of 8 percent or more.[2] Because more workers would receive deferred increases under existing contracts than through the negotiation of new agreements in 1972, it would be difficult to contain the wage gains registered by the current contracts unless some action was taken to curb the deferred increases. Moreover, the magnitude of the deferred increases could exert significant pressure on prices.

On the other hand, government intervention to limit the wage gains agreed upon by both parties long before the wage-price freeze would have severe implications for industrial relations practices. In most cases a multiyear agreement represented a comprehensive bargain between the union and management on a variety of issues. In order to win a given wage increase, the union often dropped other demands or made concessions on such issues as seniority and work rules. Any effort to reduce the amount of the deferred wage increases would undermine the complicated balance of costs and benefits worked out by the parties during the bargaining process. With some justification the union could complain of inequitable treatment if forced to forgo some of its gains while management had no equivalent burden. Some insight into the probable labor reaction was obtained by assessing the outrage expressed by the AFL-CIO when scheduled wage increases were not permitted to take effect during the freeze.

Retroactivity

Of the three major policy questions, the retroactivity issue was the least consequential in economic terms but engendered the strongest emotions and the sharpest question of principle. The problem of retroactivity arose because of the Cost of Living Council's rule denying wage increases during the ninety-day freeze period, even though they had been agreed to before August 15, 1971. The CLC viewed the denial of wage increases under these circumstances as part of a broad policy prohibiting increases resulting from future contracts. The policy was equally applicable to

2. "Special Analysis of Deferred Increases Scheduled for 1972," prepared by U.S. Bureau of Labor Statistics for the Pay Board (October 30, 1971; processed).

prices and rents. In the wage area it had the heaviest impact on school teachers. Many teachers had signed contracts during the spring and summer for higher salaries to become effective when they reported to work for the new school year at the end of August or the beginning of September. In a highly controversial ruling, the CLC had prohibited these additional amounts from being paid during the freeze.[3]

The specific issue to be considered by the Pay Board was whether these employees could claim the wage increases on a retroactive basis following the termination of the freeze on November 13, 1971. Although a large number of employees were affected by the retroactivity issue, the impact of these payments on the economy as a whole was trivial. Estimates at the time the issue was considered indicated that the total wage bill that would be incurred by retroactive payments probably would not exceed $1 billion. Subsequent calculations were significantly lower.[4] For the members of the Pay Board, however, the economic implications were overshadowed by other factors. The unions and the teachers' organizations regarded the "freeze money" as their just claim under existing contracts. The contrasting view held that various groups in the economy, including rentiers and businessmen, had also been denied increased income under the general policy barring the implementation of future contracts. Furthermore, had controls not been imposed, many workers in nonunion situations surely would have received wage adjustments as a result of ongoing personnel practices. To permit one group to have retroactive payments while denying the same right to other similarly affected groups would compound rather than remedy the inequity.

Developing Positions

After the Pay Board had identified the basic issues, its three factions proceeded to formulate their positions in separate caucuses. The process of policy development was always disorganized, usually acrimonious, and sometimes rowdy. Each group assumed that the task would be an exercise in bargaining rather than in rational decisionmaking.

The adversary aspects of this bargaining were accentuated by the ab-

3. Arnold R. Weber, *In Pursuit of Price Stability: The Wage-Price Freeze of 1971* (Brookings Institution, 1973), pp. 58–59.
4. Calculations made by the Pay Board staff following the enactment of legislation requiring the payment of retroactive salaries indicated that the total wage bill involved was probably closer to $0.5 billion than to $1 billion.

sence of any effective lines of communication among the public, business, and labor members. The labor representatives' private statements at Pay Board meetings echoed their public resentment of the administration's economic program. In addition, the background of the public members did not create the expectation that the board would lend a sympathetic ear to labor's complaints or provide an arena for the informal dealing that is the standard operating mode of industrial relations practitioners. Nor was this gap likely to be filled by the board chairman, Judge Boldt. The conviction of Dave Beck, at whose trial Boldt had presided, scarcely could have persuaded the labor members that the judge was well informed about, or sympathetic to, union goals.

The process of policy formulation was further tattered by inadequate staff resources. The Pay Board's staff was virtually nonexistent during the first days of the agency. In fact, the board had no permanent professional staff for nearly a month. Instead, personnel were assigned to the board on an indefinite temporary basis from other federal agencies (or "detailed," in civil service parlance). Some of these temporary employees remained to become members of the permanent complement; others drifted back to their home agencies after a few days. In any case the faces changed with great rapidity, and it was impossible to maintain any continuity of staff support during these early critical discussions. To the extent that any research or policy analysis was carried out, the burden was assumed by the Bureau of Labor Statistics.

The business and labor groups individually enjoyed more stable support. The business members set up headquarters in a Washington hotel suite and conscripted personnel from some of the members' firms to aid in the planning and shaping of positions. The General Electric Company was the most generous in providing professional and secretarial resources. It is accurate to state, however, that business entered the fray with a platoon of back-area troops and not an armored division. Similarly, professional support on the labor side was obtained from the AFL-CIO research staff based in Washington, and additional help was enlisted from the individual unions.

The Business Members' Proposal

The business group took the lead in formulating proposals to resolve the three critical issues. As expected in a bargaining context, the business members adopted a hard line in their initial position. Under the terms of their proposal "permissible annual aggregate increases would be limited to 5 percent of an employer's total compensation within any recognized employee category or group. . . . Total compensation includes wages, salaries, and all forms of benefits."[5] The general pay standard would be equally applicable to wage adjustments negotiated after November 13, 1971, and to deferred increases under existing agreements. The parties could apply for an exception to the general pay standard, but the criteria for waiving the 5 percent limit were not elaborated. The draft made no reference to retroactivity. By inference, payment could not be made for wage increases that were blocked during the freeze.

The only element of flexibility in the business proposal provided for a transition period between the end of the freeze and December 31, 1971. During these seven weeks pay adjustments could exceed the 5 percent standard as long as the increase was the result of "good faith negotiations in conjunction with a normal and not an accelerated expiration of a labor agreement."[6] The exact amount of the permissible increment was not spelled out. Rather, it was left to the full board for enumeration. Informally, individual business members indicated that a 7 percent ceiling would be acceptable until December 31, 1971.

The business proposal was drafted without any prior discussion with other groups on the Pay Board. Individual public and business members had conversed casually about it, but the details of the proposition were never disclosed. More seriously, these conversations created the impression among the public members that business was reaching an independent agreement, that is, "cutting a deal" with the labor members. Under the simple arithmetic of Pay Board rules, the business and labor groups could muster sufficient votes to determine the basic policies of the wage stabilization program without giving any weight to the public members' views.

The Public Members' Proposal

Originally the public members had agreed among themselves to withhold their proposal until formal statements had been forthcoming from business and labor. Although the public members eschewed a mediator's role, it seemed prudent at this early stage of the deliberations to remain silent. Once the labor and business positions were known, the public

5. From authors' personal records of Pay Board activities.
6. Ibid.

members could develop an alternative that would reflect their own views but would also be an attempt to accommodate some of the needs of the other parties. Then apprehension that labor and business would present them with a fait accompli caused the public members to alter their strategy. They hastily drafted a formal proposal to present when the business position was put on the table. But when business revealed its proposal, the public members found their concern to be unfounded. The premature divulgence of the public members' position further limited their capacity to play a constructive, if not neutral, role in the deliberations.

The public members' proposal also adopted a stringent approach to wage stabilization, partly to counteract the fictitious deal. First, it stated that there should be a numerical pay standard of 5 percent. The public members recognized that the standard, as finally approved, probably would be somewhat higher, but they considered 5 percent to be a reasonable opening position.

Second, no retroactivity would be permitted. They based this judgment on the belief that it would be highly inequitable to restore the losses incurred during the freeze by employees who were covered by collective bargaining contracts without providing the same relief to other groups that had been similarly stricken by the events of August 15. All the public members strongly supported this position in principle, but a more flexible approach was actively considered in order to win labor support for a package that would establish the stabilization program on a sound basis. Since the economic consequences of permitting retroactivity were minimal, retroactivity could be traded for a more favorable policy on the general pay standard or deferred increases without jeopardizing the overall effectiveness of the program. After extended discussion, the majority of the public members was unwilling to adopt this pragmatic approach, and a general policy of denying retroactivity was confirmed in the proposal.

Third, a formula was contrived to balance the conflicting interests associated with deferred increases. On the one hand, the public members believed that it was critical to provide some limitation on the size of deferred increases in order to preserve the credibility of the general pay standard applicable to contracts negotiated after November 13, 1971. On the other hand, it was important for the board to accommodate labor's sense of equity and to protect the stability of industrial relations practices by giving deferred increases preferred treatment. In steering between these considerations, the public members proposed that deferred increases should be honored in the amount that was specified in each existing contract. The effective date of the increase, however, would be moved forward as appropriate to reduce the adjustment to an annualized rate of 5 percent. Thus if a deferred increase of 6 percent was scheduled to take effect on January 1, 1972, the effective date would be moved forward until March 15 without reducing the amount of the increase. This "sliding" approach was designed to reduce the economic impact of the deferred wage increases, while ultimately permitting their implementation and incorporation in the wage base for calculating subsequent permissible increases.

Labor Reacts

The business and public proposals were presented to the full board on November 3. The reaction of the labor representatives was negative from the outset and welled to mountainous indignation during the course of a four-hour meeting. Leonard Woodcock dismissed the propositions "as arrant nonsense."[7] George Meany was equally vocal in his displeasure. At one point the labor members declared that it was futile to continue discussions and made preliminary motions to leave the meeting. But the session did continue, and the labor representatives moved from general expressions of scorn to detailed criticisms.

The labor members flatly stated that no proposal would be acceptable unless it permitted the payment of retroactive increases. For organized labor, redeeming the "freeze money" had become a matter of principle and extreme emotion. The labor spokesmen also insisted that all existing contracts including deferred increases should be honored. It was noted, however, that the Construction Industry Stabilization Committee, set up in March 1971 to regulate wages in the construction sector, was empowered to deal with deferred increases and had modified them in some cases, indicating that flexibility on this issue was not out of the question.

The most prolonged discussions focused on the necessity for a numerical pay standard. The 5 percent standard included in both the business and public memoranda was based on a mechanical, technical assessment of the increase in the general level of wages that would be consistent with the attainment of an inflation rate of 2–3 percent by the end of 1972. Assuming a long-term increase in national productivity of 3 percent, a general wage standard of 5 percent presumably would support the

7. Ibid.

attainment of a 2 percent price goal. Labor dismissed this figure as oppressive and unrealistic and opposed *any* formal numerical standard. Labor asserted that instead, there should be a verbal delineation of the pay standard and that each situation should be evaluated on a case-by-case basis. In labor's view the approach taken by the Wage Stabilization Board during the Korean war provided the appropriate model for emulation.

The business members aggressively pursued the argument for a numerical standard, contending that a numerical system was necessary to provide discipline for the program. Moreover, nonunion small-business employers needed explicit guidance for setting their wage policies. Without a specific numerical standard, these employers would not have a clear basis for action. Robert Bassett, who was nominally the small-business representative on the board, made this argument with special eloquence. The discussion ended inconclusively and with a quality of spent rancor. Obviously this was the first step in what would be a protracted sequence of bargaining.

Labor Proposes

The labor members presented their version of the three commandments one day later, on November 4. The policy statement incorporated many of the principles that had been expressed at the earlier meetings. As an indication of reasonableness, however, the preamble was almost a verbatim restatement of the introductory remarks in the business proposal.

Millions of workers in the Nation are looking to the Pay Board for guidance with respect to permissible changes in wages, salaries, various benefits and all other forms of employee total compensation. It is imperative to have a simple standard with as broad a coverage as possible at as early a date as possible. There is probably a need for exceptions and for individual consideration of special situations as soon as practical, and guidance to the millions whose pay relations are relatively simple is an early essential.[8]

The critical elements of the labor proposal were included in sections 4 and 5.

4. The general pay standard would provide:
   (a) On and after this date permissible annual aggregate increases would be those normally considered supportable by productivity improvement and cost of living trends.

8. "Tentative Proposal for Consideration by Pay Board: Labor Proposal of November 4, 1971, as Amended November 5, 1971."

   (b) Existing contracts and policies previously set forth would be allowed to
operate according to their terms except that specific contracts or policies are subject to review, when challenged by a party at interest or the
Board, to determine whether any increase is unreasonably inconsistent
with the criteria established by this Board.

   (c) Ongoing collective bargaining and policies shall also be permitted to
bring [employees] into an equitable position with their counterparts in
the economy.

5. Following approval of special procedures by the Pay Board with respect to
"prior approval" cases and other special situations, application may be made
for an exception to the general pay standard and for a hearing on such matters as inequities and sub-standard conditions.

The labor proposal approached the definition of the general pay standard at two levels. First, it was marked by the absence of any specific,
arithmetic standard. Instead, it referred to permissible increases "supportable by productivity improvement and cost of living trends." Second,
it provided for exceptions to reflect the "equitable position" of the employees involved "with their counterparts in the economy."

This combination of a qualitative standard and a global provision for
exceptions clearly would afford the parties—and the board—the widest
latitude in reaching judgments in individual cases. In effect, sections 4
(a) and (c) together virtually assured that the board would operate on a
case-by-case basis. Section 5 established the right of appeal for an exception and further introduced the concept of substandard conditions.
The specific meaning of "substandard conditions" was unclear, but it
appeared to restore a policy developed by the National War Labor Board
during World War II when the concept of substandard wages was used to
afford special treatment to low-wage workers.[9]

The policy toward deferred increases was enunciated in section 4(b).
Under this provision deferred increases—that is, "existing contracts . . .
previously set forth"—would automatically go into effect. The parties at
interest or the board could challenge these increases to determine whether
they were "unreasonably inconsistent" with the board's criteria. Presumably if an increase was found to be reasonable by the board's standards, it would continue without modification. If it was "unreasonably
inconsistent," some adjustment could be made. In other words, deferred

   9. *The Termination Report of the National War Labor Board*, vol. 1: *Industrial
Disputes and Wage Stabilization in Wartime* (Government Printing Office, 1947),
pp. 211–25.

increases were given full force and effect in the absence of any positive steps taken by the board. The oxymoronic formulation of "unreasonably inconsistent" was borrowed from the executive order governing the operation of the Construction Industry Stabilization Committee, which used the case-by-case approach and was generally viewed with favor by the labor representatives.

This affirmation of "existing contracts . . . previously set forth" also was intended to permit the retroactive payment of deferred wage increases that had been blocked by the freeze. The specific language in section 4(b) indicated that retroactive wage increases could be challenged, but this right was more of a formality than an effort to deal systematically with individual cases. As a practical matter, it would be impossible to modify these retroactive increases on an ex post basis once they had been implemented under the authority of section 4(b).

The labor proposal precipitated intensive discussion, much of which went over ground that had been covered previously. Again, the business and public members strongly emphasized the need for a numerical pay standard. They also expressed concern that the formula for dealing with deferred increases was too imprecise for effective review or control. The retroactivity issue received little attention because it was recognized that the labor representatives' strong feelings on this matter would only be inflamed by further discussion. The meeting ended with an agreement that the business and public members would carefully reassess their positions in the light of the labor proposition.

Framework for Consensus

The events of the meeting on November 4 were viewed as the first encouraging developments since the Pay Board had been convened. The discussion had moved from polemics to specifics. Informal communication with the labor members was still virtually nonexistent, but the formal exchange had assumed a more realistic tone. The public members decided that it would be tactically undesirable to develop a new proposal. Instead, they preferred to offer a set of principles on which to base continued discussion of the major policy issues. By stating these principles the public members hoped to establish a framework for direct negotiations between the business and labor members. At the same time, the public members might refurbish their status as constructive neutrals between the two in-

terest groups. The principles would be stated orally rather than added to
the growing sheaf of written proposals and counterproposals.

The board reconvened the next day, on Friday, November 5. George
Meany temporarily deflected the plan to define a framework for consensus when he announced that he wanted to make a statement. He declared that the labor members had listened carefully to the earlier comments and had modified their proposal to reflect the most persuasive
arguments. First, section 4(a), describing the general pay standard, was
modified by adding the phrase "or 6%." Second, section 4(b), covering
deferred increases, was supplemented by the sentence, "This right of
review shall not apply to any increase of 8% or less."

Meany asserted that these changes represented significant concessions
and should provide a basis for agreement by the board. He particularly
noted that the labor members would now go along with a specific numerical standard in order to provide clear guidance for "the little fellows"
whose plight had been so poignantly addressed by the business members.
The introduction of a cutoff point for the right to challenge and review
deferred increases also should contribute to certainty in the operation of
the program. On the other hand, this amendment provided for de facto
approval of all deferred increases of less than 8 percent.

Meany then called for a vote "up or down." His motives in demanding an immediate response were not completely clear. One contributing
factor was his scheduled departure for Bal Harbour for the AFL-CIO
convention. Reportedly, Meany was preparing to leave by train on Sunday afternoon, just two days hence. It was reasonable to assume that he
wanted to go to the convention with conclusive board action in hand so
that he could affirm or assail these policies, as the case might be.

Despite the labor members' call for quick action, the full board was
unwilling to vote. The members had seriously discussed the basic issues
at only two meetings. In addition, the boundaries of the conflicting bargaining positions had been defined only the day before. Both the public
and business members argued that it would be precipitate to have a formal
vote on the labor motion at the same meeting where it had been presented.
Instead, further discussion was necessary.

Meany insisted on a vote and tartly expressed his displeasure when the
public members indicated that if a vote was called they would all abstain.
Since eight votes were required for a board action, if the public members
abstained, any poll on the labor proposal was expected to result in five
"for" (the labor members) and five "against" (the business members).

Meany reacted to this ploy by demanding, "How long are you going to keep us prisoner?"[10]

After an embarrassed silence the public members persisted in presenting their statement of principles to serve as a basis for agreement. First, they asserted that a numerical pay standard should be adopted. In order to have a reasonable hope of achieving the 2–3 percent price goal by the end of 1972, the average rate of increase of compensation per man-hour for the economy as a whole should not exceed 6 percent. The pay standard should be consistent with this goal, although it might differ in its precise terms. Various factors intrinsic to the administration of the stabilization program or outside the control of the board probably would result in increases above the pay standard. These included equity adjustments, interindustry shifts in employment, and the possible enactment of an increase in the minimum wage. On balance, it would be prudent to endorse a pay standard that was somewhat below 6 percent in order to reach that target for increases in average compensation.

The second principle accepted the labor contention that existing contracts should be allowed to operate after November 14, 1971, according to their terms, except where the contract provided an increase in wage and benefits in excess of a stated amount. By inference this cutoff point would be higher than the general pay standard in recognition of the special considerations involved in the deferred increase issue. When the increase was above the cutoff point it could be suspended for a limited period of time if challenged by the employer who was a party to the agreement or by any member of the board. The board's ruling concerning the acceptable level of the deferred wage increase would become effective retroactively to the date originally specified in the contract. The cutoff point for challenges was not enumerated.

Last, retroactivity for pay increases banned by the freeze would be denied. The board, however, could review individual cases and approve back pay in those situations where substantial evidence showed that price increases had occurred in anticipation of the wage changes for which retroactivity was claimed.

Thus the public members' statement purported to move toward a middle position. While insisting on a numerical pay standard—which now had been conceded by labor—the principle signaled flexibility in the application of the standard. Deferred increases generally would be allowed to go into effect subject to a challenge-and-review procedure. And the

10. From authors' personal records of Pay Board activities.

slightest shift was made in the public members' stand on retroactivity to permit these payments in narrowly defined circumstances.

These principles were received without comment by the labor and business members. Judge Boldt then suggested that the two groups meet separately to determine if the principles offered by the public members provided a framework for agreement. The Pay Board would be scheduled to meet the next morning and informal discussions could go forward at that time. A meeting of the full board would be reconvened to assess the progress that had been made to identify the unresolved issues. The members agreed to this procedure and a sense of optimism flickered for the first time.

What promised to be a climactic meeting proved to be a fiasco for reasons unrelated to the substantive issues involved. All the board members, including George Meany, showed up at the Executive Office Building at 10:00 A.M. Each of the three factions settled down in individual rooms on the same floor. It was assumed that the labor and business representatives would take the initiative to meet with each other in accordance with the procedures that had been spelled out at the previous session. Throughout the morning, however, the different groups waited like expectant suitors for a call that never came. Apparently each thought that the other would make the first move or that the public members would act as convener. At one point during the morning Judge Boldt went to the room where the labor members were assembled. He stood at the door and asked whether he could be of any help. No response was forthcoming.

The morning dragged on without further communication between the separate caucuses. At about 1:00 P.M. the public members went out to lunch by themselves at a restaurant across the street from the Executive Office Building. At the restaurant Boldt received a telephone call from Meany, who said he wanted to meet with Boldt and the public members immediately. They quickly left the restaurant, to their digestive discomfort, and returned to the Executive Office Building. Meany eloquently indicated his unhappiness with the course of events and expressed the belief that the labor members had been purposely ignored. In his opening speech to the AFL-CIO convention in Bal Harbour twelve days later, Meany recounted his version of the episode and the intent that it revealed.

. . . the minutes will show that we were to meet at 11:00 A.M. They don't show much but they at least show this. We were sitting in this room, all the labor members and the people working with us there, and the Judge stuck his nose in the door about a quarter after 11:00 and said, "If you need me, I will be around." Then he *and the industry members* went to lunch and they didn't even tell us that they were going to lunch. [Emphasis added.]

We didn't see the Judge again until 4:00 o'clock that afternoon. We just sat in his room. This was deliberate. I think they were trying to goad us into walking out. At least I got that impression.[11]

The incident clearly contributed to Meany's dyspeptic view of the earlier discussions. In describing the process of negotiation, Meany stated:

I want to tell you, I have been around a long time; I don't have to tell you that; you read that in the paper. But I have been around a long time and I will tell you in all my experience never have I gone through a more frustrating, debasing experience, I would say. I have been insulted by experts in my time.[12]

Following Meany's outburst in the Executive Office Building, Boldt attempted to explain, with little success, that there had been a misunderstanding. He then reassembled the full board. Because of the morning's events, the members made no progress on substantive matters. Indeed the negotiations had retrogressed, and there was little chance of developing a unanimous policy statement—if such a possibility had ever really existed. The labor members reiterated their demand for a vote on the amended proposal. Again the public members stated their unwillingness to act at that time. Instead, they called for another meeting on the next day, Sunday. The labor members reacted coldly to the thought of a Sunday session. Meany expressed his perception of these developments to the AFL-CIO convention on November 18 in the following terms:

When they finally got to the meeting at 4:00 o'clock that afternoon, we requested a vote and we couldn't get it.

We informed them that no matter how long they delayed it, we were going to be there. They knew that I was due to come here to attend the building trades meeting, and I told them I was cancelling that and I was going to stay there, and I would stay there until midnight on December 13 if that is what they wanted. Well, I guess they understood they weren't going to force us to walk out."[13]

Following labor's rejection of a Sunday session, the members did agree to convene on Monday afternoon, November 8, at 4:30 P.M. It was tacitly accepted that the Monday meeting would be the last formal session on the major policy issues and that a final vote would be taken. Relations with the labor members had been severely strained, and it was unlikely that further efforts at accommodation could be successful.

11. *Proceedings of the Ninth Constitutional Convention of the AFL-CIO, Bal Harbour, Florida, November 18–22, 1971: Daily Proceedings and Executive Council Reports* (AFL-CIO, n.d.), p. 23.

12. Ibid., p. 22.

13. Ibid., pp. 23–24.

Inching toward a Policy Statement

The public and business members continued to meet separately over the weekend to draft resolutions that would provide the basis for the board's policy statement. The public members attempted to move as close to the amended labor position as they could while preserving their view of an effective wage stabilization program. They first agreed that the general pay standard should be set at 5.5 percent. The selection of the 5.5 percent figure reflected the coincidence of both political and economic considerations. That is, 5.5 percent was clearly a middle position between the original public and business position of 5 percent and labor's willingness to accept a 6 percent standard. At the same time, 5.5 percent was technically consistent with the attainment of the price goal whereby the rate of price increases would be reduced to the 2–3 percent level by the end of 1972. Moreover, the 5.5 percent yardstick presumably provided a 0.5 percent cushion for exceptions and other factors that might exert upward pressure on the board's approvals.

In spelling out the 5.5 percent general pay standard, the public members also endorsed the concept of flexibility incorporated in section 4(c) of the labor proposal. In reviewing new contracts and pay practices, the board would consider "ongoing collective bargaining and pay practices and the equitable position of the employees involved."[14] The confirmation of this principle was designed to placate labor; in addition, it was acknowledged to be a sound approach in dealing with the myriad cases that were sure to come to the board at the end of the freeze.

The labor position on deferred increases was accepted virtually verbatim. Contracts "previously set forth" would be allowed to operate according to their terms except "when challenged by a party at interest or by five or more members of the board."[15] The public members' formulation, however, dropped the proviso that the right of review should apply only to any increase of 8 percent or more, as originally proposed by labor. A specific cutoff was dropped in order to avert further dispute over what the proper number should be and to allow the board members greater discretion in the administration of the general policy.

The retroactivity question continued to be the most complex and contentious of the basic policy issues. Following extended discussion, the

14. "Policies Governing Pay Adjustments Proposed by the Public Members of the Pay Board" (November 7, 1971; processed).
15. Ibid.

public members modified their earlier position to permit the retroactive payment of wage increases denied during the freeze under three conditions: (1) if the employer had raised prices in anticipation of wage increases scheduled to occur during the freeze; (2) where a wage agreement made after August 15, 1971, succeeded a contract that had expired before August 16, 1971, and where retroactivity was an established practice or had been agreed to by the parties; and (3) to remedy severe inequities. This last condition, of course, was a safety valve that would permit the board to deal with other circumstances it could not foresee at the time.

The public members' final proposal was rounded out by two additional clauses adapted from earlier labor and business statements. The first declared that no "retroactive downward" adjustment, that is, pay cuts, of wage rates legally instituted would be required by the application of the general pay standard. The last clause was an innocuous proviso recognizing vacation plans, longevity increases, and related components of compensation.

On Sunday evening, November 7, a delegation of public members met with the business representatives to review their revised proposal. The business members had not progressed far beyond their original proposition. After a discursive discussion of various formulas for handling deferred increases, they indicated a willingness to support the public members' policy statement in its entirety. But as a formality they would introduce their own resolution for a vote by the board.

One last effort was made to communicate with the labor members. On Sunday evening and Monday morning, calls were made to the individual union leaders for private meetings to discuss the proposal to be presented at the board meeting on Monday afternoon. In each case the offer was accepted. During these sessions the labor members listened noncommittally and gave no hint of their final response. Each union leader was advised that similar presentations were being made to other labor representatives. This precaution was taken to avoid any suggestion that an effort was being made to reach agreements with individuals rather than with the group as a whole. Any intimation that the public members were trying to split the labor bloc would surely have exacerbated an already tender situation.

This cautionary statement did not have the desired effect. In providing his account of events that took place before the Monday meeting, Meany said:

And I can tell you there was a deliberate attempt here to divide the labor movement, because on the Monday before the vote was taken they sent an individual public member to see every labor member to try to tell that particular labor member not to worry, not to worry.[16]

When the board assembled for the decisive meeting on Monday, it underwent another one of the seemingly endless series of misadventures that had plagued this hapless body. The thermostat in the room where the sessions were held had been erratic since the first board meeting. On some occasions the heat was overbearing and reached well above 80 degrees. At other times cool air rolled out of the air conditioner like arctic mist, reducing the temperature to barely tolerable levels. On this occasion the hyperactive thermostat had dropped the temperature in the room to 56 degrees. Several of the members, including George Meany, sat at the table in their overcoats—an ironically appropriate costume for the meeting at which the policies that would end the wage freeze would be determined. After ten minutes one of the labor members rose and vehemently announced that he would not remain in the room any longer because of the frigid temperature. Judge Boldt notified the Cost of Living Council liaison representative who was posted outside the door. The CLC staff member scurried to find another meeting room. The only available space was the conference room used by the director of the Office of Management and Budget. This room was afforded a measure of reverence in government circles because it was there that top OMB officials drew up the federal budget.

The board moved to this new site, and the meeting recommenced. There was no preliminary discussion; instead, the chairman called for a vote on the amended labor resolution. The proposal was defeated by a vote of ten to five, with the public and business members voting against and the labor members supporting their own motion.

A vote was then taken on the business members' policy statement. The distinctive feature of the resolution was its continued adherence to a flat 5 percent pay standard. The resolution also was defeated ten to five, with negative votes cast by the labor and public members.[17]

Next, the public members put their proposal on the table. Before the vote was taken the labor members pursued an intensive line of questioning. They gave their attention almost exclusively to the exceptions clause, which stated that the Pay Board would consider "ongoing collective bargaining and pay practices and the equitable position of the employees involved," in reviewing new contracts that provided wage increases in ex-

16. *Proceedings,* p. 25.
17. Minutes of the Pay Board, November 8, 1971.

cess of the general standard. Since the concept had been adopted almost verbatim from the labor proposal, there was a reasonable basis for assuming that the union leaders were familiar with the intent of the clause.

Nonetheless, Meany and Leonard Woodcock aggressively pressed the matter. Their questions primarily concerned the probable status of particular agreements under the exceptions clause. Since none of the contracts in question had yet been negotiated, the inquiries had an overt hypothetical quality. Specific queries were addressed to situations in the coal, railroad, aerospace, and longshoring industries where bargaining was in process or close to completion. In each case it could be expected that settlements would exceed the 5.5 percent ceiling by a significant amount. Moreover, all the contracts had expired before the freeze, and special factors might constitute strong arguments.

The replies to this interrogation indicated a willingness to actively consider increases above the general pay standard because of special circumstances. Individual public and business members stated that the exceptions clause would provide a framework for the review of these cases. However, because the details of the contracts had not yet been agreed to by the parties themselves, no conclusive judgment could be made. As the colloquy continued, Meany said it was clear to him that the public members would take care of the "big guys" but would not be sympathetic to the needs of the "little guys." The rejoinder that the exceptions clause would be applicable to any situation that met the criteria in the policy statement did not allay this concern. In reporting to the AFL-CIO convention, Meany narrated his version of the exchange.

... we had about a half hour of discussion asking Mr. Weber how this [the exceptions clause] would work. And it was very, very interesting.

He was sitting there with the proposal in front of him and we said, how is this going to affect the West Coast longshoremen? He says they will be taken care of under (c)2.

How about the railroads? Oh, they will be taken care of under (c)2.

How about aerospace? Oh, they will be taken care of under this, that, and the other thing. And he went down the line: Railroads, aerospace, me too contracts, so on and so forth. Finally, I said, hell, what about the little guys? You are taking care of all the big guys.

Well, he said, we take care of anybody who fits into these particular qualifications.

Oh, yes, and the Teamsters were taken care of, everything, freeze pay because they had gotten some contracts oh, a little over that five and a half. Maybe three times over, something like that. But they are all right, they are going to be taken care of.

All the big unions are going to be taken care of, but not all the members of all the big unions. All the big unions that have the big contracts, so on and so forth.[18]

The board's discussion did not promote understanding. Indeed the structure of the questions and inferences was impenetrable. If the exceptions clause could not be used to review the situations that were described, then it had little significance, and the general pay standard could be construed as a rigid guide to permissible wage settlements. On the other hand, when it was indicated that the exceptions clause was conceived as a mechanism for handling the major cases identified by labor as problems in the transition from Phase I to Phase II, then the policy was aimed at mollifying the "big fellows" to the detriment of the "little fellows."

When the questions were exhausted, a formal vote was taken on the public members' resolution. The proposal was affirmed by a vote of ten to five, with the labor representatives voting against.[19]

The complete text of the public members' resolution read as follows:

1. Millions of workers in the Nation are looking to the Pay Board for guidance with respect to permissible changes in wages, salaries, various benefits and all other forms of employee total compensation. It is imperative to have a simple standard with as broad a coverage as possible at as early a date as possible. There is probably a need for exceptions and for individual consideration of special situations as soon as practical, and guidance to the millions whose pay relations are relatively simple is an early essential.

2. This general pay standard is intended, in conjunction with other needed measures, to meet the objectives which led to the establishment of this Board.

3. The general pay standard should be applicable to:
  (1) changes that need approval before becoming effective;
  (2) changes that must be reported when they become effective; and
  (3) all other changes requiring compliance but not requiring specific approval or reporting.

4. (a) Effective November 14, 1971, the general pay standard shall be applicable to new labor agreements and, where no labor agreement is in effect, to existing pay practices. The general pay standard would provide:

On and after November 14, 1971, permissible annual aggregate increases would be those normally considered supportable by productivity improvement and cost of living trends. Initially, the general pay standard is established as 5.5%. The appropriateness of this figure will be reviewed periodically by the Board, taking into account such factors as the long-term productivity trend of 3%, cost of living trends, and the objective of reducing inflation.

18. *Proceedings*, pp. 24–25.
19. Minutes of the Pay Board, November 8, 1971.

In reviewing new contracts and pay practices, the Pay Board shall consider on-going collective bargaining and pay practices and the equitable position of the employees involved, including the impact of recent changes in the cost of living upon the employees' compensation.

(b) Existing contracts and pay practices previously set forth will be allowed to operate according to their terms except that specific contracts or pay practices are subject to review, when challenged by a party at interest or by five or more members of the Board, to determine whether any increase is unreasonably inconsistent with the criteria established by this Board.

In reviewing existing contracts and pay practices, the Pay Board shall consider ongoing collective bargaining and pay practices and the equitable position of the employees involved, including the impact of recent changes in the cost of living upon the employees' compensation.

(c) Scheduled increases in payment for services rendered during the "freeze" of August 16 through November 13, 1971, may be made only if approved by the Board in specific cases. The Board may approve such payments in cases which are shown to meet any of the following criteria:

   (i) Prices were raised in anticipation of wage increases scheduled to occur during the "freeze."

   (ii) A wage agreement made after August 15, 1971, succeeded an agreement that had expired prior to August 16, 1971, and retroactivity was an established practice or had been agreed to by the parties.

   (iii) Such other criteria as the Board may hereafter establish to remedy severe inequities.

5. Following approval of special procedures by the Pay Board with respect to hearing "prior approval" cases and other special situations, application may be made for an exception to the general pay standard and for a hearing on such matters as inequities and sub-standard conditions.

6. No retroactive downward adjustment of rates now being paid will be required by operation of the general pay standard unless the rates were raised in violation of the freeze or of the general pay standard.

7. Provisions may be considered for vacation plans, in-plant adjustments of wages and salaries, in-grade and length of service increases, payments under compensation plans, transfers and the like.[20]

The meeting broke up immediately without any of the niceties that often attend the conclusion of labor negotiations. In a real sense the bargaining had just begun. At a press conference that evening Judge Boldt informed the press and the public of the Pay Board's decisions without elaboration beyond the technical details of the policy statement. His formal statement alluded to the conflict associated with the board's deliberations but ended on an upbeat note.

It is fair to state that each and every member of the board has worked on our problems with great dedication and diligence. For the past two weeks we

20. "Policies Governing Pay Adjustments."

have been working many hours every day to achieve a result as fair to all Americans, whatever their economic situation, as the complexities of the problems involved will permit.

Issues are involved which allow for wide ranges of judgment and opinion, and some of them arouse strong feelings. I would be less than candid not to admit that viewpoints have been exchanged with considerable emphasis from time to time. . . .

I believe these first policy decisions can and will provide a starting point for a program which will achieve the ultimate goal of ending inflation.

With the understanding, cooperation and support of the vast majority of Americans, the program will succeed. On behalf of my colleagues and myself, we ask the American people to give us that cooperation.[21]

Immediately after the Pay Board had acted Meany journeyed to the AFL-CIO convention in Bal Harbour. The convention was the occasion for a flood of oratory harshly attacking President Nixon's economic program in general and the Pay Board and the public members in particular. Obviously the convention delegates did not share Judge Boldt's optimism that the worst was behind the board. The report adopted by the convention concerning the Phase II system of wage controls dolorously noted:

There is little hope that economic justice can be achieved by this Board, the majority of whom [sic] are guided by the dictates of the Administration or the interests of big business.[22]

The conclave was also distinguished by the personal appearance of President Nixon, who defended Phase II and the administration's economic record. The President had requested the opportunity to speak to the delegates, and his appearance precipitated another cause célèbre. At the close of the President's speech Meany curtly announced to the convention, "We will now proceed with Act Two."[23] President Nixon on his own part made a special effort to shake hands with individual delegates in an apparent effort to make contact outside the narrow channels permitted by Meany as chairman of the convention. The event precipitated a furious exchange of public criticisms and defenses of both the President's and Meany's actions. The imbroglio entered labor annals as "the Battle of Bal Harbour" along with other notable exchanges such as John L. Lewis's attack on President Franklin Roosevelt.[24]

21. Statement of George H. Boldt, chairman of the Pay Board, November 8, 1971, as cited in the *New York Times,* November 9, 1971.

22. *Proceedings,* p. 57.

23. Ibid., p. 166.

24. For an exposition of this series of events from the AFL-CIO's point of view, see Joseph C. Goulden, *Meany* (Atheneum, 1972), pp. 446–50. Goulden coined the characterization "the Battle of Bal Harbour."

What Price Policy?

It is apparent that the Pay Board's process of policy formulation was fitful at best. From the outset it suffered severely from inadequate planning and staff resources. To a degree these deficiencies were inherent in the autonomous, tripartite nature of the Pay Board. Because the board was designed to be independent of government influence in order to win labor's participation, it could not readily call on the resources of the federal bureaucracy or be preplanned by the Cost of Living Council. These logistical problems were aggravated by the extreme time pressure under which the board operated. The board held its first business meeting on October 27; the freeze was scheduled to expire on the evening of November 13. The broad policies governing Phase II had to be determined and promulgated well before November 13 in order to inform the public, draft the supporting regulations, organize the staff, and give attention to the other minutiae of a bureaucratic enterprise. Under ordinary circumstances these would be difficult tasks; in the frenetic environment that prevailed at the time they became excruciatingly difficult.

A combination of misfortune, misunderstanding, and ineptness accentuated the organizational problems of the Pay Board. No planning system can take account of a balky thermostat; and what might have been a passing irritation was transformed into a major affront when the labor members were left waiting for a call to a meeting that never came about. Against a background of animosity the harried lunch of the public members became part of a pattern of hostile maneuvers designed to harass and embarrass labor.

At this early stage the Pay Board had most of the disabilities of tripartitism and few of the strengths. The process of policy formulation was cast in strict adversary terms. Minor points became the focus of acute disagreement. The differences in interests were not salved by personal goodwill, and communication between the labor representatives and the other members was strained at best. There was little agreement on facts, let alone principles. Undoubtedly the labor members amplified their indignation for bargaining purposes, but their suspicions and sense of grievance were real.

Despite these shortcomings the tripartite process and the Pay Board redeemed themselves in a very fundamental sense. The board did provide a forum for the airing of different points of view. It was a vehicle for the participation of various interest groups, particularly organized labor, in a process of national economic bargaining. And this participation did create a basis for acceptable policies that carried the Pay Board over its most difficult period.

More to the point, it can be argued that the policies forthcoming from the process were basically sound in view of the background and objectives of the wage stabilization program. The 5.5 percent pay standard made sense as related to the goal set for price increases in Phase II. The exceptions clause was essential for dealing with the complexities and inequities that were sure to arise in the wake of the wage-price freeze. The formula for handling deferred increases did strike some balance between the objectives of the controls program and the need to preserve stable industrial relations practices. The policy regarding retroactivity did try to provide for equity in certain circumstances while reflecting the interests of groups outside the drab meeting rooms at the Executive Office Building. No one was entirely satisfied with the policies, and labor's distress resulted almost as much from the deficiencies of the process as from the stringency of the standards. In this case tripartitism was a reasonable mechanism for decisionmaking but not for promoting consensus or tranquility. Nonetheless, the policies were set and provided a framework for the specific actions that would lie ahead.

III

Policies and Principles: Further Elaboration

After announcing the basic wage stabilization policies, the Pay Board initiated the complex task of elaborating specific rules and regulations. The 5.5 percent standard for new wage adjustments had only symbolic meaning unless accompanied by computational and substantive definitions. According to the Pay Board, exceptions might be granted on the basis of "ongoing collective bargaining and pay practices and the equitable position of the employees involved."[1] But this statement had little meaning until exception criteria were more fully developed. With respect to retroactivity, the board referred to "severe inequities" as grounds for limited exceptions but did not spell these out. As it turned out, Congress soon acted on the retroactivity issue, necessitating a new Pay Board policy.

The 5.5 Percent Standard

The Pay Board's definition of the wage standard was generally consistent with a cost-push approach to inflation. Basically applicants were asked to calculate the percentage difference between the average hourly wage and the cost of fringe benefits in the period immediately preceding their control year and at the end of that year. (See appendix A for details concerning computation and methodology.) Three exceptions to this approach are noteworthy. Legally required fringe benefits, such as the employer's share of social security taxes, were excluded from the computation. Such taxes are part of the cost of compensation per man-hour, although many economists believe they are eventually absorbed by labor.[2] The adjustment in social security taxes due for January 1, 1972, would

1. "Policies Governing Pay Adjustments Proposed by the Public Members of the Pay Board" (November 7, 1971; processed).

2. See John A. Brittain, *The Payroll Tax for Social Security* (Brookings Institution, 1972), chaps. 2 and 3.

have reduced the effective standard for other wage and fringe payments by an average of about 0.7 percent had these taxes been included in the 5.5 percent.[3] It would have had a greater impact on the nonunion sector than on the union sector, since a greater proportion of nonunion workers were likely to experience new adjustments and hence be subject to the 5.5 percent standard.

A second deviation from a strict cost-push approach can only be gleaned from early Pay Board decisions, although it was later adopted formally. Originally the 5.5 percent guideline was meant to include all forms of compensation other than legally required fringe benefits. In some cases employers experience an increase in fringe benefit costs simply to maintain existing benefits. Thus, for example, the cost of hospitalization insurance might rise as hospital room rates increase. On a strict cost basis such cost increases ought to have been charged against the allowable 5.5 percent. On equity grounds it might be—and was—argued that since an employee receives no added utility from benefit-maintenance increases, such increases should not be charged against the standard. This view did not appear in the original Pay Board announcement of the 5.5 percent standard. But it can be inferred from the public members' statement on the coal case, in which a large fringe benefit adjustment was seen as necessary to maintain pension fund solvency.[4] The Pay Board's standard governing qualified fringe benefits ultimately was modified to include the cost of additional benefits but to exclude extra costs necessary to maintain existing fringe benefits.

A third exception to the cost-push approach resulted from a compromise on escalator clauses. In general all increases were to be computed on an end-to-end basis. That is, the percentage adjustment was to be determined by comparing the hourly compensation rate of the unit just before the control year and at the end of the control year. The increase was computed regardless of the effective date of the change during the control year. An alternative would have been "time-weighting"—weighting each increase during the year by the proportion of the year in which it was effective. In other words, a 5 percent increase granted halfway through the year would count as only 2.5 percent.

The ultimate cost effect, of course, is the hourly rate paid at the end

3. See Daniel J. B. Mitchell, "The Impact and Administration of Wage Controls," in John Kraft and Blaine Roberts, eds., *Wage and Price Controls: The U.S. Experiment* (Praeger, 1975), table 4-10, p. 67.

4. See Pay Board press release PB-4, November 19, 1971. The coal case is discussed in chapter 5.

of the year. Time-weighting would have permitted large increases at the end of control years that would not have had much impact on the allowable 5.5 percent but would have inflated costs and the base wage for the next year. On the other hand, the labor members argued that units that incorporated escalators in their contracts had acted responsibly and should not be penalized. The use of an escalator permitted a guaranteed deferred adjustment, with any other monies conditional on the actual rate of inflation. Apart from any such general argument the four officials of national unions represented on the Pay Board had specific concerns; all had major contracts with escalators. Time-weighting was adopted by the Pay Board for escalator adjustments.[5]

The cost aspect of the standard also can be seen in its application to average job rates in *units* rather than to individuals or particular jobs. For control purposes employees in the union sector generally were grouped according to the collective bargaining unit. In the nonunion sector the employer had broad discretion in defining the unit, another factor that usually kept nonunion sector cases away from the board.[6] Concentration on the unit's average wage implied an aggregate cost approach. Some workers could get more than 5.5 percent as long as others got less. The wage administrators of the unit could handle problems of wage structure within the guideline as they saw fit. The Pay Board therefore did not become involved in occupation differentials as the Construction Industry Stabilization Committee did in the craft-oriented construction industry.

Deferred Adjustments

When the Pay Board bargained about the general standard for new adjustments, it was dealing with a guideline for increases that were yet to be negotiated or determined. Hence the impact of any given percentage standard was entirely hypothetical. But deferred adjustments were already spelled out in contracts when the Pay Board met. A given percentage guideline would be known in advance to affect some units but not others.

All the unions represented on the Pay Board except the Machinists had key deferred agreements. Table 3-1 shows the larger agreements already

5. This decision did not prompt a rush to adopt escalators. It did have the side effect of distorting Pay Board statistics on requests and approvals, mainly for deferred adjustments.

6. Nonunion employers could often subdivide their workers into less visible Category III units. Units could also be picked that showed lesser rates of wage increase.

Table 3-1. *Agreements Involving 20,000 or More Workers Scheduled for Deferred Adjustments in 1972*

Industry group and union	Number of workers involved[a]	Escalator present	Reported increment[b]
Food products			
California Processors—Teamsters	56,550	no	21–31¢
Apparel			
Clothing Manufacturers Association— Clothing Workers	125,000	no	20–22.2¢
N.Y. Coat and Suit Association—Ladies' Garment Workers	40,000	no	5%
Popular Priced Dress Manufacturing Group—Ladies' Garment Workers	60,000	no	5%
Rubber			
Goodyear—Rubber Workers	23,000	no	26¢
Steel			
Basic steel agreement (9 companies)— Steelworkers	350,000	yes	12.5¢ and COLA
Machinery, except electrical			
Deere and Company—Auto Workers	21,000	yes	3% and COLA
Electrical machinery			
General Electric—Electrical Workers (IUE)	90,000	yes	15¢ and COLA
General Motors—Electrical Workers (IUE)	33,000	yes	11–19¢ and COLA
Westinghouse—Electrical Workers (IUE)	36,000	yes	15¢ and COLA
Chrysler—Auto Workers	110,200	yes	11–21¢ and COLA
Ford—Auto Workers	165,000	yes	9.5–21¢ and COLA
General Motors—Auto Workers	395,050	yes	11–22¢ and COLA
Railroads			
Class I Railroads—Locomotive Engineers	35,000	no	
Class I Railroads—United Transportation Union[c]	135,000	no	
Class I Railroads—Carmen	50,000	no	10%
Class I Railroads—Maintenance of Way	77,000	no	
Class I Railroads—Railway Clerks	140,000	no	

Table 3-1 (*continued*)

Industry group and union	Number of workers involved[a]	Escalator present	Reported increment[b]
Trucking			
Central States Area, Local Cartage— Teamsters	120,000	yes	
Central States Area, Over-the-road— Teamsters	40,000	yes	50¢ and
Motor Transport Labor Relations, Over-the-road—Teamsters	23,000	yes	COLA[d]
National Master Freight Agreement (N.J., N.Y.)—Teamsters	38,000	yes	
Communications			
AT&T—Communications Workers	24,000	yes	12.5–18.75¢ and COLA
Wholesale and retail trade			
San Francisco Employers Council— Teamsters	25,000	yes	30¢ and COLA

Source: U.S. Bureau of Labor Statistics, *Wage Calendar 1972*, Bulletin 1724 (Government Printing Office, 1972), pp. 7–12.

a. Bureau of Labor Statistics estimate.

b. Increments reported to the Pay Board may have varied owing to treatment of fringe benefits, control years, unit definitions, etc. Weekly increments are divided by forty to convert them to an hourly basis.

c. The Pay Board considered whether this contract was a deferred agreement, since it had been incompletely ratified before Phase II.

d. The 50 cent increment fell into two separate control years under Pay Board rules, 25 cents in each year.

COLA = cost-of-living adjustment (escalator clause).

scheduled for 1972 when Phase II was planned. A relatively high standard for deferred wage increases would be likely to bump against the contracts of only one member of the board: the Teamsters. The railroad contracts also could come under consideration.

A summary of deferred adjustments throughout the major union sector appears in table 3-2. In the nonconstruction sector—which was most relevant for the Pay Board—the Bureau of Labor Statistics estimated that deferred increases, including escalators, would average less than 7 percent, given a 3 percent rate of price inflation. A simple application of the 5.5 percent standard to deferred adjustments obviously would have affected many contracts. On the other hand, a standard as high as 7 percent or 8 percent would have brought relatively few contracts under the scrutiny of the Pay Board. In fact, a standard of 7 percent for deferred payments was proposed by the business members, but labor insisted that a case-by-case approach was more appropriate.

Table 3-2. *Deferred Wage Adjustments Scheduled in 1972*[a]

| | Workers scheduled for deferred increases | | Mean wage increase scheduled (percent) | | |
| | | | | With escalator at 3 percent inflation[c] | Total agreements at 3 percent inflation[c] |
Industry	Total (thousands)	With escalators[b] (percent)	With no escalator		
Private nonfarm	6,728	56	8.1	6.3	7.1
Excluding construction	6,155	61	7.4	6.3	6.7
Manufacturing	3,639	65	5.9	5.4	5.6
Food and kindred products	314	50	6.3	7.7	7.0
Apparel	384	0	5.5	d	5.5
Stone, clay, and glass	104	33	6.1	7.3	6.5
Rubber	109	4	6.0	5.1	6.0
Metalworking	2,317	91	5.6	5.2	5.2
Tobacco	26	n.a.	n.a.	n.a.	n.a.
Textiles	14	n.a.	n.a.	n.a.	n.a.
Lumber and wood products	9	n.a.	n.a.	n.a.	n.a.
Furniture	29	n.a.	n.a.	n.a.	n.a.
Paper	89	n.a.	n.a.	n.a.	n.a.
Printing	59	n.a.	n.a.	n.a.	n.a.
Chemicals	69	n.a.	n.a.	n.a.	n.a.
Petroleum refining	54	n.a.	n.a.	n.a.	n.a.
Leather	48	n.a.	n.a.	n.a.	n.a.
Miscellaneous manufacturing	11	n.a.	n.a.	n.a.	n.a.
Construction	573	0	11.6	d	11.6
Transportation	1,145	56	10.0	10.9	10.5
Communications, gas and electricity	750	86	7.9	4.8	5.2
Warehousing, wholesale and retail trade	381	23	8.0	8.5	8.1
Services	99	0	6.3	d	6.3

Source: U.S. Bureau of Labor Statistics, *Wage Calendar, 1972*, Bulletin 1724 (GPO, 1972), p. 4. Numbers of workers are rounded.

a. Based on data known in late 1971.

b. Implicit proportion based on average increase reported by the Bureau of Labor Statistics for escalator, nonescalator, and total agreements.

c. A 3 percent price increase is assumed to result in a 1.8 percent wage increase in agreements with escalators; 1.8 percent has been added to reported deferred increase.

d. No escalator clauses reported.

n.a. Not available.

The board adopted the case-by-case approach but added a procedure whereby any five members could challenge a contract and bring it up for review. Thus the business members could make 7 percent a de facto standard for challenges by simply acting as a bloc to challenge all cases above that amount. This automatic challenge procedure would primarily affect categories I and II (units of 1,000 or more workers), since the smaller Category III units did not have to report deferred adjustments and thus few of their cases would reach the board.

When the business members let it be known that they would use 7 percent as a standard for challenging, the board moved to prevent blanket challenging. It required the challengers to identify in writing the contracts they designated for review.[7] Just before the withdrawal of four labor representatives from the board in March 1972, the business members had challenged seventy-four deferred adjustments.[8] After the walkout the 7 percent figure became the quasi-official point of challenge, or at least review, although in principle the board could challenge any case. The number of board members required for a challenge was reduced to two. An option of setting variable challenge standards by industry to allow staff challenges was rejected.[9] The chairman, however, was permitted to challenge cases for board attention. (See appendix B for a more detailed account of the handling of deferred adjustment cases.)

The 7 percent figure was reinforced by Pay Board reporting requirements. Beginning in February 1972 the board had to be notified sixty days in advance of all Category I and Category II deferred adjustments above 7 percent.[10] Since all Category I adjustments required prenotification in any case, this decision affected only Category II. When the board became an all-public one following the labor walkout, the Cases and Appeals Panel—a subcommittee of the full board—began to operate. The board allowed the panel to consider some of the more run-of-the-mill cases that had piled up in the backlog. It became apparent that a problem was developing in handling deferred increases. Even challenged cases could operate according to their terms. Cases would be reported to the board, but the parties would drag their feet on providing the detailed data the staff might request. Thus payments would continue to be made according to the existing contracts. The board had announced that it would not roll back a wage increase retroactively (other than one paid in willful violation of the regulations), so workers under existing contracts were in no danger of losing what had been paid. The worst that could happen would be a prospective rollback that would take effect after the Pay Board's decision.

7. Pay Board press release PB-36, January 11, 1972.
8. Ibid., PB-68, April 5, 1972.
9. Pay Board staff paper EAD-26, May 17, 1972.
10. Pay Board press release PB-48, February 9, 1972.

On June 8, 1972, the Pay Board—having just made its first cutback of a deferred wage increase (Philadelphia meatcutters)—announced new reporting procedures designed to obtain more advance warning on deferred adjustments and to provide an incentive to the parties (or at least to the union) to cooperate in supplying needed data.[11] All Category I and Category II deferred wage increases above 7 percent now had to be reported to the board ninety days in advance. Payments under deferred contracts could not be made until sixty days after the board received adequate data. This requirement in effect gave the parties thirty days to present any additional information the Pay Board staff might request.

Apart from the challenge point, the Pay Board had to define exactly what was meant by a deferred increase. This meant establishing a date to serve as the demarcation between new and old contracts and pay practices. The board decided to set November 14, 1971, the first day of Phase II, as the dividing line. Wage increases under the terms of contracts and pay practices established before that date were classified as deferred.[12]

The Pay Board, however, was to find most of its attention centering on new adjustments, not deferred increases. Relatively few deferred increases were cut back during Phase II. The 7 percent standard for deferred challenges was not especially tight, particularly after the board liberalized its standard for fringe benefits and the computation rule for escalators. Early deferred increases generally slipped through the Pay Board while it was preoccupied with rule-making and the first major cases subjected to controls. Since most union workers were under existing contracts during Phase II, and since the nonunion sector generally met the 5.5 percent standard, the Pay Board was concerned mainly with a minority of workers in a minority sector.

Although it may seem misguided or counterproductive that the Pay Board's efforts should be so narrowly focused, the concentration on new union adjustments made sense in terms of the overall objectives of the

11. Ibid., PB-95, June 8, 1972.
12. As a result of the coal case, the Price Commission and the Pay Board set different demarcation dates. When the Pay Board approved the bituminous coal agreement, the Price Commission announced that it would hold the line on wage increases by refusing to permit increases above 5.5 percent from being passed into prices. For a time the commission maintained this stance, even for deferred wage increases that were not subject to the 5.5 percent standard. When the commission later decided to permit dollar-for-dollar pass-throughs for deferred increases above 5.5 percent, it set its demarcation date as November 8, 1971, so that coal would not be considered as deferred for price purposes.

program. A cost-push program is logically aimed at the collective bargaining sector, because nonunion wages are likely to respond to a combination of market conditions plus patterns in the union sector. Precontrol contracts could not be cut back extensively without creating complaints about inequity and without risking the loss of the union acquiescence that prevailed during Phase II. Isolating deferred increases under special rules made them appear to be unique cases, not pattern-setters. The board could then concentrate on new adjustments that would gradually affect a larger fraction of the labor force and reinforce the credibility of the 5.5 percent standard for the nonunion sector.

Looking Backward: Retroactivity

As a practical matter, the Pay Board could not spend all its time in the early days of Phase II planning for the future. It had to expend considerable effort in disentangling the complexities created by freezing wage increases that had been scheduled to become effective during the Phase I period, August 15–November 13, 1971. The Bureau of Labor Statistics estimated for the Cost of Living Council that 514 major union situations (those covering 1,000 or more employees) involving 2.4 million workers had been affected in the freeze. According to the Commerce Department, retroactive wage claims of roughly $500 million were outstanding at the end of the last quarter of 1971.[13]

The Pay Board's tough position on the retroactivity issue effectively barred the retroactive payment of increases lost during the freeze. But Congress was more responsive than the board to the arguments of organized labor. In considering the extension of the Economic Stabilization Act, the House of Representatives originally considered requiring the payment of retroactive wage increases unless the magnitudes involved were "grossly disproportionate" to the standard. Later the language was changed to "unreasonably inconsistent," a phrase that presumably gave the Pay Board more leeway.[14] Meanwhile the Pay Board softened its

13. The Commerce Department reported that "wage accruals less disbursements" amounted to over $500 million during the second half of 1971. See *Survey of Current Business*, vol. 54 (July 1974), p. 15.

14. Bureau of National Affairs, Inc., *Daily Labor Report*, December 2, 1971, p. 1. The phrase "unreasonably inconsistent" appears to have originated in Executive Order 11588, March 29, 1971, which set up the Construction Industry Stabilization Committee.

stance somewhat by spelling out additional conditions in which case-by-case exceptions for retroactive adjustments might be allowed.

The board permitted units with tandem relationships to contracts negotiated before August 15, 1971, to operate if they could show that they had followed the leader unit for five years or during the last two collective bargaining agreements. Originally the contract expiration of the follower unit had to come after the expiration of the lead contract by no more than thirty days. This was later changed to ninety days. Retroactivity had to have been agreed upon during the freeze or had to have been an established past practice, and the leader and follower had to have been in the same industry.[15] These provisions were aimed mainly at smaller companies who could normally have followed the basic steel agreement concluded just before Phase I.

Wage increases for workers earning no more than $2 an hour that had been held up by the freeze also were allowed.[16] The issue was largely symbolic, however, since workers earning $2 or less would have been nonunion, and they would have been unlikely to have had a formally scheduled increase during the freeze.[17]

It was because of the Pay Board's stance on retroactivity that Congress adopted the approach whereby retroactive increases were permissible unless they were "unreasonably inconsistent" with the standard. This action virtually mandated the payment of most scheduled retroactive wages, since the Pay Board's limited criteria for exceptions had been based on "severe inequity." The board established a challenge procedure for retroactive increases similar to that set up for deferred wage hikes. Category II and Category III employers could implement scheduled retroactive increases of 7 percent or less provided they later notified the Internal Revenue Service. The board also permitted increases if prices, taxes, or productivity had been raised in anticipation of a wage increase. Category I employers had to prenotify the Pay Board but could put the increases into effect un-

15. Pay Board press release PB-5, November 19, 1971.
16. The board's decision was ambiguous in reference to whether people earning less than $2 might have their pay raised above $2.
17. The board also provided an exception for retroactive pay in cases where an employee would have been eligible for a benefit increase during the freeze and could not become eligible after the freeze. The example given in Pay Board rulings was a case where an employee was scheduled to retire during the freeze and missed out on a payout from a profit-sharing plan that the employer was prevented from funding by the freeze. See Pay Board ruling 1972-93, *Federal Register,* vol. 37 (November 23, 1972), p. 25007.

less a challenge was issued in fourteen days (later twenty-eight).[18] Smaller units with retroactive increases above 7 percent also were subject to Pay Board reporting requirements and the possibility of challenge. In fact, there were no significant cutbacks of retroactive wage gains. Virtually all scheduled increases for Phase I were probably paid eventually.

The Pay Board might have been more restrictive in dealing with scheduled retroactive increases, even in the face of congressional action. In fact, Congress had given the board the discretion to determine what "unreasonably inconsistent" meant. But a continued tough stand on retroactivity would have exacerbated Pay Board relations with Congress and would have invited lawsuits over what was essentially a symbolic issue. In addition, the economic significance of retroactivity for future inflation was doubtful.[19] Resolution of the retroactivity issue involved lump-sum transfers, not marginal costs that might affect prospective pricing decisions. Initially there had been strong feeling among board members for the original position, at least on the part of the public members. When it was reported that the Construction Industry Stabilization Committee had processed a large number of retroactive approvals, the issue became one of the first major skirmishes between the CISC and the board.[20]

The basic retroactivity rules are summarized in table 3-3. As can be seen, the Pay Board was generally more restrictive concerning retroactivity in contracts negotiated during Phase II, even if they succeeded prefreeze contracts. In such a case retroactivity was allowed only if it was a past practice or had been agreed upon before the freeze. Then, retroactivity was permitted through Phase I. But starting with Phase II, the board in effect considered the increase as if it had been effective only after the freeze. This was accomplished by excluding the retroactive adjustment from the base. If a contract expired July 31, 1971, and was renegotiated on January 1, 1972, with a 10 percent increase effective August 1, 1971, the 10 percent could be paid retroactively through November 13, 1971. As of November 14, 1971, the unit would have to submit a request for a 10 percent increase, which would be measured against the 5.5 percent standard and allowable exceptions. If the 10 percent were not excluded from the base as of November 14, the November 14 increase would have

18. Pay Board press release PB-38, January 13, 1972.

19. As congressional action neared, it was reported that the administration was no longer resisting an amendment requiring retroactive pay. See BNA, *Daily Labor Report,* November 30, 1971, p. 1.

20. Ibid., November 23, 1971, pp. 1–2; December 3, 1971, p. 2.

Table 3-3. *Summary of Pay Board Rules Governing the Payment of Retroactive Wage Increases*

Status of contract	General rules regarding retroactive payments
Existing contract continuing through freeze	Payments could be made subject only to a minimal challenge and reporting requirement. Those of 7 percent or less were virtually assured.
Contract expired and was renegotiated during freeze	Generally payments could not be made unless unit qualified under the tandem rule.
Contract expired before freeze and was renegotiated during freeze	Generally payments could not be made unless unit qualified under successor contract rule.
Contract expired before freeze and was renegotiated after freeze	Generally payments could not be made unless unit had past-practice or prefreeze agreement on retroactivity. If so, payments could be made up through Phase I. But such payments were excluded from the base used in evaluating the first control year in Phase II.
Contract expired during freeze and was renegotiated after freeze	Generally payments could not be made.

been zero, clearly within Pay Board standards. Hence the base exclusion permitted the 10 percent adjustment to be considered.[21]

Formula Exceptions

As the Pay Board began operations its rules consisted of three essential elements: a standard for new adjustments, a procedure for existing contracts, and a policy on retroactive pay. Since the 5.5 percent standard

21. Of course, if a unit had, say, a 10 percent increase for the year beginning August 1, 1971, and if it was thought that the Pay Board would cut the increase to 5.5 percent as of November 14, 1971, the unit could implement an increase effective August 1 big enough to offset the cut. The base wage at the end of the control year, however, would still only rise by 5.5 percent. Moreover, the employer might be taking a considerable risk, since costs would be very much raised if the Pay Board did not in fact make the expected cut.

constituted a goal for average compensation per man-hour rather than a ceiling, it was evident that exceptions would have to be provided. Exceptions could be given either on a case-by-case basis, a procedure that would have entailed a much larger staff than was available, or through some sort of formula. The exclusive use of formulas would fail to provide consideration in unique situations, and a small, untrained staff might misapply them. These factors led ultimately to a mixed system of formulas, individual case consideration, and limits on the amount that the automatic formulas would permit.

The Pay Board identified three major categories for exceptions from the general standard: labor shortages, traditional relationships between employee units, and a recent history of falling behind the wages of other workers. These concerns gave rise to the "essential employees," "tandem," and "catch-up" exceptions announced in December 1971. All three were capped at 7 percent, that is, 1.5 percent above the basic 5.5 percent. Moreover, exceptions could not be cumulated to obtain more than 7 percent. The 7 percent cap effectively voided the need for similar exceptions for deferred adjustments, since they operated under a de facto 7 percent standard anyway. (Appendix C further explains the implementation of the three basic exceptions.) A fourth exception for "intraplant inequities" was adopted four months after the others. It was also capped at 7 percent.

Essential Employees

The essential-employees exception was the only one with a strictly economic rationale. When wages or prices are controlled, particularly in a competitive setting, it is possible that excess demand will be created. In the labor market this would translate into excessive employee turnover and abnormally high vacancy rates. Obviously some vacancy and turnover activity is normally observed in any labor market. Certain employers find it optimal to maintain a wage premium to hold down turnover and to keep a queue of potential employees available. Others simply pay a premium, whether desired or not, because of a strong union bargaining position. Still others choose to pay comparatively low wages and put up with a relatively high rate of turnover. It is theoretically possible, however, that tight wage controls, particularly when there is a buoyant demand for labor, could create severe problems in recruiting and retaining employees.[22] The result could be disruptions in production and even black markets for labor, both of which have occurred in some European countries.[23]

With three economists among the public members, it is not surprising that the Pay Board adopted a labor-shortage exception. Business was willing to go along because of a desire to provide relief to nonunion employers who might unilaterally desire to raise wages above 5.5 percent for labor market reasons. Labor typically approached wage issues from an equity orientation. Hence this economic exception was the one category the labor members did not propose.

The nature of the exception for essential employees was determined in large measure by the level of the general pay standard. When the 5.5 percent standard was adopted, it was evident that there would be less need for exceptions and more room for firms to deal with shortages within the allowable 5.5 percent. For example, a firm with a shortage in a particular occupation could grant an increase in excess of 5.5 percent to that occupation provided that less than 5.5 percent was given to other workers. Proposals for the magnitude of the exception initially fell in the range of an additional 2 percent to 2.5 percent (7.5–8 percent, total). The exception for essential employees was eventually capped at 7 percent, the figure that seemed to characterize most formula deviations from the 5.5 percent standard.

As finally worded, the exception placed a strict burden of proof on the applicant unit. It had to be shown that increases above the standard could reasonably be expected to alleviate the shortage, that nonwage conditions of work had not deteriorated (otherwise there could be a shortage at a given wage rate), and that there had been vacancies for three months despite intensive recruiting activity. The strict wording stemmed from a concern that many units might claim shortages unless documentation was required. For example, even after the essential-employees rule was announced, the aerospace industry made a vague claim about recruitment difficulties despite retrenchment and unemployment in the industry.[24]

Because of the economic conditions that prevailed in 1972 the essen-

22. See Daniel J. B. Mitchell and Ross E. Azevedo, *Wage-Price Controls and Labor Market Distortions* (Institute of Industrial Relations, University of California at Los Angeles, 1976).

23. See J. J. Klant, "Holland After the Wage Explosion," *The Banker*, vol. 65 (January 1965), pp. 26–30.

24. The claim was also made in the related United Aircraft case. See Pay Board staff paper EAD-5, January 16, 1972.

Table 3-4. *Selected Labor Market Indicators, 1969–72*

Rates in percent

Year	Unemployment rate	Manufacturing vacancy rate	Manufacturing quit rate	Help-wanted advertising index (1967 = 100)
1969	3.5	1.2	2.7	121
1970	4.9	0.7	2.1	93
1971:1	6.0	0.5	1.7	78
1971:2	5.9	0.5	1.8	81
1971:3	6.0	0.5	1.8	84
1971:4	6.0	0.5	1.8	84
1972:1	5.9	0.6	2.1	90
1972:2	5.7	0.6	2.2	96
1972:3	5.6	0.7	2.2	104
1972:4	5.3	0.8	2.4	112

Sources: U.S. Department of Commerce, Bureau of Economic Analysis, *Business Statistics 1973* (GPO, 1973), pp. 69, 86; and U.S. Bureau of Labor Statistics, *Employment and Earnings*, vol. 19 (December 1972), p. 113. All figures are seasonally adjusted.

tial-employees exception was not used extensively during Phase II. At the time the exception was announced, the economy was slowly moving out of recession. As table 3-4 shows, all indicators of labor market conditions in late 1971 pointed to a surplus rather than a shortage. Unemployment was in the 6 percent range; both vacancies and quits were down. Only toward the end of Phase II did the unemployment rate begin to decline rapidly. But it still remained considerably above the level of the 1969 economic peak.

The board expressed interest in knowing whether the labor market was in fact tighter than it seemed. The staff reviewed evidence that demographic changes in the labor force required adjustments in the reported unemployment rate.[25] By any standard, however, the market appeared to remain loose. The staff also sought evidence of occupational labor shortages but was unable to uncover anything significant.[26] In August 1972 the Pay Board and the Price Commission asked their staffs jointly to consider options for the excess demand conditions that might occur in 1973. On the wage side the board recommended that the Price Commission permit labor cost pass-throughs of wage increases above 5.5 percent that were

25. Ibid., EAD-66, August 18, 1972. See also George L. Perry, "Changing Labor Markets and Inflation," *Brookings Papers on Economic Activity, 3:1970*, pp. 411–41.

26. Pay Board staff paper OCE-103, November 28, 1972.

justified on the basis of essential employees.[27] But the Price Commission
did not act on this suggestion.[28]

Tandem Relationships

Major contracts had been concluded in a number of industries immediately before Phase I. In many sectors smaller units follow patterns
set by key settlements, although there may be a time lag between the adjustment in the leader and the adjustment in the follower. These tandem
relationships are an important mechanism for maintaining the stability of
the wage structure within an industry or union jurisdiction, but the freeze
prevented many of them from operating. As noted previously, the Pay
Board dealt with these situations as they applied to Phase I by a tandem
rule that ultimately permitted up to a ninety-day lag. A similar rule was
applied for Phase II, with a time lag of up to six months.[29] The board
originally defined the lag in terms of the starting dates of the leader and
follower contracts but later modified it to refer only to the adjustments
themselves. This was necessary to permit second- and third-year tandem
increases to operate. Such increases by definition occur with a delay of
over twenty-four and thirty-six months, respectively, from the starting
date of the leader *contract*. But the follower *increases* may lag the leader
increases by only a few months.

As finally stated, the tandem rule applied two basic tests. First, the
follower unit had to have experienced wage increases that were generally
equal in value and directly related in timing to increases in a leader unit.
If the follower unit was nonunion, it was required to demonstrate that the
relationship had existed over at least five consecutive years. Unionized
follower units had to show that the relationship had been in effect for the
previous two collective bargaining agreements. The second test involved
the labor market and product market relationship of the two units. A
follower had to show that its leader was either in the same "commonly
recognized industry" or in the same local labor market.[30] Unlike catch-up,
the tandem exception could not be self-executed, even for increases of 7
percent or less. The board felt that permitting parties to determine for

27. Ibid., EAD-74, September 11, 1972.
28. The Price Commission might have perceived little likelihood of using this
provision, since most forecasts (including those of the Wharton School and the
UCLA Business Forecasting Project) anticipated a soft labor market.
29. Pay Board press release PB-28, December 17, 1971.
30. Ibid.

themselves whether they were following a pattern would lead to abuse of the tandem exception.

The tandem rule was useful not only for relationships between pre-freeze and Phase II contracts, but also to preserve relationships between follower units and exceptions granted by the Pay Board to key units. (An option of limiting tandems to followers of pre–Phase II negotiations—which would have been sufficient to accommodate followers of the basic steel agreement of early August 1971—was considered and rejected.) It applied also to pay practices, so that nonunion workers in partially union-ized firms who had traditionally moved in step with union workers could maintain their relationships. Although tandems were capped at 7 percent, the board permitted larger adjustments on a case-by-case basis. The labor position was that tandem exceptions should be uncapped and automatic. This turned out to be not far from what actually happened, since the board did in fact permit bona fide tandems to be followed, even if increases above 7 percent were required.

Table 3-5 lists potential candidates for tandem claims related to pre-control contracts in the major union sector in 1971. The tabulation is of interest because for reasons of bargaining structure and equity, the Pay Board was locking a portion of Phase II wage increases onto increases that had occurred in the precontrol period. It underestimates the number of workers potentially involved by omitting the nonunion and smaller-union sectors and the tandems to new exceptions the board was to ap-prove during Phase II.

The left-hand column of table 3-5 lists private sector industries and unions that experienced major expirations before Phase I. "Major" in this case refers to contracts affecting 5,000 workers or more. West Coast longshoremen have been removed, since a settlement was not reached un-til Phase II despite a June 1971 contract expiration. The right-hand column lists the number of workers in situations of 1,000 or more em-ployees whose contracts in the same industry and with the same union were due to expire in 1972. Of course, not all these workers may have had tandem relationships to prefreeze agreements. And the table un-doubtedly omits some tandems that crossed union or industry lines. In addition, the 64,000 workers listed under transportation equipment are more likely to have been tandem to the aerospace contracts that expired after the freeze began than to the few prefreeze transportation equipment expirations. Even so, omitting transportation equipment, 185,000 workers can be identified as involved in possible tandems. These workers repre-

Table 3-5. *Potential Tandems from Major Collective Bargaining Agreements Expiring in 1971 before Controls*[a]

Unions experiencing major contract expirations in 1971 before controls, by industry[b]	Number of workers in potential tandems in 1972[c]
Apparel	
Clothing Workers	37,150
Chemicals	
District 50, Allied and Technical Workers; Textile Workers; Oil, Chemical and Atomic Workers	5,850
Petroleum refining	
Atlantic Independent Union	0
Leather	
United Shoe Workers; Leather Goods, Plastics and Novelty Workers	5,750
Glass	
Glass Bottle Blowers; Glass and Ceramic Workers	9,700
Primary metals	
Aluminum Workers; Auto Workers; Steelworkers; Armco Employees; Independent Steelworkers Union (National Steel Corp.)	8,550
Fabricated metals	
Steelworkers	9,400
Machinery, except electrical	
Allied Industrial Workers; Auto Workers	2,450
Electrical machinery	
Electrical Workers (IUE); Communications Workers	13,350
Transportation equipment	
Auto Workers; Machinists	63,950[d]
Railroads	
Railway Clerks[e]; other railway craft unions	47,200[f]
Airlines	
Transport Workers	0
Communications	
Communications Workers; Telegraph Workers	21,550
Insurance	
Insurance Workers	24,500
Total	249,400
Total, excluding transportation equipment	185,450

Sources: U.S. Bureau of Labor Statistics, *Wage Calendar, 1971*, Bulletin 1698 (GPO, 1971), pp. 8–14; and ibid., Bulletin 1724 (GPO, 1972), pp. 23–33.

a. Omits West Coast longshoremen's agreement, which was not settled until Phase II.

b. Expirations involving at least 5,000 workers.

c. Contracts expiring in 1972, involving at least 1,000 workers and the industries and unions in the first column.

d. Mostly aerospace workers who were unlikely to be tandem to precontrol agreements.

e. Agreement involving the Railway Express Agency and the union.

f. Difference between nonoperating union employees reported in *Monthly Labor Review*, vol. 96 (January 1973), p. 14, and in ibid., vol. 95 (January 1972), p. 13, as having agreements with Class I railroads. The United Transportation Union agreement involving 135,000 workers was considered to be a deferred contract.

sented close to 10 percent of employment under nonconstruction contract expirations affecting agreements covering 1,000 or more workers in 1972. These expirations were clearly the target group for Phase II wage controls, and 10 percent was a significant proportion.

Unfortunately there is no way of knowing the number of tandem requests actually granted during Phase II. Many would have been in Category III, for which records are very sparse. (Those involving 7 percent increases or less in Category III would have been processed entirely by the Internal Revenue Service and would not have reached the Pay Board.) Computer records maintained by the board for categories I and II do not contain information on the reason for exceptions.[31] It may be assumed that many tandems—such as New York Telephone—were handled as a "gross inequity" because increases of more than 7 percent were requested. One indication that tandems were an important influence is provided by Category I and Category II case records regarding new union approvals in primary metals. These averaged 9.3 percent during Phase II, presumably a reflection on the precontrol basic steel agreement.

Catch-Up

The relatively high first-year wage adjustments in major contracts reached just before the freeze (about 10 percent in the first half of 1971) suggested that the union sector was making up ground lost during the inflation of the late 1960s. As chapter 11 demonstrates, there is considerable evidence that wages in some parts of the union sector did fall behind—in a relative sense—compared with nonunion wages. An attempt to block the adjustments simply would have preserved the distorted wage structure until controls were lifted. Since it was hoped that controls would have a permanent effect, it was necessary to permit catch-up increases to restabilize the wage structure but to prevent these approvals from spilling over into situations where catch-up was not required.

Board discussion of the catch-up exception was less concerned with whether there should be some provision of this nature than with how

31. It may seem surprising that computer records of the board did not indicate the nature of an exception request. Two factors explain this omission. First, as cases arrived it was sometimes difficult to know exactly what was being claimed. Requests to the Pay Board often used such words as "catch-up" or "tandem," even when the rules did not strictly apply to the units on whose behalf the requests were made. (In some cases the requests tracked the eligibility language of the exceptions but asked for more than 7 percent.) Second, the long delay in making the computer system operational due to administrative problems precluded the recording of such information (see chapter 7).

such a provision should be constructed. It was necessary to define a period over which the erosion of relative wage positions should be measured. For unions it seemed natural to pick the duration of the previous contract as an appropriate period. Presumably at the time the previous contract was negotiated the union would have been able to demand any catch-up it felt was due from earlier periods.

Union contracts had been averaging close to three years in duration. According to a survey of major union agreements covering 2,000 or more workers, 65 percent of known agreements in 1971 had a duration of three years.[32] It was therefore obvious that a three-year period should be used for the nonunion sector as well. Of course, nonunion employers who had let their wages slip before controls were unlikely to suddenly want to make their employees "whole," that is, to let them reach parity with other workers. Nonunion employers generally are free to make adjustments at will and could have prevented a slippage of wages at any time before the freeze. The only exceptions to this general rule were certain state and local employees and nonunion employers who were in tandems with union workers. Private nonunion workers who had tandem relationships with the union sector generally could have used the tandem exception. So their problem was not acute as long as a catch-up provision was accorded union workers. Some state and local employees, however, could receive adjustments only when legislative bodies convened. This sometimes involved a two-year period, as in the case of the Ohio state employees. So catch-up problems could accumulate. At any rate, as in other Pay Board decisions, it seemed necessary to provide symmetry for the nonunion sector, even though it was unlikely to be the scene of a wage push during Phase II.

The board desired to place some sort of cap on the catch-up exception as it had on the others. It noted that in the three-year period ending just before the freeze, the sum of price increases plus the 3 percent productivity factor used for the 5.5 percent standard came to nearly 7 percent a year. This suggested a 7 percent cap, although there were proposals to use the 7 percent figure as a criterion for eligibility but to cap the exception above 7 percent. The rationale was that if an employee unit had fallen behind the 7 percent criterion over the previous three years by more than 0.5 percent a year, a 7 percent exception would not bring these workers up to an equal basis with others. Some of the business members therefore

32. U.S. Bureau of Labor Statistics, *Characteristics of Agreements Covering 2,000 Workers or More,* Bulletin 1729 (Government Printing Office, 1972), p. 6.

suggested 7.5 percent; the labor members argued for 8.5 percent.[33] But the board ultimately applied the 7 percent cap used for other exceptions. It finally agreed that a unit would compute its catch-up based on the difference between what it actually got over the previous contract (union sector) or last three years (nonunion sector) and 7 percent a year. It could add this margin to the basic 5.5 percent as long as the total increase did not go over 7 percent. Unlike the essential-employees and tandem exceptions, catch-up was made self-executing—a unit that could otherwise implement a 5.5 percent adjustment without awaiting board approval (categories II and III) could also implement catch-up. The formula was sufficiently mechanical for the board to anticipate little risk in this method of implementation.

The Pay Board also debated the appropriate expiration date for the catch-up exception. The business members argued for February 1, 1972, but the initial expiration date was set at March 31, 1972, and was later extended to June 30, 1972.[34] As June 30 approached, the issue again arose. This time the board granted a final extension of the catch-up exception until November 13, 1972, the anniversary of Phase II. A new limit was imposed, however. Units would be eligible only if they averaged $3 an hour in wages or less. In effect this gave the exception to those least likely to use it. There was some initial confusion over the definition of "wages." It was first announced that wages meant straight-time pay plus "includable" benefits, that is, benefits not granted preferential treatment by Congress. Such benefits included overtime and similar premiums, holidays, and vacations and averaged 8–9 percent of straight-time pay, even for lower-wage units. After some pressure by the Teamsters representative, the board later revised the definition, stipulating $3 in straight-time pay only.[35]

The Pay Board staff estimated that roughly 40–50 percent of the applicants would have been eligible for a simple extension of catch-up, and that the $3 cap cut eligibility roughly in half.[36] Of course, some applicants might not be applying for more than 5.5 percent, particularly at the

33. The announcement of catch-up and the business and labor positions appear in Pay Board press release PB-28, December 17, 1971; and BNA, *Daily Labor Report,* pp. AA-1–AA-3. In their public statement, however, the business members made no mention of their earlier support for a 7.5 percent lid on the exception.

34. Pay Board press release PB-63, March 21, 1972.

35. Ibid., PB-92, June 7, 1972; and PB-107, July 18, 1972.

36. Pay Board staff papers EAD-22, May 9, 1972; EAD-29, May 19, 1972; and EAD-35, June 1, 1972.

Table 3-6. *Average Annual Rate of Increase in Selected Wage Indexes over the Three Years Preceding Controls and Average Median Adjustments in Collective Bargaining Settlements, 1968–70*

Percent

Description	Average annual rate of increase[a]
Hourly earnings index[b]	
Mining	6.8
Construction	9.0
Manufacturing	6.4
Transportation and public utilities	7.2
Wholesale and retail trade	6.3
Finance, insurance, real estate	6.1
Services	7.3
All sectors	6.9
Compensation per man-hour index[c]	
Private	7.2
Private, nonfarm	6.9
Effective median adjustments in major collective bargaining agreements	
Wage rates[d]	6.0
Wages and benefits[e]	6.9

Sources: U.S. Bureau of Labor Statistics, unpublished data; U.S. Department of Labor press release USDL 75-236, April 24, 1975; and *Current Wage Developments*, vol. 25 (June 1973), pp. 46–47.

a. Compound annual rate of increase for the indexes, and average of percent change effective in each year for median adjustments.

b. Private nonfarm sector, adjusted for overtime in manufacturing and interindustry employment shifts, August 1968–August 1971.

c. Wages and benefits including legally required fringes, second quarter of 1968 to second quarter of 1971.

d. Agreements involving 1,000 or more workers.

e. Agreements involving 5,000 or more workers.

lower end of the wage scale. And some might have been eligible for other exceptions, a consideration that became particularly relevant shortly after the new catch-up extension went into effect. A court decision invalidated the Cost of Living Council's definition of the working poor as those earning $1.90 an hour or less. As a result the CLC raised the exemption to $2.75.[37] Thus catch-up in some cases became little more than a way of

37. Cost of Living Council press release, July 25, 1972. The definition based on $2.75 was made retroactive by the CLC to July 15, 1972, the date of the court decision. Subsequent litigation after Phase II ended extended the definition back to late 1971, when the Economic Stabilization Act amendments were signed.

Table 3-7. *Mean Annual Rate of Wage Increase in the Nonconstruction Industries under Major Contracts Expiring in 1972 and 1973*[a]

Percent

Expiration of contract	All contracts[b]	Duration of expiring contract[c]		
		One year	Two years	Three years
1972:3	7.7	12.2	9.0	6.8
1972:4	7.4	6.5	8.3	6.8
1973	8.9	7.0	9.1	9.0

Sources: Special studies by the U.S. Bureau of Labor Statistics. See Pay Board staff papers OCE-99, November 22, 1972; EAD-22, May 9, 1972; and EAD-29, May 19, 1972.

a. Agreements involving 1,000 or more workers. Escalator adjustments are included.

b. Includes contracts of less than twelve and more than forty-eight months.

c. One-year contracts include all those with a duration of twelve to twenty-three months; two-year contracts, twenty-four to thirty-five months; and three-year contracts, thirty-six to forty-seven months.

maintaining differentials for higher-wage workers in low-wage units that took advantage of the working-poor exemptions.[38]

As in the case of the other exceptions, Pay Board records fail to indicate how frequently catch-up was used, but tables 3-6 and 3-7 suggest that catch-up probably was the exception with the broadest coverage. Table 3-6 reveals that over the three years preceding the freeze, the major wage indexes had shown an average annual increase of about 7 percent. This figure is lowered slightly by removing construction to approximate the Pay Board's jurisdiction. Hence any exception with a 7 percent eligibility criterion was bound to affect large numbers of workers.[39]

The data on effective union wage rate adjustments in table 3-6 are suggestive of the catch-up pressures that built up in the union sector during the late 1960s. The union figures exclude 1971 up through the freeze, however, since only annual breakdowns are available. Table 3-7 provides a more detailed look at major union agreements (involving 1,000 or more workers) that expired in the last half of 1972. The figures shown were taken from special studies prepared by the Bureau of Labor Statistics for the Pay Board. The data suggest that union workers, other than

38. When the final expiration of catch-up on November 13, 1972, was discussed, the Teamsters representative reported that some units were able to handle compression problems created by the working-poor exemption with catch-up.

39. Of course, the figures on average wage trends do not provide a clear indication of the distribution of workers around those trends. Moreover, in the nonunion sector the three-year period was not always applicable, as some units had shorter contract durations. The staff underestimated the proportion of workers potentially covered by catch-up when the board considered the first extension. See Pay Board staff paper EAD-15, March 20, 1972.

those in construction, under contracts expiring in 1972 had averaged roughly 7.5 percent a year under their old contracts. The BLS tabulations indicated that 43 percent of these workers had received less than 7 percent.

The $3 limit effectively cut off most union workers; thus the use of catch-up was extremely limited in the union sector after June 1972. (The Pay Board could and did grant case-by-case gross-inequity exceptions in instances where severe catch-up problems persisted.) But a transitional problem arose for contracts expiring before June 30, 1972, that were not successfully renegotiated until after that date. The Pay Board felt that it would be inequitable to penalize workers—via the $3 limitation—whose negotiations happened to go more slowly than others. In the nonunion sector, state and local government employees faced an analogous situation. Their pay practices often coincided with the fiscal year, which began July 1. In the interests of equity the board permitted contracts and pay practices that were successors to those initiated before July 1, 1972, to apply catch-up without the $3 limit.[40]

Intraplant Inequities

From the beginning the Pay Board excluded individual promotions from direct control. In essence the basic standard was meant to apply to an average of job rates within a unit, not to the workers who happened to be holding those jobs. This principle, however, could prove ambiguous in cases where the jobs in a unit were altered. That is, the computation rules made sense when workers changed jobs but not when the jobs themselves changed. Although wholesale revisions in job structures do not occur regularly, changes in technology or other similar developments sometimes make such adjustments necessary.

In principle, if a single new job—or a few new jobs—was created in an existing unit, the employer was to set the wage rate for the new job at a level equal to those of comparable jobs in the unit. If comparable jobs did not exist, the employer was required to look elsewhere in the firm, in the local labor market, or in industry, as he did if totally new units were created.[41] There was no way of closely policing this requirement, and in

40. For clarification of the catch-up extension as it applied to state and local government employees, see Pay Board press release PB-108, July 18, 1972.

41. This was basically in keeping with Phase I policy regarding new products and services. See Arnold R. Weber, *In Pursuit of Price Stability: The Wage-Price Freeze of 1971* (Brookings Institution, 1973), p. 66.

a very tight labor market it might have become a loophole. Although this danger was not imminent in Phase II, the board could not permit the new-job principle to apply to wholesale revisions of jobs, since the opportunity for evasion would become too great. If the new-job approach had been followed, it would have been possible for employers to simply reclassify jobs, with little Pay Board control, and to adjust rates to levels alleged to prevail in some vaguely identified referent. Thus even if the new-job approach is viewed as the theoretically correct way of handling job reclassifications, it was not considered a practical option. During the board's tripartite days, the labor members had argued that there should be an unlimited exception of intraplant inequities.[42] But by the time the issue came up for final consideration, the labor members had already departed.

The approach used during the Korean war period, which the board considered, basically limited corrections for intraplant inequities to situations involving small numbers of workers and minor wage adjustments. In a sense the Pay Board went in the opposite direction. It ruled that an exception for intraplant inequities—later called "intra-unit" inequities— should apply only when 10 percent or more of the jobs and 25 percent or more of the employees in a unit were affected.[43] The board felt that its basic standard, unlike the Korean war controls, permitted sufficient leeway for minor adjustments and did not want the exception to operate broadly. A unit could use up small amounts of its allowable 5.5 percent on job reclassification without creating severe inequities for employees whose jobs were not affected.

In order for a unit to meet the qualifications for an exception, evidence had to demonstrate that the job reclassifications had resulted from an orderly and detailed study of wage structure. The language of the exception paralleled that of procedures normally applied in formal job evaluation plans.[44] The study was to identify differences in job content and provide a basis for ranking jobs on the basis of content. Job evaluation plans usually break down jobs according to such factors as skill, effort, responsibility, and working conditions, all of which were mentioned in the Pay Board's exception. "Points" are assigned based on the degree to which the job reflects the various characteristics. The total number of points attributed to a job from all the relevant characteristics provides a

42. BNA, *Daily Labor Report,* December 17, 1971, p. AA-4.
43. Pay Board press release PB-79, April 26, 1972.
44. For a brief description of job evaluation, see Dale S. Beach, *Personnel: Management of People at Work* (3d ed., Macmillan, 1975), pp. 652–72.

ranking for each job. Finally, a monetary value is assigned to a point, thus providing a wage structure.

Job evaluation plans usually are not applied mechanically. The wage structure that initially results is adjusted iteratively so that key jobs that can be compared with those in the outside labor market end up with "correct" wage rates. The board did not require slavish application of job evaluation methods, and therefore adjustments based on judgment were permissible. The board, for example, said that "historical practice in an industry" should be considered.[45]

Other than in cases qualifying for the intraplant inequity exception, the Pay Board insisted on reviewing claims of wage structure distortions as individual allegations of gross inequity. For example, to comply with amendments to the Economic Stabilization Act, the board permitted increases above 5.5 percent to occur to bring the unit into compliance with federal agency wage determinations.[46] These determinations require federal contractors to pay "prevailing" wages as determined by the Labor Department. The Pay Board was unwilling to have all wages in a unit rising automatically in proportion to the wages of those under federal contracts, so it exempted only the increment *above* 5.5 percent attributable to a federal agency wage determination. Thus it was conceivable that the federal determination could use the entire 5.5 percent for a unit, leaving other workers with no adjustment at all. Such a result would compress the wage structure and might create an inequity. The Pay Board promised to hear such cases as they occurred but would agree to no formula exception for them.

A similar problem arose when the wage level defining the working poor was raised to $2.75. Although the new computation rule for the working poor did not charge the increase to $2.75 against the 5.5 percent for other workers in the unit, a compression problem could occur. This was likely if the working poor needed more than 5.5 percent to go up to $2.75. Again, the Pay Board refused to adopt a compression exception for such circumstances.[47]

45. Pay Board press release PB-79.

46. Pay Board press release PB-54, March 2, 1972. The board provided the same treatment for similar increases required by state laws. In contrast, increases due to the federal minimum wage were not chargeable. However, such increases—even if the law had been amended in 1972—would not have gone much above the then-prevailing definition of the working poor based on $1.90. Pay Board press release PB-44, January 26, 1972.

47. The board believed that the $2.75 figure was undesirably high. (The public

Gross-Inequity Exceptions

Cases that reached the full Pay Board, its Cases and Appeals Panel, or its Category III Panel (see chapter 7) involved requests for increases above what was allowed by the 5.5 percent standard and the formula exceptions. Those cases involving 5.5 percent or less could be easily handled by the staff and required only minimal processing. And if the terms of a formula exception were met, little administrative effort was involved. Hence most of the time board members spent on cases involved so-called gross-inequity claims under section 201.11(d)—later 201.30—of the board's regulations. The gross-inequity exception was in many respects the safety valve of the wage control program in Phase II. It was used to handle the widely publicized cases discussed in chapters 5 and 6 and provided a framework for the consideration of the myriad claims the Pay Board could not anticipate. (See appendix C.)

Some gross-inequity claims were made on the basis that the unit met the spirit but not the letter of one of the formula exceptions. Thus a unit with an eight-month lag in a tandem relationship might argue that although the lag exceeded the specified six-month period, the unit ought to be granted a tandem exception. Others might argue that although they met the letter of the exception eligibility rules, the 7 percent cap was insufficient relief for their problems. Still others would raise issues not dealt with at all by the exceptions. For example, issues of wage compression, misalignment with local prevailing wages, or special consideration for work rule buy-outs (productivity bargaining) might be raised.

The original section 201.11 of the board's regulations, published on the eve of Phase II, said that the board would consider "ongoing collective bargaining and pay practices and the equitable position of the employees involved, including the impact of recent changes in the cost of living upon the employees' compensation."[48] The later version of section 201.30 added language concerning productivity and "factors . . . necessary to foster economic growth, to promote improvement in the quality of governmental services, and to prevent gross inequities, hardships, seri-

---

member position had been for $2.20 at the time the Cost of Living Council's definition based on $1.90 was announced. See Pay Board press release PB-39, January 19, 1972.) Thus it in effect counted on potential compression problems to maintain some control below $2.75. Employers presumably would be reluctant to distort their wage structures, even if the regulations permitted such distortions.

48. *Federal Register,* vol. 36 (November 13, 1971), p. 21791.

ous market disruptions, domestic shortages of raw materials, localized shortages of labor, and windfall profits."[49] The added language was lifted in part from the December 1971 amendments to the Economic Stabilization Act.[50] The items listed were not very significant in practice other than as signals that the board would use broad discretion in deciding cases in which more than the 7 percent allowed by the formula conceptions was involved.

Rejected Exceptions

During its deliberations, the Pay Board decided *not* to adopt certain exceptions, including three important ones proposed by the labor members.[51] These issues involved increases of 25 cents or less, productivity bargaining (work rule trade-offs), and interplant inequities.

Cents-Per-Hour Exception

Earlier in the life of the Pay Board, the labor members had proposed a flat exemption of all wage increases of less than 25 cents, regardless of the percentage. This exception would have effectively raised the 5.5 percent standard for units with a base compensation of less than $4.55. For example, a unit with a base of $3 would have had a de facto 8.3 percent standard. It is doubtful that the labor members believed that a 25-cent-increase exception had any chance of being adopted, since the public members did not accept income redistribution as a proper goal of the anti-inflation program then in progress. A lower cents-per-hour approach, however, would have been rather clumsy. Low-wage workers in units with high *average* wages would not benefit. And high-wage workers in low-wage units might benefit. Consequently, consideration of the cents-per-hour approach was eventually dropped.[52]

Work Rule Exception

The work rule issue was more complex. Productivity bargaining had been popularized during the 1960s by experience in Britain, as well as by

49. Ibid., vol. 37 (November 23, 1972), p. 24966.
50. Section 203(b) of the Economic Stabilization Act listed these criteria for consideration in determining allowable wage and price increases.
51. See BNA, *Daily Labor Report,* December 17, 1971, p. AA-4.
52. An analysis was provided to the board of the likely effects of such an exemption. See Pay Board staff paper EAD-10, February 16, 1972.

some prominent American examples.[53] The principle is simple. A union can impose costs on employers either in the form of cash wage and benefit premiums or by lowering productivity through restrictive work practices. In either case unit labor costs are raised. If the parties agree to reallocate these costs by increasing wages and benefits in return for less restrictive work rules, there will be no increase in unit labor costs and hence no pressure on prices. In addition, since taking benefits in the form of restrictive work practices may be an inefficient way of extracting concessions from employers, unit labor costs may actually be reduced.

Unfortunately the principle is easier to state than to implement. To conclude a productivity bargain, the parties need to have some notion of the costs involved in a restrictive practice and these costs are not always easy to measure. Moreover, restrictive work practices are more common in older industries where employment opportunities are declining. Efforts to buy out such restrictive practices may involve further employment reductions. This creates distributional stresses within the union, complicating the bargaining process. Sometimes, but not always, these stresses can be alleviated through sweetened early retirement benefits, attrition plans, or retraining arrangements.[54]

The problem of productivity bargaining becomes even more complicated when an outside wage control agency is involved. The British incomes policy experience suggested that a productivity bargaining exception could easily become a loophole in a wage control program. Requests for above-standard wage increases are usually based on *prospective* cost savings of the change in work rules, and the parties to the agreement may exaggerate the estimate of cost savings. Moreover, it is difficult to retrospectively separate normal productivity improvement resulting from investment and new technology from productivity increases related to work rule reform. There have been fears that large wage increases where productivity bargaining had been successfully concluded could set a pattern for increases in units lacking such agreements. These considerations led to a Pay Board rejection of a formula exception for work rule buy-outs.

The board found that even on a case-by-case basis, work rule buy-outs could prove misleading. In early 1972 the Pay Board approved increases

53. See Allan Flanders, *The Fawley Productivity Agreements: A Case Study of Management and Collective Bargaining* (London: Faber and Faber, 1964); and R. B. McKersie and L. C. Hunter, *Pay, Productivity and Collective Bargaining* (St. Martin's Press, 1973).

54. McKersie and Hunter, *Pay, Productivity and Collective Bargaining,* p. 40.

on the railroads for the United Transportation Union (UTU) subject to the successful implementation of work rule reform. Documents submitted to the board suggested savings on the order of $156 million a year.[55] When the Pay Board sought documentation before an increase scheduled for October 1, 1972, the carriers were extremely reluctant to provide it, and what they did provide was too limited to be satisfactory.[56] After the board hinted at the possibility of a subpoena, the carriers filed a thorough report. The savings were found to be running at a rate of about $15 million, or about 0.8 percent of compensation, much less than the parties had projected and the board had anticipated.[57]

Although the Pay Board decided that a formula exception for productivity bargaining was inappropriate, it did adopt a policy for more mechanistic programs of relating pay to productivity in response to congressional wishes. Productivity had become something of an "apple pie" word by 1971. There had been a tendency to blame inflation on a lack of a productivity growth policy and to assume that productivity could be made to increase substantially more rapidly through government efforts. Economists attribute long-run productivity growth primarily to new technology, investment, and changes in the quality and composition of the labor force.[58] But on occasion government officials have acted as if they thought that exhortations would have a noticeable effect on the rate of output per man-hour. In any case Congress was in a mood to include productivity provisions in the December 1971 amendments to the Economic Stabilization Act. The so-called Percy amendment (section 203 [f][3]) was adopted with little discussion, along with a variety of directives to the National Commission on Productivity, an agency originally created by the Nixon administration to fend off demands for wage-price controls.[59]

55. This figure appeared on a sheet submitted to the board by the UTU when it was considering the case. Also indicated on the sheet were potential savings several times the initial $156 million. See Pay Board staff paper EAD-1, January 16, 1972.

56. Pay Board staff paper EAD-41, June 16, 1972, notes that the initial information supplied by the railroads did not permit a dollar estimate of cost savings.

57. Pay Board staff paper EPCA-EAD, Micro-103, August 28, 1972.

58. See Edward F. Denison, *Accounting for United States Economic Growth, 1929–1969* (Brookings Institution, 1974).

59. The Pay Board was instructed by another December 1971 amendment to the Economic Stabilization Act (sec. 203[i]) to consult with the executive director of the National Commission on Productivity on productivity-related matters. The commission, however, was basically dormant during Phase II. A perfunctory meeting with the executive director was held early in 1972, but the board's policies on productivity matters was self-generated.

This amendment, sponsored by Senator Charles H. Percy of Illinois, stated that wage controls could not be used to preclude wage payments made "in conjunction with existing or newly established employee incentive programs which are designed to reflect *directly* increases in employee productivity." (Emphasis added.) After analyzing the legislative history, the general counsel of the Pay Board determined that programs described in the Percy amendment were plant-wide. However, the board saw little point in making a significant differentiation between plant-wide and less than plant-wide plans.

Productivity incentive programs range from simple piece-rate systems to elaborate bonus schemes that include mechanisms to induce labor-management cooperation in raising output. According to a BLS survey, about 14 percent of urban plant workers during 1968–70 were paid on an incentive basis, down from 20 percent in 1961–63.[60] Only an insignificant handful of office workers were on incentive programs in either period, probably because of the difficulty in defining their output. Three percent of plant workers in 1968–70 were paid according to group productivity bonus plans, which include programs of the much touted Scanlon Plan variety.[61] Under such plans productivity savings are shared with workers according to prearranged formulas. It was probably Scanlon-type programs, which cover a negligible portion of the labor force, that had actually impressed Senator Percy. Therefore the Pay Board conceivably could have taken a very narrow view of the coverage of the Percy amendment without directly affronting Congress.

In fact, the board decided that existing productivity incentive programs, of whatever scope, would be allowed to operate according to their terms.[62] The board assumed that existing programs could not have been designed to circumvent wage controls, although they offered the potential for doing so. In effect such programs could raise the *rates* at which they paid benefits by 5.5 percent a year. But if covered employees raised their productivity, they could obviously raise their take-home pay by more than 5.5 percent.

Some obvious questions of equity were raised regarding workers under incentive plans and workers paid on the basis of time rates. To have fol-

60. John Howell Cox, "Time and Incentive Pay Practices in Urban Areas," *Monthly Labor Review*, vol. 94 (December 1971), p. 54.

61. Frederick G. Lesieur, ed., *The Scanlon Plan: A Frontier in Labor-Management Cooperation* (MIT Press, 1958).

62. Pay Board press release PB-50, February 23, 1972.

lowed a different policy, however, would have effectively forced an end
to many established plans. For this reason, even without the Percy amendment, the board probably would have adopted a similar policy for existing incentive plans. Existing arrangements could be compared with deferred contracts, which had already been granted preferential treatment.
While it was true that board rules would permit earnings of units under
incentive plans to rise by more than 5.5 percent, it was also true that the
rules allowed greater than 5.5 percent to units where more workers than
usual happened to have been promoted or to have accrued overtime.

In the case of new plans or modifications of old plans, the board faced
a different problem. Obviously such plans could be rigged to get around
wage controls. Evidence from Western Europe indicated that the phenomenon of wage drift due to incomes policy occurred partly through the
piece-rate mechanism.[63] Over a period of time, productivity in a typical
unit usually rises as new equipment and technology is introduced. A bona
fide productivity incentive system will correct for this factor, but the simple expedient of not making such adjustments has the effect of accelerating the increase of earnings.

The board decided to handle new or modified plans as it did existing
plans, provided it received assurance that the new or modified plans were
bona fide. Hence the board required new plans to meet a variety of criteria—based on standard personnel practice—in order to confirm that
the bonus payments directly reflected worker effort. Proposals for new
plans had to be cleared with the board before implementation. In practice the review of the proposals was left to the executive compensation
staff, although most plans did not involve executives. This turned out to
be a wise choice, since executive pay plans often commingled profit and
productivity-based programs. The board did not view profits as a form of
executive productivity, since profit fluctuations are primarily a reflection
of the business cycle. It was therefore unwilling to permit profit-based
plans to take advantage of the productivity incentive regulations.

The Pay Board, of course, could not police the details of new or modified productivity incentive plans. It relied on the descriptions supplied
by the parties. The expectation that the exception would not become a
major loophole in a temporary program proved correct. There was no
rush to implement new plans. Employers generally were unwilling to

63. Lar Aavig, "Wage Drift in Norway," *British Journal of Industrial Relations,*
vol. 2 (July 1964), pp. 182–83.

transform their payment systems for years to come in order to circumvent a short-term program operating in a loose labor market.[64]

Interplant Inequities

Although the board eventually adopted an exception for *intraplant* inequities, it was unwilling to provide the same flexibility for dealing with *interplant* inequities. Interplant inequities arise when traditional wage relationships between plants in the same company, industry, or labor market are disrupted. To the extent that strict tandems had been disrupted by controls, the tandem exception was available. Hence interplant inequities as discussed by the board had the looser connotation of a unit whose wages had somehow fallen below those of some other comparison unit(s).

It is a common practice in collective bargaining for wage demands to be made in conjunction with a comparison of the unit's workers with workers in some other unit where wages happen to be higher. Management, of course, responds with examples of units paid at the same level or a lower level than its employees. This ritual is made possible by the difficulty in defining what characteristics an appropriate comparison group should have.

Precisely because of this difficulty, the board ultimately decided that an interplant inequity formula could not be constructed and that an attempt to do so might create a substantial loophole. Claims were made from time to time, however, on a gross-inequity basis that included comparisons with other employee groups. For example, the state of Ohio submitted a claim involving comparisons with civil servants in other states. Sometimes applicants would simply point to BLS data on surveyed wages in their industry or area. In some instances interplant inequity issues were intertwined with arguments about labor shortages resulting from an inability to pay prevailing wages.[65] Unless a case was made to prove a gross inequity, the board generally took the view that any effort to establish a uniform interplant wage structure would have to await the end of the stabilization program.

---

64. A few instances of such behavior did occur, however. See Mitchell and Azevedo, *Wage-Price Controls and Labor Market Distortions,* chap. 5.

65. For example, an exception was granted for faculty salaries at the University of California on the grounds that the university's salary rank had slipped relative to other comparison institutions.

Table 3-8. Employee Progression Plans in Agreements Covering 2,000 or More Workers, 1971[a]

Industry	Number of workers in surveyed agreements[b]	Percent of workers in agreements with progression plans				
		Total	Automatic only	Merit only	Automatic and merit	Unknown
All industries[c]	4,863	43	21	12	9	2
Manufacturing	2,575	53	17	21	11	3
Ordnance	61	96	65	0	31	0
Tobacco	18	69	43	0	0	26
Apparel	217	63	62	1	0	0
Furniture	7	43	0	0	0	43
Paper	26	63	11	0	52	0
Chemicals	44	42	24	5	13	0
Petroleum refining	15	82	15	0	20	47
Rubber and plastics	68	34	0	0	0	34
Machinery, except electrical	101	45	24	8	11	2
Electrical machinery	340	80	13	24	41	3
Transportation equipment	805	84	15	56	8	4
Instruments	24	100	8	0	92	0
Miscellaneous	13	79	79	0	0	0
Communications	524	100	78	3	18	0
Gas and electric utilities	63	97	50	8	35	4
Retail trade	174	56	48	3	5	0

Source: U.S. Bureau of Labor Statistics, *Characteristics of Agreements Covering 2,000 Workers or More*, Bulletin 1729 (GPO, 1972), p. 27. Figures are rounded.
a. Not all workers in an agreement with a progression plan are necessarily covered by that plan.
b. Includes 620 agreements. No railroad or airline contracts were surveyed.
c. Industries are shown separately if more than one-third of workers are covered by agreements with progression plans.

Merit Plan Policy

Merit systems provide formal procedures whereby employees are evaluated and given wage increases based on performance. According to a BLS survey, 9 percent of urban plant workers were paid according to a merit system during 1968–70.[66] Another 12 percent were paid through a system based on longevity and merit. The proportions were considerably higher for office workers: 36 percent and 22 percent, respectively. Since merit plans by their nature give an employer a degree of flexibility in determining pay, it is not surprising that their incidence among union workers appears to be less than among nonunion workers. As table 3-8 illustrates, however, merit and merit-plus-automatic plans covered a significant minority of workers under larger union agreements in 1971.

From the beginning the Pay Board decided that pay increases resulting from bona fide job promotions were not to be charged against the 5.5 percent standard. This ruling was in keeping with the philosophy of controlling average increases in job pay rates but not individual pay rates. It was also in keeping with Phase I practices. Obviously it would not have been possible for the Pay Board to police the legitimacy of promotions in order to determine whether they might have been given merely as a means of evading controls. On the other hand, it seemed likely that employers would not lightly upset their job structures to evade a temporary program.

Although promotion policy was easy to formulate, the issue became more complex when it came to other forms of progression. Some units use automatic longevity plans that provide higher wages simply as a function of time on the job, assuming satisfactory job performance. Longevity increases presumably are a reward for doing a given job better, an accomplishment formally assumed to come with experience. But the distinction between doing a given job better and moving to a better job is not always clear. In a sense longevity increases might be regarded as quasi-promotions. Since longevity plans established before Phase II could not have been created to evade controls, and since their mechanical approach generally precluded manipulation, the board exempted longevity and related increases within a rate range as one of its first decisions.[67]

The possibility of manipulating a merit plan, on the other hand, could

66. Cox, "Time and Incentive Pay Practices," p. 54.
67. Pay Board press release PB-1, November 13, 1971.

not be ignored. In theory a merit plan is meant to be more precise in measuring employee productivity than a longevity plan. Instead of a strict time approach, supervisors are supposed to make judgments about the relative merits of their employees. Often a supervisor will be given a checklist of characteristics that are considered meritorious, and he will be responsible for giving his employees a rating according to these criteria. Supervisors are sometimes given discretion in awarding merit raises, but limits are generally placed on the number of merit awards that can be distributed.

Promotion systems, longevity plans, and merit plans have one common characteristic. If all that is involved is employee progression, the plans need not raise average costs. This point is often confusing with merit plans, since firms sometimes allocate budgets to merit increases. These budgets, however, are partly a way of preventing the system from degenerating into a general across-the-board increase. Merit systems need not raise average labor costs as long as the proportion of individuals at each wage level remains constant. This condition presumably will arise when a firm reaches a steady-state employment pattern.

In practice, steady-state conditions need not apply. A rapidly growing firm may have a disproportionate number of relatively young and inexperienced employees. When growth slows, the average age and experience level of the firm's work force often rises, increasing average compensation per man-hour. Another spurt of growth would again lower average costs. Hence business cycle (demand) and demographic influences (supply) will affect average labor costs under a merit system.

In principle, personnel managers frown on using merit systems to provide general wage increases. If across-the-board increases are needed, they prefer to label them as such rather than to simply increase the annual portion of deserving employees. Nonetheless, across-the-board increases sometimes are made through merit systems, particularly in nonunion firms. In nonunion firms merit plans can be less formal than in union firms, and the employer may have more discretion, although practices vary widely. Despite advice from the personnel department, management may see a virtue in avoiding the appearance of across-the-board increases, which may create expectations of such increases in the future. Management may decide that it is preferable to let employees keep up through more liberal merit policies. Or it may be that the merit system is used unofficially to provide general increases because line supervisors feel a need to keep turnover down as wages outside the firm rise.

Originally the board decided to permit merit increases within rate ranges under existing union merit plans to be excluded from the calculation of a unit's wage increase. Adjustments to the rate ranges themselves would be counted against the allowable increase. Thus if a union plan had a rate range of $4 to $4.50 an hour, a worker receiving a merit increase from $4.20 to $4.40 would not have this increase charged against the 5.5 percent standard. Even if the average compensation of all employees in the range rose from, say, $4.25 to $4.35, no charge would be made. In effect the Pay Board was willing to assume that union plans, because of their formality, would be operated honestly and that changes in average wages simply reflected exogenous business cycle and demographic factors. This approach was heavily promoted by UAW Vice-President Pat Greathouse, whose union had many members covered by such plans. Indeed because of Greathouse's interest the merit issue anomalously received initial consideration by the board within the framework of collective bargaining contracts.

The board was unwilling to make the same assumption for nonunion plans, which had a greater discretionary element. A confusing press release was issued stating that increases under nonunion plans would be charged against the 5.5 percent pay standard.[68] The release failed to spell out a computation rule for making these charges. Thus nonunion employers complained bitterly about discriminatory treatment relative to the union sector and about inability to go ahead with even allowable increases because of imprecise regulations.

In its policy on nonunion plans the board was groping toward what was later called the "double-snapshot" computation rule. In effect the board wanted nonunion employers to project what the average wage would be at the end of the control year and to compare it with the base-period average wage to calculate the percentage increment.[69] The problem with this method was that it included not only whatever general increase had been tucked into the merit plan but also the demographic and business cycle effects. That is, the change in the average wage encompasses more than the average wage rate increase. In retrospect it appears that the changing composition of the labor force during 1972 would have reduced average pay in units applying the double-snapshot rule by about

68. Ibid., PB-6, November 23, 1971.
69. In other words a "snapshot" taken just before the control year that could be compared with one taken at the end of the control year.

0.5 percent.[70] In effect such units would have been eligible for a de facto 6 percent standard on the average, with variations among units.

The problem for the Pay Board was that it knew what it wanted but found it difficult to translate its objective into operational terms. It wanted the "true" merit portion of merit plans to be excluded from the wage increase calculation, along with the demographic and business cycle influence. And it wanted the general increase portion to count. In principle the board could have asked employers to estimate what this year's labor force would have earned under last year's merit plan. This would have theoretically provided a way of extracting the general increase. But so much guesswork and room for creative accounting would have resulted that the board decided to put its trust only in union plans, in which the general increases are presumably reflected only in rate-range adjustments. Suggestions that nonunion plans that were operated in good faith and under well-defined rules should be treated the same as union plans were initially rejected. The feeling seemed to be that good faith would be an insufficient control.

The Pay Board was caught by surprise by the outcry that followed its first decision on merit plans. Subsequent discussion revealed that not all board members had understood fully the computational problems involved in rules for nonunion plans. Confusion also marked later staff discussion concerning merit plans, particularly over the issue of whether merit plans automatically created upward wage drift. The criticism of the Pay Board on the merit issue has to be understood in relation to the circumstances. The Pay Board was in the midst of disposing of the five major cases discussed in chapters 5 and 6 when the merit rules were announced. Complaints were mounting over an alleged pro-union bias in case decisions, and the merit exclusion of nonunion plans seemed to be another symptom of the bias.

By mid-December 1971, the board decided to revise its merit policy. But the press of board business prevented immediate revision, and the board simply voted to reconsider merit plans at the earliest possible date.[71] Labor members of the board dissented, fearing that the position of

70. This estimate was made by comparing the age profiles of employed persons aged fourteen and over in December 1971 and in December 1972 as reported in *Employment and Earnings*. Age groups were weighted by mean yearly incomes of full-time workers as reported in *Current Population Reports*, Series P-60, no. 83 (GPO, July 1972), table 6. Using the fixed incomes, 1972 income was 0.5 percent below that in 1971.

71. Pay Board press release PB-26, December 17, 1971.

union merit plans might be imperiled. In a statement released with the board's decision, the labor members disclaimed any responsibility for disparity of treatment between the union and nonunion sectors.

The board reviewed a variety of options when it reconsidered the merit issue in February 1972. The labor position was basically that all merit plans should operate according to their terms, as far as increases within rate ranges were concerned. Business took the view that existing plans— union and nonunion—should be subject to the 5.5 percent standard and the double-snapshot approach. New or successor plans could be implemented providing they met specified criteria. In both cases any wage increasing the effects of labor force composition on changes in the wage bill could be removed from the calculation.

The public members proposed a similar plan but suggested capping the percentage increase at the same 7 percent that had been applied to other exceptions. On February 8 the public members' plan was adopted.[72] Merit policy remained unchanged until the regulations of the board were recodified in November 1972. At that time the board felt impelled to remove the de facto double exception of the computation rule and the 7 percent cap, since staff studies uncovered several cases where increases substantially above what was contemplated were being provided.

Qualified Fringe Benefits

As noted earlier, the Pay Board initially decided to include all fringe benefits within the 5.5 percent standard. Units were to be left with the task of allocating the proportion of their allowable increase they wished to spend on wages versus fringe benefits. The composition of compensation was not to be of concern to the board. The only deviation from this cost-oriented approach was that increased expenditures needed to maintain existing benefits were not included for reasons of equity.[73]

Once Pay Board policy was announced, two interest groups mobilized to persuade Congress that the board should grant preferential treatment to fringe benefits. The insurance industry, which provides and manages many fringe benefit packages, was anxious lest Pay Board policy depress what had been a growing market for their services. Insurance companies

72. Ibid., PB-47, February 8, 1972.
73. As noted earlier, this was not an explicit policy originally. Rather, it was implied by the public members' position on the coal case.

feared that if the 5.5 percent standard squeezed the amount available for a compensation increase, compensation would be redirected toward visible cash in the pay envelope. In particular the industry was concerned that since the start-up costs of creating a new benefit, such as a pension program, were high, there might not be enough room within the allowable 5.5 percent to establish new programs. The insurance industry was joined by organized labor in lobbying efforts.[74]

Originally, proposed language in the Senate's version of the revised Economic Stabilization Act would have limited preferential treatment for fringe benefits to units with less than 1,000 employees. Eventually, however, the House version prevailed. In the House version the size of the unit was not a factor. The final bill provided authority to stabilize wages and salaries but excluded from their definition

(1) any pension, profit sharing, or annuity and savings plan which meets the requirements of section 401(a), 404(a)(2), or 403(b) of the Internal Revenue Code of 1954;

(2) any group insurance plan; or

(3) any disability and health plan.[75]

Limits on such benefits were permitted, however, if the contributions made to support them were "unreasonably inconsistent" with the standards for wage or price stability.

Congress in effect had given the Pay Board three options. The board already had a 5.5 percent standard, which now applied to wages and benefits not mentioned by Congress (so-called includable benefits). One possibility would be to totally exclude the congressionally favored benefits from consideration. This alternative would have provided tremendous incentive for units wishing more than 5.5 percent to channel the coverage into fringe benefits.

Arguments had been made in Congress that such benefit increases would not be inflationary because they were a form of saving. The Pay Board did not accept this view. First, such benefits add to labor costs and therefore put pressure on prices in the same manner as wage increases. Second, there was no guarantee that forced saving for employees would not be offset by dissaving. For example, a worker given a life insurance

74. Democratic Senator Lloyd M. Bentsen, Jr., of Texas played a major role in the congressional action favoring fringe benefits.

75. P.L. 92-210 (1971), sec. 203(g). Section 401(a) of the Internal Revenue Code refers to qualified pension, profit-sharing, and stock bonus plans. Section 404(a)(2) refers to annuities. Section 403(b) refers to annuity plans of government, educational, and charitable organizations.

or pension plan would have less incentive to buy his own life insurance plan privately or to save for retirement. Moreover, not all the benefits mentioned by Congress were truly forms of saving. Health insurance plans are mainly a procedure for risk-pooling, not saving. Third, even if net saving did increase as a result of a benefit exemption, this was not an appropriate prescription for 1972. During the previous wartime programs when the saving argument was first advanced, the force behind inflation had been excess demand. But during Phase II the economy would be moving out of a recession. Phase II was aimed at cost-push, hypothetical or otherwise, and excess demand was not viewed as a problem.

A second option for the Pay Board was to maintain a 5.5 percent standard for wages and includable benefits and to require separate reporting on congressionally favored fringe benefits. The board could then decide on a case-by-case basis whether the reported benefit increases were "unreasonably inconsistent" with the standard. Under this approach the board would be forced to look at every case, even those reporting wage and includable benefit increases of 5.5 percent or less. The Pay Board staff could not handle the "unreasonably inconsistent" question unless specific guidelines were issued. And for that matter wage-setters would have no idea of what was permissible unless some rules were announced. Given the slow process of policymaking, however, the board exercised this option for a limited period. From the time the December 1971 amendments to the Economic Stabilization Act were passed until the new fringe benefit policy was announced on February 23, 1972, the reporting forms issued by the board excluded congressionally favored fringe benefits from the regular calculations. Such benefits appeared in a separate section of the forms.[76]

The board felt, however, that it must eventually adopt some sort of numerical standard for what were then called exempted, or excludable, benefits but which later became known as qualified benefits (QBs). As table 3-9 shows, in 1970 such benefits made up a significant fraction of what the Pay Board defined as compensation.[77] The table shows that lower-wage units of employees tended to have a smaller proportion of their total compensation in QBs than did higher-paid units. Similar re-

76. The forms issued in this fashion were designated PB-1 (for unionized units) and PB-2 (for nonunion units).

77. Some benefits that were not technically qualified are included in the QB total of tables 3-10 and 3-11. The Bureau of Labor Statistics does not break down pension plans or other benefits into qualified or unqualified. It was assumed that all pension and thrift plans were qualified.

Table 3-9. *Composition of Employee Compensation, 1970*

Percent

Type of compensation	All employees	Office employees	Nonoffice employees	Manufacturing employees	Nonmanufacturing employees	Employees in establishments with 500 or more workers	Nonoffice employees	
							Union establishments	Nonunion establishments
Straight-time pay	84.2	83.1	84.7	80.6	86.0	79.7	81.4	89.3
Includable fringes[a]	9.5	10.4	9.3	11.9	8.5	12.2	10.8	7.5
Qualified benefits[b]	6.3	6.6	5.9	7.1	5.4	8.2	7.8	3.2
Pensions	3.2	3.9	2.7	3.2	3.1	4.2	3.5	1.4
Health and welfare	2.8	2.3	3.0	3.7	2.2	3.6	4.2	1.7
Savings plans	0.2	0.4	0.1	0.2	0.1	0.4	0.1	0.1
Total compensation[c]	100.0	100.0	100.0	100.0	100.0	100.0	100.0	100.0
Addendum:								
Monetary compensation[c] (dollars per hour)	4.31	5.57	3.65	4.64	4.14	5.02	4.57	2.89

Source: U.S. Bureau of Labor Statistics, *Employee Compensation in the Private Nonfarm Economy, 1970*, Bulletin 1770 (GPO, 1973), pp. 15–18, 21. Figures are rounded.

a. Premium pay, pay for leave, severance pay, supplemental unemployment benefit funds, and nonproduction bonuses.

b. May include some benefits that were not technically qualified under Pay Board rules.

c. Excludes social security, unemployment insurance, and workmen's compensation.

Table 3-10. *Private Nonfarm Compensation Trends, 1968–70*

Type of employee, establishment, and compensation[a]	Compensation per hour worked (dollars)		Compound annual rate of change, 1968–70 (percent)	Change in qualified benefits as percent of total compensation at annual rate, 1968–70[b]
	1968	1970		
All employees				
All establishments				
Qualified benefits	0.21	0.27	13.4 ⎱	
Total compensation	3.70	4.31	7.9 ⎰	0.8
Establishments of 500 or more workers				
Qualified benefits	0.32	0.41	13.2 ⎱	
Total compensation	4.34	5.02	7.5 ⎰	1.0
Nonoffice employees				
All establishments				
Qualified benefits	0.16	0.21	14.6 ⎱	
Total compensation	3.19	3.65	7.0 ⎰	0.8
Union establishments				
Qualified benefits	0.27	0.35	13.9 ⎱	
Total compensation	3.97	4.57	7.3 ⎰	1.0
Nonunion establishments				
Qualified benefits	0.06	0.09	22.5 ⎱	
Total compensation	2.53	2.89	6.9 ⎰	0.6

Sources: U.S. Bureau of Labor Statistics, *Employment Compensation in the Private Nonfarm Economy*, issues for 1968 and 1970, Bulletins 1722 and 1770 (GPO, 1971 and 1973), pp. 14, 17, 20 (1968) and pp. 15, 18, 21 (1970).

a. Qualified benefits include pensions, health and welfare, and thrift plans. Total compensation excludes social security, unemployment insurance, and workmen's compensation.

b. Simple average of interpolated qualified benefit increment, 1968–69 and 1969–70, divided by total compensation for 1968 and that interpolated for 1969, respectively.

sults appear for small establishments relative to large ones and for nonunion establishments relative to union ones. Moreover, as table 3-10 shows, in recent years the tendency had been to increase QBs faster than other forms of compensation. From 1968 to 1970 total compensation per hour worked increased at an annual rate of just under 8 percent, while hourly QBs rose at a rate of over 13 percent. These divergent trends had in fact been evident throughout the postwar period.

Table 3-10 also indicates that a standard for a QB increase expressed as a fraction of the compensation base would be more likely to hit union employees than nonunion employees. During 1968–70 QB compensation in nonunion establishments rose faster in percentage terms than in union establishments. This partially reflected the institution of new plans in the nonunion sector. The low incidence of such plans in the past resulted in

Table 3-11. *Expenditures on Qualified Benefits by Establishments with Positive Expenditures, 1970*[a]

	Benefit as percent of total compensation	
Plan[b]	BLS definition[c]	Pay Board definition[d]
Pension	4.0	4.1
Health and welfare	2.9	3.0
Savings	1.0	1.0
Total[e]	7.9	8.1

Source: U.S. Bureau of Labor Statistics, *Employee Compensation in the Private Nonfarm Economy, 1970*, Bulletin 1770 (GPO, 1973), pp. 29, 31, 35.
a. Includes only those establishments that had the benefit programs.
b. Some plans may not have been technically qualified under Pay Board rules.
c. Includes social security, unemployment insurance, and workmen's compensation.
d. Excludes social security, unemployment compensation, and workmen's compensation.
e. It is technically improper to sum expenditures on the three types of plans, since some establishments may have had zero expenditures in certain categories and would have been excluded from the calculations.

a higher percentage increase as new plans came into operation. When the increase was expressed as a fraction of the compensation base, however, the annual increase was only 0.6 percent, compared with 1.0 percent for the union sector. Similarly, a standard as a percentage of the base was likely to impinge on larger units relative to smaller ones. Thus if the Pay Board used a percentage-of-the-base standard, it would accomplish two aims. Recent experience indicated it would provide more leeway to the smaller units, about which Congress was especially concerned; and it would focus the impact of controls on the union sector, just as the 5.5 percent standard did.

The initial proposals of the public members made a distinction between units with relatively high base-period compensation earmarked for QBs and other units. It was thought desirable to distinguish between units that already had QBs and those contemplating the installation of new programs. A unit that had QB programs in operation typically would have devoted 8.1 percent of total compensation to them (table 3-11), as opposed to the all-unit average of 6.3 percent (table 3-9). Moreover, BLS data indicated that if unionized units with QBs were considered, the average would be closer to 10 percent. Hence 10 percent became the dividing line in initial public member proposals for the QB standard. Units with less than 10 percent in QBs were to have an especially generous formula.

One of the public members' early proposals was that units with less than 10 percent of base-period compensation in QBs should have a basic standard of 1 percent of the compensation base for control-year QB increases. This might be supplemented by a catch-up provision for up to another 3 percent. Units with 10 percent or more in QBs would have a 0.5 percent standard plus 1.5 percent in catch-up. In addition, units with less than 10 percent in QBs could install new plans without limitation, while the units with at least 10 percent in QBs had no such provision.[78]

In the course of the negotiations that followed, the 10 percent distinction was removed in all but one form of exception. This action was not surprising. The 10 percent distinction had the effect of favoring the non-union sector, where fringe benefits are less prevalent than in the union sector. Labor members obviously favored an across-the-board standard for QBs as long as it was higher than the 0.5 percent that would have been the guideline for most major union situations. In addition, it is significant that every union with representatives on the board had achieved a record of negotiating generous fringe benefits for many members in their jurisdictions.

As a compromise, a 0.7 percent standard was imposed for all units, bringing the Pay Board's total compensation standard to 6.2 percent (5.5 percent + 0.7 percent). QB catch-up remained but was kept at the 1.5 percent originally proposed for the units with at least 10 percent in QBs. (Units that had gotten less than 1.5 percent over the last three years could make up the difference and add it to the basic 0.7 percent.) A tandem exception was added, originally paralleling the tandem rule for wages, except that no cap was specified. Eventually the tandem lag period between the lead unit and the follower unit was lengthened from the six-month period of the tandem wage rule to twelve months because fringe benefit increases were sometimes loaded into the second year of a contract. Units with less than 10 percent in QBs in the base period were allowed to rise to 10 percent, but by an increment no larger than 5 percent. (A unit with 3.5 percent in QBs in the base period could come up to 8.5 percent; a unit with 6.5 percent in QBs could come up to 10 percent.) And the board decided that unlike the wage standard, the QB standard would cumulate. That is, if a unit used only 0.2 percent of the allowable 0.7 percent in one year, it could carry over the remaining 0.5 percent to subsequent years. QB catch-up was also permitted to be carried over for one year only.

The Pay Board was anxious that benefit trust funds not be used as escrow pools for impermissible wage increases. To prevent manipulations

78. Pay Board press release PB-51, February 23, 1972.

of trust funds for this purpose, technical language was included to block improper manipulation with regard to such items as the actuarial assumptions underlying the plan. The Board, however, did permit savings from previously overpessimistic assumptions to be used to finance new benefits at no charge against the allowable QB standard. And as noted earlier, increased contributions to maintain existing benefit levels were not counted against the standard.

Executive Compensation Regulations

The attitude of the Pay Board toward executive compensation was ambivalent. On the one hand, the board wished to concentrate on policies and cases that related to its largest audience: ordinary wage earners. On the other hand, the compensation of top executives was highly visible, and the board wished to avoid the appearance of unequal treatment between executives and nonexecutives.

During Phase II the board was forced to give more attention to executive pay than it had planned to do. First, congressional critics, especially Senator William Proxmire, chairman of the Joint Economic Committee, complained that the regulations governing executive pay were too loose.[79] Surveys of the compensation increases of top executives during 1972 suggest that had Phase II continued during the time that the surveys were released, the board might have agreed. (Available data on executive pay are discussed in chapter 10.) Second, the work load on executive compensation cases was larger than had been expected. The rules were expected to be largely self-executing, and few exception requests were anticipated. In fact, 17 percent of the Pay Board work load consisted of executive compensation cases.[80] Third, the "executive compensation industry," that is, the management consulting firms that design executive

79. See Proxmire's statements during a special hearing to review Pay Board policy on executive pay. This hearing was called shortly after the chairman of the Pay Board had testified before the Joint Economic Committee on the general scope of the wage program. Proxmire's interest was sparked by accounts in the press of large compensation increases received during 1971 by some well-known top executives. *Review of Phase II of the New Economic Program,* Hearings before the Joint Economic Committee, 92 Cong. 2 sess. (GPO, 1972), pp. 309–24.

80. Pay Board computer records indicate that as of March 12, 1973, 13,816 cases were closed. Of these, 2,337 were listed as executive compensation cases. The board did not officially count Category III cases processed by its Category III Panel as the board's work load. For details, see chapter 7.

pay plans, proved to be very vocal. They watched Pay Board regulations closely and did not hesitate to complain about alleged inequities. During the summer of 1972 when the Pay Board conducted public recodification hearings, discussion of executive compensation took up much of the hearing time. When the Pay Board published its forty-five pages of recodified regulations in the *Federal Register,* November 23, 1972, nine pages dealt specifically with executive and variable compensation.

Structure of the Executive Pay Rules

Executives often receive a portion of their compensation under some sort of predetermined plan that permits variation in income. Of course, executives are not the only category of employees who experience income fluctuations as a result of their compensation programs. Salesmen, for example, often receive commissions in lieu of a straight salary, and production workers sometimes are paid on the basis of piece rates and production bonuses. The executive compensation section at the Pay Board handled cases relating to variable pay plans for nonexecutives as well as executives. But the earnings of private-sector executives as a group generally fluctuate much more than those of other types of employees.

Although the executive compensation regulations were quite complex, it is useful to focus on three aspects of the rules: those relating to regular salaries, to incentive bonuses, and to stock option plans. In order to design the regulations, the Pay Board established a subcommittee chaired by Sheldon Cohen, a former commissioner of the Internal Revenue Service. Cohen was assisted by an alternate from the Teamsters (Abraham Weiss) and one from the business members (A. B. Slaybaugh, vice-president of Continental Oil). Essentially, the rules the subcommittee recommended to the board were adopted in full.[81] There was little debate, since the board was preoccupied with other matters.

As far as regular salaries were concerned, the same rules applied to executives as to other types of workers. That is, their units could receive a 5.5 percent increase (plus allowable exceptions) on the base that existed just before the control year. As it developed, the seeming equality of treatment was sometimes more apparent than real. In nonunion situations firms had a great deal of flexibility in determining the scope of the appropriate unit for the purpose of applying Pay Board rules. Executives

81. The rules are described in Pay Board press releases PB-27, December 17, 1971; and PB-31, December 27, 1971.

Table 3-12. *Percent of Firms with Bonus Plans for Three Highest Paid Executives, Percent with Deferred Payment, and Relation to Salary, by Major Industries, 1961–71*

Industry	Percent of firms with executive bonus plans						1971[a]	
	1961	1963	1965	1967	1969	1971[a]	Percent of plans with deferred payment	Median bonus as percent of salary
Manufacturing	45	49	53	63	65	67	38	36
Retail trade	46	51	41	48	40	50	20	43
Fire, marine, and casualty insurance[b]	n.a.	25	22	16	30	40	27	16
Commercial banking	19	12	8	10	19	23	28	11
Life insurance[b]	9	6	8	11	10	16	22	14
Gas and electric utilities	2	0	5	4	7	8	56	[c]

Sources: The Conference Board, *Top Executive Compensation*, report 573 (Conference Board, 1972); and ibid., reports 186, 193, 204, 213, and 501, published biennially, 1962–70.
a. In 1971 the number of firms surveyed were: manufacturing, 634; retail trade, 60; fire, marine, and casualty insurance, 65; commercial banking, 249; life insurance, 143; and gas and electric utilities, 115.
b. Stock companies only.
c. Sample too small for a meaningful computation.
n.a. Not available.

were always nonunion. Thus it was possible to combine the relatively few executives with larger units of other employees. A slight decrease in the amount allowed nonexecutives (or lower-rung executives) in the unit could be turned into large percentage increases for the top executives.

Although it was technically possible to treat straight salaries of executives under the same rules that applied to other workers, bonuses presented a more complex problem. Data on incentive bonuses are scarce and not comprehensive. Some indication of the importance of bonuses can be gathered from table 3-12, based on a survey of compensation practices for the top three executives in firms reporting to the Conference Board. It is evident from the table that the incidence of bonus plans varies widely by industry. In manufacturing 67 percent of the firms had such plans in 1971, while only 8 percent of utility companies had them. The differences may reflect the degree to which executives are thought to be able to influence company performance.

Bonuses are often geared to profits or profit-related variables and therefore will be sensitive to economic conditions. In a bad year the plans may provide little or no payments; in good years large bonuses can be expected. Presumably an executive knows that whatever the payoff is in a given year, over the long run a better performance will result in improved compensation.

The subcommittee recommended that bonus plans have a choice of base year in order to avoid inequities created by profit fluctuations. Specifically, it permitted units a choice of the best year of the previous three "plan" years.[82] The bonus for the unit could increase by 5.5 percent of the base during the first year under controls. To the extent that a bonus plan paid more than 5.5 percent, the excess had to be charged against the allowable 5.5 percent for wages and salaries of the unit.

The ability of bonus units to choose base years provoked criticism. It was pointed out that ordinary wage earners had no such choice.[83] Of course, even if ordinary workers had a choice, they would almost always have picked the latest year as a base, since wages ordinarily do not fall from year to year. Nevertheless, the choice of base for executives could

82. Plan years were the annual periods during which the plan historically operated. They were analogous to the control years in union situations in which traditional timing differed from the twelve-month period beginning on the starting date of Phase II. Short plan years were not permitted, however, although short control years were allowed in union situations to bridge the gap from the starting date of Phase II to the anniversary date of the contract.

83. See *Review of Phase II*, Hearings, p. 314.

Table 3-13. Percent of Firms with Qualified and Other Stock Option Plans for Three Highest-Paid Executives, by Major Industries, Various Survey Years, 1961–71[a]

Year	Manufacturing		Retail trade		Fire, marine, and casualty insurance[b]		Commercial banking		Life insurance[b]		Gas and electric utilities	
	Qualified	Other	Qualified	Other	Qualified	Other	Qualified	Other	Qualified	Other	Qualified	Other
1961	c	77	c	66	c	n.a.	c	12	c	26	c	28
1964	c	75	c	60	c	33	c	20	c	33	c	30
1966	65	9	63	10	28	2	21	2	26	2	16	8
1968	78	5	75	0	37	2	23	3	32	2	15	1
1969	90	8	81	2	51	2	30	4	35	3	18	1
1971[d]	87	27	83	18	38	9	36	4	46	7	19	3

Sources: The Conference Board, *Top Executive Compensation*, report 573 (Conference Board, 1972); and ibid., reports 186, 193, 204, 213, and 501, published biennially, 1962–70.
a. "Qualified" includes firms that have qualified option plans only and those that have both qualified and nonqualified plans; "other" includes firms that have nonqualified plans only and those that have both qualified and nonqualified plans. The total number of firms from which the percentages are derived includes those with no plans.
b. Stock companies only.
c. Not applicable; the qualified stock option plan was created in 1964 in amendments to the Internal Revenue Code.
d. In 1971 the number of firms surveyed were: manufacturing, 634; retail trade, 60; fire, marine, and casualty insurance, 34; commercial banking, 249; life insurance, 87; gas and electric utilities, 115.
n.a. Not available.

permit a very large percentage increase on a year-to-year basis, and this in turn could create the appearance of favored treatment for high-paid executives.

A second problem related to bonuses was Pay Board treatment of performance-share plans. Such plans set performance goals on a longer-run basis than many incentive bonuses and are considered by some compensation experts to have better-designed targets. Performance-share plans run for several years, and their ultimate payout (often in stock) is unknown until the end of that period. Before the recodification of the regulations in November 1972, Pay Board treatment generally discouraged the establishment of such plans. The Board charged the full amount of the payout to current-period wages and salaries, *on the assumption that the target was fully achieved.*

Stock option plans presented a problem similar to bonuses in that their payouts are likely to fluctuate from year to year. They also presented a valuation problem, since it is impossible to know what the ultimate value of an option will be until it is actually exercised. In addition, the board was faced with two basic types of stock option plans: those that met the Internal Revenue Code qualifications and those that did not.

Under the Internal Revenue Code a stock option plan is "qualified" if it is approved by the stockholders, provides that the options must be granted within ten years of the plan's adoption, provides that the option must be exercised within five years of the grant, issues options at the fair-market price as of date of issue, and meets other regulatory requirements. The definitions for a qualified plan were first laid out in 1964 and then tightened in 1969. The chief advantage of a qualified plan is that if the option is exercised after a three-year waiting period, the difference between the option price and the market price at that time is taxed preferentially as a capital gain.

Table 3-13, based on the Conference Board survey cited earlier, summarizes the availability of stock options for the top three executives in reporting companies. The survey indicates that after 1964 most firms shifted to qualified stock option plans. Most recently, and probably because of the tightening of the law in 1969, nonqualified plans began making a comeback. Qualified plans, however, were still the most general form of stock option during Phase II. Eighty-seven percent of the manufacturing firms surveyed by the Conference Board provided qualified stock option plans to their top three executives in 1971. The proportions were lower in the other sectors shown in table 3-13.

The Pay Board initially limited the issuance of options under existing qualified plans to the average annual number issued during the three fiscal years preceding Phase II. Because of the erratic nature of the issuance of options, complaints arose that the three-year limit created arbitrary results, and the board agreed to reconsider the issue during recodification.

Nonqualified plans resulted in charges against wages and salaries. If the plan provided the option at less than the fair market price at the time of issuance, the difference between the market price and the option price was charged to wages and salaries. In addition, another charge of 25 percent of the fair market value of the stock was made. This percentage was taken from a crude estimate of the average discounted worth of an option, based on historical data. An additional charge was made if the gain on the option exceeded 25 percent at the time of exercise.

Case Processing

A special Executive Compensation Panel served as an advisory body to the staff until September 1972.[84] This panel was essentially the old Executive Compensation Subcommittee, headed by Sheldon Cohen, which recommended the initial Pay Board policies on executive pay. It would make recommendations on precedent cases presented by the staff, and these recommendations would then be implemented for similar cases. Appeals from staff decisions were heard by the Category III Panel, a special staff-operated tribunal for small-unit cases, even for the small proportion of executive compensation cases involving units larger than Category III. After September 1972 the staff took precedent-setting cases directly to the Pay Board.

As noted earlier, the volume of executive compensation cases was underestimated when staff resources were initially allocated. Executive compensation was originally a two-person operation (with secretarial support). By the end of Phase II the executive compensation section had ten employees. Whether this was the optimum allocation of Pay Board staff depends on the weight placed on the importance of the executive compensation cases relative to other types of cases. Executive compensation cases were numerous but typically involved small units. Hence the

---

84. The panel was used only in an *advisory* capacity because of legal impediments stemming from its operating procedures. In fact, the staff always followed its decisions.

number of employees in the backlog of such cases was smaller than the number, say, in Category I and Category II cases involving regular wage and salaried employees. Although it is hard to characterize the degree of pressure to hold the executive compensation backlog down, some of this pressure appeared to be a response to the conspicuousness of the executive compensation cases in the business community. To some extent executives judged the efficiency of the Pay Board by the speed with which it processed their cases.

Significance of Executive Pay Raises

It is evident from the previous discussion that Pay Board concern with executive pay revolved mainly around the appearance of equity in the treatment of the highest-paid employees. In terms of the economic impact of executive pay, the relatively small portion of employees covered by the Pay Board's rules regarding bonus and stock option plans was an obvious limiting factor. Moreover, many executive pay practices appear to have only a small impact on pricing decisions. For example, plans that pay bonuses geared to profits might be viewed as analogous to profit taxes, which—in the short run in any case—will theoretically leave prices unaffected. The granting of stock options is likely to "water" a company's stock—if the options are exercised. Whether this effect would have any significant impact on pricing decisions is also open to question.

In principle the nonsalary component of executive pay is supposed to provide an incentive to increase managerial efficiency and thus could have an anti-inflationary impact. Naturally the management consultants who promote these plans argue strongly that this is actually the case and point to the willingness of stockholders to approve the programs as evidence of their efficacy.

The executive compensation staff felt that the Pay Board slighted the executive aspect of Phase II wage controls. Unlike the Korean war situation, when a special executive salary agency was created, the Pay Board retained control of executive compensation. But the board was not able or willing to devote its major attention to such compensation at the time the initial policies were created. The board farmed out the policymaking role to a subcommittee, whose recommendations it followed with little debate. In fact, the Pay Board probably delegated more authority— formally and informally—to the executive pay staff than to any other operating division.

Reconsideration

The main policies of the board were basically laid out by March 1972. But as noted in the case of catch-up, the board was willing to reconsider policies that had already been announced in the light of new evidence or changing circumstances. In some cases unforeseen technical hitches required Pay Board attention. The executive compensation rules in particular had a boundless potential for raising new issues. But other areas were involved as well. For example, the small-business exemption that decontrolled most firms with sixty employees or less, excluded the health sector. This meant that private medical doctors who incorporated themselves for tax purposes suddenly found that they were "employees" under Pay Board regulations and subject to the wage and benefit standards. The board devoted considerable time to discussing doctor problems, basically because of an accident in the regulations.

Three key areas of reconsideration, however, occurred after the initial regulations were released. The first was the extension of catch-up, which has already been discussed. After June 1972, following two extensions, catch-up—with its $3 limitation—was scheduled to end on the anniversary of Phase II. There was perfunctory discussion of a third extension before the termination date, November 13, 1972.[85] The board felt that catch-up should be ended, particularly since defining the working poor as those earning $2.75 or less an hour had relaxed controls for much of the group that could benefit from catch-up.

A second area of reconsideration dealt with the basic standard. The Pay Board had said from the beginning that the 5.5 percent figure would be reconsidered in the light of changing economic circumstances. When it originally created the 5.5 percent guideline, the number stood in something of a vacuum. It was formulated as a compromise target on compensation per man-hour. Without knowledge of the regulatory framework that was to follow, it was difficult to predict whether the target and the guideline were consistent. By June 1972 the staff had begun to assess whether labor market behavior would be consistent with the 2–3 percent inflation goal

85. The staff pointed out that a simple extension of catch-up would have produced an anomalous result. A unit that had received 5.5 percent during Phase II—that is, less than 7 percent—might have been entitled to catch-up simply because of its compliance. See Pay Board staff paper EAD-88, October 25, 1972.

POLICIES AND PRINCIPLES   109

that had been the foundation of the program. The basic goal by this time was to keep unit labor costs in the 2–3 percent range. Productivity was expected to rise more rapidly than the long-run 3 percent a year, owing to the economic expansion. This meant that compensation per man-hour for growth in the 6–6.5 percent range became the target.[86] (The lifting of the target from the original 5.5 percent in part reflected the boost in the de facto standard to 6.2 percent by the QB rules.)

The Pay Board asked the staff to provide a general economic analysis of issues surrounding the target in preparation for a review of the standard in August 1972. Reports were prepared on wage and productivity trends, based on official statistics, Pay Board data, and general trends in the economy.[87] Basically the board considered two options. One was to lower the standard. A second was to maintain the existing standard with a proviso that if units negotiated in advance for 5.5 percent in their 1973 control years, the Pay Board would guarantee to accept it. This might have provided some incentive for advance negotiations from the labor viewpoint, providing it was thought likely that the board would later lower the standard for 1973. Ultimately the board simply endorsed its existing standard and made no change.

A third area of reconsideration involved recodification. The purpose of recodification was to improve the technical drafting of existing Pay Board regulations, to obtain public comments on the regulations, and finally to redraft them, partly on the basis of the comments. The regulations also were to include restatements of the rules based on problems the staff had detected. As part of the recodification procedure, public hearings were held in several major cities during the summer of 1972. Much of the public discussion was taken up with matters relating to executive compensation.

One of the major decisions reached was to discontinue the 7 percent exception for merit plans whose control years began after November 14, 1972. Staff analysis suggested that the double-snapshot method of computation was providing significantly more latitude for many units than had been anticipated. The demographic and business cycle factors operating during 1972 often reduced the percentage computation under this method. Moreover, the Pay Board's merit rules provided that applicants could adjust their computations if the double-snapshot approach hurt them but

86. Pay Board staff papers EAD-38, June 5, 1972; and EAD-53, July 10, 1972.
87. Ibid., EAD-56 through EAD-64, all August 4, 1972.

did not have to adjust if it biased their reported percentage downward.[88] The board decided that the double-snapshot approach itself was a sufficient exception for merit plans and so discontinued the 7 percent rule. Thereafter, merit plans were subject to the basic 5.5 percent. A staff study of a sample of Pay Board cases suggested that double-snapshot by itself would be worth another 1–2 percent on the average.

The other exception that was altered by recodification was the tandem rule. Originally the tandem regulation was worded so that second- and third-year tandems could not be followed. This resulted from the six-month lag being based on contract expirations of the leader and follower units rather than on the timing of the actual wage adjustment. The board did not wish to disrupt second- and third-year tandems and therefore revised the regulatory language accordingly.

An expanded definition of "deferred adjustment" was added to include wage reopener clauses established before the freeze. The reopener had to establish a specific date; it could not be conditional on price movements or other economic circumstances. This meant that wage adjustments under such reopeners would have a more liberal standard than if, as before recodification, they had been classified as new adjustments. Category II and Category III units were allowed to institute increases of up to 7 percent and simply postreport them. Increases of more than 7 percent required Pay Board approval. Category I had to have all reopener adjustments approved by the Pay Board, but it was probable that anything up to 7 percent would have been permitted.[89]

According to BLS data, 168,000 workers under private agreements covering 1,000 or more workers in the nonconstruction sector were

88. It has been suggested that few units knew how to adjust for this effect. See Thomas R. Goin, "Phase II Stabilization Policies and Concepts," in U.S. Department of the Treasury, Office of Economic Stabilization, *Historical Working Papers on the Economic Stabilization Program, August 15, 1971–April 30, 1974* (GPO, 1974), pt. 1, p. 369. However, the downward bias found in a sample of Pay Board cases caused by the double-snapshot method seemed larger than the 0.5 percent suggested in note 70. It is possible that some units engaged in some creative accounting in estimating their merit adjustments. An exaggerated projection of workers at the lower rungs could cause this bias.

89. The issue of whether reopeners in existing contracts should be treated as deferred adjustments was raised in the course of a public recodification hearing by a union spokesman. It was argued that negotiators dealt in various ways with uncertainty about the future in multiyear contracts. Some negotiated scheduled adjustments (deferred ones), some negotiated escalators, and some negotiated reopeners. Since the board gave deferred adjustments and escalators preferential treatment, an equity case was made that the same should be true of reopeners.

scheduled to be affected by wage reopeners in 1973; almost 4 million workers were scheduled for contract expirations.[90] Thus the potential impact of reopeners was small. Moreover, none of the key negotiations scheduled for 1973 contained an eligible reopener clause.

The rest of recodification dealt mainly with executive compensation problems. Some of these problems arose from inadvertent drafting of the initial regulations. For example, variable compensation plan (bonus plan) rules originally permitted only one 5.5 percent increase rather than 5.5 percent a year. The rules were changed in recodification to allow successive increases. In addition, the original language for bonus plans and stock option plans did not take account of changes in the number of individuals covered. Thus if the covered pool of individuals was reduced, more was available for the remaining individuals. If the opposite were true, the members of the pool would be especially restricted. This anomaly was corrected by including an adjustment factor for the number of plan participants.

Were There Alternatives?

This review of policy formulation suggests that the Pay Board made reasonable judgments, given the economic environment and the constraints imposed by the Cost of Living Council for Phase II. There appears to be a logical drift in policy when it is recounted after the fact. An analogy might be made with the history of science. A high school student is impressed with the gradual accretion of knowledge from medieval alchemy to modern chemistry. He fails to learn about the false theories and false starts that occurred along the way, because the natural tendency is to forget and omit errors. The Pay Board also took false steps that disappeared from the documentation left behind and from the memories of the participants.

It can be asked, however, whether the basic design of the program was the best alternative. That is, was a numerical standard with exceptions and a category system the best possible design? The board did have available an alternative model, namely the one used by the Construction In-

90. David Larson and Lena W. Bolton, "Calendar of Wage Increases and Negotiations for 1973," *Monthly Labor Review,* vol. 96 (January 1973), p. 5.

dustry Stabilization Committee.[91] Could the case-by-case CISC approach
have been applied to the nonconstruction sector?

Naturally if *all* constraints are taken as given, the answer has to be
No, simply because case-by-case analysis was incompatible with a comprehensive program and a limited staff. As will be seen in chapter 7, even
with the board's approach, the backlog of Category III cases was threat-
ening to become a severe problem by the end of Phase II. And in many
respects the well-publicized 5.5 percent standard served as a control over
those who never filed cases with the board or the Internal Revenue Service. Simply adding more staff would not necessarily have permitted case-
by-case analysis at the Pay Board. The staff would have required substantial training in industrial relations before responsibility could be
delegated to it. In short, more would have been involved than merely
providing additional staff.

The nature of the CISC approach was basically structural. The CISC
operated on a wage distortion theory. According to this theory, traditional
wage relationships between craft groups and areas had been disrupted in
the 1960s. This set off a competitive readjustment process that turned out
not to be self-stabilizing. Instead, a leapfrogging process was set in motion that by 1971 had led to large wage increases well out of line with the
rest of the labor market.

The CISC could bring the process to an orderly conclusion by approving adjustments likely to restore the old structure and disapproving those
that were destabilizing. A particular numerical standard was not appropriate in the CISC's view, because the appropriate adjustments might be
less than 5.5 percent. The CISC usually looked at differentials in cents-
per-hour terms rather than in percentages, a practice that also limited the
usefulness, in its view, of a percentage guideline.[92] The possibility of an
approval for less than 5.5 percent was also important, since local union
leaders were often unresponsive to the threat of nonunion competition.

91. It is not clear that all board members fully appreciated the difference in the
CISC approach in the very early days of the Pay Board. The original "Order Number Two" issued by the board just before Phase II delegated to the CISC the task of
administering in construction "the policies of the Pay Board." See Pay Board press
release PB-1, November 13, 1971. Later the board issued "Amended Order Number
Two" which recognized the CISC approach. See ibid., PB-45, January 28, 1972.

92. For an exposition of the CISC view, see D. Quinn Mills, "The Problem of
Setting General Pay Standards: An Historical Review," in Gerald G. Somers, ed.,
Proceedings of the Twenty-Sixth Annual Winter Meeting, 1973 (Industrial Relations
Research Association, 1974), pp. 9–16; and idem, "Explaining Pay Increases in Con-
struction: 1953–72," *Industrial Relations,* vol. 13 (May 1974), pp. 196–201.

National leaders recognized the danger but needed the CISC to control their locals.

A key question is whether the CISC structural approach was applicable to sectors other than construction. The sharp craft divisions found in construction are not generally characteristic of the union labor force, although they do exist in some sectors.[93] Moreover, the CISC was able to offer an enticement to union cooperation in construction that could not be duplicated in all sectors. In order to obtain union cooperation in early 1971, the President suspended the Davis-Bacon Act. This law requires the payment of "prevailing" wages—which usually means union wages—by federal construction contractors. It thus shields union contractors and wage scales from nonunion competition. When labor agreed to participate in the CISC, the Davis-Bacon Act suspension was revoked. Although the CISC consistently downplayed the importance of the suspension, it probably was a significant factor in obtaining union cooperation.

The CISC was also able to offer the national construction unions something that might not be as enticing in other sectors. Construction bargaining is typically carried out at the local level. It was felt that the lack of coordination that local bargaining entailed served to make union wages in construction more prone to the type of explosion that occurred in the late 1960s. In other sectors, particularly those organized by industrial unions, national bargaining is more common. Leapfrogging is not endemic. Even in the industrial setting, questions of interoccupational wage differentials arise, but these are worked out within the internal political mechanism of the union. The CISC was able to offer the national unions in construction more control of their locals. But this offer would not be especially relevant to a union such as, say, the Auto Workers.

The Pay Board, of course, did arrive at a modified structural approach. This can be seen most clearly in the tandem and catch-up exceptions. The tandem rule was designed to maintain traditional interunit differentials. And catch-up was intended to permit units that had fallen behind to re-

93. An attempt was made in Phases III and IV to set up a committee for wages in retail food stores modeled after the CISC. There are craft elements in retail food that have some similarities with construction. The evidence on the success of the CISC model in the food sector seems to be mixed. Albert Rees, who served on the food committee, believes that the wage structure was "rationalized" but suggests that its tripartite structure was somewhat less successful than an all-governmental body would have been in adhering to a wage increase target. See Rees, "Tripartite Wage Stabilizing in the Food Industry," *Industrial Relations,* vol. 14 (May 1975), pp. 250–58.

gain their traditional position in the wage structure. Pay Board exception rules were intended to permit units to deviate from the crowd only so they could take up their old positions. The modified structural approach can also be seen in the board's willingness to adopt special procedures for two sectors of the labor force: government employees and nonunion construction workers. (See appendix D for details.)

A unit basis, rather than a strict craft basis for controls, permitted the Pay Board to use more general standards. There may be an appropriate relationship between average wages in rubber versus steel. But the differential does not have to be measured out to the last penny. Slight errors will not be destabilizing. Moreover, to the extent that the board set controls on key union units, it could be expected that follower union and nonunion units would continue to establish their traditional differentials on their own. As chapter 10 points out, if the Pay Board had left the wage structure in a distorted position, there should have been a wage surge when the looser rules of Phase III were announced. But no wage bubble became evident.

It would be wrong to infer that the Pay Board carefully worked out a structural theory and then simply wrote regulations applying that model. What the Pay Board experience suggests is that if there are important structural elements within a regulated market, reasonable regulators will become aware of those elements. Awareness will come through a combination of trial and error and from previously held knowledge. The resulting program will reflect that awareness.

IV

Coverage

The comprehensiveness of controls was one of the striking aspects of the pay program. When Phase II began virtually all wage and salary workers were covered (table 4-1). The only important exception was employees of the federal government. And even in this category controls were applicable to government enterprises such as the Postal Service and the Tennessee Valley Authority. After small businesses were exempted in May 1972, over 70 percent of all wage and salary workers remained subject to controls. And the so-called working-poor exemption was not in fact an exemption at all in terms of reporting requirements. It was instead handled as an exception for which eligibility had to be established.

The wide coverage of Phase II is surprising in view of the public discussion that took place during Phase I, when the format of the next stage of the controls program was still uncertain. Some administration officials stressed that controls were not intended as a permanent addition to economic regulation and that excessive bureaucracy was an evil to be avoided.[1] This view seemed to foretell a relatively limited program. At the same time, experts testified before Congress that extensive controls were unnecessary.[2]

Why Comprehensive Coverage?

Four factors contributed to the decision to impose comprehensive controls during Phase II: economic considerations, administration, equity, and public support. The four have obvious overlaps but can usefully serve to highlight the various pressures influencing the decision.

Economic considerations focused on the presumed nature of the inflationary process. If controls have a rationale, it is rooted in some variant

1. For example, see the statement of Commerce Secretary Maurice H. Stans in Bureau of National Affairs, Inc., *Daily Labor Report,* August 24, 1971, pp. A-16–A-17.
2. See the statements of Otto Eckstein, Charles L. Schultze, and John Sheahan in ibid., August 19, 1971, pp. A-13–A-14; August 20, 1971, pp. A-9–A-12.

Table 4-1. *Coverage of Phase II Wage Controls*

Type of employment	Number of workers, 1972 (thousands)	Initial coverage (percent)	Coverage after small-business exemption (percent)
Private nonfarm payroll employment	59,474	100	68
Hired farm workers	1,146	100	a
State and local employment	10,640	100	Local, 96[b]
Federal employment	2,650	27[c]	27
Total	73,910	99	72

Sources: U.S. Bureau of Labor Statistics, *Handbook of Labor Statistics, 1974*, Bulletin 1825 (Government Printing Office, 1974), pp. 103, 116; U.S. Bureau of the Census, *Statistical Abstract of the United States, 1973* (GPO, 1973), p. 229; and Cost of Living Council press release, May 1, 1972.
a. Exemption had a significant but unknown effect on coverage.
b. Exemption had no effect on state coverage.
c. Federal enterprises only.

of the cost-push theory. Often this theory is based on a presumed association between economic power in the marketplace and inflationary wage and price decisions. One version imputes a continual upward pressure on wages and prices from the mere existence of such power. Relatively few economists would accept that view without qualification; a more widely accepted one suggests that economic power may retard the subsidence of inflationary pressures.

This discussion, of course, begs the issue of what constitutes economic power. In both the labor and product markets, it is often assumed that size is a proxy for such power. But this need not be the case. The wage explosion in construction seemed to arise from a leapfrogging action within relatively small local units of construction workers. It is also true, however, that most of the wage settlements that are regarded as pattern-setters are identified with larger units containing thousands of workers. The settlements in basic steel, automobiles, electrical equipment, and trucking are obvious examples.

In the labor market, size and unionization also are often correlated. Even when small-business employers are unionized, they are often combined in associations for purposes of collective bargaining with a particular union. Multi-employer bargaining is found in the apparel industry, trucking, and longshoring. Thus if size is defined as the number of workers in the bargaining unit rather than as, say, the sales volume of individual employers, the correlation between size and unionization is enhanced. And in a labor market context, the presence of unionization is at least a necessary condition for the exercise of economic power in wage determination.

From an economic viewpoint, therefore, it seems logical to direct controls at large collective bargaining units, with perhaps selective controls on those smaller units in which autonomous wage pressure can be identified. The bulk of the labor force is employed in nonunion units, where controls would seem to be redundant. In nonunion units, wage determination is based on labor market conditions, plus the employer's probable desire to remain nonunion. When the labor market is relatively slack, as it was during Phase II, nonunion employers are unlikely to place upward pressure on wages unless they are trying to maintain some degree of parity with the union sector. And if the union sector is controlled, then pressures for parity on nonunion employers are dissipated.

Administrative considerations and economic factors usually go hand in hand. Obviously the amount of resources required to administer controls (including resources expended by those being regulated) is a factor in the overall weighing of costs and benefits. The fewer the number of units controlled, the lower the administrative costs will be. In addition, to the extent that there is concern about the establishment of a permanent bureaucracy, that danger is lessened if the controls can be administered by a relatively small staff.

When a concern about equity is added to the analysis, however, it is unclear whether a comprehensive or selective system is appropriate. Creditable arguments can be made on both sides. Across-the-board controls achieve a rough sort of equity in that all segments of the economy are subject to a uniform set of rules. Conversely, the comprehensive approach may not produce equal burdens on all sectors, even if the rules are seemingly uniform. In particular, the ability of smaller units to ply their way through the intricacies of obscure regulations in the *Federal Register,* to supply required data, or to file appeals, may be questioned.

Finally, there were the intangible considerations concerning the public perception of an effective program of wage controls. Comprehensive coverage signals the determination of the authorities to fight inflation. There may be an illusion here—that bigger is necessarily better—but it is apparent that public support is an important determinant of the efficacy of the program. Even in a selective program, many individuals will be touched by the restraints. If the very selectivity of the program makes it appear weak and ineffective, then the limited cooperation requested may not be forthcoming. This is especially important if it is implicitly conceded that no controls program can work if it requires close bureaucratic regulation of all wage-determining units but essentially must be founded on voluntary compliance.

Analyzing the conflicting considerations regarding the appropriate scope of coverage is easier than making the decision itself. A number of factors, however, pushed in the direction of blanket coverage. First, the Phase I controls appeared to be popular, according to public opinion polls, although, paradoxically, many people seemed to be unsure of their effectiveness.[3] Since Phase I itself was a comprehensive program in its coverage, there was an incentive not to appear "soft" by shifting to a drastically different type of program. Second, the Economic Stabilization Act of 1970, on which the authority for presidential controls was based, had been amended early in 1971 when construction was singled out for a selective wage control program. Congress made it difficult for future selectivity, apparently on the assumption that comprehensiveness and fairness went together.[4] Finally, the AFL-CIO, whose cooperation with controls was believed to be essential, had long taken the position that it is necessary to control all income shares, as had been the case in wartime, if any controls were to be imposed.[5] These factors overrode other considerations, and in late September 1971 President Nixon made it clear that controls would "cover the whole economy."[6]

The decision to adopt comprehensive coverage did not resolve administrative doubts about the dangers of a large bureaucracy. What was needed was a plan that was comprehensive in principle but that would in fact focus on the key situations. If this dialectical approach could be achieved, the administrative burdens would be significantly lightened. Thus it might be possible to create a comprehensive system that would avoid some of the encumbrances associated with an across-the-board program.

3. A question on controls was added to a regular Census Bureau survey at the request of the Cost of Living Council. Because the results were not especially supportive of the CLC program, the data were released quietly. Support for the idea of controls remained strong, however. See ibid., November 4, 1971, pp. A-13–A-15.

4. Section 3(b) of P.L. 92-15, the Economic Stabilization Act as amended on May 18, 1971, reads: "The authority conferred on the President . . . shall not be exercised with respect to a particular industry or segment of the economy unless the President determines, after taking into account the seasonal nature of employment, the rate of employment or underemployment, and other mitigating factors, that prices or wages in that industry or segment of the economy have increased at a rate which is grossly disproportionate to the rate at which prices or wages have increased in the economy generally."

5. President Meany of the AFL-CIO called for a board modeled after the World War II National War Labor Board. See BNA, *Daily Labor Report,* August 27, 1971, pp. AA-1–AA-2.

6. Speech at the Economic Club of Detroit, cited in *New York Times,* September 24, 1971.

This approach was implemented by creating a hierarchy of reporting requirements based on the size of the unit. For price purposes, size was defined in terms of an enterprise's dollar sales volume. This definition was inappropriate on the wage side, since the unit of wage determination was not necessarily coterminous with a pricing unit. For wage control purposes, therefore, the rules defined size in terms of the number of workers in the bargaining unit (union workers) or wage determination unit (nonunion workers). Units of different sizes were grouped into "categories," the term chosen early in Phase II to differentiate the Pay Board's reporting classifications from the Price Commission's "tiers."

The category system, as noted earlier, differentiated between units of 1–999 employees, 1,000–4,999 employees, and 5,000 and more employees (categories III, II, and I, respectively). The cutoff points of 1,000 and 5,000 corresponded to levels used by the Bureau of Labor Statistics for statistical studies of the union sector. Category III units were not required to report unless they wished to exceed the basic standards for new adjustments. This meant that any increase up to 5.5 percent plus allowable fringe benefits was entirely self-executed. Where the Pay Board's catch-up exception applied, increases up to 7 percent could be instituted without filing a report. Category III employers, however, were subject to spot checks from the Internal Revenue Service. Category III was treated even more generously with regard to "old" adjustments, wage increases scheduled under pre–Phase II contracts and pay practices. Such increases did not have to be reported at all, regardless of the amount. But a Category III employer could challenge such an adjustment if he wished, as could the Pay Board.[7] In theory, and to a lesser extent in practice, the demarcation of Category III would sharply reduce the administrative requirements of the controls program without diminishing coverage.

Category II was in an intermediate position in the hierarchy. All adjustments of whatever magnitude had to be reported, but increases that met Pay Board standards could be put into effect without awaiting board approval. Such increases had to be postreported within ten days of implementation. New adjustments that exceeded the standard had to await board approval. As eventually adopted by the Pay Board, the policy on old adjustments required a ninety-day prenotification for adjustments above 7 percent. At the end of the ninety-day period, these adjustments could be made effective even if the board had not taken formal action.

Categories I and II shared a common procedure for old adjustments.

7. See the Pay Board's recodified regulations, sec. 202.30, in *Federal Register,* vol. 37 (November 23, 1972).

But for new adjustments Category I units had to notify the Pay Board sixty days in advance of all increases in compensation. No new adjustments, even those below 5.5 percent, could be implemented without prior approval. In effect, therefore, the system concentrated attention on categories I and II, especially Category I.

At the time the category system was created, the Cost of Living Council estimated that 83 percent of covered employment in 10 million units fell into Category III.[8] Seven percent of covered employment in 4,000 units was believed to fall in Category II, and the remaining 10 percent were in Category I. Excluding federal employees outside the Postal Service, roughly 70 million workers can be assumed to have been in covered employment in late 1971 when the category system was designed. About 11.9 million workers were assumed to fall into categories I and II. Since the Bureau of Labor Statistics estimated that there were 10.9 million workers in late 1970 under union agreements covering 1,000 or more workers in the private sector alone, the CLC apparently believed that the two categories would be heavily dominated by union workers.[9] This assumption was grossly inaccurate—Pay Board data indicated that unionized workers constituted 49 percent of the employees included in categories I and II.[10]

Although the system won high marks for bureaucratic ingenuity, it was vulnerable for assuming the size of the employee unit was always correlated with its importance in the labor market. In the heavy industry sector—manufacturing, mining, and transportation—the key settlements could be expected to fall into categories I or II. Several sectors, however, had small units that could be pattern-setters. These included retail food stores, health services, tool and die shops, trucking, and certain service establishments.

Even where the key settlement did fall into categories I or II, the general exemption of Category III from reporting old adjustments created potential problems of equity. If the Pay Board rolled back a deferred adjustment under a pre–Phase II contract, a search would have to be made for tandem adjustments in Category III to challenge. In one key case involving the Teamsters, the task of finding the tandems was so over-

8. BNA, *Daily Labor Report,* November 10, 1971, pp. F1–F3.
9. Leon Bornstein and Lena W. Bolton, "Calendar of Wage Increases and Negotiations for 1971," *Monthly Labor Review,* vol. 94 (January 1971), pp. 31–44.
10. For more information on Pay Board data, see chapter 11.

whelming that the board decided to deduct the overage from the successor contract, a decision effectively nullified by the switch to Phase III.[11]

Efforts to Reduce Coverage

During Phase II several decisions were made to reduce the scope of the stabilization program's coverage. These steps represented refinements of the program and were also part of a tacit process of decontrol that began shortly after the outset of Phase II. In one case, that of the working poor, all three branches of government—legislative, executive, and judicial—were involved. The small-business exemption resulted from legislative and executive actions. Exemptions for federal workers (before Phase II) and professional athletes were purely executive determinations.

Small Business

Soon after the Pay Board began operation, it became apparent that there would be much to gain by exempting small businesses. File cabinets at the board began to fill with plaintive letters from barber shops and other tiny enterprises inquiring about allowable pay increases. At the same time, Congress, in extending the Economic Stabilization Act, included vague language urging consideration of special relief for small business.

It is the sense of the Congress that . . . . such exemptions shall be provided for small business enterprises as may be feasible without impeding the accomplishment of the purposes of [the act].[12]

It is clear that the Cost of Living Council had wide discretion under this amendment to make policy concerning a small-business exemption. No particular size definition appears in the legislative history of the amendment, which was phrased as a general desire rather than a specific directive.

The coincidence of congressional directives, the desires of labor and business at the Pay Board, and administrative necessity made it a virtual certainty that a small-business exemption would be adopted. The Cost of

11. BNA, *Daily Labor Report,* December 26, 1972, p. A-12.
12. Sec. 214, Economic Stabilization Act Amendments of 1971, P.L. 92-210, December 22, 1971.

Living Council took a preliminary step when it exempted an estimated 1.5 million "ma and pa" stores with annual sales volumes of less than $100,000 from price controls on January 19, 1972. A more general exemption had to await a decision concerning the appropriate cutoff point.

Although cutoffs of various sizes were considered, none came near the de facto exemption of most Category III units under Phase III. When the CLC asked the Pay Board for recommendations, the labor walkout was taking place. At the time, however, representatives of the Auto Workers and the Teamsters were still on the board as labor members. They recommended that a small business be defined as one having 100 employees or less. The business members were divided. One thought that any exemption for small businesses was premature. Another thought that fifty employees was an appropriate level. The other three recommended an initial cutoff point of twenty employees.

The five public members supported a resolution calling for a cutoff of fifty employees, excluding employers who were covered by larger master collective bargaining contracts involving 10 percent or more of their workers. This proviso recognized that the employee unit in such cases was not the firm but the master contract itself. Under the public members' resolution, employers whose firms grew after exemption would be permitted to retain their exclusion from controls until their employment level reached sixty workers.[13]

It is important to note that while reams of data concerning the number of workers potentially affected by alternative definitions were made available, the figures were at best imprecise estimates. The CLC and the Pay Board staffs made independent studies at the time the small-business exemption was under consideration.[14] But there were no comprehensive data on the distribution of employment and the number of enterprises classified by number of employees. Initially the CLC supported a fifty-employee cutoff, but at the last moment raised it to sixty employees, reportedly because of new data estimates.

The sixty-employee cutoff was announced on May 1, 1972.[15] Firms with 50 percent or more of their work force covered by master contracts involving over sixty employees remained subject to controls regardless of size. If a firm had sixty employees or less, and if less than 50 percent were covered by a master contract, only the covered employees would remain

13. Reported in Pay Board, "Weekly Status Report," April 3–7, 1972.
14. Pay Board staff paper EAD-10, February 16, 1972.
15. Cost of Living Council press release, May 1, 1972.

subject to controls. (That is, the firm would still be exempt on the price side and with regard to other workers.)

The health and construction sectors were excluded from the small-business exemption. The construction exclusion was based on a labor market consideration: the prevalence of small-business employers in the unionized sector where the precontrol wage explosion had taken place. It was believed that the Construction Industry Stabilization Committee could not operate an effective program if workers employed by small businesses were exempted and permitted to leapfrog controlled workers. The health industry exclusion was based on price considerations, that is, the general concern about rising medical costs. An inadvertent by-product of the health exclusion was the creation of the "doctor problem" for the Pay Board. Doctors who had incorporated their practices and who employed themselves found that their wages and fringe benefits were subject to controls, leading to a loss of the tax advantages of incorporation.

The exemption also applied to small government agencies.[16] The CLC estimated that altogether about 26 percent of payroll employment was removed from coverage by the small-business exemption, including 7 percent of local government employment. Later, because of problems on the price side, small firms with more than $100,000 of sales in the lumber industry were again placed under controls. Employees in the lumber industry who had received wage increases during the period of temporary decontrol were allowed to keep them. These increases were charged against the allowable 5.5 percent for the control year, so that those who had received 5.5 percent or more became ineligible for further increases.

The small-business exemption had a lesser impact on the work load of the Pay Board and the Internal Revenue Service than the number of workers involved suggests. There was no cutback at all in health or non-union construction, since these sectors were unaffected by the exemption. Moreover, Category III cases came mainly from the union sector. Non-union employers generally did not wish to exceed the 5.5 percent standard and hence did not have to file reports. Unionization within Category III usually occurred in the larger firms, that is, those with more than 60 but less than 1,000 workers. And those firms that had sixty or less employees and were unionized were often part of master contracts and therefore were not covered by the exemption anyway.

16. To some extent, increases in small government units were later recontrolled. This occurred in connection with state-mandated minimum salary increases for local governmental units. See appendix D.

Federal Employees

Under the terms of the original Economic Stabilization Act, the President was given the power to control all "prices, rents, wages, and salaries."[17] No specific exclusion was included for federal employees, whose wages are set by Congress or pursuant to procedures established by Congress. When the act was amended in May 1971, Congress reacted to the establishment of the Construction Industry Stabilization Committee by making it more difficult for the President to invoke selective controls. But no exclusion of federal employees was added at that time.

Federal civilian employees were not in line for a wage increase during Phase I, so the matter of the applicability of the freeze to them was moot. However, a pay raise had been scheduled for January 1, 1972, a few weeks after the start of Phase II. The President initially delayed the federal wage increase for white-collar workers until July 1, 1972.[18] He exercised this authority under the terms of the statute governing pay for classified employees of the federal government. The President's intent was to retain his own authority over federal salaries and not to put them under Pay Board control directly. There was some sentiment at the Pay Board for including federal workers, but this was eventually overridden by the CLC. The CLC did provide that employees of government enterprises, such as the Tennessee Valley Authority and the Postal Service, would be subject to Pay Board controls.[19] In 1971 these two enterprises accounted for over one-fourth of federal civilian employment.

The decision of the President to delay scheduled pay increases for those federal employees outside government enterprises did not meet with favor in Congress. With little opposition, a provision was added to the Economic Stabilization Act Amendments of December 1971 restoring the federal pay raise for January 1. Congress did specify that the magnitude of the wage hike should be limited by the Pay Board's 5.5 percent guideline, even if the normal formula for federal pay suggested a larger increase.[20]

17. P.L. 91-379, sec. 202, 1970.
18. BNA, *Daily Labor Report,* September 1, 1971, p. A-14. A raise for military personnel during the freeze was blocked by the CLC.
19. Application of the freeze to postal workers had been upheld in a federal court case. See ibid., October 21, 1971, p. A-13. (*National Association of Letter Carriers* v. *United States Postal Service,* U.S. District Court for the District of Columbia, Civil Action 1755–71, October 20, 1971.)
20. Economic Stabilization Act Amendments of 1971, sec. 3.

Thus while Congress wished to assert its customary jurisdiction over federal pay adjustments, it showed a willingness to limit itself to the guidelines of the economic stabilization program. This precedent was followed again when the question of a wage increase for the District of Columbia police force was considered. Congress requested an informal review of the police case by the Pay Board before it enacted the adjustment.

Professional Sports

In many respects the professional sports issue was similar to that involving the control of executive pay. It was largely a matter of symbolism, since professional athletes were often in the public spotlight. And like executive pay, the sports question took up more Pay Board time than could be justified from an economic viewpoint.

Beyond the question of symbolism, the professional sports industry possesses a number of unique characteristics, both in the product market and in the labor market.[21] Team sports have enjoyed varying degrees of cartel power, exemption from antitrust laws, and special tax advantages. These features are directed primarily toward the product market, but they often have the indirect effect of limiting the potential number of employers. Moreover, the major team sports have long held monopsony power in the labor market. Players are limited—or were in 1972 at any rate—by "reservation systems" in their ability to induce wage competition among the various teams.

The systems varied from sport to sport, but their essential feature was to tie players to individual teams. Professional athletes could not simply offer themselves to the highest bidder. In general, mobility could not occur without either the permission of the owners or some sort of compensation arrangement between the team that gained the player and the team that lost him. In effect the reservation system gave owners an equity interest in their players and permitted them to pay wages significantly below marginal revenue product.

Similar controls applied to new entrants. Professional sports operated under various draft systems, whereby new players were allocated to teams, usually with the lower-quality teams receiving first pick. Deviations from

21. For a review, see Roger G. Noll, ed., *Government and the Sports Business* (Brookings Institution, 1974).

the draft order could be arranged, but again compensation had to be paid to the original team, thus giving its owners an equity interest in the player.

The monopsonistic arrangements in the labor market of professional sports were usually justified on the grounds that they acted to balance the strengths of competing teams. According to this argument, the result was more evenly matched contests, which maintained spectator interest. Free competition for players would lead to concentrations of talent on a few teams, to the detriment of the sport as a whole and even to the quality teams.

Economists who examined this rationale for labor market monopsony expressed doubts about the actual effect. Player resources seemed to move to high-quality teams despite the reservation and draft systems, although the systems did transfer some of the revenues produced by this movement to owners. In addition, questions have been raised about the social desirability of attempting to create leagues of equally matched teams since the tastes of sports fans with regard to hometown winners may vary across cities.[22] For better or worse the monopsony features of the professional sports labor market were well established when Phase II arrived, and it was hardly the job of the Pay Board to make general public policy in this area.

The Pay Board, however, did have to come up with some sort of policy regarding wage determination in the sports industry. In this respect the monopsony element presented an unusual economic circumstance. Under conditions of monopsony, upward pressure on wages—such as that being exerted by the fledgling player associations—was unlikely to lead to corresponding pressure on prices, at least not in the short run. It could be assumed that the labor supply to the industry was relatively inelastic and that the player associations (and the small number of superstar athletes who had special negotiating advantages) were engaging the owners in zero-sum bargaining. A more or less fixed pie was available for slicing, and the outcome would have no immediate effect on ticket prices or the prices charged for broadcasting rights.

The most simple option for the Pay Board was to apply the same rules to professional athletes that governed all other covered employees. Employers of athletes could have been permitted to define employee units on a team, league, or other reasonable basis, and the 5.5 percent standard could have been applied. The basic difficulty with such an approach was

22. See ibid., especially chaps. 1, 2, 3, 6, and 10.

the erratic nature of professional sports careers. Some players rise to the top with dramatic suddenness and receive equally dramatic pay increases. Their careers may be relatively short-lived, so that a Pay Board limitation of their peak earnings could have created inequities. Star athletes also usually develop considerable bargaining power in negotiating their salaries. The ability of a team to meet such demands may be critical to the retention of its top players and its competitive quality. A lesser problem was that in some sports, such as hockey, teams from Canada were an important part of the leagues. American controls did not affect employees of Canadian teams, and obvious inconsistencies could arise if only the American portion of a league were subject to wage restraints.

Because of the interest of the general public—and perhaps of some board members as well—the Pay Board ultimately spent a great deal of time (including public hearings) on the sports issue. A variety of alternative options were considered, and much staff work was generated. The end result was a recommendation to the Cost of Living Council for decontrol on the wage side, a proposal the CLC adopted in July 1972.[23]

The Working Poor

Incomes policies in Europe often have provided some special treatment for low-wage workers.[24] During the 1960s the wage side of the Kennedy-Johnson guideposts also afforded preferential treatment for low-wage workers.[25] The Phase I regulations provided an exemption only for workers below the federal minimum wage (then $1.60). This decision was

23. An initial resolution excluding compensation resulting from postseason playoffs and all-star games was adopted early in the deliberations. At the same time the board voted to study what was termed the Bassett resolution (named after Robert Bassett, a business member). The Bassett resolution—which was viewed as the owner's position—maintained some Pay Board control while allowing employer flexibility. One factor that may have led to the decision for decontrol was the realization that athletes were in fact popular figures whose exemption would not cause public resentment. The seeming parallel with largely anonymous corporate executives, whose compensation also took up considerable board time, was seen as illusionary.

24. Lloyd Ulman and Robert J. Flanagan, *Wage Restraint: A Study of Incomes Policies in Western Europe* (University of California Press, 1971), pp. 226–27.

25. An exception to the 3.2 percent wage guidepost was provided "where wages are particularly low." See *Economic Report of the President, 1965* (Government Printing Office, 1965), p. 108.

carried over into the early Phase II regulations of the CLC and the December 1971 amendments to the Economic Stabilization Act.[26]

The advisability of using wage controls to correct inequities in income distribution creates difficult problems. First, an emphasis on this objective can divert attention from the fundamental goal of controlling *costs*, not incomes. Second, controls are an extremely blunt instrument for dealing with income distribution. At most, controls can provide the latitude for a wage increase; they do not ensure that one will be given. Third, the hourly wage rate—which is the basic element controlled—does not translate easily into a standard of living. The standard of living is determined by such factors as hours worked, number of family members, and the availability of sources of income other than the earnings of the particular worker affected. Notwithstanding these technical difficulties, there were strong reasons for giving special treatment to low-wage workers. Few economic commentators would argue that the burdens of vanquishing inflation should fall equally on the rich and poor alike, especially when low-wage workers probably had a limited capacity to protect themselves against inflation in the first place.

The Pay Board probably would have permitted some form of low-wage relief even without congressional action. When the board initially considered the issue of retroactivity for Phase I adjustments scheduled under precontrol contracts, it permitted an exception to its hard-line stance for workers earning $2 an hour or less.[27] Such workers could automatically receive increases scheduled during Phase I.

The working-poor episode during Phase II in many respects was an example of decisionmaking at its worst in all three branches of government. Congress began the process by adopting vague language on the issue. The Senate version of the 1971 amendments to the Economic Stabilization Act provided the following:

No order or regulation . . . shall apply to the wages or salary of any individual receiving substandard earnings. The President shall prescribe regulations defining for the purposes of this subsection the term "substandard earnings." In no case shall such term be defined to mean earnings less than these resulting from a wage or salary rate which yields, on an annual basis, an income below the poverty level for a family of four (or an appropriate equivalent in the case

26. Economic Stabilization Act Amendments of 1971, sec. 203(f), and Pay Board minutes of November 11, 1971. The CLC proposed the exemption of workers earning less than the minimum wage and the Pay Board endorsed the proposal.

27. Pay Board press release PB-5, November 19, 1971.

of workers employed in part-time or seasonal occupations) as prescribed annually by the Office of Management and Budget.[28]

The annual poverty-level budget to which the Senate version referred had last been issued for the year 1970 at the time the amendments were being considered. For 1970, poverty-level income stood at $3,968. The Senate version did not prescribe a precise formula for translating this annual figure into an hourly rate, although it suggested that some assumption concerning annual hours worked might be divided into the budget.

In the conference committee designed to iron out differences between the Senate and House bills, the Senate acceded to the even more vague House version of the working-poor amendment.

. . . wage increases to any individual whose earnings are substandard or who is a member of the working poor shall not be limited in any manner, until such time as his earnings are no longer substandard or he is no longer a member of the working poor.[29]

The legislative history of the House bill made reference to the "lower budget" for a family of four issued by the Bureau of Labor Statistics, rather than to the poverty budget of the Office of Management and Budget. This lower budget represented an austere but not poverty level of income and was chosen arbitrarily by the BLS for comparison with its "intermediate" and "higher" budgets. The latest figure available at that time for this BLS budget was $6,960 as of spring 1970. While the BLS budget provided a higher standard of living than the OMB budget—suggesting that the House wished to be more liberal than the Senate—the House version did not even suggest the appropriate translation from an annual budget to an hourly wage. Would the Cost of Living Council be permitted to adjust for secondary sources of income? Did it have to assume a four-person family, or could it use average family size as a definition? The language of the House version suggests that the CLC had greater leeway in arriving at an hourly wage under its terms than under the Senate's version. But the scope of this latitude could not be known in advance.

Two factors seem to have influenced the CLC's initial definition of the working-poor wage. First, when the Pay Board was established, it was granted autonomy in deciding individual cases.[30] The CLC in turn jeal-

28. BNA, *Daily Labor Report,* December 2, 1971, p. X-1.
29. Adopted as section 203(d) of the Economic Stabilization Act Amendments of 1971.
30. BNA, *Daily Labor Report,* October 12, 1971, pp. AA-1–AA-5. The so-called Meany Memo was issued in order to pave the way for labor participation on the Pay Board.

ously guarded its remaining authority over exemptions. Hence the CLC and the Pay Board held no informal consultation concerning an appropriate definition of the working poor. The board was presented with a fait accompli in the form of a letter from the CLC after the decision was made. Second, Congress was considering an increase in the federal minimum wage, and the administration hoped to keep the new figure at $2 or less. A higher standard for the working poor might be taken as an admission that a lower figure was inadequate.

The decision of the CLC was to define the working poor as those employees who received less than $1.90 an hour. The labor members of the board were outraged, since a 5.5 percent increase for a worker earning just above that level would be only 10 cents, a meager increase in absolute terms.[31] The board, however, was unable to agree on an alternative figure to suggest to the CLC. At the meeting when the definition of the working poor was discussed, the staff presented the board with an analysis of the many alternative definitions that might be adopted. One of the calculations took the lower budget of the BLS, updated it for price changes, and divided it by a compromise figure for annual hours that reflected multiple wage earners in the family but that assumed a workweek of only thirty-seven hours. The latter figure simply reflected average weekly hours in the nonfarm sector for nonsupervisory workers. It was suspect, since it represented an average of full- and part-time workers, but it had been used in the AFL-CIO's argument challenging the CLC definition. The resulting hourly wage was about $2.20, a figure adopted by the public members in the subsequent debate.

After considering and rejecting proposals for $1.90, $2.20, and $3.50, the board simply voted to issue a press release declaring:

It is the sense of the Pay Board that the $1.90 figure recommended by the Cost of Living Council is inconsistent with the purposes of the Amendments to the Economic Stabilization Act and supporting analysis.[32]

In effect a majority agreed that $1.90 was too low, but no alternative number could muster the needed eight votes for an endorsement. Nonetheless, it was significant that a majority of the board—consisting of a coalition of labor and public members—adopted a forthright statement opposing the CLC's determination.

31. The official labor reaction is contained in a lengthy memorandum from Nat Goldfinger, chief economist of the AFL-CIO, to the board, January 17, 1972. It appears in Pay Board, "Weekly Status Report," January 17–21, 1972.

32. Pay Board press release PB-39, January 19, 1972.

Despite the Pay Board's criticism, a wage of $1.90 an hour or less remained the operational definition of the working poor until a court decision nullified the CLC's decision. The board adopted a regulation that simply exempted wage increases given to bring low-wage workers up to $1.90 from the calculation of the unit's percentage wage adjustment. While seemingly a straightforward approach, the regulation had a peculiar consequence. It permitted higher-paid workers contained in a unit with some working-poor employees to receive more than the allowable 5.5 percent.[33]

What was originally a minor aberration in the Pay Board's rules assumed critical importance after a federal district court decision in July 1972 nullified the definition based on $1.90.[34] In their suit the union plaintiffs charged that the CLC had flaunted the will of Congress in setting the working-poor level so low. To understand the issue involved, it is necessary to review the CLC's method of justifying its calculation.

The CLC started with the BLS lower budget of $6,960. If this budget is simply divided by 2,080 hours, that is, forty hours a week for fifty-two weeks, the resulting hourly wage is about $3.35. Essentially this procedure is what the unions pressed the CLC to follow. The procedure appears closer to what might be construed as the Senate's intent with regard to the OMB poverty budget, although the Senate version was ultimately rejected by Congress. Accepting the division by 2,080 as the correct procedure for either budget, then $1.90 appeared to be approximately in line with Senate desires ($3,968/2,080 = $1.91), although it did not allow for inflation occurring subsequent to the estimate of the budget.

33. Consider a unit composed of ten workers earning $1.80 and ten earning $2. The average wage in the unit is $1.90. Without the working-poor exemption the allowable 5.5 percent increase, if applied proportionately, would be 9.9 cents for the lower-paid workers and 11 cents for the higher paid. On an hourly basis the payroll expenditure is 20 × $1.90 = $38. Hence the cost of a 5.5 percent increase would be $2.09 an hour ($38 × 0.055) across the entire unit. With the working-poor exemption based on $1.90, however, the entire $2.09 could be used to raise the salaries of the higher-paid workers. Since the hourly payroll of the higher-paid employees is $20 (10 × $2), the percentage increase allowed for them could be $2.09/$20 = 10.5 percent if only 5.5 percent were given to the working poor. This peculiar result occurred because the working poor were included in the base as part of the unit, but did not count in the calculation of the increase. It appears that the board did not realize the implications of the rule when it was originally adopted. The staff was aware of the anomaly, but it was never brought back for reconsideration because so few units had significant numbers of workers earning less than $1.90.

34. The decision is reprinted in BNA, *Daily Labor Report,* July 14, 1972, pp. G-1–G-6. (*Jennings* v. *Connally,* 347 F. Supp. 409.)

In its letter to the Pay Board, the CLC had made passing reference to the OMB poverty budget, which seemed to support the argument that congressional wishes had been frustrated. The bulk of the CLC analysis, however, was based on the lower budget of the BLS. The key element in the CLC analysis was the assumption that a working-poor family would contain 1.7 wage earners. The 1.7 figure came from a Census Bureau study of all families. If 1.7 wage earners work 2,080 hours a year, they would each have to average $1.97 an hour to earn the $6,960 set by the BLS. Other minor adjustments the CLC made for taxes, changes in the cost of living, family size, and so on, further reduced the figure to $1.90.

The key argument of the plaintiffs in the legal challenge to the choice of $1.90 was that the assumption of 1.7 earners was inappropriate. In part this point was argued on moral grounds, that is, a one-earner family should be able to earn at least the BLS lower budget. The plaintiffs also produced data showing that low-income families typically had fewer than the 1.7 wage earners. This argument was correct and predictable, since the number of earners is a key determinant of total family income. A more relevant statistic would have been the average number of earners in families *headed by a low-wage worker*. It is not uncommon for families with low-wage heads to have additional workers in the labor market.

Once the $1.90 cutoff was invalidated, the Pay Board halted the processing of wage rollbacks in all cases. Pay Board regulations were based on the unit, a point Congress neglected when it enacted an exemption for individuals. Whether a given case contained any working poor was not indicated on Pay Board report forms, which dealt only with the average wage in the unit. Worse, in its decision the court had not suggested what might be the appropriate new definition of the working poor or how it might be calculated. And if the CLC decided to appeal the court's decision, the process of coming up with a new figure might be further delayed.

A decision was made to accept the court's decision and to try to come up with an acceptable figure that would not be too high. There was widespread agreement at the board and the CLC that the $3.35 demanded by the plaintiffs was too high. A number of industries, such as apparel, retail trade, leather, and lumber, had substantial numbers of workers below $3.35. And the original public members of the Pay Board, who now were a majority of the revamped all-public board, had favored $2.20 when the issue was first considered.

One difficulty in determining a new number was the uncertainty about exactly what the court wanted. The general impression left by the decision was that the court had "smelled a rat" but had been unable to determine the exact location of the odor. The lowest-risk strategy was to pick a number at the higher end of the acceptable range to minimize the danger of another court reversal.

The new definition was pegged at $2.75 after informal consultation with the AFL-CIO. The CLC explained this figure in a press release aimed more at the court than at the public.[35] The key adjustment this time was based on Census Bureau data, which showed that families with low-wage heads typically received about $2,300 from income sources other than the head. Much of this can be assumed to have come from other labor force participants. This amount was subtracted from the BLS budget, and the remaining income gap was then subjected to some minor adjustments. Finally, a variety of assumptions concerning the number of hours worked per year were used, producing a spectrum of estimates from $2.25 to $2.74. Since $2.75 was just above the range, the CLC believed it was clearly acceptable.

In fact, however, the stabilization program operated under a cloud concerning the acceptability of the definition based on $2.75. The court did not render a final decision upholding the definition until Phase III had begun. Although the $2.75 figure itself was upheld at that time, the CLC decision to make the new definition effective on July 14, 1972, the date of the initial invalidation, was not accepted by the court.[36] The effective date, according to the court, was December 22, 1971, the date the 1971 amendments to the Economic Stabilization Act became law. As a result, employers were given retroactive approval to implement working-poor pay increases during the period from December 22 to July 14 that would have previously been disallowed.

After the CLC established the definition based on $2.75, the Pay Board found itself with an inadequate set of regulations. As already noted, the rules adopted in connection with the $1.90 figure permitted increases for the working poor to be passed on to higher-paid workers. With a figure as high as $2.75, this procedure was not acceptable to the board.

The essential problem for the board was to break the unit up into its working-poor and higher-wage components, so that separate wage bases could be calculated for the two groups. In essence, board policy was to limit the higher paid to 5.5 percent but to permit low-wage workers an increase up to $2.75, or 5.5 percent, whichever was greater. If an employer chose to grant low-paid workers an amount greater than 5.5 per-

35. Cost of Living Council press release, CLC-127, and fact sheet, July 25, 1972.
36. The decision is reprinted in BNA, *Daily Labor Report,* March 2, 1973, pp. F-1–F-6.

cent and if this increase raised them above $2.75, the excess above 5.5 percent was charged against the whole unit, so that higher-paid workers would receive less than 5.5 percent. The easiest way for an employer to implement the exemption would be to give everyone in the unit—working poor and higher paid—a 5.5 percent increase and then raise the working poor up to or toward $2.75.[37]

The technical aspects of the exemption at the $2.75 level were increasingly complex and intruded on other aspects of the wage stabilization program. It specifically rejected a special "compression" exception for higher-paid workers in units where traditional differentials were narrowed due to the exemption. The computational aspects of the rules were intricate, particularly if a unit wished to know the maximum increase the exemption would allow. In order to calculate the wage base for higher-paid workers, the employer had to include those working-poor employees who would cross the $2.75 line *after* the increase was granted. That is, an employer had to know what he was going to do before he decided what he wanted to do.

In sum, Congress enacted a vague definition that created uncertainty over the exact definition of the working poor; the CLC permitted extraneous factors to influence its initial determination of $1.90; and tripartite procedures prevented the Pay Board from arriving at a consensus on any other figure, although it is conceivable that such a consensus might not have influenced the CLC.[38] The court invalidated the definition based on

37. Units composed entirely of the working poor were subject to limitations on their wages only above the $2.75 level. If it took more than 5.5 percent to raise them to $2.75, no further increase would be permitted. (The board considered and rejected the option of allowing the working poor an increase to $2.75 *plus* 5.5 percent.) Qualified fringe benefits of the working poor were subject to the basic 0.7 percent standard plus exceptions. A unit composed only of the working poor was allowed to raise "includable benefits" by 5.5 percent on top of whatever other wage increases were provided. Roll-up effects of the raise up to $2.75 were not charged against the allowable increase for qualified or includable benefits. See chapter 3 and appendix A for details on fringe benefit computations and roll-up.

38. The Pay Board in principle could have adopted regulations giving a de facto exemption to workers earning less than some figure above $1.90. But it did not choose to attempt to override a CLC decision. A milder suggestion was to permit a cents-per-hour standard or 5.5 percent, whichever was greater. For example, if the board permitted a cents-per-hour increase of 12.1 cents, workers earning less than $2.20 per hour (the public members' suggestion for the working-poor level) would get more than 5.5 percent. They would not get much more, however. A worker earning $1.90 would receive only 6.4 percent. Because of its limited value, a cents-per-hour standard was dropped. See staff paper in Pay Board "Agenda and Policy Papers" (March 20, 1972; processed), sec. 2, pp. 1–9.

$1.90 without providing any precise guidelines for producing an acceptable definition. It then permitted the issue to remain open for another seven and one-half months until the decision on the $2.75 figure was finally ratified.

Impact of the Exemptions

One of the exemptions, that of professional sports, is not easily susceptible to a quantitative impact analysis, since there is no readily available index for athletes' salaries. Federal employees who were exempted from Pay Board controls were still subject to the 5.5 percent standard indirectly, since Congress mandated that magnitude of increase for them during Phase II.[39] The major question of impact thus revolves around the small-business and working-poor exemptions.

Since the correlation between employer size and wage levels is strong, the effect of the two exemptions cannot be statistically disentangled. Chapter 10 provides a detailed impact analysis, thus an extensive review will not be made at this point. It is worth anticipating some of the conclusions of that chapter, however.

As a general rule, during Phase II high-wage unionized industries experienced faster rates of wage increase than others. Much of this dispersion can be explained by catch-up wage pressures that had built up as a result of the accelerating inflation of the late 1960s. The unionized areas of the economy were slower to react than the nonunion because of the institutional characteristic of long-term wage contracts in the former sectors. Hence a more rapid growth of union wages relative to nonunion wages was to be expected during Phase II, despite the exemptions allowed low-wage small businesses, which are less likely to be unionized.

The exemptions provided to small businesses and the working poor had little economic significance, simply because there was no pressure in those sectors to drive wages up faster than the allowable 5.5 percent. Even a before-and-after test of wage increases affected by the definition of the working poor based on $2.75 showed no tendency for low-wage earnings to jump ahead of others. In fact, a reverse tendency was found.

39. Basic federal wage *scales* rose 5.4 percent from July 1, 1971, to July 1, 1972, owing to the increase on January 1, 1972. The average hourly earnings of federal executive branch workers, however, rose 7.5 percent, indicating a significant wage drift. See *Current Wage Developments,* September 1972, pp. 39, 52.

Earnings in higher-wage industries accelerated after July 1972, but no acceleration occurred in the lower-wage sector.

Undoubtedly some workers benefited from the exemptions, even if it is impossible to detect them from aggregate data. The board received reporting forms from units applying for the working-poor exemption after the definition was based on $2.75, but unfortunately no records were kept on the number of workers or cases involved. In fact, even the lower $1.90 figure affected some workers in at least one prominent case: employees of the state of Ohio.[40] On an aggregate basis, however, the impact of the exemptions on income distribution was negligible.

Final Considerations

There is always a danger in historical studies of attributing more rationality to key decisions than actually was the case. The ex post key decision in determining the scope of Phase II controls was opting for comprehensive coverage. With hindsight, the forces underlying this action seem clear. Phase I had been extensive and had met with public approval. Congress had reacted negatively when selective controls were imposed only on union construction in March 1971. And while there were some obvious pros and cons regarding extensive coverage, the absence of a clear model that could weight the alternatives led to pressure to cover almost everything and then see what happened.

Once the coverage decision was made, other characteristics of the program were effectively determined. The program had to have broad general rules, such as the 5.5 percent guideline, so that the many units affected would know what was required without a case-by-case Pay Board review. And after the program had gotten under way with extensive coverage, there was a natural caution in changing this fundamental characteristic. No one knew what would happen under a comprehensive program if some significant element of the labor force were to be abruptly decontrolled. Despite the reams of data that might be produced in advance of a decision, the CLC and the Pay Board were basically groping in the dark.

As noted in chapter 10, the sudden move to Phase III in January 1973

40. Thanks to the computational anomaly that applied to the definition of the working poor based on $1.90 an hour, some of the benefit of the exemption spilled over to higher-paid state of Ohio workers.

did not produce a wage bulge, despite Phase III's de facto removal of most of Category III from economic controls. This suggests that exemptions during Phase II could probably have been more extensive than they were without sparking a wage explosion. If a decision to engage in more extensive decontrol had been made during Phase II, however, it might have been desirable to consider some basis other than employer size or hourly wages. Presumably a move to cut the coverage of a wage control program is designed to obtain two dividends: less strain on both public and private resources needed for compliance and the ability to look more carefully at sectoral problems. While the former dividend can be realized with virtually any method of exemption, the latter requires an industry-by-industry analysis.

An industry-by-industry approach would most likely involve the type of wage structure approach favored by the Construction Industry Stabilization Committee or the kind used during phases III and IV in retail food.[41] In both cases no small-business exemption was applied. The working-poor exemption was irrelevant in the high-wage construction industry and was an administrative nuisance in retail food. An exemption by wage level—if it affects significant numbers of workers—potentially threatens wage relativities, the heart of the wage structural approach.

Controls are by nature an executive function. Congress must provide authorization, and the courts must prevent gross abuses. Neither Congress nor the courts are particularly effective at making specific policy or case decisions. It seems clear that future wage controls would be better served if a more collaborative relationship could be achieved between the executive and legislative branches at the time of the initial authorization. Congress may wish to indicate some general directions for the program, but vague restrictions that open the door to litigation and alternative interpretations—as occurred with the working-poor exemption—are potentially disruptive. Moreover, such restrictions are unlikely to benefit their target groups in any substantial way. The working-poor exemption did not distribute income more equitably. If in fact it had had much effect, it probably would have compressed wage differentials, thus creating inequities and engendering subsequent pressure for wage inflation.

41. Albert Rees, "Tripartite Wage Stabilizing in the Food Industry," *Industrial Relations,* vol. 14 (May 1975), pp. 250–58.

V

The Last Cows in the Barn

The Pay Board had barely issued its basic policies and assembled a skeleton staff when it was called upon to reach decisions in five highly visible cases. These cases involved collective bargaining agreements in the bituminous coal, railroad, aerospace, and West and East Coast longshoring industries. They posed a major test of the board's credibility and inflamed the conflicts that arose during the first days of Phase II. Ultimately the decision in one of these cases, that of the West Coast longshoremen, precipitated the walkout of four of the board's five labor members. The five cases shared common characteristics that ensured that their outcome would have a profound, if not determinate, effect on the course of the wage stabilization program.

First, each situation encompassed a large number of workers, ranging from 13,000 covered by the West Coast longshoremen's agreement, to 100,000 in aerospace, and 150,000 on the railroads.

Second, all but one of the industries were critical to the short-term stability of the national economy. The longshoremen and railroad cases involved key elements of the national transportation system. An adequate supply of bituminous coal was vital to electric power production and basic industries such as steel. Only aerospace could be considered peripheral to the main currents of the economy.

Third, in three of the cases—coal, and the West and East Coast longshoremen—collective bargaining agreements had been reached following lengthy strikes. The railroad settlement was the product of two years of maneuvering by the parties at the bargaining table, sporadic strikes, and congressional intervention. Because the agreements had been reached by a test of strength in the first place, any Pay Board action to trim the unions' gains was likely to precipitate worker resentment and another walkout. Each of the unions involved had a reputation for militance, so this threat was more than hypothetical. A renewal of the work stoppages could inflict serious damage on the economy and dampen the recovery then in process.

Fourth, each case was newsworthy, and the board's decisions would surely condition the public's perception of wage controls and hence the overall stabilization effort. The 5.5 percent pay standard and the related fine print were at once precise and vague. It was possible that the special circumstances in a given situation would justify board approval of a wage increase significantly in excess of the 5.5 percent limit. This action would very likely be viewed by the public as evidence that the board lacked the will or capacity to enforce its own standards and would cast doubt on the integrity of the overall anti-inflation program. Both the size of the bargaining units involved and the fact that the board was taking its first swings against big league pitching ensured close scrutiny of its performance.

Last, and most troublesome, each of the cases represented the end-product of labor-management negotiations that had commenced before the imposition of controls on August 15, 1971. Thus the settlements reflected expectations and conditions that antedated the establishment of standards, reporting requirements, and other paraphernalia of the stabilization program. This problem was compounded because the settlements came at the end of the 1971 bargaining round that had established a generous goal for union bargainers. Only fifteen days before the freeze the United Steelworkers of America and the basic steel companies had signed an agreement providing for a first-year increase of 16 percent in wages and fringe benefits. Indeed concern about substantial union wage gains during a period of considerable slack in the labor market had contributed to the pressures for wage controls in the first place.[1] Because of their position in the bargaining cycle relative to the initiation of controls, these five cases were dubbed "the last cows."[2] Three of them, the coal, railroad, and aerospace cases, will be discussed in this chapter; the other two are the subject of chapter 6.

The Bituminous Coal Case

Of all the unions in the American labor movement, the United Mine Workers of America (UMW) probably has the longest and most vivid record of militance. The UMW was established at the turn of the century

1. See Arnold R. Weber, *In Pursuit of Price Stability: The Wage-Price Freeze of 1971* (Brookings Institution, 1973), pp. 1–9. See also Marvin H. Kosters in association with J. Dawson Ahalt, *Controls and Inflation: The Economic Stabilization Program in Retrospect* (American Enterprise Institute for Public Policy Research, 1975), pp. 7–10.

2. The metaphor, "the last cows," was coined by Virgil B. Day, a business member of the Pay Board.

and has a history of alternate growth and contraction in the face of un-remitting management resistance. Some of the most sanguinary chapters in American labor history are associated with UMW efforts to achieve employer recognition or to protect wage standards from the erosion of nonunion competition.[3] Under the leadership of John L. Lewis and in the congenial climate of public policy during the 1930s, the UMW emerged as a dominant force in the industry and in the labor movement. Indeed Lewis created the Congress of Industrial Organizations (CIO), and the miners' union provided many of the resources and shock troops for the unionization of the mass production industries, such as steel and auto-mobiles. Coal miners in the United States, as in other industrialized nations, have revealed a strong sense of independence, a high propensity to strike, and a sense of separation from the rest of society that frequently has been manifested in a disregard of government authority.[4]

In 1971 the traditional militance of the UMW was also associated with unaccustomed political instability. During his long tenure as president, John L. Lewis had come to exercise iron control over the decisionmaking apparatus of the union.[5] Building on this internal control, Lewis main-tained almost complete discretion in collective bargaining. He frequently negotiated industry-wide agreements on a one-to-one basis with repre-sentatives of the Bituminous Coal Operators Association (BCOA). Once Lewis and his management counterparts reached an agreement, it be-came effective without the niceties of formal ratification by the rank and file, as is the practice in most union situations.

Initially this consolidation of power within the UMW was a functional response to the need for discipline in the face of harsh employer resistance and competition from nonunion mines. With the passage of time, how-ever, the autocratic structure of the UMW reflected Lewis's style of lead-ership and the Mosaic role he had defined for himself in the union and the labor movement at large. Because of his control and enormous per-sonal prestige among the miners, he wielded power in the UMW without any real challenge until he stepped down as president in 1960.

3. Selig Perlman and Philip Taft, *History of Labor in the United States, 1896–1932* (MacMillan, 1935), vol. 4, pp. 326–42, 469–88, 562–71.

4. Clark Kerr and Abraham Siegel, "The Interindustry Propensity to Strike: An International Comparison," in Arthur Kornhauser, Robert Dubin, and Arthur M. Ross, *Industrial Conflict* (McGraw-Hill, 1954), pp. 191–93.

5. Wellington Roe, *Juggernaut: American Labor in Action* (Lippincott, 1948), p. 95. See also Saul Alinsky, *John L. Lewis: An Unauthorized Biography* (Putman's, 1949).

The end of the Lewis era predictably gave rise to stirrings of democracy in the union. Lewis's immediate successor, Thomas Kennedy, was a transitional figure who took office at an advanced age and died after three years. In contrast, the next UMW president, W. A. (Tony) Boyle, sought to entrench himself in the leadership of the union, exploiting the undemocratic practices that had been refined by Lewis. This time, however, an overt opposition group, the Miners for Democracy, emerged to directly challenge the incumbent. The opposition movement was led by Joseph Yablonski, a dissident member of the UMW who contested Boyle for the presidency in 1969. The election campaign was marked by allegations of violence and irregular voting practices. Ultimately the Department of Labor intervened on the grounds that the conduct of the election had violated the safeguards included in the Labor-Management Reporting and Disclosure Act. In the course of these events, Yablonski was murdered. After prolonged investigation, Boyle was indicted in 1973 and subsequently convicted for conspiracy in the crime.

Stormy Bargaining of 1971

In this turbulent context negotiations commenced in the summer of 1971 over the terms of a new labor contract between the UMW and the BCOA. The existing agreement had been negotiated in 1968, covered 80,000 miners employed by over 300 bituminous coal operators, and was scheduled to expire on September 30, 1971. The UMW adhered strictly to a policy of "no contract, no work," so that failure to reach agreement by that date would almost certainly result in an industry-wide strike.

As is customary, negotiations proceeded at a leisurely pace at the outset. Before any real progress had been made, a major uncertainty was introduced into the bargaining process with President Nixon's surprise announcement of the wage-price freeze on August 15. On the one hand, the contract was scheduled to expire during the ninety-day freeze period. On the other hand, the standards and regulations governing wage agreements after the freeze could not be known until the Phase II policies and administrative machinery were put in place. In fact, the blueprints for Phase II were not unveiled until October 7, and the general policies governing wages were not announced until November 9.

This uncertainty exacerbated an intrinsically difficult bargaining situation. When the parties failed to reach a new agreement by September 30, the UMW immediately called an industry-wide strike. Shortly after the shutdown began, Secretary of Labor James Hodgson sought a preliminary assurance from the Cost of Living Council that any agreement concluded by the UMW and BCOA would receive a favorable ruling by the CLC. He argued that this assurance was necessary to facilitate the end of the strike and that special treatment was justified because negotiations had started before the freeze had been instituted. The CLC rejected Hodgson's request on the grounds that the issue should be considered by the appropriate Phase II agency. In addition, a flexible response to Hodgson's petition would have undermined the rigid position the CLC had taken in blocking the payment of deferred wage increases during the freeze.[6]

The strike continued without resolution through all of October and into November. Although coal users had built up inventories before the contract expiration date, they were increasingly concerned that the stoppage would have a depressing effect on industrial activity. As coal stocks dwindled, several electric utilities announced brownouts and other curtailments of service. In the latter stages of negotiations Governor Arch A. Moore, Jr., of West Virginia joined the discussions as a mediator. West Virginia, of course, is a major coal-producing state, and its public officials had a deep interest in the settlement of the strike. Moreover, Moore was running for reelection as governor in 1972, and it seemed apparent that he would face strong opposition from John D. Rockefeller IV, who had used West Virginia as a launching site for a career in Democratic politics.[7] Moore's identification with a constructive settlement obviously would create political capital for the future campaign. The governor's intervention heightened the political sensitivity of the case. An agreement was finally reached late on November 13—the last day of the freeze. Thus when the Pay Board officially hung out its shingle the next day, the first client was already camped on the doorstep.

Contract Terms

Although the strike settlement called for a three-year contract as a matter of general policy, the Pay Board's scrutiny was limited to the wage and benefit increases scheduled for the first year. Within this time frame,

6. Weber, *In Pursuit of Price Stability*, p. 30.
7. Moore subsequently defeated Rockefeller to win reelection as governor of West Virginia in 1972.

the agreement exceeded the 5.5 percent standard by a generous margin. As reported to the board, the new contract provided for first-year wage increases ranging from $3 to $4.50 a day, depending on the job classification. (Compensation for coal miners traditionally has been quoted as a daily rate.) When this increase was translated into hourly rates, it amounted to a 55 cent hike, or approximately 9.2 percent on a base of $5.98 an hour in total compensation. An additional 6 cents was attributed to an improvement in shift differentials, an extra paid holiday, and one added day of vacation.

The total cost of the economic package was sharply increased by changes in funding designed to restore the financial integrity of the UMW pension and welfare plan. The UMW Welfare and Retirement Fund had been established in May 1946 following an industry-wide strike. During the course of the strike, President Truman ordered the seizure of the coal mines by the government under the terms of the War Labor Disputes Act. Truman then directed Secretary of the Interior Julius A. Krug to negotiate a labor contract with the UMW. The resulting agreement called for a royalty payment into a new Welfare and Retirement Fund of 5 cents for each ton of coal produced. The fund would be controlled by three trustees; one representing the union, one representing the coal operators, and one neutral. Miners who retired at age sixty-two with twenty or more years of service were eligible for retirement benefits of $100 a month.[8]

From its inception the Welfare and Retirement Fund suffered financial stress because of the ambitions of the union, the economic deterioration of the industry, and demographic trends in the coal mine work force. After establishing the fund the UMW pressed successfully for extensive medical services for its members, including a chain of hospitals throughout the mining areas of West Virginia and Kentucky where few such facilities existed. This expansion and the increase in the number of miners eligible for retirement benefits put heavy pressure on the fund. The retirement program did not operate on an actuarial basis whereby adequate reserves would be established to fund the past service liabilities of the work force. Rather, benefits were financed on a pay-as-you-go basis from the accumulation of the tonnage royalty payments.

To meet the rising demands of the fund, the royalty payment was raised to 40 cents a ton through successive increases over the years. The

8. United Mine Workers of America, "A Chronology of the U.M.W.A. Welfare and Retirement Fund, Covering the Period between 1945 and April 26, 1951" (Washington, D.C.: UMW Welfare and Retirement Fund, n.d.; processed).

capacity of the industry to assume further pension and welfare costs was limited, however, by the decline in the economic importance of coal as an energy source throughout the 1950s. During this period coal production declined from 516 million short tons in 1950 to 416 million short tons in 1960, and employment dropped from 416,000 to 169,000.[9] Coincidentally, the average age of the work force rose steadily so that by 1965 about 60 percent of the miners were forty-five years of age or more and only 6.6 percent were under thirty years of age.[10] Under these circumstances the Welfare and Retirement Fund faced recurrent problems of solvency that led to the closing of several UMW-operated hospitals and a cutback in supplementary benefits.

The fiscal problems of the Welfare and Retirement Fund were compounded by the political conflict within the UMW. When Yablonski announced that he would contest Boyle for the presidency in the next UMW election, scheduled for 1969, Boyle looked for dramatic means to demonstrate his solicitude for the rank and file. An obvious demonstration of largess would be to increase the retirement benefits, which were $115 a month. Because a three-year contract had been negotiated in 1968, it was not possible to raise the benefit level by collective bargaining. Instead, Boyle won the approval of the other two trustees of the fund to hike pension benefits to $150 a month. While the merits of the raise were undeniable in terms of the miners' needs, the improvement was mandated without any increase in the employers' contribution to the fund. Consequently the benefit program was pushed to the edge of insolvency. In October 1971 the payout from the fund was approximately $35 million a month, and the total reserve was estimated to be $70 million—enough to support current benefits for only two months.[11]

Against this background, the UMW gave the highest priority to an increase in the tonnage royalty payment during the 1971 contract negotiations. Under the terms of the agreement the tonnage royalty payment would be doubled in three years to a total of 80 cents. Half of the increase, or 20 cents a ton, was scheduled for the first year. This jump in the tonnage royalty translated into an increase of 45 cents an hour for the first year and 90 cents for the life of the contract. Thus the cost of bolstering

9. U.S. Bureau of the Census, *Statistical Abstract of the United States, 1975* (Government Printing Office, 1975), p. 684.

10. Data provided to the Pay Board by the Bituminous Coal Operators Association, November 17, 1971.

11. Testimony of Joseph Brennan, economist for the United Mine Workers, before the Pay Board, November 18, 1971.

the Welfare and Retirement Fund was almost equal to the gain in money wages and lifted the total cost of the economic package to 17.5 percent of average hourly compensation during the first year of the contract and to 41 percent over the three-year period, far above the Pay Board's 5.5 percent standard.

As noted, at the time of the new contract the base hourly rate of wages and salaries was $5.98. The breakdown and total cost of the bituminous coal agreement in dollars per hour was calculated by the board's staff as follows:[12]

	First year	Three-year period
Straight-time pay	0.55	1.50
Welfare and retirement	0.45	0.90
Shift differentials	0.02	0.02
Holidays	0.02	0.02
Funeral leave	. . .	. . .
Protective clothing	. . .	. . .
Vacation pay	0.02	0.04
All wages and salaries	1.06	2.48

Pay Board Deliberations Begin

The Pay Board scheduled consideration of the bituminous coal contract for November 18, a scant four days after the agreement had been reached. This expedited treatment reflected the importance of the case and not the simplicity of the issues or the efficiency of the board's staff. It was recognized that the Pay Board's decision would be viewed as a major test of the standard and the board's capacity to make it stick in difficult situations. In view of the history of bargaining in the coal industry and the particular circumstances surrounding the negotiations in 1971, the board could not have selected a worse case for its inaugural effort.

Before it could deal with the substance of the agreement, the board had to make a technical determination of some importance. Pay Board rules, as sketchy as they were at the time, provided for different treatment of new and existing labor agreements. New contracts were those negotiated after November 13, 1971, when Phase I terminated, and generally were

12. "Cost of Bituminous Coal Settlement," Pay Board staff draft, November 19, 1971. Increases for funeral leave and protective clothing were less than 1 cent an hour in each case. It should be noted that the staff estimate probably understated the total economic cost of the settlement. Because the Pay Board's rules and procedures were primitive at this stage, no effort was made to calculate roll-up, or the effect of the increase in the basic wage on wage-related benefits.

subject to the 5.5 percent standard. Existing contracts, on the other hand, were those that were in effect on or before November 13, 1971, when the freeze ended. The basic policies adopted by the board stated that these agreements would be allowed to operate under their own terms provided that the wage gains included in the contracts were not "unreasonably inconsistent" with the 5.5 percent pay standard. Although the guidelines for existing contracts had not yet been formulated, all factions on the Pay Board recognized that wage increases up to 7 percent would be acceptable.

When the coal negotiations sputtered to a conclusion, the settlement was signed early on the morning of November 14, implying that it should be designated as a new contract. At the board's request, the Internal Revenue Service determined the exact sequence of events. The report indicated that the negotiators reached agreement on all the issues in the early afternoon of November 13. By 6:00 P.M., the board of directors of the BCOA had approved the settlement. The National Scale and Policy Committee of the UMW considered the contract at 9:00 P.M. and ratified it by 11:45 P.M. In a hurried ceremony the negotiators signed the agreement at 12:30 A.M. on the morning of November 14.

Thus the sequence of events revealed that agreement had been reached on November 13, but the contract had not been formally executed until November 14. The general counsel of the Pay Board reviewed the circumstances and advised that for the board's purposes the coal agreement qualified as an existing contract. According to the counsel's memorandum, it was a settled principle in the administration of the National Labor Relations Act that a collective bargaining agreement had been reached when there was a "meeting of the minds" of the negotiators and all material issues were resolved in the bargaining.[13] Similarly, during Phase I the Cost of Living Council had accepted the so-called handshake principle to determine whether a labor agreement had been concluded before August 15, 1971, when the freeze commenced.[14] The circumstances of the coal settlement were clearly consistent with these precedents, and the Pay Board voted unanimously to designate the agreement an existing contract.

13. Memorandum from Jack McGregor, acting general counsel to Judge George H. Boldt, chairman of the Pay Board, November 17, 1971. The memo cited a decision of the National Labor Relations Board for *Plywood Workers Local 3181* v. *Georgia-Pacific Corporation,* July 13, 1970 (case no. 26-CB-534).

14. Weber, *In Pursuit of Price Stability,* p. 69.

When the full board convened to consider the coal agreement on Thursday, November 18, seven of the regular members were absent and were represented by alternates. The only labor member present was Frank Fitzsimmons, the president of the Teamsters.[15] Three of the five business members—Robert Bassett, Leonard McCollum, and Benjamin Biaggini—also were represented by alternates. All of the public members were on hand for the proceedings.

The meeting was held in an unadorned conference room in the Pay Board's new quarters, a commonplace modern building that was still in the final stages of completion. Like the board itself, the premises had an improvised, haphazard quality. The offices and the conference room were constructed of insubstantial temporary partitions (for easy relocation to accommodate the needs of the next tenant) that were joined in a complex maze of corridors. The board's conference room was about 40 feet long and 20 feet wide. A large rectangular table was set in the middle of the room for the members and witnesses. Judge George Boldt, as chairman, sat at the head of the table, with the public members clustered near him on both sides. The business representatives flanked the table in the middle, and the labor members were all positioned at the far end. Establishing a pattern that prevailed as long as the labor members remained on the board, the UAW representative, usually Pat Greathouse, sat at the foot of the table facing the chairman. A single row of chairs lined the wall for staff members, alternates, and witnesses; otherwise, the quarters were bare.

The meeting was attended by representatives of the parties to the agreement. Tony Boyle appeared for the UMW. The coal operators were represented by John Corcoran, president of the Consolidation Coal Company; and R. Heath Larry, vice chairman of the board of directors of United States Steel. Larry had served as chief negotiator for the BCOA in the recent bargaining round. U.S. Steel, which owned the so-called captive mines, had long played an important role in the BCOA, and Larry was an experienced negotiator for the basic steel companies. In addition to these principals, Governor Arch Moore of West Virginia requested and was granted the right to make an appearance before the board because of his involvement in the final settlement.

The session began with a long, rambling statement from Boyle, who

15. Three of the labor representatives, George Meany, Floyd Smith, and I. W. Abel, were occupied with activities associated with the AFL-CIO convention in Bal Harbour, Florida.

did not discuss the details of the agreement or their relationship to the stabilization program. Instead, he reminded the board that the contract had been reached after a long strike and that there was a shortage of coal above ground. He further stated that regardless of any action taken by the board, "you can't mine coal with bayonets"[16]—a shibboleth of coal miner militants. He asserted that the agreement should be approved without modification because it was fair and afforded equitable compensation for dirty, dangerous work.

Boyle was followed by Joseph Brennan, the economist for the UMW, who worked through a more analytical justification for approval of the contract. He argued that wages in the steel and coal industries historically had moved closely in tandem. The current coal settlement should be confirmed because it was linked to the steel agreement that had been negotiated on August 1, 1971, two weeks before the freeze. The steel contract included a first-year increase in labor compensation of approximately 16 percent. Brennan also declared that the contract provided a fair share of productivity gains in the coal industry and reflected the need to catch up for the erosion of real wages caused by inflation since the last contract. Finally, he described the special problem of the Welfare and Retirement Fund and argued that the increased tonnage royalty was necessary to stave off insolvency and put the fund on a sound actuarial basis.

The management spokesmen generally restated the arguments presented by the UMW representatives. One new justification was added, however. Corcoran declared that the wage increase was necessary to attract new, young recruits to the industry labor force. Without a generous increase in wages, the industry could not recruit the labor force necessary for expanded output. Governor Moore joined this chorus calling for approval. He made a brief statement noting that the agreement had been reached after a long strike that had imposed a high cost on West Virginia. The contract should be approved because it helped the "poor people" and was important to the economic stability of the state.

After two hours the hearing was concluded and the board reconvened in executive session. The members engaged in a cursory discussion of the issues raised by the presentations, requested the staff to compile additional information, and adjourned until the next day. Following the pattern established early in the life of the board, the process of decision-making went forward through the deliberations of the individual caucuses.

16. From authors' personal records of Pay Board activities.

A Divided Ruling

From the outset it was clear that the five labor members would vote to sustain the coal agreement without modification, and no effort was made to discuss a possible compromise approach with them. In contrast, the public members agreed among themselves that the settlement was excessive and should be reduced. The public members' position was based on a loose analysis of the substantive issues and a political judgment of what actions might be acceptable to the parties while signaling the resolve of the Pay Board to the public at large.

First, it was determined that over the course of the prior labor agreement coal miners (both union and nonunion) had registered an 18.9 percent increase in average hourly earnings, while the consumer price index had risen by 15.8 percent. Therefore there had not been an erosion of real earnings.[17] In addition, it was noted that the three-year contract provided for a wage increase of $1.50 an hour and a total package of $2.48, or 41 percent.

Second, the data provided by the BCOA gave little credence to the argument that an above-standard wage increase was necessary to attract new workers to the industry labor force. From 1968 to August 1971 the number of production workers in the bituminous coal industry had increased from 109,000 to 130,000. More significantly, the percentage of the bituminous labor force that was under thirty years of age had jumped from 11.4 percent in 1967 to 20 percent in 1970.[18]

Third, a comparison of wages in the coal and basic steel industries revealed that coal wages had risen somewhat faster than steel wages during the previous decade. Bureau of Labor Statistics data indicate that average hourly earnings in bituminous coal mining rose by 46 percent over the period 1960–70, compared with 37 percent for steel.[19]

The major question considered by the public members was the weight to be given to the special problem of the Welfare and Retirement Fund. Although there was a strong belief that the financial difficulties of the fund were self-inflicted, the public members acknowledged that the need

17. Data were provided by the U.S. Bureau of Labor Statistics.
18. Data provided to the Pay Board by the BCOA, November 17, 1971.
19. The coal industry is defined as Standard Industrial Classification 12 for purposes of the text, while the steel industry is defined as SIC 331. Figures on average hourly earnings are from U.S. Bureau of Labor Statistics, *Employment and Earnings, United States, 1909–75*, Bulletin 1312-10 (GPO, 1976), pp. 16, 120.

would have to be met. Moreover, disallowing the special claims of widows and retired coal miners hardly seemed the appropriate basis for the board to take a hard line. Accordingly, it was agreed that the full amount of the increased contribution to the pension fund should be approved.

All these considerations had to be brought together in a single acceptable number. While any formula had elements of arbitrariness, there should be some reasonable justification. The public members ultimately settled on 12.5 percent; 5.5 percent under the general pay standard, 4.1 percent for the contribution to the Welfare and Retirement Fund, and the remaining 2.9 percent "to reflect inter-industry wage relations."[20]

Despite this laborious effort, the public members received no support from the business representatives. As a group, the business members took the position that the agreement should be approved without change. Their formal position, as later expressed in the resolution affirming the coal settlement, was that the extra payment for the welfare fund was necessary to finance existing benefits and therefore could have been implemented any time before or during the freeze. For this reason, the business members alleged, the higher tonnage royalty had no impact on total compensation and "[did] not adversely affect the objective of reducing inflation."[21] The balance of the increase was justified in the light of "the equitable position of the employees involved," the "ongoing collective bargaining relationships which have traditionally been applied in the coal industry," and "the imperative need of the industry to . . . attract new employees into its work force."[22]

This tolerant approach was inconsistent with the tough position the business members had adopted during the formulation of the board's general policies. Although there were strong considerations of equity in the coal case, other factors probably contributed to the business members' position. Because the agreement was the product of an eighty-nine day strike that resulted in a coal shortage, brownouts had occurred in some areas, giving rise to a valid concern that a cutback of the settlement would prolong the turbulence in the industry and threaten the economic recovery. In addition, there were intimations of pressure from the White House to approve the contract in toto. The pressure presumably reflected the ad-

20. "Resolution Proposed by the Public Members of the Pay Board, November 19, 1971," an attachment to Pay Board press release PB-4, November 19, 1971.
21. "Resolution Proposed by the Business Members of the Pay Board, November 19, 1971," an attachment to Pay Board press release PB-4, November 19, 1971.
22. Ibid.

ministration's concern about the impact of a continued strike on the economy and its unwillingness to be pushed into a direct confrontation with organized labor so early in the game. These allegations of White House intervention were never proved.

When the business members' position became known, the public members tried to develop support for some symbolic reduction. At a separate caucus, the public members argued that approval of such an outsized settlement in the board's first case would deal a major blow to the stabilization program. During an acrimonious discussion they suggested that the business representatives were adopting a position that reflected their narrow interest rather than the national interests that presumably were embraced by the program.

These discussions failed to alter the original positions of the two blocs, and when the full board reconvened the next day, on November 19, it approved the first year of the coal agreement without modification. The public members' initial resolution that would have reduced the settlement to 12.5 percent was voted down by a ten-to-three margin. The business members' resolution was then approved by the same ten-to-three vote. The alignment was the same on both votes; all the labor and management representatives voted to approve the contract, and three public members—Kermit Gordon, William Caples, and Arnold Weber—supported a cutback. Neil Jacoby disqualified himself from voting because he was a member of the Board of Directors of the Occidental Oil Company, which also had coal holdings. He indicated, however, that if he had voted, he would have supported the cutback. Judge Boldt supported the public members' resolution, but as a self-imposed convention he voted only when his ballot would affect the outcome.

As a portmortem to the board's action, there was deepening concern on the part of the public members that the wage stabilization program would be undermined by the tendency of the business members to protect their special interests by forming alliances of convenience with labor on a case-by-case basis. Consequently the public members cast about for some way to "stiffen management's backbone," that is, to impose costs on business for this alleged behavior. At the request of the public members, a meeting was held with C. Jackson Grayson, chairman of the Price Commission, on the same day that the coal decision was handed down. At the time, the Price Commission's rules and procedures were in the same embryonic stage as those of the Pay Board.

Grayson expressed a similar concern that the apparent willingness of the business members to support large wage settlements would make it difficult to maintain the integrity of the stabilization program. Since it seemed likely that the Price Commission would have to permit price increases on some cost pass-through basis, the approval of wage increases far in excess of the 5.5 percent standard would make it difficult to attain the 2.5–3.0 percent goal for price increases.

As a result of this discussion, Grayson and the public members of the Pay Board agreed that it would be desirable for the Price Commission to adopt a policy stating that it would only allow wage increases up to the Pay Board standard of 5.5 percent as a cost justification for price hikes. Presumably this policy would embolden the business members on the Pay Board—and management officials elsewhere—to take the pay standard more seriously. The Price Commission subsequently did adopt such a policy.[23] In any case the Pay Board had taken its first uncertain steps in implementing the general pay standards with inauspicious results.

The Railroad Cases

When the Pay Board had extricated itself from the bituminous coal case, ingloriously or otherwise, it was immediately drawn into another thicket of even greater density. This situation involved two related wage settlements between the National Railway Labor Conference, an association of major railroads, and the Brotherhood of Railroad Signalmen (BRS) and the United Transportation Union. As in the coal case, the railroad agreements were industry-wide in scope and the focus of prolonged controversy between the parties. But whereas the bituminous coal contract was a product of bargaining with one comprehensive union, collective bargaining on the railroads took place in a highly intricate, multiunion structure. The problems posed by the structural factors were magnified by the direct involvement of the federal government at almost every step of the bargaining process that brought the BRS and the UTU agreements to the Pay Board.

Complex Industry Bargaining Structure

The bargaining structure in the railroad industry had evolved over fifty years. From the outset of unionization in the industry, the workers gen-

23. C. Jackson Grayson, Jr., with Louis Neeb, *Confessions of a Price Controller* (Dow Jones-Irwin, 1974), pp. 97–99.

erally grouped themselves in separate craft organizations for purposes of representation and collective bargaining. At one point, as many as twenty-two different craft unions reflected the different skills and functions of the various groups of workers.[24] The largest and most important of the five major clusters of employee organizations encompasses the so-called operating employees such as locomotive engineers, firemen and enginemen, trainmen, and switchmen. The second major grouping includes the clerks and other white-collar employees. The third grouping covers maintenance-of-way employees and food service workers, such as Pullman porters. The fourth cluster spans the shopcraft and repair workers. And last, there is a miscellaneous group including train dispatchers and signalmen.

Because the individual craft unions are limited in size, have overlapping work jurisdictions, and are closely linked to each other in the conduct of collective bargaining, there has been some disposition toward mergers. The most significant combination in recent union history involved the formation of the United Transportation Union. On January 1, 1969, the UTU brought together four important operating unions, including the Brotherhood of Railroad Trainmen, the Brotherhood of Locomotive Firemen and Enginemen, the Order of Railway Conductors and Brakemen, and the Switchmen's Union of North America. This merger made the UTU the largest single railroad union, representing about 180,000 employees. The only operating union of significance that remained outside the UTU was the Brotherhood of Locomotive Engineers, the aristocrats of the railroad work force.

The various railroad unions bargained with the carriers on an individual basis. Because there were so many different unions, great instability marked the conduct of collective bargaining, including forms of indiscipline known as "whipsawing" and "leapfrogging."[25] Improvements in wages and benefits obtained by one union obviously would be sought by another, and many unions tried to exceed the previously established pattern. In addition, the employers were highly vulnerable to union power

24. Jacob J. Kaufman, *Collective Bargaining in the Railroad Industry* (King's Crown Press, 1954), p. 45.

25. Although the terminology is imprecise, whipsawing takes place when a union strikes the most vulnerable employer to gain a favorable settlement and then imposes the same terms on other employers who otherwise would have resisted had they not been outflanked. Leapfrogging occurs when a union uses a settlement with one employer as a basis for obtaining a more generous agreement with another employer.

because a strike by any individual craft could shut down all railroad operations.

In order to buttress their position, the carriers grouped together in multi-employer associations to facilitate collective bargaining. Initially these associations were organized on a regional basis, but in 1963 an umbrella organization was founded that covered all the major railroads in the country. This organization, the National Railway Labor Conference, hoped to speak for the industry with a single voice in dealing with the unions. Collective bargaining was carried out by a single employer bargaining committee. This process of consolidation created a complex, highly visible bargaining structure.

Under these circumstances it is not surprising that the federal government came to play an important, if not determinate, role in the conduct of the industry's collective bargaining. The legal framework for railway labor relations is defined by a separate statute, the Railway Labor Act, which was passed in 1926, nine years before the National Labor Relations Act (Wagner act) extended the protected right to organize to almost all industrial workers. Although the act was hailed as a model law, over the years it has given rise to a pattern of government intervention that has become an integral part of the strategy of both parties to collective bargaining. The statutory procedures include formal notification of intent to terminate an existing contract, mediation of disputes by the National Mediation Board, the offer of binding arbitration, and finally, the convening of a special emergency board appointed by the President of the United States to review unresolved issues and make recommendations for settlement.[26]

In theory, these procedures would minimize the likelihood of strikes and promote constructive collective bargaining. The prestige of a presidential emergency board and general public support of its recommendations were expected to induce the most intransigent party to reach agreement. Although the initial experience was positive, the efficacy of the Railway Labor Act procedures sharply deteriorated over the years. In many cases the parties would not settle their bargaining disputes until an emergency board had been convened and had made recommendations. Even then, if the board rejected labor's claims, the union could threaten to exercise the legal right to strike. Because of the economic consequences of a nationwide work stoppage, this action always raised the prospect of

26. Railway Labor Act, 45 U.S.C. (1964 ed.) 151 et seq.

further government intervention by Congress or the White House. In fact, either party might seek to precipitate such intervention when it believed this tactic would strengthen its hand at the bargaining table. The result was long-term debilitation of voluntary collective bargaining; the act that once had been viewed as a model eventually was scorned in many quarters as the most notorious example of the harmful effects of government intervention in labor-management relations.

This pattern—with a few extra wrinkles—was reflected in the railroad cases that came before the Pay Board. In late 1969 the major railroad unions initiated a new round of bargaining with the National Railway Labor Conference by filing legal notice of intent to terminate the existing labor agreements. These so-called Section 6 notices were filed in September by the Railway Clerks, Maintenance of Way Employees, and Hotel and Restaurant Employees. The BRS and the UTU followed with their own notices in October. The last of the important operating unions, the Locomotive Engineers, made the appropriate submission in November.

Demands Lead to Emergency Board Intervention

The demands of the individual unions varied, but they all called for generous wage increases. The UTU, the largest union, asked for a 15 percent wage increase effective January 1, 1970, another 15 percent on January 1, 1971, and a cost-of-living escalator clause. Additional items included improvements in the contract terms governing vacation pay, holidays, expenses away from home, and sick leave.[27]

The carriers countered with their own demands for sweeping changes in the work rules that controlled the management of the industry labor force, the use of equipment, and the system of compensation. These work rules were the product of local practice and collective bargaining for over sixty years and were legendary for their scope and complexity. The work rules issue had been a source of controversy in railroad labor relations as early as 1919 and had been the subject of an endless series of presidential commissions, emergency boards, and other special study groups. Beginning in the early 1960s, the carriers launched a concerted effort to modify or abolish what they viewed as the most onerous—and costly— work rules. This campaign had been marked by only moderate success, and in 1969 management was still seeking relief from many restrictive

27. "Petition to Pay Board by United Transportation Union" (n.d.; processed), pp. 2–3.

rules. The carriers' demands related to the work practices of all the rail-road crafts; the most important target, however, was those rules included in the contracts with the UTU. Among the changes demanded by the carriers were the establishment of interdivisional runs, the combining of yard and road work, the relaxation of interchange rules, and the elimination of provisions that barred or penalized the use of radios.[28]

Negotiations between the carriers and the major unions proceeded slowly within the framework prescribed by the Railway Labor Act. In late January 1970 the National Mediation Board (NMB) entered the dispute. The mediation efforts dragged on inconclusively until the end of July. At that time the NMB proffered arbitration as authorized by the Railway Labor Act. The four major unions—the UTU, Railway Clerks, Maintenance of Way Employees, and Hotel and Restaurant Employees— all refused. On August 10, 1970, the NMB sent a letter to the disputants advising them that the mediation effort had failed. The release of the case by the NMB permitted the unions to strike after a thirty-day cooling-off period, on or after September 10, 1970. At the request of the Department of Labor, this period was extended for another four days. When no agreement was forthcoming, the UTU and the Railway Clerks called selective strikes against three major railroads, the Southern Pacific, the Chesapeake and Ohio, and the Baltimore and Ohio. The selective strike strategy apparently was motivated by a desire to avoid a complete shut-down of the national railroad system and thereby avert further government intervention. This strategy failed, however, when the U.S. District Court in Washington, D.C., issued a temporary restraining order. On September 18, President Nixon convened Emergency Board No. 178, which consisted of five neutrals, to investigate the dispute and to make recommendations for settlement. This board was authorized to consider the disputes involving the UTU, Railway Clerks, Maintenance of Way Employees, and Hotel and Restaurant Employees. By law, the establishment of the Emergency Board barred a strike for a minimum of sixty days.

28. "Interdivisional runs" refers to the practice of operationally segmenting rail-roads into divisions of 100 miles or less. Under existing rules the carriers generally were required to either change crews at division points or pay premium rates to crews making runs between divisions. Yard and road work also generally involves separate crews, with complex rules and pay provisions governing the circumstances and the allocation of work between yard and road crews. Interchange rules concern the use of road crews to deliver or receive full trains to connecting carriers. Finally, "arbitraries," or flat premiums, were imposed for the use of radio communications in yard or road service. See Pay Board, Economic Analysis Division, "Workrule Concessions in the United Transportation Union Case," EAD-1, January 16, 1972.

The Emergency Board submitted its findings and recommendations to President Nixon on November 9, 1970.[29] Although each of the unions had submitted somewhat different demands, the board treated them as a unit in formulating wage recommendations and proposed a three-year agreement with the following schedule of wage increases:

First year: 1970
  January 1   5 percent
  November 1   32 cents an hour
Second year: 1971
  April 1   4 percent
  October 1   5 percent
Third year: 1972
  April 1   5 percent
  October 1   5 percent

According to the Emergency Board, this settlement constituted a realistic approach that reflected collective bargaining developments outside the railroad industry, recognized the accelerating pace of inflation, and compensated the union for entering into a three-year agreement. Most significantly, the board took a strong position in favor of the extensive modification of work rules to promote greater efficiency in the operation of the railroads.

Prolonged Settlement Process

The Emergency Board's recommendation proved to be a pause in a prolonged process that seemed to strain everyone's forbearance but the negotiators'. After reviewing the Emergency Board's report, the unions rejected the proposals and once more prepared to strike. At this point the government had exhausted all remedies available under the Railway Labor Act. The unions set a deadline of December 10, 1970, and as the date approached, Congress entered the picture to impose its own alternative to free collective bargaining. The strike had barely commenced when Congress enacted Public Law 91-541, which propelled the dispute to still another stage. The law prohibited the unions from engaging in a work stoppage until March 1, 1971. Congress mandated that in the interim, the railroads must put into effect the first two wage increases that had been recommended by the Emergency Board: 5 percent effective January 1,

29. *Report to the President by Emergency Board No. 178, November 9, 1970* (GPO, 1971).

1970, and 32 cents an hour effective November 1, 1970. Both increases were retroactive to the specified dates. It is noteworthy that the law did not require the adoption of the work rule changes that also had been endorsed by the board.

The first break in the impasse came in February as time was running out on the statutory strike ban. All the unions involved in the dispute except the UTU agreed to settlements that substantially conformed to the Emergency Board's recommendations. In addition, the carriers and the unions agreed to extend the terms of the contract for six months, to July 1, 1973. An extra wage increase of 25 cents an hour was provided in consideration of this extension.

Despite this breakthrough, the UTU refused to accept the Emergency Board's recommendations as a basis for settlement. Because the heaviest burden of the work rule revisions fell on the UTU, the union had an interest in either limiting the scope of the changes or increasing the compensatory economic package. At this point the pattern of railroad contracts had a paradoxical quality. That is, the size of the economic package in the emerging industry pattern was justified in part by the changes in the work rules; the economic gains, however, had been achieved by those unions that had relinquished least, while the union that controlled the largest stakes had yet to come to an agreement.

When the legal restriction on the right to strike had expired, the UTU again initiated selective work stoppages, this time against the Burlington Northern and the Seaboard Coast Line. The strike precipitated another complicated series of legal maneuvers that ultimately upheld the UTU's right to call selective stoppages if two weeks' notice was given to the designated railroads. Once the right to strike was upheld, the UTU resumed negotiations with the carriers without exercising it. Negotiations were still fruitless even though the pattern had become more firmly established when in May 1971 the Locomotive Engineers reached an agreement that was consistent with the earlier contracts negotiated by the Railway Clerks, Maintenance of Way Employees, and Hotel and Restaurant Employees.

Frustrated by the eighteen-month impasse with the UTU, the carriers announced their intention to unilaterally institute all the proposed work rule changes on July 2. The UTU responded with another selective strike against four major railroads on July 16. Two more carriers were shut down on July 24. With little ammunition left in their arsenals, the UTU and the National Railway Labor Conference finally staggered to a tentative agreement on August 2, 1971, thirteen days before the wage-price freeze. In addition to providing for substantial wage increases, the new contract included the major changes in work rules that management had demanded. The agreement was not formally ratified by the union until December—a factor that would greatly complicate the Pay Board's consideration of the case. But the agreement did mark the conclusion of an epic exercise in collective bargaining that was unique even by railroad industry standards.

Following the UTU settlement, the last act in the bargaining round was performed by the Brotherhood of Railroad Signalmen. Along with the rest of the crafts, the BRS had submitted its demands for a new contract to the carriers back in the fall of 1969. Negotiations had followed the customary tortuous route through mediation, an offer of arbitration, and ultimately, the establishment of Emergency Board No. 179 on March 4, 1971. The thrust of the BRS's demands was that its members should receive equal wage treatment with the electricians, a separate railroad shopcraft. The electricians, who were represented by the International Brotherhood of Electrical Workers (IBEW) had already received a wage increase as the result of an earlier contract signed in December 1969 and were seeking additional gains as part of the new bargaining round that had been kicked off by the operating unions.

Emergency Board No. 179 generally supported the contentions of the BRS concerning parity between the signalmen and the electricians.[30] Its recommendations, announced on April 14, 1971, provided for a two-stage wage increase. The adjustment in 1970 would equal the increase that had accrued to the electricians under the shopcrafts agreements in 1969, and the hike in 1971–72 would follow the recommendation of Emergency Board No. 178. When the shopcraft unions, including the IBEW, more or less accepted the operating unions' pattern for 1971–72 on October 7, 1971, the BRS soon fell in line and reached agreement with the carriers on similar terms on November 16. Thus the sequence of bargaining in the railroad industry was completed three days after the onset of Phase II. The pattern of wage increases for the various unions produced by this complex series of events is shown in table 5-1.

Complex Task for Pay Board

Although all the railroad agreements were closely interrelated, the process of case review was such that the Pay Board could only enter the

30. *Report to the President by Emergency Board No. 179, April 14, 1971* (GPO, 1971).

Table 5-1. *Wage Increases Granted under Collective Bargaining Agreements between the Railroads and Affiliated Unions, 1970–73*

Effective date of wage increase	Wage increase (percent)						
	Agreements reached before August 15, 1971					Agreements reached after August 15, 1971	
	UTU[a]	BRAC[b]	BLE[c]	BMWE[d]	HRE[e]	Shopcraft unions[f]	BRS[g]
1970							
January 1	5.0	5.0	5.0	5.0	5.0	5.0	5.0
February 19	...	...	...	...	...	1.7	...
April 1	...	...	...	...	...	1.0	...
August 1	...	...	...	...	...	1.0	...
November 1	8.4	8.4	8.4	8.4	8.4	...	6.9
1971							
January 1	...	...	...	...	...	2.6	2.6
April 1	4.0	4.0	4.0	4.0	4.0	2.9	2.9
October 1	5.0	5.0	5.0	5.0	5.0	5.0	5.0
1972							
April 1	5.0	5.0	5.0	5.0	5.0	5.0	5.0
October 1	5.0	5.0	5.0	5.0	5.0	5.0	5.0
1973							
January 1	3.0	3.0	3.0	...	...	...	...
April 1	2.0	2.0	2.0	5.0	5.0	5.0	4.7
Total increases[h]	37.4	37.4	37.4	37.4	37.4	34.2	37.1

Source: Pay Board staff paper EAD-3, January 16, 1972.

a. United Transportation Union; agreement reached August 2, 1971.
b. Brotherhood of Railway, Airline and Steamship Clerks, Freight Handlers, Express and Station Employees; agreement reached February 25, 1971.
c. Brotherhood of Locomotive Engineers; agreement reached May 13, 1971.
d. Brotherhood of Maintenance of Way Employees; agreement reached February 10, 1971.
e. Hotel and Restaurant Employees and Bartenders International Union; agreement reached February 10, 1971.
f. Shopcraft unions included the International Association of Machinists and Aerospace Workers; the International Brotherhood of Boilermakers, Iron Shipbuilders, Blacksmiths, Forgers and Helpers; and the Brotherhood of Railway Carmen of the United States and Canada. Agreement reached November 13, 1971.
g. Brotherhood of Railroad Signalmen; agreement reached November 16, 1971.
h. Sum of the columns. Does not allow for compounding factor.

maze from a side door. In the first place, four major agreements had been reached long before the onset of wage-price controls and could not be considered on a timely basis by the Pay Board. These agreements covered the Maintenance of Way Employees, Hotel and Restaurant Employees, Railway Clerks, and Locomotive Engineers. The first three were negotiated in February 1971; the Locomotive Engineers' contract was ratified in May 1971. Under Pay Board rules these agreements were considered existing contracts, subject only to the challenge procedure that was applicable to deferred increases. Thus the first wage increase the board could consider was scheduled for April 1, 1972. Even then, the adjustment was limited to 5 percent, within the Pay Board's general standard. The scheduled increases would exceed Pay Board standards only in October 1972, when the employees were slated to receive another 5 percent increase, which would bring the total for the control year to 10 percent.

These circumstances meant that the Pay Board's immediate authority for review and determination was limited to the agreements negotiated by the UTU and the BRS. Of the two agreements, the UTU settlement was clearly dominant. Indeed the negotiations between the carrier's conference and the UTU constituted the keystone for the industry bargaining structure. The carriers' desire to obtain relief from work rule restrictions contributed in large measure to the sizable wage gains registered by the railroad agreements. The general outline of the wage settlement delineated by Emergency Board No. 178 became the basis of the agreements reached by the Maintenance of Way Employees, Railway Clerks, and other craft unions. A similar pattern of increases for 1971–72 was followed in the Signalmen's case, although the magnitude of the adjustment was justified by wage comparisons with the electricians. In addition, it is significant to note that the BRS agreement covered 9,840 employees, while the UTU contract covered 134,500 workers.

Notwithstanding the great divergence in the weight of the two agreements, the sequence of the Pay Board review was controlled, if not manipulated, by the timing of the parties' submissions. Although the UTU had reached a temporary agreement on August 2, the agreement did not become official until it had been ratified by the union. The process of ratification was obscure and was controlled by Charles Luna, the president of the UTU. Throughout the freeze and the first two months of Phase II, Luna gave no evidence that he was willing to move toward formal approval of the agreement and thus trigger its consideration by the Pay Board. One explanation for this dilatory behavior—aside from Luna's personal idiosyncrasies—was that he was delaying in order to determine the specific details of the wage regulations and to build support for approval of the UTU contract. In any case the first railroad agreement to come before the board involved the BRS and not the UTU. The contract between the national carriers and the Signalmen had been formally reached on November 16, 1971. Therefore it was designated as a new contract for Pay Board purposes. The contract was submitted to the board before the end of November and was placed on the agenda for hearing on December 9, 1971. The Signalmen's agreement was taken up shortly after the decision had been reached in the bituminous coal case but before the deliberations on aerospace.

The board's first task was to determine the status of those wage increases that were retroactive to dates before the wage-price freeze and the beginning of Phase II. As indicated in table 5-1, the BRS agreement provided for four different wage increases between January 1, 1970, and April 1, 1971. Another 5 percent hike was scheduled to take effect on October 1, 1971, during the freeze. It was agreed without dissent that the board would not review those wage increases that were retroactive to dates before November 13, 1971. The legal authority of the board to conduct such a review was questionable, some of the wage increments had been mandated by congressional action as a consequence of the central dispute with the operating unions, and any rollback would be subject to sharp attack on grounds of equity.

Most attention focused on the wage increases scheduled to take effect in the postfreeze period. Table 5-1 shows that the BRS contract exceeded the 5.5 percent pay standard by a significant margin even when the most favorable assumptions were made in calculating the magnitude of the gain. If all the wage increases retroactive to dates before August 15 were included in the wage base, the contract still called for a full year's increase of approximately 10 percent—5 percent on April 1, 1972, and an additional 5 percent on October 1, 1972. The last wage adjustment under the contract terms, effective April 1, 1973, would fall in another control year and therefore would require separate calculations. When the 1972 wage gains were incorporated in the new base, the total increase in wages and benefits scheduled for April 1973 totaled 5.4 percent, which was within the 5.5 percent standard as it was then interpreted.

Thus as the railroad cases developed, it was apparent that the Pay Board could get only a precarious handhold on the contracts. On the one hand, it was forced to deal first with the Signalmen's agreement, which occupied a secondary position in the railroad industry bargaining structure. On the other hand, the board had review authority over only a small proportion of the total wage gains incorporated in the agreement—those scheduled for April 1 and October 1, 1972. Despite these constraints, considerable importance was attached to the railroad cases because they followed the blow to the board's credibility in the bituminous coal decision and because the *total* wage increase of 37 percent over forty-three months loomed so large in the public's perception.

Consideration of the cases went forward in a quick series of procedural skirmishes. The public members argued that action on the BRS contract should be postponed until the UTU contract had been submitted to the board. They asserted that the BRS agreement was clearly a pattern-follower and that judgment should be postponed until the pattern-setting contract had been reviewed. Further, the Signalmen's contract, unlike the UTU agreement, did not include any major work rule concessions that could be considered as justification for wage increases in excess of the 5.5 percent pay standard.

The leading spokesman for the management members was Benjamin Biaggini, the president of the Southern Pacific Company. The Southern Pacific was a member of the National Railway Labor Conference and was a party to the various labor agreements. Biaggini stated that the Signalmen's contract was the product of a long and controversial bargaining process and that industry stability required the timely review of the agreements as they came to the Pay Board. He submitted a motion calling for the approval of the BRS agreement without modification. The resolution dealt with the public members' concerns by stating that the deferred increases scheduled for April 1, 1972, October 1, 1972, and April 1, 1973, would be subject to the general prenotification and challenge procedure. As noted previously, the effect of this resolution would be to delay any opportunity for Pay Board action until October 1, 1972, when the cumulative control year wage increase would exceed the 5.5 percent standard.

The public members were not placated and made a motion to table the Biaggini resolution. The motion was defeated by a vote of eight to six. Two of the business members voted for the motion and Judge Boldt abstained. As expected, all the labor representatives voted against the move to table the motion. After additional parliamentary wrangles, the Biaggini motion was approved by a vote of nine to three. Only the public members present voted against the resolution. By blessing the tail, the

Pay Board had taken a major step toward granting grace to the main corpus of the railroad case. The discussion of the BRS contracts had taken a little over two hours.

Following this action, consideration of the railroad settlements was held in abeyance while the board turned its attention to another highly controversial case involving the aerospace industry. The board lacked authority to expedite the matter on its own initiative, since the UTU was still playing a cat-and-mouse game with both the carriers and the government over the ratification of the tentative agreement that had been reached on August 2. In the intervening period, the railroads had not received any word from Charles Luna concerning the final ratification of the settlement. Nor had the terms of the contract been put into effect. Consequently there was no legal basis for a review of the contract by the board.

Luna never did formally notify the employers that the August 1971 agreement had been ratified. Instead, during the second week in January 1972, after the board had disposed of the aerospace case, he submitted the UTU-National Carriers Agreement directly to the Pay Board for approval. As the railroad spokesmen later testified, this was the first indication they had received that the contract had in fact been ratified by the union.

Coming to Terms on Work Rules

When the contract materialized at the board's offices, immediate steps were taken to bring the matter to a decision. Because of the importance of the case and the general public interest in it, the board convened a public hearing on January 18, 1972. The meeting followed what was now a set format, including lengthy opening statements by the parties and a round of questions from members of the Pay Board. Spokesmen for both the UTU and the carriers recounted in excruciating detail the process of bargaining and governmental intervention that had led to the agreement. The union argued that the work rule concessions provided more than an adequate justification for the total wage package. Estimates of the savings from the work rule changes ranged from $54 million to $156 million a year.[31] Further, Luna argued that the total package over the three-and-a-half-year period was moderate because the Emergency Board had spread the wage increases over forty-three months in order to minimize the cost

31. Pay Board, "Workrule Concessions."

of retroactive payments by the carriers. The union had accepted this pattern of wage increases in recognition of the railroad's financial problems. Therefore, additional burdens should not be imposed on the workers.

The management spokesman, William H. Dempsey, chairman of the National Railway Labor Conference, had a more delicate task. First, he had to persuade the Pay Board that the work rule concessions justified the wage package. Second, the railroads undoubtedly were concerned that any public declaration of savings derived from the work rule changes would make it more difficult for the carriers to obtain the approval of the Interstate Commerce Commission (and the Price Commission) of prospective applications for rate increases. The carriers danced around this problem by declaring that the work rule concessions held the *long-run* prospect of substantial savings; in the short run, however, the cost reductions would be limited because of the time required for implementing the changes and because the contract included income guarantees to those employees whose earnings would be adversely affected by the introduction of the new working arrangements.[32] The carriers' spokesman stoutly resisted efforts by various Pay Board members to pin him down to a more precise estimate of the schedule of savings.

The UTU contract was considered in the framework that had been elaborated in the Signalmen's case. The Pay Board accepted all the wage increases through October 1, 1971, and limited its review to the 5 percent increases scheduled for April 1, 1972, and October 1, 1972. As in the Signalmen's case, the 1973 increase fell in the subsequent control year and therefore was not vulnerable to immediate Pay Board action.

The controversy that arose within the board over the UTU contract involved the integrity of the review process rather than the magnitude of the wage increase. In an effort to remedy what they considered to be the procedural deficiencies of the BRS decision, the public members introduced a resolution that approved all wage and salary increases "which have been or will become effective on or before April 1, 1972." The resolution further stated, however, that

all wage and salary increases pursuant to said agreements which are scheduled to become effective after April 1, 1972, shall require prenotification to the Board and be subject to challenge and review by the Board for consideration of consistency with Board standards. At that time the Board will give special

32. "Statement of the National Railway Labor Conference before the Pay Board Concerning the Tentative Agreement with the United Transportation Union" (n.d.; processed), pp. 14–16.

consideration to progress in the implementation of work rules changes covered by the agreement.[33]

In other words, the board would not directly disapprove or modify the terms of the settlement. Instead, it would limit approval to the April 1 increase of 5 percent and retain the authority to intervene in the subsequent increase scheduled for October 1, 1972. At the same time, the resolution made it clear that approval of the October increase would be conditioned by evidence that progress had been made in implementing the work rule changes—which ostensibly justified the total wage package.

Biaggini again took the lead in seeking board approval of the UTU contract. His resolution conceded the board's authority to review subsequent wage increases but more or less committed the board to prospective approval. The key section of the Biaggini resolution read as follows:

Resolved: . . . that the agreement is approved and that the Pay Board intends to approve deferred increases scheduled to be paid in 1972 and 1973 subject to a showing by the parties at the time of prenotification required for such increases that the work rules changes covered by the agreement are being implemented in accordance with the applicable provisions of the contract.[34]

This statement of initial approval and future intentions was viewed as necessary to obtain the UTU's cooperation in giving full faith to the work rule concessions. Without this approval of the entire contract in principle, it was argued that the union would be reluctant to move quickly on the new operating rules. Indeed there were rumblings of strike action in the event that a blanket approval was not forthcoming from the Pay Board.

The debate proceeded within this talmudic framework. When the board had spent itself in making these involuted distinctions, an initial vote was taken on the Biaggini resolution. The outcome was indecisive—seven votes for the resolution and six against. Because a majority of eight votes was necessary for an official Pay Board action, the resolution failed to pass. All five public members and one business representative voted against the resolution. (Judge Boldt cast a vote in this instance, since his ballot affected the outcome.) The other four business members and three labor members voted for the Biaggini resolution. Two labor members, William Winpisinger of the IAM and Pat Greathouse of the UAW, abstained.

The abstention of the two labor members was a unique occurrence and reflected the vagaries of interunion politics. Apparently Winpisinger and

33. Minutes of the Pay Board, January 19, 1972, Exhibit 3.
34. Ibid., Exhibit 2.

Greathouse felt sufficiently aggrieved over the decision in the aerospace case to cut the wage increases included in the IAM and UAW contracts to be unwilling to support a contract they considered less meritorious. In addition, they indicated displeasure with Luna's maneuvering in bringing the UTU contract to the board. At any rate the board was confounded when the two members abstained, resulting in a tie vote.

The situation became further clouded when the board voted on the public members' resolution. The vote in this instance was also a deadlock, six to six. Winpisinger and Greathouse continued to abstain and were joined by a member from the business ranks. In an attempt to break the stalemate, the public members introduced an alternative resolution that edged somewhat closer to the Biaggini approach: "All wage and salary increases . . . effective after April 1, 1972, shall require prenotification . . . and be subject to challenge and review by the Board." However, rather than making progress in implementing the work rule changes a flat condition for approval, the substitute resolution stated that "the Board will give special consideration to progress in the implementation of work rules changes covered by the agreement."[35] With the decisionmaking process in disarray and some members playing unaccustomed roles, the board decided to table the motion until its next meeting on January 25, six days later.

When the board reconvened, significant shifts in opinion quickly became apparent. In the period between meetings, the two balky labor members and one management representative had changed their positions and now voted with the bloc calling for blanket approval of the UTU agreement. This reflected a judicious reconsideration of the issues, a response to acute pressure, or both. Little preliminary discussion preceded a vote on the public members' revised resolution. This time Winpisinger and Greathouse did not abstain but cast their ballots against the resolution, and hence it was defeated eight to six.

The stage was now set for consideration of the Biaggini resolution. The key sections of the final version of the resolution read as follows:

2. That the Pay Board . . . approves wage and salary increases scheduled to have become effective April 1, 1971, and October 1, 1971, pursuant to terms of the agreement.

3. That the Board takes notice of the changes in work rules covered by the agreement and recognizes that encouragement of increases in productivity is in the National interest; and

35. Ibid., Exhibit 3.

4. That the Board intends to approve deferred increases in wages and salaries for the year 1972 under terms of the agreement provided that on the pre-notification dates required for such increases, the work rules changes covered by the agreement are being implemented in accordance with the applicable provisions of the agreement.[36]

The Biaggini resolution was approved by a vote of eight to five. Three business members joined the labor members in supporting the resolution. One management member abstained, as did Chairman Boldt. The net effect of the Pay Board action was approval of the UTU contract, and therefore of the related railroad agreements, through 1972 and a slender procedural victory for the opponents, who had preserved the right to review the progress made in carrying out the work rule changes. It was fitting that the Pay Board's determination in the UTU case, like collective bargaining in the railroad industry itself, should hang on technicalities and result in prolonging the dispute.

As an epilogue, it may be noted that in the summer of 1972 the Pay Board did request submissions from the railroads concerning the progress that had been made in implementing the work rule changes as a preliminary to consideration of the wage increase scheduled for October 1. The board's staff reported that the most generous estimate indicated that the annual savings from the changes would total $15–20 million, far below the original projections. The report also stated that the failure to realize the anticipated savings was not the result of obstructionist tactics by the union. Rather, the shortfall was the consequence of management's slow pace in putting the work rule changes into effect.[37] On this basis, the October wage increase was approved by the board without dissent.

The Aerospace Case

Although the coal and railroad agreements moved through the review process unscathed, the aerospace contracts were the first of the last cows to be nicked by the Pay Board. Like the other major cases, that of the aerospace industry involved difficult questions of equity and interpretation. In addition, the decisionmaking process was marked by a high level of controversy and ineptness that reinforced the divisions on the board. Nonetheless, this case marked the first time that the array of interests and issues made it possible for the board to cut a negotiated wage settlement.

36. Ibid., Exhibit 2.
37. Pay Board staff paper EPCA-EAD, Micro 103, August 28, 1972, pp. 1–8.

The basic bargaining structure of the aerospace industry encompassed five major companies and two unions. The firms included McDonnell Douglas, North American Rockwell, Boeing, Lockheed, and Ling-Temco-Vought (LTV). The two unions were the UAW and the IAM, both of which organized the employees on an industrial basis, combining production and craft workers in comprehensive bargaining units. The two unions had staked out the aerospace industry as their jurisdiction following the split between the American Federation of Labor (AFL) and the Congress of Industrial Organizations in 1937.[38] After the AFL-CIO merger in 1955, the UAW and IAM had coexisted more or less peaceably. Relations between the IAM and the UAW were not disturbed when the latter withdrew from the labor federation in 1962. The UAW was the dominant union in North American Rockwell and LTV, while the IAM enjoyed exclusive bargaining rights in Boeing and Lockheed. Each union had two large locals in McDonnell Douglas, reflecting the distribution of representation rights when McDonnell and Douglas were separate companies.

Bargaining relationships in the aerospace industry had been a mixture of passivity and militancy. For several years the UAW had attempted to link aerospace bargaining developments to the pattern it had established in the automobile industry. This strategy generally had been unsuccessful. Contract provisions for aerospace and auto workers had some similarities, but the industries succeeded in maintaining separate approaches. This separation was abetted by the fact that aerospace negotiations lagged the auto pattern by a year, and the industries were differentiated significantly by occupational composition, the nature of the product market, and the geographical location of major production facilities. In addition to disputes over bargaining structure, some employers had taken a hard line on basic questions of union security. For example, Lockheed and the IAM had engaged in a long, bitter strike over the demand for a union shop clause. On the other hand, because the federal government was a major customer for the aerospace industry, management and the unions often found a basis for cooperation in lobbying for government programs of mutual economic interest. Thus the IAM had joined Lockheed in vigorously lobbying Congress to enact a special loan guarantee program for that company in 1970.

The origins of the 1971 aerospace agreements—and of a large part of

38. Walter Galenson, *The CIO Challenge to the AFL: A History of the American Labor Movement, 1935–41* (Harvard University Press, 1960), pp. 506–09.

the Pay Board's difficulties in this case—can be traced back to the preceding contract. In 1968 the five major aerospace companies had won union acceptance of a "cap" on the existing escalator clause. Under the terms of the original escalator clause, wages increased without limitation by 0.4 cent for each one-point increase in the consumer price index. The 1968 agreement, in contrast, included an 8 cent limit on the escalator clause for each of the first two years of the three-year contract. In separate letters to the UAW, however, North American Rockwell and McDonnell Douglas agreed that any wage increase that would have accumulated through the operation of the escalator clause in the absence of the cap would be paid, effective October 3, 1971, two days after the 1968 agreement was scheduled to expire. Such a letter was not provided to Lockheed, Boeing, or LTV, although their bargaining agreements also included a cap on the escalator clauses. Nonetheless, because the five aerospace companies generally adhered to the same pattern, the residual cost of living increase was expected to be paid under the same terms spelled out for North American Rockwell and McDonnell Douglas. By October 1971, 34 cents had accumulated under the cap on the escalator clauses applicable to the five aerospace companies.

The lead agreement in the 1971 bargaining round in the aerospace industry involved the UAW and North American Rockwell. The existing contract was scheduled to expire on October 1, 1971. When the parties failed to agree on the terms of a new contract, the old agreement was extended on a day-to-day basis. Obviously, because the negotiations took place during the wage-price freeze, considerable uncertainty characterized the bargaining process. Indeed Leonard Woodcock, president of the UAW, had expressed concern about the impact of the wage stabilization program on aerospace negotiations during the heated Pay Board discussions of the basic standards.[39]

Negotiations continued through the freeze and into November without resolution, but a new contract was finally signed by North American Rockwell and the UAW on December 6, 1971. The other units then fell in line and ratified identical or closely similar agreements. McDonnell Douglas, Boeing, and Lockheed came to terms within a week after the North American Rockwell agreement, and LTV settled on December 18.

The Pay Board moved quickly to consider the aerospace contracts,

39. See chapter 2.

nudged by the UAW and IAM representatives on the board. The full board initially considered the North American Rockwell settlement alone on December 14. At that time, it decided that all the major aerospace cases should be handled on a consolidated basis.

The COLA and Roll-Up Issues

From the outset, the critical issue in the aerospace decision was the status of the residual cost of living adjustment (COLA) of 34 cents carried forward from the previous agreement. Without this increment, the economic terms of the new contract were within reach of the 5.5 percent standard. The impact of the residual COLA on the wage package in the North American Rockwell case, the lead agreement for the industry, is shown below in dollars per hour: [40]

	Residual COLA excluded	Residual COLA included
Wage and benefit base	4.979	5.319
Wage increase	0.173	0.513
Benefits increase		
Holiday	0.025	0.025
Roll-up	0.027	0.068
Total wage and benefit increase	0.225	0.606

The spread in the percentage effect of including or excluding the residual COLA in the base was striking. If the adjustment was considered to be "old" money that was committed by the previous contract, then the 34 cents would be included in the base wage and the first-year increase would be limited to 22.5 cents, or 4.5 percent. If, on the other hand, the residual COLA was treated as "new" money, then the total increase in wages and related benefits was 60.6 cents or 11.4 percent of the old base.

The arithmetic problem of determining the true economic cost of the labor agreement was compounded by ambiguity concerning the status of "roll-up." Roll-up is the idiomatic term used to describe the additional cost in wage-related benefits generated by increases in the basic wage rate. For example, if holiday and vacation pay are computed on the basis of the

40. "Cost Analysis of First Year of Agreement between North American Rockwell and UAW," Pay Board staff memorandum, December 14, 1971. Wage and benefit base includes company contributions to pension plans, group insurance, and legally required payments.

employee's hourly rate, then the cost of these benefits to the employer will increase when the base rate is raised. Although the Pay Board subsequently required the inclusion of roll-up in the calculation of wage increases, this question was not a settled point in the early days of Phase II when the aerospace case was considered. As the tabulation above indicates, the cost of roll-up could be considerable. When the residual COLA was counted as part of the wage increase, roll-up amounted to 6.8 cents; when it was included in the base, roll-up was 2.7 cents. Confusion over the inclusion of roll-up in the calculation of the total allowable wage increase added significantly to the controversy in the aerospace decision.

Fringe Benefits

In addition to the problems of residual COLA and roll-up, the circumstances of the aerospace case created questions concerning the treatment of pensions and insurance plans. When the Pay Board promulgated the general pay standard, it explicitly determined that the 5.5 percent would include the cost of any improvements in pensions, health insurance, and related fringe benefits. Similarly, the cost of the existing benefit plans would be incorporated in the base wage or hourly compensation. In response to strong pressures from organized labor and the insurance companies, however, Congress specified that a separate standard must be applied to fringe benefits. The amendments to the Economic Stabilization Act became law on December 22, 1971, shortly after the Pay Board began its consideration of the aerospace contracts. Under these circumstances, the policy concerning the treatment of the cost of improvements in pension and insurance benefits was in limbo. The original rudimentary rules for incorporating these costs in Pay Board calculations were no longer appropriate, but the new policies had not been formulated, and the likelihood that this complicated matter could be resolved for timely application to the aerospace contracts was virtually nil. It was possible, of course, to defer the case until the necessary standards had been promulgated, but under the pressure of events this alternative did not receive serious consideration.

The cost of the fringe benefit improvements included in the aerospace agreements was significant. As part of the industry pattern, retirement benefits had been increased from $5.75 to $8 a month per year of service, and the health insurance program had been upgraded. The consequences of including the cost of current benefits in the wage base and the cost of the improvements in the total economic gain in the North American Rockwell agreement were as follows in dollars per hour:[41]

	Residual COLA excluded	Residual COLA included
Wage and benefit base		
Excluding pensions and insurance	4.979	5.319
Including pensions and insurance	5.894	6.235
Increase in health and insurance plans	0.018	0.018
Increase in pension benefits	0.156	0.156

The cost increase of insurance and pension improvements as a percentage of the total base (including costs of existing plans) was 2.8 percent, including residual COLA, and 3 percent, excluding residual COLA. Overall, then, the cost of the total economic package won by the UAW in the North American Rockwell contract was approximtaely 15 percent.

One additional complication muddied the water. Although the actual pension and insurance benefits were more or less equivalent among the five aerospace companies, there were significant variations in the costs. These variations reflected differences in methods of financing the pension plans and differences in the demographic and occupational characteristics of the work force in each of the companies. The most striking variation was in the cost of North American Rockwell's existing pension plan and those of the four other companies. The hourly cost of the North American Rockwell plan was 48.9 cents; for McDonnell-Douglas, it was 21.9 cents, and for Boeing, it was 27.9 cents. This spread was attributable to the fact that North American Rockwell funded the past service liability on a ten-year basis, while the other two companies spread the cost over twenty years, permitting a lower hourly contribution by the employer. The effect of these differences on the percentage increases attributed to pension and insurance improvements among the various aerospace companies are shown in table 5-2.

The Pay Board entered this labyrinth on December 21 when it convened the formal hearing in the aerospace case. Spokesmen for the UAW and IAM and management officials from all five aerospace companies were present. (By this time, LTV had also reached an agreement with the UAW.)

In their statements the company and union spokesmen adopted a common front and appealed for board approval without modification of the

41. Ibid.

Table 5-2. *Increased Costs of Benefit Adjustments as Percent of
Total Wage and Benefit Base, Aerospace Collective Bargaining
Negotiations, 1971*

	Increased costs of pension and insurance improvements as percent of total wage and benefit base	
Company	Residual COLA included in base	Residual COLA excluded from base
North American Rockwell	2.7	2.9
McDonnell Douglas	3.8	4.0
Boeing	2.4	2.5
Lockheed (Georgia)	4.0	4.2
Lockheed (California)	4.3	4.6
Ling-Temco-Vought	1.9	2.1

Source: Derived from Pay Board staff analyses.

contract terms. Management officials from North American Rockwell
made the basic presentation, focusing on the status of the residual COLA
payment. They asserted that as far back as 1968 a commitment had been
made to include the residual COLA in the employees' wage rates on the
first day the terms of the new contract were in effect. Therefore, the higher
wage, including the 34 cent payment, was already in effect on October 3,
1971, and should be counted as part of the base rather than as part of the
wage increase. Under this approach the first-year increase in wages and
benefits was approximately 6 percent. As a clincher, it was noted that if
the fringe benefits covered by the recent amendments to the Economic
Stabilization Act were excluded from the calculations, the economic gains
were reduced to 3.5 percent. All the companies explicitly or implicitly
supported this argument. As an additional justification for approval of the
contracts, it was stated that the entire wage increase was necessary to
retain highly skilled "essential" workers who otherwise would be bid
away by other employers.

UAW and IAM officials extended these arguments with great conviction. They contended that the terms of the letter of agreement concerning
the carry-forward of the residual COLA in the case of North American
Rockwell were part of the industry pattern and therefore were applicable
to all companies, whether or not a formal letter was exchanged. They alleged that the aerospace agreement could also be approved as tandem to
the pattern established in the automobile industry in 1970. They further
pointed out that most aerospace workers had not received a wage increase

in eighteen months and that equity demanded the approval of the full amount. With respect to the complexities of calculating insurance and pension costs, the board should focus on the need to raise and equalize the benefits involved, rather than on the costs.

The hearing was distinguished by an incident that vividly illustrated the difficulties, if not the anomalies, of tripartitism. As the hearing opened, Leonard Woodcock took his place with the other Pay Board members on the dais. When the UAW was called upon to make a statement, however, Woodcock took one of the seats reserved for the witnesses and made a strong defense of the aerospace contracts. Thereafter, he withdrew from the proceedings, and his place was taken by Pat Greathouse, his alternate and a vice-president of the UAW.

A Test for Tripartitism

There was little doubt that the labor members would stand firmly for approval of all the aerospace agreements as negotiated. In addition to the broad considerations of equity and labor solidarity, it was significant that two of the labor members were officers of unions that were a party to the new contracts. As one of the labor spokesmen noted pointedly, "It's all right to talk about the coal miners and railroad workers, but now you're playing in our pea patch."[42]

The business members, on the other hand, adopted a hard line. They found the arguments for approval unpersuasive and expressed a consensus view that the wage increase should be reduced to 7 percent, which was the "high" standard implicitly accepted by the board as a guide in dealing with situations that posed strong considerations of equity. This was the first case in which the business representatives had pressed for a wage reduction.

The public members concurred that the aerospace contracts should be modified but disagreed among themselves concerning the size of the wage reduction. One group believed the wage increase should be cut to 7 percent; another group felt that an intermediate figure between 7 percent and the total wage increase of 11.4 percent, as calculated in the North American Rockwell contract, would be appropriate. The willingness to go beyond 7 percent was due to two factors.

First, although there was no support for the contention that the 34 cent residual COLA was already in effect when the new contract was

42. Comment made to Arnold Weber.

signed, a creditable argument could be made that it should be given some weight in the board's decision. Clearly the arrangements for the carry-forward of the residual COLA had been agreed to as early as 1968, and the unions involved had expected it to become the platform from which additional wage increases could be negotiated.

Second, the aerospace case provided the initial opportunity for the public members to play a traditional role in a tripartite wage stabilization process—that of mediating or defining the middle position between the extremes. In the first two cases considered by the board, the public members had taken what proved to be an explicit adversary position vis-à-vis the business and labor representatives. To be sure, the public members felt that their position generally should be determined by the merits of individual cases in the light of the objectives of the stabilization program. But they recognized the desirability of trying to develop a middle ground that might increase labor's acceptance of the wage stabilization program and willingness to work for its success.

With this objective in mind, the public members initiated a series of discussions with the labor representatives in an effort to find a mutually acceptable disposition of the aerospace contracts. Rather than enhancing the public members' role as conciliators, however, these events resulted in bitter misunderstanding and further strained relations within the Pay Board.

Moving toward a Cutback

Following the open hearing, the board convened in executive session. At that time it was decided to defer the final determination in the aerospace case until January 5, 1972, after the Christmas and New Year period. The three groups then retired to separate caucuses to work out their positions and strategies. As the afternoon progressed, various board members left to return home for the Christmas holiday. In the early evening the remaining public members—Gordon, Weber, and Judge Boldt—approached Greathouse and Winpisinger, the UAW and IAM representatives, to discuss their current thinking concerning the aerospace contracts. In view of the informal nature of the conversations and the pre-eminent interest of the UAW and the IAM in the case, the other labor representatives were not invited.

The meeting was held in Judge Boldt's office. The public members led the discussion. They thought that the wage settlement would have to be reduced and that a majority could be mustered for this action. On the other hand, they were disposed to approve the pension and health insurance improvements without change because of the ambiguity of the new legislation and the complexity of the issues raised by any effort to achieve uniform treatment across the five companies. Within this context the public members were considering reducing the settlement to about 9.5 percent, or 47 cents. This approach implied a reduction of 13.5 cents in the wage settlement. Of the 13.5 cents, 10 cents would be moved forward and approved as part of the second-year wage increase. The remaining 3.5 cents would "disappear"; that is, be cut from the settlement. This formula had the attraction of appearing to impose a large reduction but cushioning its effect by permitting the payment of most of the reduction in the following year.

The public members viewed this proposal as a basis for further discussion rather than as a firm offer. Because two of the members, Jacoby and Caples, were not present and a firm consensus had not yet taken shape within the group, it was not possible to make a commitment. The union representatives listened noncommittally and asked that consideration of the proposal be deferred until after the Christmas recess. Both Greathouse and Winpisinger were alternates and obviously did not have the discretion to reach an agreement. In addition, the UAW and the IAM had strong democratic traditions, and considerable spadework would have to be done with the local union leadership and the rank and file. Although the public members believed they had made it clear that the proposal was merely exploratory, within the peculiar psychological framework of conventional collective bargaining the union representatives had some basis for assuming that a firm offer had been laid on the table.

Any expectation that these discussions would lead to a constructive agreement was dissipated when the board members reassembled on January 4, one day before the next formal meeting. First, the business members balked at the approach that had been developed by the rump group of public members and continued to press for a deeper cut in the wage settlement. Second, the formula itself did not stand the test of detailed application and was rejected by the labor representatives as a basis for their tacit acquiescence to a wage cut.

On the morning of January 4, a separate meeting was again held in Judge Boldt's office that included all the public members, Leonard Woodcock, Greathouse, and Ken Bannon, another UAW vice-president. The meeting began with a statement from Woodcock that even though the union might go along with a reduction, it should be understood that the UAW would file suit in the federal courts and argue that the Pay Board had erred in its decision by treating the residual COLA as new money rather than as a commitment under the previous contract. The public members indicated that they understood the need for this action and had no objection in principle.

Woodcock then asked for a confirmation of the details of the proposed formula. Specifically he inquired if the 9.5 percent increase to be approved was all "real pennies" or included roll-up. By real pennies Woodcock meant actual increases in the base wage of the employees covered by the collective bargaining agreement. In fact, the Pay Board had no explicit policy governing the inclusion of roll-up in its calculations, and the concept itself had not been clearly articulated. Moreover, the issue had not been considered in the earlier discussions of the proposed 9.5 percent approval. Within this void, the public members replied that the 9.5 percent did indeed include roll-up. The implications of this off-the-cuff determination were direct and severe from the union's point of view. Instead of receiving 47 cents in real pennies, the amount would be reduced to about 40 cents, with the additional 7 cents committed for roll-up. Therefore the overall loss to the employees would be 10 cents for one year and an additional 10.5 cents on a permanent basis—the cost of the roll-up and the 3.5 cents slated to "disappear."

When Woodcock learned of the inclusion of roll-up in the proposed allowable increase, he exploded. In a stream of angry comments he attacked the public members' integrity and competence, individually and collectively. The outburst obviously aborted the effort to fashion a compromise and further inflamed labor's mistrust of, and hostility toward, the wage control program.

When the attempt to build a compromise between the public members and the labor members failed, the process of decisionmaking shifted back to discussions between the two groups. As noted previously, the business representatives originally called for a reduction of the wage increase to 7 percent. The public members continued to press for a more moderate cut. Whether Woodcock's behavior had been a spontaneous display of wrath or a bargaining tactic of the moment, it clearly had exerted pressure on the public members to act in a restrained manner.

The formula adopted was a more stringent version of the approach that had been developed in efforts to strike a compromise with the labor representatives. The allowable wage increase had two components: an amount equal to the general pay standard of 5.5 percent, or 27.4 cents in the case of North American Rockwell, and 17 cents for one-half of the residual COLA carried forward from the previous contract. These two elements totaled 44.4 cents. Although the public and business members rejected the notion that the residual COLA was part of the base calculation, they recognized the strong equitable claim involved and decided to approve half a loaf. In addition, the remaining half, or another 17 cents, would be given prior approval as a meritorious supplement to the second-year wage adjustment prescribed by the contract. This prospective approval was counterbalanced by the deduction of the amount that was expected to be generated by the application of the escalator clause in the three months that had passed since October 1, 1971, the effective date of the contract. This amount was estimated to be 3 cents. Furthermore, roll-up was included in the gross amount that was approved. Therefore the approved wage increase (which the board rounded to 34 cents) consisted of the following elements (in cents):

Allowable under the general pay standard of 5.5 percent	27.4
One-half residual COLA	17.0
Minus COLA increase since October 1, 1972	− 3.0
Allowable wage increase	41.4
Minus roll-up	7.0
Net allowable wage increase	34.4

Last, the decision provided for the approval of all pension and health insurance improvements without change. This formula of 34 cents plus all fringe benefits was applied to the five aerospace contracts. Because of differences in the base and in the method of funding benefits, the percentage varied from case to case.

The finale to the aerospace case came in a meeting of the full board convened on January 5, 1972. At the beginning of the session, Pat Greathouse, Woodcock's alternate, introduced a resolution calling for the approval of the five aerospace contracts in accordance with their terms. He followed with a long and detailed defense of the agreements. After some formal debate, the motion to approve was defeated, nine to five, with all the labor members voting for the resolution and all the business and public members voting against (Judge Boldt abstaining). Woodcock, who was also present but who deferred to Greathouse for most of the discussion, then stated that he was withdrawing all the contracts between the UAW and the aerospace companies from the board's consideration. Judge Boldt responded by ruling that a unilateral withdrawal was ineffective and that the board would not relinquish jurisdiction over the cases.

After extended haggling, the public members submitted a resolution formally disapproving the five aerospace contracts on the ground that they were "unreasonably inconsistent with the purposes and objectives of the Economic Stabilization Act . . . and . . . contrary to the standards and criteria established by the Pay Board"[43]—the ungainly rhetoric that had been fashioned by the board's lawyers to lay a foundation for a wage reduction. The resolution was approved, nine to zero, with the labor members abstaining, presumably to show their unwillingness to accept the board's authority.

With these preliminaries out of the way, the final resolution was introduced stating the terms of the board's approval. The resolution was structured so that it gave the chairman the right to approve the aerospace contracts that met the standards of the formula of 34 cents.[44] When the outcome of the vote was foreordained (nine to five in favor), the labor and business members asked for a delay. A majority of the board granted the delay until the next day and then agreed to an extension until January 13 so that the unions and companies involved could discuss the implications of the prospective board decision and begin to renegotiate the terms. The resolution was formally approved on January 23, 1972. The original terms were unchanged, but some variations were permitted in their application in recognition of the special circumstances in individual cases.

In this characteristically halting, if not confused, manner the Pay Board had achieved its first cutback. When the entire economic package was considered, the action was not draconian, but the impact on the public and the board itself was considerable.

43. Minutes of the Pay Board, January 5, 1972, exhibit 1.
44. Ibid. The resolution gave the chairman the right to approve the five agreements that had been "heretofore disapproved" as long as the enumerated conditions were met. In fact, it was intended that the chairman have some discretion.

VI

More Last Cows

The last two of the "last cows" were of the same species, although they were significantly different in their detailed markings. Both cases involved agreements between longshore unions and maritime employers. The first contract considered was between the International Longshoremen's and Warehousemen's Union (ILWU) and the Pacific Maritime Association (PMA) and came to the Pay Board in March 1972. The second case concerned the International Longshoremen's Association (ILA) and various employer groups along the East and Gulf coasts and was decided in early May 1972. When the Pay Board issued its ruling on the ILA agreement, it finally completed the transition from the precontrol period of free collective bargaining to the encumbrances of Phase II.

These cases were considered in a context quite unlike that which had characterized the first three disputes. By March 1972 the Pay Board had completed formulating the major policies and supporting regulations that would govern the wage stabilization program for the duration of Phase II, except for minor changes. This meant that both longshore contracts would be subject to review in the light of explicit standards and computational rules. The absence of such guidance had permitted wide latitude for the introduction of novel concepts of equity and other notions that lacked precision. Indeed in the early days of the Pay Board sharp controversies had developed over issues that would have been routinely disposed of under subsequent board rules. For example, under the regulations developed *after* the bituminous coal case had been decided, an increase in payments necessary to maintain an existing level of benefits was not counted as part of the cost of the contract. Therefore the additional royalty of 45 cents a ton agreed to in the coal case would have been allowed automatically.

By the time the ILWU case reached the Pay Board, the agency had been established as a going concern and had partially repaired its credibility. In January the board had instituted the first pay cut in a major case, that of the aerospace industry. The railroad decision served notice that the Pay Board had the will to maintain its presence in a case whose impact on the economy would stretch over a long period of time. In addition, the machinery had been established for the systematic review of deferred increases in the contracts that had been negotiated before the outset of Phase II. Under these circumstances the public and business members of the board did not feel compelled to take a tough position for broad institutional reasons that might influence their perception of the merits of individual cases.

The West Coast Longshoremen's Case

The West Coast longshoremen's case had many of the same ingredients as the railroad dispute—prolonged negotiations, a major strike, government intervention in various forms, and work rule changes and productivity as central to the final outcome. One of the major differences between the two cases, however, was the nature of the longshoremen's union and the industry bargaining structure. The ILWU was formally constituted in 1937, when it became the successor to the Pacific Coast District of the ILA. The founding of the ILWU was part of the resurgence of unionization associated with the formation of the CIO and broad industrial organization. Thus the ILWU had a ready-made history of bitter employer resistance and a high incidence of conflict, if not bloodshed. Unionism had won a foothold in the West Coast longshore industry in the 1890s. But major strikes were lost in 1901 and 1916, and the longshoremen's union went into a long twilight period during the 1920s when for all intents and purposes it ceased to function.[1]

Labor-Management Relations

Labor organization along the West Coast was rekindled in the thirties. In an epic eighty-four-day strike in 1934, the longshoremen's union won employer recognition. Widespread violence marked the strike, which precipitated a general strike by all unionized workers in San Francisco in support of the longshoremen. The 1934 strike was the first battle in a prolonged guerilla war between the employers and the union. Between 1934 and 1948 a series of strikes and "job actions" occurred that made

1. See Charles P. Larrowe, *Shape-Up and Hiring Hall: A Comparison of Hiring Methods and Labor Relations on the New York and Seattle Waterfronts* (University of California Press, 1955), p. 91.

the West Coast longshoring industry one of the most turbulent sectors on the American labor scene. These skirmishes culminated in a ninety-five-day strike in 1948, an episode that exhausted the parties and persuaded them that mutual acceptance, even at a price, was preferable to unremitting hostility. After the 1948 strike, labor-management relations in the West Coast longshoring industry were generally peaceful.[2] Indeed, as noted below, the relationship was distinguished by one of the most far-reaching innovations in contemporary American collective bargaining.

During this painful evolution of labor-management relations in the West Coast longshore industry, the progress of the ILWU was linked with the leadership of Harry Bridges. Bridges spent his early years in Australia, came to the United States in 1920, and was deeply involved in efforts to unionize the West Coast waterfront. He became president of the ILWU in 1937 and continued to hold that position through 1971 and 1972 when the events associated with the Pay Board case took place. Over the years Bridges was an outspoken advocate of left-wing causes and ideology. In 1941 the U.S. government unsuccessfully tried to deport Bridges on the grounds that he had concealed his early political affiliations.[3] In 1950 the ILWU was expelled from the CIO—along with ten other unions—for being Communist-dominated. Despite these attacks by both the established labor federations and the government, Bridges maintained an unassailable position within the union. After being ousted from the CIO, the ILWU operated on an unaffiliated basis. With the passage of time, it has lost much of its stigma and is viewed with respect, if not approval, by the rest of the labor movement.

The Pacific Maritime Association, the counterpart organization on the employers' side, was founded in 1949 as the successor to an array of separate employer associations. The PMA consisted of 122 member companies in three industry groupings: ship-operating companies; stevedoring companies and terminal operators; and public agencies, such as port authorities. The primary function of the PMA was to act as the negotiator for its members in their dealings with the various maritime and longshore unions. The leadership of the PMA has been distinguished for its skill and capacity to innovate in labor-management relations.

The bargaining unit for negotiations between the ILWU and the PMA included all the major ports along the West Coast. This unit determina-

2. Ibid., pp. 130–31.
3. See Charles P. Larrowe, *Harry Bridges: The Rise and Fall of Radical Labor in the United States* (Lawrence Hill, 1972), pp. 324–25.

tion was made by the National Labor Relations Board in 1938. The ILWU had requested a multiport unit in order to help insulate it from potential raiding by rival unions. A single master agreement covered most aspects of wages, hours, working conditions, and fringe benefits in all the ports.[4] Supplementary agreements were negotiated for individual ports, but they had limited economic significance.

The Mechanization and Modernization Agreement

The most noteworthy achievement in the ILWU-PMA bargaining relationship was the negotiation of the so-called Mechanization and Modernization (M&M) Agreement in October 1960. This agreement marked the beginning of a new era in West Coast longshore union-management relations. Up to this time the ILWU had followed the path trod by most unions in the transportation industries. Great emphasis was placed on detailed work rules to preserve employment and earning opportunities for the longshoremen. The price of these work rules was a severe limitation on the employer's discretion in controlling stevedoring operations and a lackluster record in productivity and labor cost. The labor agreements rigidly prescribed crew size, sling loads, and loading procedures, all to the detriment of efficiency. For example, certain contract clauses prescribed the multiple handling of cargo whereby shipments trucked to the dock and unloaded on a pallet had to be removed from the pallet and placed directly on the "skin of the dock" before the longshoremen could handle the cargo.

This traditional, restrictive approach was changed radically by the M&M agreement. Under the terms of the contract, the employers were now given wide discretion in the introduction of new technology and work methods. Management in return agreed to establish a $27.5 million fund over a period of five and a half years to provide a wide range of benefits for the incumbent work force. All longshoremen and clerks with a history of extended attachment to the industry labor force (Class A men) were qualified for payments for thirty-six months or a lump sum of $7,920 in addition to their regular benefits of $220 a month upon normal or early retirement. By mutual consent the union and the PMA could also require mandatory early retirement at age sixty-two. Longshoremen subject to mandatory early retirement would receive $320 a month, rather than $220, until they reached sixty-five years of age. Still

4. Ibid., pp. 127–29.

another benefit afforded disability payments for longshoremen with as few as fifteen years of service. In this manner the M&M agreement established a variety of programs to induce attrition and thereby reduce the number of claimants for available employment. Moreover, those who did work were covered by a wage guarantee that became operative when actual hours of work dropped below thirty-five a week.[5]

The original contract was extended for five years in 1966. The companies pledged an additional $34.5 million to improve the various retirement, income support, and disability benefit programs. The wage guarantee was dropped from the contract at the union's behest, since job opportunities had not declined significantly during the five-year term of the first agreement. The surplus in the wage guarantee fund was distributed to the "A" men as lump-sum payments on a pro rata basis.[6]

Thus for the eleven years preceding the 1971 negotiations, the employers had enjoyed considerable flexibility in introducing new work methods and manning requirements. Although measuring output in the longshore industry is a difficult task because of variations in cargo mix, careful estimates indicate that labor productivity rose by 130 percent over the eleven-year period. This prodigious increase contributed to a one-third decline in the labor cost per ton handled.[7] By any standard this was a spectacular performance and justified the claims of the parties that the M&M agreement had broken new, fertile ground in American labor-management relations to the benefit of both the parties and the public.

Troubles at the Bargaining Table

Despite—or because of—this auspicious record, the negotiation of the new ILWU-PMA contract promised to be complex and contentious. First,

5. "Mechanization and Modernization Agreement," Technical Paper 9, EPCA-EAD, Micro 10, in "Pay Board Staff Submission Papers," PMA-ILWU (March 14, 1972; processed), pp. 62–67. Also see *Improving Productivity: Labor and Management Approaches,* prepared for the National Commission on Productivity by the U.S. Bureau of Labor Statistics (Government Printing Office, September 1971), pp. 8–9.
6. "Mechanization and Modernization Agreement."
7. "Productivity in the West Coast Longshore Industry," Technical Paper 10, EAD-13 in "Pay Board Staff Submission Papers," table 2, p. 74. For a detailed exposition of the problems of productivity measurement in the longshore industry and experience under the M&M agreement, see Paul T. Hartman, *Collective Bargaining and Productivity: The Longshore Mechanization Agreement* (University of California Press, 1969).

five years had passed since the last agreement, and many inevitable problems had developed that could only be resolved at the bargaining table.
Second, the winding down of the Vietnam war had reduced the tonnage
handled by ILWU members on the West Coast. The union's concern over
employment and earnings also was heightened by the spread of containerization. This method of handling cargo trimmed labor requirements
and, equally serious, shifted work to union members in the Teamsters'
jurisdiction. Third, there was some indication that political opposition to
Bridges's leadership was taking shape within the ILWU in response to
this uneasiness about the impact of the M&M agreement and diverse internal factors.

The long, quarrelsome course of bargaining began November 16, 1970,
seven and a half months before the scheduled expiration of the contract
on June 30, 1971. Discussions continued until mid-December when they
were suspended on procedural grounds. They resumed again in February,
but no real progress was made. By June the parties were still at logger-
heads. The main points in dispute were the overall size of the wage increase and the ILWU's insistence on the reinstitution of a pay guarantee
plan to provide income protection for its members in the face of the new
economic uncertainties confronting the industry.

As the contract termination date approached, the parties initiated continuous discussions in an effort to reach an agreement. The last-minute
concessions were insufficient to close the gap, and on July 1 the ILWU
struck, shutting down virtually all port facilities along the West Coast.
The strike was peaceful, but additional efforts to conclude an agreement
were unsuccessful. In September President Nixon, who was en route to
greet Emperor Hirohito in Alaska, met with Harry Bridges in Portland,
Oregon, to impress upon the union leader his personal interest in an
early settlement to the strike.

The meeting of President Nixon with Bridges, the venerable left-wing
labor leader, was heavy with irony.[8] It did not facilitate a settlement. On
October 6, after the strike had been in progress for 100 days, the federal
government invoked the national emergency provisions of the Taft-Hartley Act and, as directed by the court, the workers returned to the docks for
an eighty-day cooling-off period. At the end of the eighty days, the union

8. When President Nixon was a senator from California in the late 1940s and
in the 1950s, he had developed a reputation as a militant anti-Communist, both in
U.S. domestic affairs and in international relations. As noted earlier, Bridges had
been something of a cause célèbre during this era.

members voted on the PMA's last offer, as prescribed by the Taft-Hartley Act. Consistent with prior experience in other industries, the employers' last offer was overwhelmingly rejected by the rank and file members.

After exhausting these procedures the parties reverted to normal bargaining procedures. Again, efforts to break the impasse were inconclusive, and the strike resumed on January 17. As the impact of the strike on the national economy became more severe, management and union representatives were summoned before the labor committee of both the House of Representatives and the Senate. The clear implication of this step was that unless the ILWU and the PMA soon reached a voluntary agreement, Congress would impose a settlement. Experience during the prolonged railroad dispute indicated that Congress would overcome its distaste for intervention in collective bargaining and would set the terms of an agreement if the case involved an essential industry. Under this duress the ILWU and the PMA finally reached a two-year accord on February 10, 1972. The settlement was ratified by the rank and file on February 20.[9] After fifteen months of negotiations and a cumulative strike of 134 days, the longshoremen returned to the docks. In the intervening period, the nation had been plunged into direct wage and price controls and the Pay Board had painfully evolved its basic policies and standards. The parties submitted the agreement to the board on February 25, 1972.

The most distinctive feature of the agreement, aside from its overall cost, was the new pay guarantee plan. All fully registered longshoremen and clerks (Class A members) whose earnings had been reduced as a result of technological change were guaranteed a weekly minimum of thirty-six hours of straight-time pay. The so-called Class B men, who had less work experience in the industry, were guaranteed eighteen hours of pay a week. These guarantees would be financed by the proceeds of a $1 tax paid by the stevedoring companies on containers that were "stuffed" or "stripped" within fifty miles of the port dispatch hall by workers other than ILWU members. If the proceeds of the tax were inadequate to defray the total cost of the guarantees, the balance would be paid directly by the employers. It is significant to note that the pay guarantee was designed as a replacement for the prior M&M agreement whereby the employers had been committed to pay $34.5 million over a five-year period for special retirement and disability benefits.

9. "History of the Current Settlement," in "Pay Board Staff Submission Papers," p. 2.

Table 6-1. *Increase in Total Compensation, PMA-ILWU Agreement,*
First Year

Dollars

Item	Amount of increase
Total compensation in base period (including all fringe benefits)	7.123
Average wage increase	0.806
Includable fringe benefits	0.105
Pay guarantee plan	0.105
Roll-up	0.257
Qualified fringe benefits	0.677
Life insurance	0.077
Sickness and accident benefits	0.015
Other insurance	0.112
Pensions	0.473
Increase in total compensation	1.845
Addenda:	
Percent increase, wage and includable fringe benefits	16.40
Percent increase, qualified fringe benefits	9.50
Total percent increase	25.90

Source: "Staff Calculation of Percentage Change in First Contract Year," and "First Contract Year Increments," Pay Board Staff Submission Papers (March 14, 1972; processed), pp. 12–14.

Pay Board Steps In, Labor Walks Out

The Pay Board review of the ILWU-PMA agreement indicated that it was far in excess of the board's standards. The staff analysis was more refined (if not more rigid) than in earlier cases and showed the effects of bureaucratic elaboration (table 6-1).

The PMA-ILWU contract came before the full Pay Board on March 14, 1972. As was now the standard practice in major cases, a public hearing was convened and appearances were made by the principles, including Harry Bridges for the ILWU. The union and management spokesmen presented a common front in calling for Pay Board approval of the agreement without modification. The greatest emphasis was given to the fact that the new contract maintained the parties' commitment to technological change and productivity improvements. Their performance under the previous M&M agreements had demonstrated that these productivity gains were not illusory. Further advances in efficiency could be expected from the increased use of containerization and LASH (lighter aboard ship)—a method for loading and unloading complete units on cargo ships. Both containerization and LASH held the promise of major improvements in longshore productivity. Thus approval of the contract was wholly consistent with the board's statutory mandate "to foster economic growth" and indeed was required to protect "the equitable position of the employees involved."[10]

On a less lofty level, both the union and management noted that the contract was the product of fifteen months of negotiations and a 134-day strike. Moreover, the settlement had been reached under direct pressure from Congress. In discussing the subpoena to appear before the House Subcommittee on Labor, the spokesman for the PMA said, "Without a doubt, the parties were convinced to settle voluntarily or 'be legislated.' "[11] Any attempt by the Pay Board to alter the terms of the settlement would have upset the balance that had been achieved so painfully. Although never stated directly, the obvious implication was that a negative Pay Board ruling could precipitate another strike with deleterious consequences for the economy.

In addition to these appeals on principle, the parties pressed two important technical arguments. First, they asserted that the Pay Board should make an allowance for the discontinuance of the M&M fund in calculating the cost of the settlement. Under the prior contract the employers' contributions to the fund had been equivalent to 31.2 cents for each man-hour worked. The new agreement abolished the fund and established the pay guarantee plan. The plan served the same purpose as the fund in providing income security for longshoremen who otherwise would be adversely affected by technological change. Therefore the board should allow an M&M offset equal to the full 31.2 cents per hour.

Second, the parties argued that the first-year cost of the pay guarantee plan should be valued at 2.6 cents an hour, not 10.5 cents, as calculated by the board staff. The 2.6 cents was justified on the basis of estimates of the amount of revenue that would be generated by the container tax during the first year. On the other hand, the estimate of 10.5 cents was based on PMA projections of the probable disbursements that would have to be made for the pay guarantees. Under the terms of the contract the difference between the container tax revenues and the actual payments under the guarantee would be an out-of-pocket cost to the employers.

10. Pay Board Regulations, sec. 201.11(d).
11. "Statement of Pacific Maritime Association before U.S. Pay Board" (PMA, n.d.; processed), p. 5.

Following the open hearing the public members took the lead in developing the Pay Board ruling in the case. It was agreed that the M&M offset should be allowed for the reasons stated by the parties. This adjustment, along with other technical changes, reduced the increase in "excludable fringes" to 4.9 percent; board regulations allowed 1.9 percent. Nonetheless, the public members agreed to approve all these fringe benefit improvements on the grounds that they were necessary to maintain union support of the productivity improvement program.

The disposition of the wage increase (including roll-up and includable fringe benefits) was more difficult. The public members agreed that the higher figure of 10.5 cents should be used for costing the pay guarantee plan, since this amount constituted the probable payout under the plan. Using this calculation, one faction among the public members pressed for cutting the wage increase from 16.4 percent to 7 percent, the maximum amount for which the longshoremen qualified under the board's "catchup" formula. It was argued that the overall settlement was so large that it had to be reduced by this amount in order to maintain the integrity of the board's pay standard. Allowance had already been made for the special productivity sharing arrangements by approving the total package of qualified fringe benefits. This line of reasoning was countered by the contention that a reduction of the wage increase to 7 percent would be too harsh and would undermine the ILWU's incentives to preserve the constructive industrial relations climate that had prevailed since 1960. Moreover, so sizable a cut would arouse the support of other unions in the AFL-CIO who otherwise would not be particularly sympathetic to the ILWU.

Ultimately the public members worked out a compromise formula. The total cost of employer contributions to the M&M fund since 1960 was ascertained (about $60 million) and then distributed on a cents-per-hour basis for all man-hours worked under the agreement since 1960. This distribution amounted to a wage increase of approximately 3 percent a year. The 3 percent a year was accepted as the "productivity increment" and was added to the 7 percent for a total allowable wage increase of 10 percent. The total package approved by the board would be 14.9 percent, incorporating the improvements in qualified fringe benefits.

The public members then approached the business members, who agreed to the compromise approach without modification. The last hurdle was the labor bloc. The labor members listened to the details of the proposed decision without comment. The public members were prepared for further discussion about the terms of the decision and were surprised by the passive response. Even the usual haggling over calculations was absent. The Pay Board decision in the West Coast longshore case was announced on March 16, 1972, and conformed to the formula that had been developed by the public members. Any disposition toward self-congratulation for shaping an acceptable package was nullified, however, when seven days later four of the five labor members walked off the Pay Board, citing the ILWU decision as evidence of the inequity of the wage stabilization program.[12]

The East Coast Longshoremen's Case

The resolution of the ILWU-PMA dispute set the stage for consideration of a companion case involving the East Coast longshoremen. The Pay Board action in this case followed the West Coast decision by five weeks. In the interim the board had been reconstituted on an all-public basis following the departure of the four labor members. In effect the first major decision of the reorganized board was the last of the last cows.

East-West Differences

The East Coast and West Coast longshore cases had some obvious similarities and equally important differences. Each dispute involved different geographical segments of the same industry. Both bargaining agreements included complex guaranteed income plans with conjectural cost estimates. And each settlement had been a product of protracted negotiations, a major strike, and direct government intervention. These similarities did not mean that the East Coast dispute could be disposed of by the mechanical application of the ILWU-PMA decision. Instead, the West Coast case provided a standard for comparison that had to be given weight for political purposes but preserved the flexibility for differential treatment based on the special characteristics of union organization, bargaining structure, and bargaining practices along the East Coast.

The longshoremen in ports reaching from Maine to Florida and along the Gulf Coast from Alabama to Texas were represented by the International Longshoremen's Association. Although the ILA was an AFL affil-

12. See *Statement Adopted by the AFL-CIO Executive Council, March 22, 1972* (AFL-CIO, n.d.).

iate, it had long adopted a live-and-let-live policy toward the ILWU. Except for a few footholds gained during the 1930s, the ILA had been content to leave the West Coast to the ILWU. Similarly, the ILWU generally had respected the ILA's jurisdiction along the Atlantic and Gulf coasts. The maintenance of these separate spheres of influence was feasible because ports on the West and East coasts were not competitive with each other in any real sense. For the greater part they served different shipping companies and different maritime routes. Only under very special circumstances would it be attractive to transfer shipping from one coast to the other in response to labor cost differentials. Each union could operate in its own preserve without great sensitivity to the other's policies and bargaining strategy. In fact, there were significant differences in bargaining policies. As indicated earlier, the ILWU had taken a very progressive approach to the problem of work rules and productivity. In contrast, the ILA had moved very slowly in this area, and only in the late sixties did it show noticeable flexibility on the productivity issue.[13]

Perhaps the sharpest difference between the ILWU and the ILA was ideological. The ILWU had long been identified as a left-wing union and in the late 1940s had been involved in work stoppages with strong political overtones. The union's opposition to the Marshall Plan contributed to its expulsion from the CIO in 1950. In contrast, the ILA adhered to a conservative position on foreign affairs and domestic issues. Indeed its leadership was frequently identified with expressions of patriotism—if not jingoism—and outspoken anti-Communism. For many years, the ILA had a policy of encouraging its members not to load or unload ships from the Soviet Union.

If the ILA was a bastion of conservative ideology, it was also distinguished for its long history of undemocratic practices and racketeering. For many years the union had been closely controlled by its president, Joseph P. Ryan. At one stage, his authority was so complete that the membership was inspired to elect him as president for life. ILA locals, particularly in the New York City area, gained great notoriety during the 1940s and 1950s because of their complicity in various schemes involving extortion of the shipping companies, favoritism, payoffs in hiring, and the systematic pilfering of cargoes. These activities were the topic of journal-

13. "Work Rules," Technical Paper 3, EPCA-EAD, Micro 31; and "Productivity, Unit Labor Cost, Prices, and Capital Investment," Technical Paper 8, EPCA-EAD, Micro 36, in Pay Board, "East and Gulf Coast Longshore: Summary and Analysis of PB Forms" (May 2, 1972; processed).

istic exposés, government investigations and, perhaps the highest compliment, a popular motion picture.[14] The exposés culminated in bi-state legislation passed by New York and New Jersey that set up a government-supervised hiring hall for the port of New York and interposed other legal restrictions on labor-management relations on the waterfront. During the course of these events the ILA was expelled from the AFL for corruption and violation of the federation's Code of Ethical Practices.[15] Under these severe external pressures, the ILA underwent a significant transformation during the late 1950s and 1960s that partially restored its respectability and revitalized its capacities as a bargaining agent. In 1959 it was permitted to reaffiliate with the AFL-CIO.[16]

The 1972 agreement that came to the Pay Board for review was part of this continuing process of rehabilitating collective bargaining in the East Coast longshore industry. By 1972 the ILA's unsavory reputation had receded and was familiar only to movie buffs and students of labor history. Nonetheless, the ILA was still sharply distinguishable from the ILWU in ideology and bargaining practices. In the contemporary setting, the ILA had been identified with the "hard hat" movement of labor conservatives who had actively supported the Nixon administration.

Consolidating Negotiating Units

The most significant difference between the ILWU and ILA concerned the structure of collective bargaining. As noted previously, the ILWU for many years had conducted collective bargaining on a coast-wide basis, dealing with a single employer association. This arrangement had promoted uniformity of wages and working conditions among the ports along the West Coast. It had also created a framework for the development of stable union-management relations and innovations in collective bargaining.

In contrast, the bargaining structure within the ILA's jurisdiction had remained in a state of partial consolidation. For many years the ILA bargained with the employers on a port-by-port basis. Typically, the bargaining round commenced with negotiations covering the local unions in the port of New York. When these locals reached an agreement with the

14. The film was *On the Waterfront,* starring Marlon Brando. See "Waterfront Film Dramatizes the Real," *Business Week,* August 7, 1954, pp. 94–98.

15. *New York Times,* September 23, 1953.

16. Ibid., August 18, 1959.

New York Shipping Association, the employers' collective-bargaining organization, the settlement would establish the bench mark for the other ports. Bargaining would then proceed on an individual port basis down the Atlantic and Gulf coasts. Although the New York agreement set the pattern, there were significant differences in wages and other conditions of employment among the various ports. Emphasis was placed on uniform *improvements* rather than on common contract terms.

Because of the instability generated by this loose structure, the ILA pressed the employers for coast-wide bargaining within the Atlantic Coast District, that is, from Searsport, Maine, to Hampton Roads, Virginia. The employers rejected this demand, preferring the discretion afforded by negotiations on an individual port basis. In 1956 the ILA launched a concerted drive for a multi-port bargaining unit. After a long strike, the employer associations in the North Atlantic ports other than New York agreed that New York could execute a master contract whose terms would cover the entire district. The ports covered by this arrangement included New York, as the pattern-setter, Boston, Providence, Philadelphia, Baltimore, and Hampton Roads. The terms of the master contract applicable to these ports would be limited to five issues: (1) wages, (2) hours of work, (3) contributions to welfare plans (but not benefit levels), (4) contributions to the pension plans (but not the level of pension benefits), and (5) the duration of the agreement.[17]

This limited master agreement approach was introduced in 1956 and continued to be used in negotiations in 1959, 1962, 1964, and 1968. Shortly before the 1971 bargaining round began, the employer associations in the ports covered by the master contract converted their loose alliance into a formal organization that included all employers in the Atlantic Coast District. The new association, the Council of North Atlantic Shipping Associations (CONASA), could now speak with a single voice for the employers in the six ports. The votes were distributed among the ports on a roughly proportional basis, the New York employers holding 40 percent of the votes. Before the 1971 negotiations the ILA and CONASA agreed to add two new issues to the topics covered by the master contract: containerization and LASH.

Parallel steps were taken to consolidate employer negotiating units in

17. "Joint Application of the Council of North Atlantic Shipping Associations (CONASA) and the International Longshoremen's Association, AFL-CIO, to the Federal Pay Board, March 31, 1972," in "East and Gulf Coast Longshore Submissions of the Parties" (n.d.; processed), pp. 3–8.

ports outside the Atlantic Coast District. Employers in ports from Lake Charles, Louisiana, to Brownsville, Texas, formed the West Gulf Maritime Association (WGMA). The stevedoring companies in New Orleans, on the other hand, continued to bargain through a separate organization, the New Orleans Steamship Association (NOSSA). The CONASA covered approximately 28,000 waterfront workers; the WGMA, 11,000; and the NOSSA, 10,200.[18] The association-wide contracts were supplemented by local agreements covering work rules and other special issues. In this complex structure, the ILA and CONASA negotiations obviously would dominate, but there was still the opportunity for local discretion, if not disruption.

The Issue of Guaranteed Annual Income

Negotiations between the ILA and the CONASA over the terms of a new agreement commenced on August 18, 1971. Bargaining immediately hit a procedural snag. The ILA demanded that the guaranteed annual income (GAI), which was designed to facilitate productivity, be designated a master contract item applicable to all ports represented in the CONASA. The East Coast stevedoring industry, like its West Coast counterpart, had long been beset with work rules and practices that had severely constrained labor productivity. In 1963, following one of the recurrent industry strikes, the U.S. Department of Labor offered its services to study the situation and to propose new mechanisms for stabilizing labor-management relations. This study paved the way for an employer proposal whereby the union would permit the mechanization of longshoring operations in return for income guarantees for the ILA members. The proposal also was part of a broad effort to decasualize the labor market. That is, the plan would offer stable, high-level earnings for workers with a high degree of industry attachment. Longshoremen who had been paid for 700 hours or more in the previous year would be guaranteed 1,600 hours of work or pay at straight-time rates. In return the ILA agreed to a reduction in gang-size and increased flexibility in work assignments. The plan was accepted by the ILA in New York and adopted with modifications in other Atlantic ports. It was liberalized in 1968, when the guarantee was increased to 2,080 hours for all qualified ILA members.

In seeking the designation of the GAI as a master contract issue, the union argued that technological change affected the job opportunities of

18. "East and Gulf Coast Longshore: Summary and Analysis," p. 1.

all its members and therefore the issue should be negotiated on an association-wide basis. The CONASA rejected this demand on the grounds that the plan had developed uniquely in each of the ports and that discussions should be continued at the local level in order to permit the parties to shape it to their special circumstances. The dispute was resolved on August 31 when the ILA acceded to the CONASA's position and agreed that the GAI should be considered on a port-by-port basis. The CONASA in turn agreed that local negotiations on the guaranteed income plan should precede coast-wide bargaining on the seven master contract items. Thus the ILA could hold the master contract terms hostage to the successful resolution of the GAI issue as it was considered in the individual ports.

This bargaining sequence proved to be an impediment to reaching an agreement before the existing contract expired on September 30, 1971. Because the parties were unable to settle the GAI issue on a local basis, they were not able to resolve, or to even discuss in detail, the master contract items. Consequently the New York longshoremen struck on October 1 and were followed to the picket line by ILA members from Maine to Texas. The strike dragged on through October and well into November. The deadlock over changes in the GAI in the port of New York was not broken until mid-November. On November 17 the ILA and the CONASA finally turned their full attention to the seven master contract issues. Bargaining along the Gulf Coast and in New Orleans marked time until a settlement had been reached in the Atlantic Coast District. As the strike dragged on, its economic impact intensified. On November 24 President Nixon convened a Board of Inquiry under the emergency strike provisions of the Taft-Hartley Act. Acting on the recommendation of the Board of Inquiry, the U.S. Attorney General obtained a temporary restraining order against the strike on November 26. This order was the preliminary to an eighty-day cooling-off period prescribed by the statute.

Under this pressure the ILA and the CONASA announced a tentative agreement on the master contract issues on January 6, 1972. This settlement did not end the strike, however, since local issues still had to be resolved. On January 21 the ILA and the New York Shipping Association (which was a component of the CONASA for purposes of negotiating master contract issues) finally reached an agreement on all local items. Once this bottleneck was dissolved, the ILA could make progress in negotiations with the WGMA, the NOSSA, and the other employer groups in the individual ports within the CONASA. This complicated process of multiple-tier negotiations edged forward through January and into February 1972. Although the Taft-Hartley injunction expired on February 14, the ILA agreed to continue discussions for thirty days without reinstituting the strike. Agreements were reached in most of the ports before the expiration of this grace period.[19]

The announcement of tentative agreements did not restore labor peace to the docks. The contracts required ratification by the individual ILA locals in each port. When the first vote was taken, the agreements were rejected by the membership in Philadelphia, Boston, Baltimore, and Providence. The leadership instituted an intensive selling campaign to the rank and file before resubmitting the contracts for their approval. This campaign was effective, and the last local agreement was ratified in Philadelphia on March 29, 1972. The conclusion of the East Coast longshore dispute was barely noticed in the furor surrounding the walkout of the four labor members from the Pay Board a few days earlier.

The key settlement in the bargaining structure—and the Pay Board's deliberations—involved the ILA-CONASA contract. The economic terms of the contract as presented by the parties and as calculated by the Pay Board staff are shown in table 6-2.

After lengthy discussions at the staff level between the parties and the Pay Board, the two economic analyses of the ILA-CONASA contract agreed in almost all details. The base compensation rate was estimated at $8.36 an hour, the increase in the straight-time hourly rate was 70 cents and the total cost of all benefit improvements, including roll-up, was 31.2 cents. The royalty item involved a costing of future payments to be made by the employers for using containerization, LASH, and other bulk storage and loading techniques. In effect, these royalties were a tax exacted by the union for granting management the privilege of utilizing this new technology. The royalties were used to liberalize various fringe benefits and, in some cases, for supplemental cash payments. Both the Pay Board analysis and the ILA-CONASA submission agreed that the total *gross* cost of the agreement was $1.012.

The major point of controversy between the Pay Board and the parties involved cost estimates of changes in the GAI. When the plan was introduced in 1963, it was estimated that the pay guarantee would cost about $3 million a year. The total outlays moved up steadily, however, and by 1968–69 the GAI cost New York shippers $6 million. In 1969–70

19. Ibid., pp. 1–3.

Table 6-2. *Terms of the ILA-CONASA Collective Bargaining Settlement,
as Submitted by the Parties and as Determined by Pay Board
Staff Analysis*

Dollars

Basic compensation rate and adjustments	ILA-CONASA submission	Pay Board staff analysis
Basic compensation rate	8.360	8.358
Straight-time hourly rate increase	0.700	0.700
Includable benefit adjustments (roll-up only)	0.212	0.212
Qualified benefit adjustment	0.100	0.100
Health and welfare	0.018	0.018
Pensions	0.038	0.038
Royalties	0.044	0.044
Total increase	1.012	1.012
Less claimed offset from guaranteed annual income	0.337	...
Total adjustments	0.675	1.012
Addenda:		
Adjustments as percent of base compensation Straight-time hourly increase and includable benefits	6.9	10.9
Qualified benefits	1.2	1.2
Total	8.1	12.1

Source: Pay Board, "East and Gulf Coast Longshore: Summary and Analysis of PB Forms" (May 2, 1972; processed), p. 20.

the total cost was $24.3 million, and by 1970–71 the employers were required to pay $29 million to meet their obligation under the plan. Thus when contract negotiations began in 1971, the New York employers were intent on changing the provisions of the plan to reduce costs and maintain control in the future.

Cost escalation was associated with several practices and arbitration decisions that had conditioned the administration of the program. First, the pay guarantee was used to compensate covered employees for travel time. Under existing procedures an unemployed longshoreman showed up in the hiring hall each morning for job assignment. Assignment for the day was made in the morning so that the employee could collect some of his guarantee for travel time to the pier to which he was assigned. Second, the debiting rules stated that debiting was limited to the number of job offers. If only one job was available and ten men declined the offer, only the longshoreman with the lowest seniority was charged for the day against his guarantee. Third, an unemployed longshoreman could refuse employment outside his job category. There were ten categories, and if the available job opportunities did not match the occupational identification of the unemployed longshoremen, some jobs would go unfilled and the idle longshoremen would receive a guarantee payment instead. Although the job categories incorporated specific skills and functions, it was recognized that in many cases a longshoreman in one category could do a job in another. Perhaps most righteously, the employers complained that the cost of the GAI had increased because a longshoreman who legally refused a job could accept employment for the day off the docks and receive his pay guarantee while being compensated by a nonlongshore employer.

These issues were discussed with great intensity during the ILA-CONASA negotiations. Ultimately the ILA agreed to major concessions. The number of job categories for purposes of assignment was reduced from ten to three: holdmen, other ship labor, and terminal labor. The debiting rules were changed so that the number of longshoremen debited for refusing the job was not limited by the number of jobs available. The pay guarantee was to be reduced by the amount of compensation received from employment in other industries. And the ILA agreed to a "prior-day-order" system whereby longshoremen were given their job assignments the day before and were required to report on the job at the normal working time rather than accruing travel time under the terms of the guarantee. Indeed the New York employers were so adamant on this point that they refused to extend the GAI beyond September 30 unless the union agreed to a prior-day-order system. The ILA accepted this change on December 6, 1971, before the other terms of the agreement had been spelled out and the new contract signed.

As a result of these changes, the parties estimated that the annual payout from the GAI fund would not exceed $10 million, or $30 million over the term of the contract. To demonstrate their confidence that these savings could be realized, they agreed to a 54 percent cut in the tonnage assessment that financed the GAI and other fringe benefits. Under the old contract each ton of cargo moving through the port of New York was assessed $3.23 to meet these costs. As of February 15, 1972, the tonnage charge was reduced to $1.50. If the payouts did exceed $10 million, however, the employers were obliged to pay the full guarantee, drawing on other funds established by the contract.

Complex Route to a Pay Board Decision

In their submissions to the Pay Board, both parties argued strenuously that they should be given an offset for the savings that would result from the changes in the pay guarantee. The estimated savings were $19 million a year, calculated on the basis of the $29 million cost incurred in 1970–71. When these savings were related to the total man-hours worked, they resulted in a reduction of 33.7 cents an hour in the size of the total wage increase. If a credit was given for the GAI offset, the chargeable adjustment under Pay Board rules was reduced to 67.5 cents, or 6.9 percent of the base compensation. Because the longshoremen qualified for a catch-up increase of 7 percent, the entire wage gain would be permissible. The total cost of the economic package would be reduced commensurately from 12.1 percent to 8.1 percent.

In addition to these complexities, the Pay Board's task was further complicated by external considerations. First, the East Coast longshore case was the board's first major decision since the dramatic walkout of the four labor members. For this reason the board's action would receive special scrutiny. On the one hand, the public would be taking the measure of the board to determine if it still had the capacity to act effectively in its new all-public incarnation. On the other hand, the decision would be analyzed to determine whether the board was acting harshly, if not vindictively, against labor because of the blow-up at the end of March. Whether or not these sensitivities reflected the reality of public opinion, the Pay Board members were acutely aware that their decision should appear to rise above both labor's harangues or any public perception of incipient weakness.

Second, although the ILA case was clearly separate from the West Coast longshore decision, the two situations were linked tactically. When the board reviewed the ILWU-PMA agreement, there was concern that Harry Bridges and the ILWU would never accept a reduction in the settlement and that any cutback would precipitate a new strike. In reaching its decision, the Pay Board innocently or otherwise ignored this threat. When the board announced its decision, the ILWU did not react overtly. Nor did the union take any steps to modify the agreement in the light of the Pay Board's decision. In effect the case remained in suspension awaiting some announcement or concrete action by the union's leadership. When the East Coast case came to the board for review, reports were circulated that the ILWU's inactivity was part of a larger strategy. It was broadly hinted that the ILWU was awaiting the board's action in the ILA case before taking a new initiative. Reportedly, if the Pay Board cut the East Coast longshore agreement, an alliance of convenience would be forged between the ILWU and the ILA, who would then act jointly to stop all shipping on both coasts. There was no way to evaluate the credibility of this threat, but the prospect of a nationwide longshore strike added a jittery quality to the proceedings.

Third, the ILA case was linked indirectly to portentous foreign policy considerations. For many years the ILA had directed its members to refuse to load cargo on Russian vessels for shipment to the Soviet Union. In 1972 the Nixon administration negotiated an agreement with the Soviet Union providing for the purchase of large amounts of U.S. wheat by the Russians. The sale was part of a complex strategy to win the Soviet Union's support for a settlement of the Vietnam conflict and was a preliminary to what was later described as U.S.-Soviet détente. As part of the negotiation process, the Nixon administration had persuaded Thomas W. Gleason, Sr., the president of the ILA, to lift the ban on loading American wheat on Russian ships. Apparently the Soviet Union attached considerable importance to this action. All these maneuvers were part of the preparations for President Nixon's trip to Moscow later in May to implement a global strategy that had been underscored by the President's earlier visit to Peking. Thus the Pay Board was somewhat concerned that if it cut the ILA settlement, the union would reinstitute the ban, disrupt the delicate chain of events linking the wheat sale to the strategy of détente, and dim the prospect of Soviet aid in resolving the long festering Vietnam conflict.

The members of the Pay Board glumly contemplated these implications. It hardly seemed appropriate that this much-abused, disparate group should have any influence, however minuscule, on matters of global consequence. The question of whether the board should accommodate its decision to these foreign policy considerations was discussed explicitly by the members. Informally they decided that if the White House intervened, they would adjust their decision to foreign policy considerations. In the absence of any White House communication, these factors would be ignored, and the board would go ahead on its own.

The board opened formal consideration of the East Coast longshore agreements at a public hearing on May 2, 1972. A joint submission was made by the ILA, the CONASA, the WGMA, and the NOSSA calling for board approval of the agreements in their entirety. (Gleason was the leading spokesman.) The arguments presented by the parties followed a familiar pattern. Gleason stated that approval of the contract was more than justified by the productivity increases that had taken place on the docks in recent years and by the prospective gains promised by the new contract. He asserted that from 1964 to 1971 labor productivity in the port of New York had increased by 58 percent, while employment had declined from 25,000 longshoremen to 15,750. In addition, total hours worked had dropped from 44 million in 1965 to less than 31 million in 1971. Gleason also asserted that a full credit should be given for the expected savings in the cost of the GAI. Finally he noted that the contracts had been the product of a long, turbulent process of bargaining and that vigorous measures had been taken to sell the contracts to the rank and file. Pay Board approval of the contracts was necessary to restore peace to the docks and to preserve a climate for continued technological change.[20]

After a desultory round of questions, the board retired to executive session to discuss the case. These deliberations were distinguished by the continued participation of Frank Fitzsimmons, president of the Teamsters. Fitzsimmons had refused to leave the board with the other labor leaders and had been designated a "public" member with a special labor interest. He had rarely attended board sessions, however, either before or after the reconstitution of the agency.[21] Fitzsimmons's presence reflected the Teamsters' interest in the case because of its long association with the ILA in contiguous jurisdictions. As the proceedings unfolded, Fitzsimmons played an important role as an intermediary between the board and the leadership of the ILA.

The board first considered—and rejected—the formal request for approval of the contract without modification. In the board's judgment little credence could be given to the claims of past productivity gains because the available data were so imprecise. Although the evidence indicated that the number of tons handled per man-hour in the port of New York had increased over 50 percent between 1964 and 1971, these findings were discounted because it was not possible to adjust the data for changes in cargo mix. As indicated in the ILWU case, shifts in the cargo

20. See presentation of Thomas W. Gleason, Sr., in "Transcript of Hearing in re: Joint Application of International Longshore Association, CONASA, et al" (Washington, D.C.: Miller-Columbian Reporting Service, May 2, 1972; processed), pp. 42–58.

21. Pay Board minutes indicate that Fitzsimmons attended five board meetings between November 9, 1971, and the dissolution of the board in January 1973.

mix could have an important effect on labor productivity independent of technology. Furthermore, while this gross measure of productivity showed a significant increase in New York, there was a wide dispersion of gains among the other Atlantic Coast ports. For example, using comparable data, labor productivity had increased by only 32 percent in Boston, 35 percent in Philadelphia, and a bare 6 percent in the port of Baltimore. At the same time, all but one major port covered by the ILA agreements had shown an increase in labor costs per ton of cargo handled. In New York the labor cost per ton of cargo had risen between 1965 and 1971 by 6 percent, and in Baltimore it had increased by 33 percent.[22]

A majority of the board also was unwilling to credit the parties with the projected savings associated with the changes in the rules governing the GAI. The past performance of the plan had been so dismal there was little confidence that the $19 million cost reduction would be realized. If, in fact, these savings did accrue, they could be taken into account when the board considered the second-year wage increase under the agreement. Some adjustment could be made at that time, not under the current circumstances of tenuous good intentions.

Having discarded the formal arguments, the board sought an acceptable basis for reaching a determination in the case. From the outset it was recognized that some basis of comparability would have to be established with the board's action in the ILWU case. Consequently the board adopted a "penny tandem" approach whereby the increment approved for the ILA would be comparable to the actual wage increase that had been authorized by the ILWU decision. In the latter case, the wage increase had been reduced from 80 cents to 50 cents an hour. The board would be willing to accept an identical 50 cent wage increase for the ILA. The amount of the reduction would be somewhat less, however, because the wage hike included in the ILA-CONASA agreement totaled only 70 cents an hour.

Fitzsimmons pressed aggressively for approval of the contract without change. When this position was rejected, he asserted that the ILA should receive a wage increment greater than 50 cents. He believed that a wage increase of 60 cents plus approval of all benefit improvements would be acceptable to the union leadership. On several occasions the Pay Board recessed while Fitzsimmons consulted informally with the officers of the ILA who were on hand at a hotel in Washington. The implication of Fitzsimmons's proposal was that this formula would minimize the possi-

22. "Productivity, Unit Labor Cost, Prices, and Capital Investment," pp. 73–75.

bility of a coalition between the ILA and the ILWU and a nationwide shutdown of the longshore industry.

After prolonged discussions the board agreed to raise the approved wage increase to 55 cents. Further arguments by Fitzsimmons were rejected, and on May 8 the board announced its decision. The ruling was applicable to the CONASA agreement, the West Gulf Coast, and New Orleans. Because the base rates and benefit programs varied significantly among the individual ports, no effort was made to tailor the decision to the details of each agreement. Instead, a blanket approval was given for all benefit improvements and a wage increase of 55 cents. The consequences of the decision would then be determined by the parties in each bargaining unit. When the agreements had been modified in accordance with the board's ruling, they would be resubmitted to the chairman for approval. In this manner different local unions and employer associations could make adjustments in the light of their particular circumstances but within the limits of the approved package cost.

After releasing the decision to the press, the board awaited the reaction of the union. At this juncture the board received an assist from external events. About six hours after the board announced the decision in the ILA case, President Nixon went on television to inform the nation that he had ordered U.S. armed forces to mine Haiphong harbor in North Vietnam.[23] This action was taken as part of the effort to pressure the North Vietnamese into seriously pursuing truce negotiations. Whatever the attributes of the ILA might be, its leaders were patriotic in the traditional sense. The ILA was unlikely to call a strike or join with the ILWU in a simultaneous work stoppage that would cripple American shipping. In fact, a strike was not called, nor was there evidence that it was seriously considered. Ultimately the employers and the local unions in all of the East Coast and Gulf Coast ports worked out accommodations within the framework of the Pay Board decision. The last of the last cows had been run through the board without kicking over the barn.

Whither the Last Cows?

The disposition of the last cows was a matter of broad significance in the evolution of the Pay Board. The five cases described the transition

23. "The Situation in Southeast Asia," text of the President's May 8, 1972, address to the nation, *Weekly Compilation of Presidential Documents,* vol. 8 (May 15, 1972), pp. 840–41.

from an environment of free collective bargaining to the restraints of a full-blown controls program. They provided visible evidence of the board's resolve—or lack of resolve—in applying its own standards. And they tested the capacity of tripartitism to work under conditions other than wartime when there were persistent conflicts of interest among the parties to the stabilization program.

Beyond these considerations, what light does this saga of the last cows shed on the development of the wage stabilization process during Phase II? Overall, the five cases clearly illustrate the maturation of the regulatory process. In this respect the differences in handling the bituminous coal case at the outset of Phase II and the East Coast longshore case six months later are striking. In the time between the two decisions the general pay standard had been amended by Congress and further amplified by the board to take account of such issues as fringe benefits, catch-up, and roll-up. Some precision had been given to otherwise vague industrial relations concepts such as tandem relations and merit increases. Most important, the rules for calculating the increases in the various categories of compensation had been greatly amplified. In this sense the regulatory process applied a discipline and calibration to the outcome of negotiations that the parties themselves often evaded. In collective bargaining, both management and unions frequently measure the costs and benefits of an agreement in a manner that is responsive as much to political needs as to the objective qualities of simple arithmetic.

Thus at one level the lesson of the last cows is that wage controls cannot be self-administered in any rigorous manner and that the notion of a "cafeteria" controls program is probably misguided. Instead, the analytical requirements of special cases and the bureaucratic momentum of the program require the elaboration of specific rules. To some extent this process describes the difference between wage controls and what has been more ambiguously characterized as "incomes policy." Whether or not the exercise in rule-making is worth the effort is another matter, but it is an intrinsic element in a wage controls program.

Although the elaboration of rules helped to define the issues, it is important to recognize that when each of the last cows passed before the board the decisions were essentially arbitrary and judgmental. These judgmental aspects were sloganized by the concept of a "gross inequity." This ponderous term was a judicial reference to the possibility that in any given case the board might give conclusive weight to factors other than those formally incorporated in the regulations. The bituminous coal de-

cision was largely determined by the belief that it was inadvisable to reduce employer contributions to the welfare and retirement fund; few
regulatory agencies, especially those of a tripartite nature, can bear the
burden of inflicting costs on the aged, widows, and orphans. In the aerospace case the board disallowed the residual cost-of-living adjustment increment, then sought to assuage the parties by giving prior approval to
the 34 cents in the second year. In the East Coast longshore dispute, the
board sweetened the penny tandem with the West Coast longshore decision by 5 cents in order to accommodate Frank Fitzsimmons and to minimize the possible formation of an East Coast–West Coast coalition.
Whether or not the intrusion of these judgments is viewed as a constructive aspect of wage controls is a matter of taste; nonetheless, it should
be recognized that this flexibility is present. In a distorted and sometimes
grotesque manner the regulatory process replicates the actual bargaining
process involving the two parties alone. At the regulatory level, however,
it is presumed that the influence of these factors is limited by the economic
objectives of the stabilization program itself.

The path traveled by the last cows also reveals that once the regulatory
process is set in motion it is difficult, if not impossible, to consider each
case in splendid isolation. Every decision left a residue that colored the
board's actions in subsequent cases. For example, the ruling in the UTU
case was conditioned by the earlier action concerning the Signalmen. The
cutback of the wage increase in the aerospace agreements was explained
in part by the board's belief that assertive action was necessary to restore
the credibility that had been lost in the bituminous and railroad decisions.
And clearly the two longshore decisions were connected in the board's
deliberations even though the pattern of bargaining and market conditions
were different. Despite the cumulative legalisms produced by the board,
"equitable considerations" created by prior decisions had a heavy influence on subsequent actions. Shortly before its dissolution, the board
showed signs of being sufficiently self-confident to decide individual cases
with a close regard for the formal rules. In disposing of the last cows,
however, the Pay Board modified the application of the rules so that there
was some internally defined order to this series of decisions.

If internal considerations were dominant in deciding the five major
cases, the most important linkage of the Pay Board to the external environment was not so much the labor market as that amorphous collection of perceptions and attitudes described as "public opinion." That is,
none of the cases involved extremely large numbers of workers or a

situation that would have major spillover effects on wage determination in other industries. The bituminous coal, railroad, and longshore industries all tended to be self-contained bargaining systems rather than parts of a complex pattern of interindustry wage relationships. Bargaining in the aerospace industry also was unique and occurred after the UAW had reached agreements for automobile workers and agricultural implement workers. Thus when the board weighed the external impact of its decisions, it was largely in terms of their effect on public opinion, particularly at the early stages of Phase II. To the extent that the Pay Board really operated under a dual system whereby it hoped its decisions in the major cases would have a coercive effect on instances of wage-setting that never came to the board's attention, this sensitivity to public opinion was a vital element in its overall strategy.

The public relations aspects of the actual decisions involving the last cows had an anomalous character. Even when cutbacks were made, in every case the board approved settlements that were far in excess of its standards. Including the cost of fringe benefits, none of the approved settlements were less than 10 percent. In the case involving the most drastic cutback—the West Coast longshoremen—the total economic package was reduced from approximately 21 percent to 15 percent. The final figure was still almost three times the general pay standard. If public opinion was served in this and other decisions in which cutbacks were levied—and it seemed to be—it was because attention could be focused on the magnitude of the reduction rather than on the size of the approved increase.

Despite transient public relations considerations, the history of the last cows further indicates that a more durable problem was one of retaining effective control over the situations in which the Pay Board nominally had taken a tough stand, that is, making the decisions stick. In several of the cases, the parties subsequently managed to modify or evade the board's decision, virtually nullifying the economic effects. Despite the Pay Board's controversial efforts to retain authority over the work rule issue in the railroad cases, this proved difficult, if not impossible, to do. When the board finally managed to extract a report on the progress that had been made in implementing the work rule changes, the results fell far short of preliminary estimates. The board reviewed these findings and discreetly laid them on a shelf. Similarly, in the aerospace case, the UAW managed to reverse the board's decision by court action more than two years after that cause célèbre had occurred. And in the West Coast longshore case, the ILWU ultimately found a way to restore most of the wage reduction that had been ordered by the board. If the story of the last cows had a happy ending, it was not recounted in the epilogue.

Beyond these postmortems, a more positive evaluation may be offered. Despite the uncoordinated nature of the process, the capacity of the board to resolve complex issues in highly contentious circumstances is the cause for modest acclaim. If the record of the last cows reveals the deficiencies and realpolitik of wage regulation, it also provides evidence of its workability. The Pay Board managed to take action in portentous cases while it was still fashioning the rules that governed its activities. Overall, the decisions struck a rough balance between the need to recognize that collective bargaining existed before Phase II and that the general pay standard would pose a real limit on other bargains. The board maintained its organizational poise despite the walkout of the labor members. It dealt with powerful unions and obdurate managements without precipitating a confrontation that impaired the workings of the economy or the stability of national political institutions, as has been the case in other Western industrialized nations. The board demonstrated that an instrument of economic policy can function on its own terms within a hyperpolitical environment. While these achievements do not cast any light on the overall efficacy of wage controls, they do indicate that the preconditions of organizational survival and operational effectiveness can be met, even under highly adverse circumstances.

VII

Structure and Administration

The design and function of the Pay Board's administration can be understood only in relation to the original goals of the controls program. Since avoiding a large bureaucracy was a primary objective, staff resources would be limited. This meant the board would have to set a fairly high wage standard that would catch only those collective bargaining settlements that were grossly out of line. With a high standard as a trigger point and some reasonable judgments as to which cases were important, fewer professional industrial relations experts would be needed for the staff.

Another condition that affected the administrative design of the program was the early decision to separate the wage and the price functions. To some extent this decision further squeezed effective staff resources, since the economies that might have been attained through a unified control program were not available. It also meant that contact between the staffs of the Pay Board and the Price Commission would be relatively limited.

Finally, the labor market was not expected to become a source of demand-generated wage pressure during 1972. Thus the relatively high wage standard in many cases would be met with little policing. And where policing was required, it could be delegated to agencies other than the Pay Board.

Formation of the Staff

The first organizational task was the formation of the Pay Board staff. Because of its tripartite nature, the Pay Board did not assemble a permanent staff for several weeks after Phase II began. During that early period the board was staffed by an assemblage of "detailees" from other agencies who ranged from highly competent personnel to marginal elements of the Washington-area civil service. Some potential staff members were frightened off by the widely publicized tripartite wrangling. The first public affairs director, for example, left in exasperation after the board members gave the press what amounted to fifteen separate explanations of the aerospace decision.

In early January the Pay Board managed to have two staffs. One consisted of detailees who were returning to their home agencies after an initial review of their performances or for personal reasons. At the same time, new employees were hired and mixed with those detailees who had decided (and were allowed) to become the permanent staff of the board. A large part of the staff came from other government agencies.

As might be expected, the staff had a high proportion of relatively young and inexperienced employees. An air of well-intentioned chaos pervaded the workings of the Pay Board. Those who came to work for the board were very uncertain about their duties. Until January 20, 1972, for example, no one at the Pay Board or the Internal Revenue Service had authority to approve cases in which wage increases of less than 5.5 percent were reported. These cases and others piled up in the absence of a delegation. Staff members were unsure of their role relative to the tripartite board. The public members viewed the staff as their aides, but the labor and business members also were free to make requests for service. In addition, a great deal of disarray characterized standard administrative procedures in the early days. It was months before the mail system was reliable. Cases appeared and disappeared mysteriously.

The Pay Board never lost its crisis atmosphere, but a degree of order eventually emerged. A sort of camaraderie-in-travail developed among the staff; veterans of the early days reminisced about past crises and learned to take new ones in stride. This atmosphere was fostered by the small size of the staff. Even the Xerox operators were only a few steps down the organization chart from the executive director.

Staff Organization

The Pay Board began with a formal ceiling of 137 employees. This level was soon breached. Until the delegation of authority to the Internal Revenue Service, a large volume of Category III cases was arriving daily, and 137 employees simply could not handle the load, let alone the larger Category I and Category II submissions. The ceiling was raised in May 1972 to 174 employees, but this step merely made official what had already occurred. Although the ceiling remained at 174 for the rest of Phase II, it too was raised by a variety of special appointments that somehow did not have to be counted against the ceiling.

It is difficult to describe "the" Pay Board organizational structure, since a number of administrative reshuffles took place during the life of the board. At the end of the program, the board had eight operating divisions, as shown below.

	Number of employees
Chairman and offices of executive and administrative directors	13
Executive Secretariat	19
Public Affairs Office	6
Congressional Affairs Office	5
Case Management and Analysis Office	83
Office of the General Counsel	23
Office of the Chief Economist	20
Office of Operations Services and Systems	49
Office of Administration	22
Total	240

The executive director had a legal and managerial background in private industry, and he placed heavy emphasis on the case-processing aspect of staff activities. His personal background was balanced by that of the administrative director, who had long experience at the managerial level in the federal government. The administrative director generally concentrated on the support aspects of the staff—for example, personnel, budget, and contracts.

Although the functions of the various offices were modified with the changing priorities of the board, it is useful to describe the general functions of each. The Executive Secretariat prepared the board's agenda and kept terse minutes of the meetings. It served as a general communications link through which board members made requests to other offices. The Executive Secretariat became the home of Category III operations, and this accounts for its relatively large staff. In addition to Pay Board staff workers, approximately twenty IRS personnel were detailed to the secretariat to work on Category III cases.

The Public Affairs Office issued official Pay Board press releases, arranged newspaper interviews, monitored press coverage, and provided speech-writing services. (In sharp contrast to the Price Commission, the Pay Board chose not to engage in an elaborate public relations effort.) A related office, Congressional Affairs, had—in the economists' phraseology—a macro and a micro aspect. At the macro level, there were senators and congressmen with an interest in the overall thrust of the stabilization program, both wage and price. On the micro level, constituents who sought to have their cases expedited sometimes called their congressmen or senators. Inquiries from Congress about particular cases generally did speed up the processing of these cases. Despite this special service, in no instance did a congressional inquiry influence the decision on a case.

The Case Management and Analysis Office (CMA) was the heart of case adjudication, except for cases going to the Category III Panel. The CMA reviewed exception requests and prepared analyses of those requests for the board. Those cases that raised novel legal issues were sent to the Office of the General Counsel. Cases involving economic issues went to the Office of the Chief Economist.[1] Within the CMA, special subdivisions handled nonunion construction and executive compensation cases.

The Office of the General Counsel had four major functions. First, it drafted the regulations that implemented Pay Board policies. This was a time-consuming process because as the program developed, Pay Board policies became more detailed. Second, apart from drafting the regulations, it interpreted them for the public. Third, it handled litigation generally in coordination with the Cost of Living Council and the Justice Department. In processing cases that raised novel legal issues, it wrote the decisions and orders for cases that could not be handled by one of the standard forms used by the board. Fourth, as its name implies, the Office of the General Counsel provided general advice to the Pay Board concerning the scope of its authority and the implications of various proposed policies.

Two major divisions operated within the Office of the Chief Economist. A case-handling section provided analysis of cases forwarded by CMA that raised questions of economic interest (productivity agreements, labor shortages, questions of costing, and so on). This section also provided a number of option papers on technical issues and played a major role in redesigning Pay Board reporting forms. A second section provided the board with general analyses of economic trends. The Office of the Chief Economist also was responsible for maintaining the accuracy of Pay Board computer files on Category I and Category II cases.

The Office of Operations Services and Systems maintained the computer and mail systems for the board. The computer system was used to keep track of cases and to obtain aggregate economic data on Pay Board decisions. This office also handled routine cases—those involving in-

1. The Office of the Chief Economist and the divisions of the CMA were originally united in a single office known as Economic Policy and Case Analysis.

creases within the guidelines—and screened all incoming cases for preliminary costing and to determine whether or not they were routine.

Finally, the Office of Administration handled support services such as personnel, purchases of supplies, coordination of automobiles, and travel. Budgetary matters were the responsibility of "Admin," which maintained relatively strict controls on expenditures. It might be noted that despite the pressures of setting up a new agency overnight, there were no known cases of employee dishonesty or misallocation of funds.

Case-Processing Machinery

The handling of cases remained a major issue at the Pay Board throughout its existence. Externally the board was criticized continually for delays and inefficiency. Senator William Proxmire suggested that inefficient case-handling was being used as a ploy to control wages without due process.[2] Union spokesmen also vigorously criticized the board's delays and inefficiencies. Wage pressure allegedly was being contained by simply not hearing cases for increases.

Internally there was pressure—especially from the executive director of the board—to prove that the board, unlike the earlier wartime programs, could handle a large volume of cases with a small staff. In analyzing the Pay Board's actual record, it is important to recognize that there were actually different case-handling mechanisms for different types of cases.

Major Cases. Major cases were those that involved a great deal of media publicity and that were regarded as pattern-setters. The earliest examples of such cases—coal, railroads, and aerospace—were in fact handled with little staff preparation, since there was no permanent staff at the time. Later cases were handled by teams of staff members assembled from various offices. Usually the staff would meet several times with the parties to discuss the papers being prepared for the board.[3] These papers, along with any documents submitted by the parties, would then

2. Senator Proxmire asserted that the program was deliberately designed to delay wage cases in order to slow down wage increases. In his words, "Delay is the name of the game." *Review of Phase II of the New Economic Program,* Hearings before the Joint Economic Committee, 92 Cong. 2 sess. (Government Printing Office, 1972), p. 184.

3. The staff felt that it had an obligation to present the best arguments that could be made for major cases, even if the parties failed to do so. This sometimes confused the press into thinking that the staff "favored" a particular application. See *New York Times,* March 15, 1972.

be reviewed at a public hearing. Final decisions on major cases were made behind closed doors, often with the staff absent. After an above-standard increase had been approved, the staff was authorized to approve tandems on an accelerated basis.

Ordinary Category I and Category II Cases. Category I and Category II cases (those of units of 1,000 or more workers) simply involved reports of adjustments within the basic standards and required only cursory cost checks. Experience with an assembly line system of processing suggested that merely passing such cases from desk to desk led to delay and lost cases. As a result, a team system was established in which a group of staff members was given responsibility for individual cases throughout the entire adjudication process.

In some cases, of course, requests were submitted for adjustments greater than the basic standards permitted. These generally were sent to the Cases and Appeals Panel unless novel issues were raised. Unique cases went before the Pay Board for a full hearing. Ordinary Category I and Category II cases were generally given the benefit of the doubt in all stages of review and there was pressure to reduce the backlog and increase the volume. Generally an applicant's description of a proposed increase was assumed to be accurate.[4]

Category III Cases. Although Category III units (less than 1,000 workers) were not required to file reports if they remained within the standards, the large number of such units was sufficient to generate a substantial administrative case load. This load usually went first to Internal Revenue Service district offices. As it operated initially, the IRS system was frustrating to applicants who were not eligible for one of the Pay Board's 7 percent exceptions. A unit requesting 8 percent had to go through the routine of a denial by the district office, since the IRS was not authorized to grant any but the 7 percent exceptions. It was necessary to go through the motions of requesting an increase known to be unapprovable by the IRS in order to be able to file an appeal with the Pay Board. This problem was alleviated by permitting the IRS to shunt such cases directly to the board.

At first, Category III cases that reached the board were handled by the

4. One example of the hasty methods applied was the treatment of multiple submissions for a given unit within a control year. In principle, if a unit asked for 4 percent at the beginning of the year and 3 percent more a few months later, the second application should not have been routinely approved, since the total request exceeded 5.5 percent. In fact, it appeared that in some instances the case analysts were not aware of earlier submissions.

same procedures used for categories I and II. But it became apparent that it was impossible for the Pay Board and the Cases and Appeals Panel to hear the tremendous volume of Category III cases. As a result, a new Category III Panel was created in July 1972. This panel was composed entirely of Pay Board staff members and represented the broadest delegation of authority the board gave to the staff during Phase II. The panel consisted of three members and was chaired by the administrative director, Millard Cass, a former deputy under secretary of labor. Its authority was limited to advising the chairman of the Pay Board on the appropriate disposition of Category III cases in accordance with previous board precedents. Cases that presented novel issues for which no precedents existed were sent to the Cases and Appeals Panel.

All board members had the right to review Category III Panel decisions. Any two members could certify a case to the Cases and Appeals Panel if they disagreed with the advisory opinion. In fact, only the Teamsters alternate reviewed cases—a monumental job—and it was understood that the chairman would always endorse his certification. Aside from this review process, applicants who were not satisfied with the initial Category III Panel decision could request a review. Their appeals went back to the panel, not to the Pay Board.

More than any other part of Pay Board case-processing, the Category III Panel was a volume operation. Category III cases were not given Pay Board case numbers; thus they did not appear in Pay Board computer records unless they were certified to the Cases and Appeals Panel. As a result, the official Pay Board backlog did not include cases awaiting action by the panel, although these cases were a significant but unknown proportion of the backlog.

It is also fair to say that the adjudicators who were conscripted for periodic service to the panel did not give the same attention to these cases as to those in Category I and Category II. In part this reflected the type of information included in the initial submissions. It was not unusual for Category III units to report their increases incorrectly. Although some applicants employed legal counsel to write their briefs, these documents frequently included material that was irrelevant to Pay Board decision criteria.

Special Cases. Because nonunion construction cases and executive compensation cases were subject to different regulations, the Case Management and Analysis Office contained separate sections to handle them. (The IRS did not handle these cases.) Nonunion construction cases were processed according to a set of rules agreed upon at a series of joint meetings of members of the Pay Board and the Construction Industry Stabilization Committee. Nonunion construction units were permitted wage increases consisting of the higher of 5.5 percent or the increment in cents per hour approved by the CISC for the same area and craft in the union sector. This meant that nonunion construction case-processing consisted largely of identifying the appropriate CISC approval. At first the nonunion construction section was hampered in its operations by the general dispute between the Pay Board and the CISC over access to the latter's data. After a basic agreement had been reached, however, the section was permitted to obtain the necessary information.

The nonunion construction section also handled certain cases that were closely related to union construction workers. For example, truck drivers who delivered to construction sites were under Pay Board jurisdiction but often could claim some sort of tandem relation to workers under CISC jurisdiction. Requests for exceptions of these groups often were handled by the nonunion construction section. The section chief would personally present these cases to the Category III Panel or to the Cases and Appeals Panel.

Although the small-business exemption applied to most industries, it did not apply to construction. This meant that the many tiny units in the construction industry remained subject to controls. It is difficult to make any estimate of the number of small nonunion construction units that might have granted wage increases of more than 5.5 percent during Phase II. It does seem clear, however, that most of the really small businesses in nonunion construction were not familiar with Pay Board rules and were not reporting their increases. The large nonunion firms, of course, were careful to comply.

The executive compensation section, despite its title, processed cases relating to both executives and other types of employees. Much of its activity did involve cases concerning the stock option and incentive compensation (bonus) programs that often characterize executive pay. But the section also handled sales commission and productivity incentive plans plus a variety of other types of miscellaneous reports required by Pay Board regulations. The section had about thirteen employees at the end of Phase II.

The majority of executive compensation cases involved Category III units. When such cases raised issues that required a decision of the Category III Panel, personnel from the executive compensation section would

Table 7-1. *Closed Pay Board Cases as of March 12, 1973*[a]

Category of cases	Number closed
Category I[b]	1,097
Category II[b]	3,606
Category III[b]	5,406[c]
Nonunion construction[d]	1,370
Executive compensation[d]	2,337
Total	13,816

Source: Pay Board computer records.
a. Includes retroactive cases. Each submission is counted as a case.
b. Excluding executive compensation and nonunion construction.
c. As of February 28, 1973, the Category III Panel had processed 3,331 cases, but for reasons given in the text these cannot be added to the total.
d. Most of these cases were in Category III.

make the presentations. Most reports and requests received by the executive compensation section arrived in completely different formats from other Pay Board cases. They did not have to be costed, since the request involved the approval of a plan, not a specific increase.

Case Processing: the Statistical Record

Table 7-1 summarizes the case-processing record as it appeared in Pay Board computer records as of March 12, 1973. By that date most Phase II cases that had been closed on or before the Pay Board's termination date (February 28, 1973) had been entered in the computer files. A "case" in table 7-1 is defined as a submission for a new, old, or retroactive adjustment; multiple submissions within a control year are counted as multiple cases.[5] The table shows a total of 13,816 submissions to the Pay Board. Phase II and the termination period lasted a total of sixty-eight and a half weeks, suggesting that weekly processing averaged about 200 cases a week.[6]

As indicated previously, once the Category III Panel began to operate, Category III cases normally were not given Pay Board case numbers and were not considered official Pay Board cases. Hence the 5,406 Category

5. In chapter 11 all submissions by a unit within a control year are considered a single case. The submission approach used in this chapter, however, is more relevant for the analysis of the case work load.

6. The effective period of case-processing was less than sixty-eight and a half weeks, since practically no cases were processed until the permanent staff began to form early in 1972.

III cases shown on the table represent cases processed before the creation of the Category III Panel, certifications from the Category III Panel to the Cases and Appeals Panel, and cases that were allowed to come directly to the board because they were tandems to major Pay Board decisions. Despite the substantial exclusion of Category III cases from the Pay Board's computer records, these cases still amounted to 39 percent of what the board officially considered to be its work load.

The Category III Panel made recommendations on 3,331 cases. Some of these cases were picked up in the 5,406 figure because they were certified to the Cases and Appeals Panel and because the Category III Panel handled cases in its early days that arrived when Category III cases were still given Pay Board case numbers. Therefore, the 3,331 Category III Panel recommendations cannot be added to the 13,816 cases reported by the Pay Board for a grand total. A reasonable estimate of the total number of cases handled by all units of the Pay Board would be 15,000 to 16,000.

Table 7-2 summarizes the data concerning the time required to process Category I and Category II cases. The table has been limited to cases that closed on or before January 12, 1973. After that date the board used an expedited case-processing system to clean out its backlog during the termination period under Phase III. Cases are broken down into "old" and "new" classifications. Old cases are deferred adjustments during Phase II under pre–Phase II contracts or practices. New cases involve adjustments established during Phase II.

The table shows that 53 percent of the new cases were processed in thirty days or less, compared with only 35 percent of the old cases. This tendency for cases involving deferred increases to have a longer waiting time stems partly from the early confusion over the circumstances under which deferred increases could be challenged. At first, all deferred adjustments were placed on a list that was circulated to the board to see if any challenges were forthcoming. The 7 percent de facto standard for deferred increases evolved gradually and really became an internal working rule only after the labor walkout. In addition, just before the board became all-public, the business members challenged a large number of cases, which then piled up for a long period of time.

Deferred increases originally were permitted to go into effect sixty days after notification unless the Pay Board ordered a rollback. In some cases, units dragged their feet in responding to Pay Board requests for additional data. They knew that the board never cut deferred increases retroactively

Table 7-2. *Length of Time Required to Process Pay Board Category I and Category II Cases*[a]

Number of days to process case[b]	Old cases		New cases	
	Percent of total cases	*Percent of total workers*	*Percent of total cases*	*Percent of total workers*
0–10	6.5	3.6	6.5	5.8
11–20	12.8	7.4	21.4	18.2
21–30	15.2	8.0	25.0	19.7
31–40	11.4	22.8	12.3	10.9
41–50	10.1	5.7	10.0	11.0
51–100	25.8	40.5	14.8	20.9
More than 100	18.1	12.1	10.0	13.5
All durations	100.0	100.0	100.0	100.0

Source: Pay Board computer records.

a. Sample of cases closed through January 12, 1973, for which duration data are available. The sample consisted of 1,118 old cases affecting a total of 12.2 million workers and 2,341 new cases affecting 11.9 million workers.

b. Days elapsed from date received to date closed.

once payment had begun. The worst that could happen would be a prospective cut. And even that became more difficult for the board as time passed and as payments continued to be made.

The Pay Board tightened up its deferred adjustment rules on June 8, 1972, by lengthening the prenotification requirement to ninety days and by forbidding implementation until sixty days after satisfactory supplementary data had been supplied on challenged cases.[7] In general the supplementary data request consisted of a special questionnaire designed by the board for all challenged deferred increases.

Deferred increases remained a problem of case-processing. Despite the improved reporting requirements, the board was reluctant to grant additional authority to the staff to approve deferred adjustments above 7 percent. It should be recalled, however, that from the viewpoint of the parties, deferred adjustments were different from new ones. Newly negotiated contracts in Category I awaited board approval, whatever their magnitude. Since it was generally not possible to determine what the increase would amount to ninety days before its scheduled implementation date, delay by the board meant delay for the workers involved. The same was true for Category II requests for exceptions to the standards in new cases. In contrast, deferred adjustments were known far in advance. As long as the parties were prompt in notifying the board and in supplying data, they

7. Pay Board press release PB-95, June 8, 1972.

Table 7-3. *Duration of Category I and Category II Cases,*
by Selected Closing Dates

	Mean duration (days)	
Closing date	New cases	Old cases
August 25, 1972	39	63
September 29, 1972	37	73
October 27, 1972	55	67
November 24, 1972	38	75
December 29, 1972	29	76
January 12, 1973	31	52
All cases	43	63

Source: Pay Board computer records.

could be sure of implementation on the scheduled date, in the absence of a cutback. Thus for cases involving deferred increases, delay at the board did not necessarily mean delay for the workers.

Computer data on the duration of case-processing became more comprehensive as Phase II progressed. Table 7-3 gives the mean duration of cases processed in categories I and II for six selected closing dates during the latter part of the program. (All cases sent to the closing station were closed on the last day of the week. Hence each date shown represents a week's worth of cases.) Although the data can hardly be said to exhibit a smooth trend, the new cases do show reduced durations toward the end of the program. This presumably resulted from the computerized processing system, which was able to expedite the review of cases that were within the standards. However, for the entire case load in categories I and II for which data are available, mean processing time was forty-three days for new cases and sixty-three days for deferred adjustment cases.

Category III cases proved to be more resistant to the Pay Board's administrative efforts. Had Phase II continued, the board would have had to implement new procedures for these cases. In fact, just before the end of Phase II, the board turned its attention to this area in the hope of improving the system. The Category III record during Phase II was heavily influenced by the program's early history. IRS personnel were expected to handle Category III cases from the beginning, but they had no authority. In the early weeks of the program, the IRS was simply forwarding cases to the board. Then, after they were given authority to handle the formula exceptions, the IRS staff required a period of training. And when the IRS system was finally able to function, applicants for increases beyond the formula exceptions were originally forced to wait for an IRS denial before appealing to the board.

The net effect of these complications was that an inventory was built up in the IRS. When the IRS received its delegation of authority, the Pay Board sent it all Category III cases that the board had not processed. As of May 16, 1972, a total of 1,882 cases was transferred to the IRS. Many units whose requests were denied by the IRS filed administrative appeals within that agency. A total of 1,355 wage appeals had been filed with the IRS by May 16.[8] Most of these appeals were also denied or were in the process of being denied at that time. Thus a wave of Category III cases previously transferred to the IRS was heading back toward the Pay Board.

When the Category III Panel was created, it was faced with this legacy. It had to deal with cases that had been in the mill for a long time, and others were arriving daily in large numbers. As has been noted earlier, these cases were generally excluded from the board's case-processing system, and no inventory data are available. In order to obtain a rough idea of case-processing time, a sample of 101 cases was drawn from the files. Only cases handled before the end of Phase II (January 11, 1973) were included, since the expedited case-processing in the termination period was not typical of the normal operation. From the cover sheets on the cases, the time from the application to the IRS to the date of an appeal to the Pay Board was calculated. The time from the appeal date to the date the decision and order was mailed was also tabulated. In cases where an appeal was made to the Pay Board after an adverse board decision, only the original decision date was used.[9]

The sample represented about 5.6 percent of the cases processed by the Category III Panel through January 11, 1973. The weighted average wage increase requested for these cases was 12.3 percent, close to the 12.1 percent average request reported by the panel through that date. Cases that were not appeals from the IRS—that is, those forwarded by the IRS to the Pay Board without decision—were not included. Table 7-4 summarizes the sample data.

The mean duration from application date to appeal date was ninety

8. See "Economic Stabilization Program Weekly Performance Summary, Twenty-sixth Week, May 9–16, 1972," in "Pay Board Weekly Status Report: Week of May 15 through May 19" (1972; processed), pp. 23, 25.

9. A review, if requested, lengthened the ultimate decision time. A certification to the Cases and Appeals Panel also lengthened the duration of cases.

Table 7-4. Length of Time Required to Process Pay Board Category III Cases

	Elapsed time								
	From application to IRS to appeal to Pay Board			From appeal to Pay Board to board's mailing of decision and order			From application to IRS to Pay Board's mailing of decision and order		
Days required for processing	Number of cases	Number of workers affected	Weighted wage increase requested (percent)	Number of cases	Number of workers affected	Weighted wage increase requested (percent)	Number of cases	Number of workers affected	Weighted wage increase requested (percent)
1–30	8	621	15.6	1	10	9.4	0	0	...
31–60	19	2,242	9.8	8	1,242	8.5			
61–90	28	4,233	11.2	29	3,103	11.5	5	107	10.6
91–120	24	2,031	19.6	23	3,114	14.0			
121–150	12	1,118	10.5	18	1,944	12.0	41	4,535	11.2
151–180	3	356	13.7	14	2,803	12.8	26	3,764	14.2
181–240	7[a]	1,876[a]	9.2[a]	8[a]	261[a]	14.6[a]	18	2,686	12.3
241–300	b	b	b	b	b	b	11	1,385	10.5
301 and over	b	b	b	b	b	b			
All	101	12,477	12.3	101	12,477	12.3	101	12,477	12.3

Addenda

	From application to IRS to appeal to Pay Board	From appeal to Pay Board to board's mailing of decision and order	From application to IRS to Pay Board's mailing of decision and order
Mean number of days	90	114	204
Standard deviation (days)	47	46	62

Source: Sample of 101 cases drawn from Pay Board files that were closed during Phase II.

a. May include data for 241 days and over.

b. If any cases fell in this range, they were included in data for 181–240 days.

days. Another 114 days elapsed, on the average, between the appeal date and the mailing of a decision from the Pay Board. Thus a total of 204 days elapsed for the average case in the sample. Median time was over six months. While a larger sample might have provided more accurate results, it is obvious that whatever the true mean duration was, it took a long time for a Category III applicant to obtain a Pay Board decision.

During its twenty-five weeks of existence, the Category III Panel processed 1,812 exception requests and 185 appeals, or about 80 cases a week. It probably averaged two daylong meetings a week. Although this suggests an average of about 40 cases a day, there were some days when the panel rendered opinions on over 100 cases.[10] The Category III operation was suffering from what the staff sometimes called the "8 cent appeal" problem. Basically this meant that once an applicant had prepared a case, it cost 8 cents—the price of a first-class letter—to appeal a denial. Since the IRS had only limited authority to grant exceptions, it was inevitable that many Category III cases would eventually reach the board.[11]

Staff Size and Efficiency

It is hard to define a "satisfactory" level of efficiency for the Pay Board. Despite allegations to the contrary, no attempt was made to delay cases in order to hold down wages.[12] Such a policy would have been self-defeating, since it ultimately could not succeed. A wage bubble would have resulted at the end of Phase II if the Pay Board had been engaged in a deliberate policy of delay. In fact, no bubble occurred. Nonetheless, it is true that the work load was high relative to the size of the staff available to handle it. The process started out with two strikes against it.

First, the delay in hiring a permanent staff built up a backlog problem. The problem was sufficiently large by the time a staff was formed to hinder the start-up process. For example, in order to train new staff, it was necessary to take existing staff away from case adjudication. This meant that the backlog would grow unless the staff already working on cases con-

10. Data were drawn from the tally sheets maintained by the Category III Panel.
11. As of January 12, 1973, the IRS reported receiving 15,683 exception requests for Category III. About one-third of these were either withdrawn by the parties or returned to them by the IRS. Most of these withdrawals and returns involved cases where unnecessary reports had been filed by parties who failed to understand the reporting rules.
12. *Review of Phase II*, Hearings, p. 184.

tinued to do so. The problem at the Pay Board level was mirrored at the IRS. IRS personnel could be trained only by Pay Board personnel.

Second, the small staff permitted the Pay Board left no margin for error. Normal administrative problems, such as mail delivery and computer operations, might have been taken in stride by a larger organization. At the Pay Board they precipitated major crises. Pressure on the staff to speed up processing also became counterproductive. For example, the tendency of some adjudicators to hide their backlog led to incorrect management information. The adjudicators' high rate of error in preparing cases for closing was symptomatic of the pressures on case adjudication. These errors sometimes prevented closing a case and forced the adjudicator to spend time correcting old work instead of moving on to new cases.

A further aspect of the staff-size constraint related to due process provided to applicants. In order to handle the volume, quality had to suffer. Adjudicators did not have the luxury of reviewing all the details of the cases they processed. To counteract the loss of quality, the system was geared to err on the side of the applicant. But naturally some errors were made on the other side. It could not be assumed that applicants who received erroneous decisions would always request a staff review. Some firms and unions possessed better resources for coping with the complexities of Pay Board rules than others.

With the benefit of hindsight, it seems apparent that it would have been better to run the risk of having an oversized staff rather than one that was too small to handle the job. The aversion to a large bureaucracy would not have been violated if the Pay Board had been 50 percent or even 100 percent larger. An agency composed of, say, 400 employees would hardly have been viewed as a bureaucratic leviathan, and some of the private costs of dealing with the regulatory system might have been reduced.

Pay Board Relations with Other Agencies

In the course of its operations, the Pay Board dealt with other government agencies. Data for cases, policy papers, and general economic analyses were often sought from the Bureau of Labor Statistics and the Commerce Department. In some instances the Pay Board was asked to provide data to these agencies. The economics staff maintained contacts with economists at the Council of Economic Advisers and the Federal Reserve Board and exchanged data with them. For example, a task force on the stabilization program met several times under the auspices of the Council of Economic Advisers for the purpose of evaluating the stabilization effort.[13] The Pay Board also had to coordinate its activities with those of other government agencies in the stabilization program, such as the Price Commission, the Construction Industry Stabilization Committee, the IRS, and the Cost of Living Council.

The Price Commission

The pay and price functions were separated in Phase II so that the Pay Board could be tripartite. During Phase II the members of the Pay Board and the Price Commission held two joint meetings. As a prelude to the first meeting in June 1972, staff members of the economic office of the Pay Board met with counterparts from the Price Commission, where pressure for the meeting seemed to have developed. The Price Commission's staff appeared to be concerned that Pay Board liberality was responsible for difficulties on the price side. Whether the members of the commission shared this view is unclear. By the time the meeting was held, wage pressure had subsided.

A second joint meeting was held in August, *after* the Pay Board had decided to retain the 5.5 percent standard. Much of the meeting was devoted to the explanation of the board's decision. Both agencies agreed that excess demand might become a problem in 1973 and asked their staffs to consider ways of dealing with it as a joint project. A resulting Pay Board recommendation that the Price Commission permit cost passthroughs where labor shortages required wage increases in excess of 5.5 percent was not adopted by the commission.

More frequent contacts occurred at the staff level. A joint staff effort was made when the Pay Board cut a deferred wage adjustment for New York City newspaper workers. Earlier deferred wage adjustment cuts had been criticized on the grounds that windfall profits could result if the deferred increase was already in effect and if the Price Commission did not take action to roll back prices. Thus on November 14, 1972, a joint press release announced both wage and price rollbacks for the news-

13. The task force issued a report on April 3, 1972, predicting that the 2–3 percent price inflation target for the end of 1972 would not be achieved. Although the report was meant to be internal, word of it appeared in the press.

papers.[14] The Pay Board and the Price Commission staffs worked together to carry out these rollbacks.

The Construction Industry Stabilization Committee

Relations between the Pay Board and the CISC were never better than strained. The CISC originally was created in March 1971 to control new wage adjustments in unionized construction, but under the executive order establishing the Phase II machinery it was made subsidiary to the Pay Board.[15] Although the official organization charts showed this relationship, the CISC never really accepted it and tried to preserve as much autonomy as possible. The rationale for this behavior went along the following lines: the CISC had a program for the construction industry before the creation of the Pay Board and could be expected to outlive the Pay Board; therefore it needed no outside guidance. In addition, the CISC generally enjoyed the support of its labor members, while union representatives on the Pay Board viewed the agency with undisguised hostility. Furthermore, in its early days the Pay Board was hardly in a position to guide another body; it had more than enough problems in its own house. Finally, at the time of the labor walkout from the Pay Board, the CISC wanted to isolate itself from the Pay Board in order to preserve its own structure.

Pay Board concerns about construction were based on stabilization objectives as well as on administrative relationships. Union construction wages had experienced an extraordinary degree of inflation during the late 1960s and early 1970s. In 1970 first-year wage rate changes in major union construction settlements ran at 17.6 percent, compared with 10.9

14. Pay Board press release PB-142, November 14, 1972. It should be noted, however, that this cooperation was preceded by a period in which the Price Commission did not accept Pay Board decisions regarding deferred increases or qualified benefits that exceeded 5.5 percent. Some of these discrepancies were not corrected during Phase II.

15. Executive Order 11640, January 27, 1972 (as amended by Executive Order 11660, March 23, 1972), states in section 15(b): "The Chairman of the Pay Board, acting in accordance with the majority vote of its members, shall continue to perform all functions vested in the Secretary of Labor by Executive Order No. 11588 with respect to (1) the certification of determinations that a proposed wage or salary increase is not acceptable pursuant to section 5 of that Order, (2) the approval of rules and regulations issued by the Construction Industry Stabilization Committee, . . . and (3) the issuance of rules and regulations pursuant to section 10 of that Order." Executive Order 11588 established the CISC. Section 5 of that order describes the procedure to be followed in the event of a CISC denial. Section 10 states that CISC rules were subject to the approval of the secretary of labor.

percent in other sectors.[16] Many labor economists believed that this inflation was in danger of spreading—or had already spread—to other industries. The CISC was formed after voluntary methods had failed and after President Nixon had suspended the provisions of the Davis-Bacon Act.[17] Although CISC officials downplayed the importance of the President's action to obtain tripartite cooperation, both the union contractors and the labor unions themselves had a great incentive to restore the Davis-Bacon Act, which was in fact reinstated after the CISC was established.

The CISC offered union contractors the hope of restraining their wage costs. At the same time, it followed a strategy of strengthening the national union leaders in their dealings with the relatively autonomous local unions. The CISC did not set a specific wage standard but based its decisions heavily on the restoration of historical wage differentials between crafts. A major assumption of the CISC approach was that a distortion of these differentials was responsible for the inflation of construction wages.[18] The public members of the Pay Board generally accepted the CISC approach but were skeptical of its probable success. In addition, at an informal meeting between the public members of both the Pay Board and the CISC in early November 1971 before the board's basic policies were announced, the CISC members flatly asserted that the prospective 5.5 percent pay standard was "unrealistic" and "unattainable" with respect to the unionized construction sector.

Construction bargaining typically occurs in the spring and summer. Hence data on the outcome of the CISC approach would not be available until several months had passed. Aside from the new contracts, the CISC was given authority over deferred adjustments under Phase II. Deferred adjustments of 11.6 percent were scheduled in major construction contracts in 1972, compared with close to 7 percent (including escalators) in the nonconstruction sector.[19]

16. Department of Labor press release USDL-72-57, January 28, 1972.

17. The Davis-Bacon act (46 Stat. 1494) provides that contractors must pay their workers "prevailing" wages, which generally means union wages, for construction financed by the federal government. Thus it deprives nonunion contractors of the advantage of the lower wages they typically pay.

18. See D. Q. Mills, "Construction Wage Stabilization: A Historic Perspective," *Industrial Relations*, vol. 11 (October 1972), pp. 350–65, especially pp. 352 and 356.

19. Michael E. Sparrough and Lena W. Bolton, "Calendar of Wage Increases and Negotiations for 1972," *Monthly Labor Review*, vol. 95 (January 1972), pp. 3–14. It is estimated that deferred increases in the nonconstruction sector scheduled for 1972 (with escalators) would have been 6.3 percent with a 3 percent increase in consumer prices. Since the price increase was actually 3.4 percent (December 1971 to December 1972), the average deferred adjustment (including escalators) would have been closer to 7 percent.

In view of union wage developments in construction, the Pay Board's interest in CISC operations was unavoidable. Furthermore, the sparse data available in the early months were not encouraging. According to a Bureau of Labor Statistics preliminary estimate, the CISC had approved wage increases averaging 14.6 percent in the first quarter of 1972, although the CISC was quick to note that these cases were all from the pre–Phase II backlog.[20] This backlog however, had been approved by the CISC itself without prior consultation with the Pay Board, sparking an early controversy between the two agencies. I. W. Abel, president of the Steelworkers and a member of the tripartite Pay Board, complained in a well-publicized telegram of a lax standard in construction relative to the Pay Board's jurisdiction.[21]

The Pay Board-CISC relationship had two important administrative aspects. First, there was the executive order giving the Pay Board responsibility for, and an oversight role in, CISC policies. Second, the non-union construction sector remained in Pay Board jurisdiction, and it was evident that some sort of cooperation was necessary. An initial series of meetings between Pay Board and CISC representatives produced Pay Board Order Number 2, which authorized the CISC to review wage adjustments effective on or after August 16, 1971, the date Phase I began. At a subsequent meeting, it was agreed that this order should be amended to provide specifically for CISC "substantive policies." But in general, Pay Board-CISC relations were steadily deteriorating.[22]

Judge George Boldt, the chairman of the Pay Board, felt obligated to exercise his authority under the executive order. He desired either that the CISC acknowledge his authority by permitting Pay Board monitoring or that the executive order be amended to remove his responsibility for the CISC. The depth of his feeling on this issue—as a federal judge—was probably not appreciated by the CISC. In any case, the dispute over Pay Board authority centered on the issue of the data that the CISC would provide to the board.

20. U.S. Bureau of Labor Statistics, *Current Wage Developments* (June 1972), p. 37.

21. "Abel Heats Up an Ancient Union Feud," *Business Week,* March 11, 1972, pp. 108–09.

22. Amended Order Number 2 was announced in a press release issued jointly by the Pay Board and the CISC on January 28, 1972 (Pay Board press release PB-45). However, the CISC repeatedly requested that its publication in the *Federal Register* be delayed. The Pay Board unilaterally published the order on April 25, 1972, in the *Federal Register* (vol. 37, pp. 8140–41).

The various moves and countermoves over the data question presented a picture of interagency bickering, if not intrigue. The Pay Board issued a series of requests for data, generally through its economics staff. The most important data requested were those relating to CISC actions on deferred wage increases. When these requests did not produce results, the board notified the Cost of Living Council and asked for its assistance. The CLC's attitude was equivocal, and the matter continued to smolder.[23] At one point, top CLC officials gave serious consideration to removing the CISC from the Pay Board's authority and making it directly accountable to a subcommittee of the council. This plan was never carried out, probably because of a concern that the action would be viewed as a victory for the unions and a blow to the Pay Board's credibility. The issue surfaced at the Joint Economic Committee hearing of April 19, 1972, when Judge Boldt was questioned by Senator Jacob Javits about the matter and announced his intention to exercise his authority.[24]

Matters came to a head when Judge Boldt sent a letter to the chairman of the CISC requesting certain data. Pay Board staff were sent to the CISC offices on April 27, 1972, with orders to come back with either permission to begin data collection or a flat denial. After an unpleasant meeting, the Pay Board representatives—together with a "witness" from the CLC—were asked to leave the CISC offices.[25] This action precipitated a White House meeting attended by Judge Boldt, CISC Chairman Dunlop, Treasury Secretary George Shultz (also chairman of the CLC), and Labor Secretary James Hodgson. At this meeting, the judge insisted that he would resign if the matter was not resolved. The outcome was an agreement for a meeting between members of the Pay Board and the CISC to work out the question.

The resulting meeting, and others that followed, finally led to a tacit agreement to provide data on new and deferred CISC approvals. In part this agreement stemmed from an agreement in another area: Pay Board policies on nonunion construction. The Pay Board agreed with the CISC that it would permit nonunion construction agreements of 5.5 percent, or the CISC cents-per-hour approval for the same craft or area, whichever

23. The Pay Board's Office of the General Counsel attempted to obtain an opinion from the Justice Department concerning the board's authority over the CISC under the executive orders. But the department shied away when the issue became an apparent "hot potato."

24. *Review of Phase II,* Hearings, pp. 214–15, 228.

25. Memorandum from Dan Mitchell to Judge George Boldt, April 27, 1972.

was greater.[26] In order to implement this agreement, the Pay Board had to have data on CISC approvals, both new and deferred. Thus the data could be provided for case-processing rather than for monitoring. Toward the end of Phase II a system was being developed whereby the Pay Board would have direct access to CISC computer records.

The Pay Board never really used CISC data for detailed monitoring after they began to arrive. The CISC did not provide any aggregates for its deferred adjustment approvals, and the resources available in the economics office could not keep up with the data inflow. Obviously if Pay Board members had intended to initiate detailed monitoring, the resources could have been found.

Although the running controversy between the Pay Board and the CISC had all the tedious elements of conventional bureaucratic bickering, it did reflect genuine issues of program design and operation. Both the standards and operating principles of the CISC were sharply different from those of the Pay Board. The CISC eschewed a general pay standard and instead made its judgments on a case-by-case basis, taking account of the history of wage changes in a particular craft and the relationship between the wages paid to the different crafts in a given labor market. In most cases CISC's determinations were the product of elaborate negotiations carried out by the public, business, and union representatives. The leadership of the international unions supported the CISC as a mechanism to exercise control over otherwise errant local unions whose individual actions had contributed to the wage explosion in the construction industry. This support was strengthened by the great confidence of the parties in chairman Dunlop. Dunlop was the preeminent academic expert on labor relations in the construction industry and had built up a network of close personal relations with union and management officials over a period of thirty years.

In this collegial environment the CISC perceived the procedures and bureaucratic requirements developed by the Pay Board with antipathy, if not distrust. Any effort to apply the board's standards to CISC activities could disrupt the delicate process of stabilizing the intercraft wage structure. Detailed public disclosure of the CISC's activities might inhibit the backroom bargaining that was an integral part of its operating procedures.

26. The CISC, which did not use a numerical guideline, was not happy with the 5.5 percent proviso for nonunion construction. The Pay Board, however, did not have the resources to adjudicate all nonunion construction adjustments, particularly because of the lack of a small-business exemption in that sector.

And to concede that the CISC was accountable to the Pay Board in any real sense might tar the former with the controversy associated with the board and weaken organized labor's commitment to a tripartite process of wage stabilization in the construction industry.

These programmatic reasons for keeping the Pay Board at arm's length were reinforced by an incident that took place shortly before the CISC was established in March 1971. When there were strong indications that the CISC would be formed and blessed by the Nixon administration, opposition to this move developed in management quarters outside the construction industry. This opposition was expressed most vocally by Roger M. Blough, the retired chairman of the Board of Directors of United States Steel, who had since become the moving figure in the activities of the Construction Users Anti-Inflation Roundtable. The Roundtable consisted of major industrial corporations (who were therefore construction users) who joined together to implement policies that would counter union power in the construction industry. Blough met with President Nixon to express his concern over establishing a wage stabilization agency for the construction industry that ceded authority to the parties to the problem. Although Blough was unsuccessful in dissuading Nixon, he was marked as an adversary of the CISC and the construction unions. Therefore, when Blough appeared as an adviser to the business members of the Pay Board, it was easy for the CISC to impute a certain malevolence to the board's intervention.

On the board's part, there was no intention to control CISC operations in any real sense. As noted above, the board generally accepted the CISC's approach to wage stabilization in the construction industry. The public and business members, however, feared that the line between collegiality and collusion within the CISC would become obscure. Consequently they believed it was important to extract a CISC pledge of fidelity to the general pay standard and, further, to establish specific reporting requirements. The broad objective of these tactics was to exert pressure on the CISC to conform to the objectives of the wage stabilization program and not to regulate the committee closely.

In this context institutional sensitivities were exacerbated by a series of misunderstandings and interpersonal frictions that plagued, or were intrinsic to, the wage stabilization program. The request for information concerning CISC action on deferred increases then became a cause célèbre that required a peacemaking effort by the White House. By objective standards, however, the feud had a happy ending. Judge Boldt did not resign, the CISC maintained its relationship with the Pay Board as part of a comprehensive wage control program, and the board received its reports from the CISC while conceding that discretion was the better part of valor. Most important, the CISC did carry out its task with a high degree of effectiveness, so that the rate of wage increase in the unionized sector of the construction industry declined dramatically during 1972 and into 1973.

The Internal Revenue Service

The IRS handled several aspects of the Pay Board's program. It provided information and interpretations at the local level for persons seeking information about Pay Board rules. During Phase II it received about 694,000 such requests.[27] The IRS also handled complaints and enforcement. Although complaints were comparatively rare on the wage side (rent and price complaints were much more frequent), about 4,000 were received, especially in connection with publicized salary increases of government officials. Compliance and enforcement investigations were initiated as a result of complaints received from the public. They also resulted from requests by the Pay Board to investigate suspicious-looking cases.

On a day-to-day basis, the most important aspect of IRS service to the Pay Board was the processing of Category III cases. The mechanics of the Category III system have already been described. In terms of interagency relations, this aspect of the IRS function on the wage side was the one most closely watched by the board.

It is important to note that the IRS did not report directly to the Pay Board on wage matters. It reported to the Cost of Living Council, an arrangement deliberately planned to give the CLC responsibility over program coverage and enforcement activities. In practice this meant that the IRS was willing to take limited direction from the Pay Board on case-processing as long as the requirements did not exceed available resources. But matters related to available resources and compliance had to be worked out in consultation with the CLC. In fact, a joint agreement between the Pay Board, the IRS, and the CLC left the overall responsibility for compliance with the CLC.

On a personal level IRS-Pay Board relations were reasonably good. But the Pay Board lacked confidence in the quality of IRS case-process-

27. Data through January 12, 1973, supplied by the IRS.

ing. Initially, for example, IRS personnel who worked in stabilization were not eligible for grade increases. This created a turnover problem, since the IRS staff had no desire to remain with the stabilization program for more than a few months under those conditions. The Pay Board also complained early in the program that the IRS was using the same staff members for wage, price, and rent cases when specialization would have been more effective. Although the Pay Board did not want to assume Category III adjudication, it did want to play a supervisory role. Concern about this issue mounted during Phase II.[28] Just before the end of Phase II, the executive director of the Pay Board requested that an increased number of IRS case adjudicators be detailed directly to the board's Washington office to work under the immediate supervision of Pay Board staff.

While it was true that most of the IRS staff had no background in labor relations, this was also true of many Pay Board case adjudicators.[29] Moreover, the IRS had to take the heat for the Pay Board's slow decision-making process on basic policies at the beginning of the program. Before the IRS received authority to shunt cases directly to the board, it also was forced to process cases that its staff knew could not be approved at the IRS level. The IRS resented the unwillingness of the Pay Board to delegate it more authority to decide exceptions. Indeed the IRS resisted the system under which it had no authority to rule on exception claims but had to shunt these to the board.

Another difficulty stemmed from the relative remoteness of the IRS case adjudicators from the Pay Board. Adjudicators at the Pay Board periodically attended board meetings and sometimes made case presentations. They were familiar with the exceptions process used by the board for "gross inequity" claims. At the local IRS level, the granting of exceptions by the Pay Board may well have appeared to be a capricious overriding of the board's own rules. And word must have gotten back to local IRS personnel of the limited time the Category III Panel was able to spend on a case.

A similar problem arose in matters of compliance and enforcement. IRS personnel would discover a violation, typically a payment above the

28. Part of the concern was based on the board's perception of the national IRS office as seeming to have relatively limited authority over the local offices. Thus practices in handling Category III cases appeared to vary across the country.

29. It was alleged at the board that IRS personnel preferred to work on the price side, which required the auditing of books and therefore was more consistent with their backgrounds and career goals. In contrast, most Pay Board adjudicators had legal backgrounds.

guidelines made without the approval of the IRS or the board. Units caught in such situations would generally file exception requests. Sometimes these requests would then be granted, but technically, payment before permission was granted constituted a violation. The Justice Department would not handle such cases because it felt that most judges would be unwilling to impose penalties for something later found to be legal. The fact that few violations ever resulted in penalties reportedly demoralized compliance investigators. In addition, the IRS had a reputation for administrative efficiency and effective enforcement machinery, and its top staff found the improvised operations of the Pay Board marginal at best.

It is not apparent that the Pay Board would have done the job better if it had operated its own local offices, as earlier wartime programs did. The unhappy experience at the Pay Board does not suggest that a more efficient case-processing system—purely from an inventory management viewpoint—would have been developed in local bureaus, given the short start-up time available. In obtaining case adjudicators, the Pay Board would have run up against the same problem the IRS faced in its recruitment efforts. Furthermore, the IRS had local offices for tax collection purposes already in place when Phase II began.

The Cost of Living Council

The CLC was charged with overseeing the entire stabilization program, both wage and price. It was not a review body for cases but did have jurisdiction over the basic program. Thus it was the CLC that implemented the small-business and working-poor exemptions. The CLC kept a representative at Pay Board meetings who acted as a conduit for information in both directions.

The Pay Board and the CLC had some disagreements. When the CLC defined the working poor as those who earned $1.90 an hour or less, it provoked the Pay Board into issuing a press release that indicated this level was not in line with congressional intent.[30] After the council's decision was overturned by a federal district court, the CLC seemed to drag its heels in pressing appeals, despite the inability of the Pay Board to is-

---

30. The board adopted the following resolution, which was cited by Judge William Jones in his opinion overturning the definition: "It is the sense of the Pay Board that the $1.90 figure recommended by the Cost of Living Council is inconsistent with the purpose of the Amendments to the Economic Stabilization Act and supporting analysis." See Pay Board press release PB-39, January 19, 1972.

sue case denials until the issue was resolved. Friction also arose over the CLC's ambiguous stand with regard to the Pay Board-CISC dispute. Staff relations between the Pay Board and the CLC, however, were generally good. At each meeting of the council, the CLC liaison representative to the Pay Board made a report on major board activities. He also conveyed Pay Board requests for actions within the jurisdiction of the CLC.[31] CLC meetings were split between executive sessions and meetings open to staff. A representative from the Pay Board staff often attended such meetings.

During the planning of Phase III, CLC Chairman Shultz met with the members of the Pay Board during a series of consultations. In general the board members cautioned against rapid and widespread decontrol. Judge Boldt testified to this effect before the Joint Economic Committee while recognizing that the President and the Congress had the responsibility for modifying the controls program.[32] The ultimate design of Phase III revealed that the CLC endorsed a more sweeping concept of decontrol.

Some Final Thoughts on Pay Board Organization

Two questions emerge from this excursion through the administrative procedures of Phase II wage controls. First, it can be asked whether the framework that was created would have been viable on a long-term basis. The answer seems fairly clear. Criticism of the program was often based on the assumption of a long-term program.[33] On a long-term basis, having three agencies perform one function is inefficient. The reason for in-

---

31. For example, the Pay Board requested the CLC to give it authority over all wage adjustments that were due to the operation of state-mandated minimum salaries. Such minimums establish floors under the wage scales of local government authorities, and some of the minimums would escape Pay Board coverage by virtue of the small-business exemption. The board felt that in the absence of action by the CLC, Pay Board actions in cases involving such minimums would create inequities between exempt units that would obey the state law and the larger units that would have to obey the board. At the CLC meeting on August 30, 1972, the Pay Board's request was approved.

32. *Price and Wage Control: An Evaluation of Current Policies,* Hearings before the Joint Economic Committee, 92 Cong. 2 sess. (GPO, 1972), pt. 1, p. 59.

33. See, for example, James W. Smith, "The Nixon Administration's Wage Controls: A Labor Viewpoint," *Labor Law Journal,* vol. 24 (August 1973), pp. 532–39. Smith described the difficulties of having a case processed, particularly in Category III. But he began with the assumption that some system of wage controls would be a permanent fixture of the economy and proceeded to describe why the Phase II procedures were not viable on a long-term basis.

volving the Pay Board, the IRS, and the CLC in the wage program was partly to avoid establishing a more permanent system. Furthermore, while there was considerable room for improvement in the case-processing system, it could not have been much improved without additional personnel.

A second question is whether—given the objectives of running a short-term program—a more efficient method of administering the program was possible. The Pay Board could have set up regional offices, for example, but this would have been an expensive and uncertain approach. The IRS was already on the scene, and the birth pains of the board could easily have become unbearable if it had been forced to recruit staff and administer offices scattered about the country. In short, expertise at the local level was sacrificed to availability.

Even allowing for the need for an instant program and structure, the procedures of the board could hardly be characterized as efficient and in many cases were unfair. The appeals procedure was often random or capricious, especially for small units. In delegating authority to the hard-pressed staff, minimal standards of due process were often ignored. And inordinate delays in case-processing persisted throughout Phase II. Although some improvements were forthcoming, each administrative change created new problems intrinsic to the size of the work load and the complexities of interagency coordination.

With more time and planning the administration of the program undoubtedly could have been improved. However, the Pay Board's experience indicated that it is not possible to implement a comprehensive program with a minuscule staff. In a perverse way, the administrative structure was adequate to the program's goals because the basic tactical approach was to give wide credence to the 5.5 percent wage standard and not to regulate compensation in every small unit. The energy and dedication of the staff helped to achieve this tactical objective, but this observation offers slight solace to the employees of a unit whose case was lost or diverted. Within the framework of Phase II, administrative efficiency in the conventional sense was an early casualty of the program's design.

VIII

Compliance and Enforcement

Under Phase II wage controls, covered units were required to accurately report prescribed information on changes in data and to refrain from, or modify increases in, compensation in accordance with Pay Board regulations and orders. Failure to comply could result in penalties of $5,000 for willful violations and might further precipitate injunctive and contempt proceedings. As with any regulatory program, wage controls had to be buttressed by a system of compliance and enforcement.

In analyzing Phase II's compliance machinery, three factors are important. First, no program can catch all violators. For Phase II, with its limited manpower resources, any attempt to seek out and prosecute large numbers of violators would have been impossible. On the other hand, it was important to make the expectation of apprehension real enough to deter violations. Second, Phase II was billed as a largely voluntary program. In the sense that compulsion by law was used, it was not voluntary. "Voluntary" more accurately meant that it was hoped that most people would go along with the program without intensive policing. Third, complaints from the public could be expected to be relatively rare. Few people complain about being overpaid. And few would go to the Internal Revenue Service to complain about other people who were paid in violation of the rules. An employer who was forced to pay more than the allowable amount due to illegal union action might complain. But to the extent an employer had agreed to pay more than was permissible, he too was in violation of the regulations. In short, wage violations generally would have to be sought out if they were to be found and prosecuted.

Although newspaper accounts managed to summarize Phase II wage controls in a single number, 5.5 percent, the regulations actually were highly complex. The 5.5 percent had to be applied to a specified base wage. It was applicable for a particular period and had to be estimated in accordance with costing routines established by the board. Special computations had to be made for exceptions to the standard, such as catch-up. In order to take advantage of the low-wage exemption, an employer had to fill out a special attachment to his report form that required

237

him to separate his work force into low- and high-wage workers. For most employers the computations required for an exception request were complicated, and in the early months of the program, they were required to make these calculations on forms rendered obsolete because of the congressional amendments to the Economic Stabilization Act.[1] Thus a pay violation could possibly occur when there was no intent to go beyond the permissible limits. The compliance problem was therefore accentuated by both the complexity of the regulations, which might engender benign violations, and the peculiar incentives, which made it difficult to identify willful violations.

Operation of the Enforcement Mechanism

During Phase II the Internal Revenue Service was the enforcement arm for both the Pay Board and the Price Commission. Although it acted as their agent in the field, the IRS did not report directly to these agencies. Instead, it reported to the Cost of Living Council. In matters of enforcement and compliance, the CLC directed IRS activities.

A number of factors limited Pay Board involvement in the enforcement area. First, since the CLC had the ultimate responsibility for compliance, the Pay Board staff had to pass along all major recommendations for action. This meant that compliance decisions always had to be made as part of a three-way interagency agreement, an intrinsically cumbersome arrangement. Second, the Pay Board had limited resources available to devote to compliance. In its early days, the staff concentrated on processing cases and assisting the board in policy decisions, and there was a willingness to let someone else worry about enforcement. Third, the staff of the Pay Board did obtain a promise that all cases referred to the Justice Department for litigation would be cleared through the board's general counsel.

1. The initial Pay Board reporting forms, PB-1 for union units and PB-2 for non-union units, were in preparation at the time Congress was debating the exemption of qualified fringe benefits. Since it was unknown how the board would deal with the congressional action, the forms were designed to isolate qualified fringe benefits from other labor costs. Percentages were calculated ignoring qualified fringe benefits in the base and in the increment. This procedure did not turn out to be in keeping with the Pay Board's ultimate decision on qualified benefits. A new form (PB-3) with the correct computation did not appear until June 1972. A short form with simplified computations for Category III employers did not appear until November 1972 (PB-3A).

Table 8-1. *Internal Revenue Service Compliance Activities during Phase II*

Activity	Total	Wage	Price	Rent
Compliance checks[a]	251,367	24,261	210,474	16,632
Special investigations[b]	6,317	1,034	2,743	2,540
Fact-finding investigations[c]	366	70	283	13
Complaints received	155,909	4,025	86,058	65,826

Source: U.S. Internal Revenue Service.
a. Investigations directed by the stabilization agencies or the national IRS office. After June 30, 1972, includes investigations initiated by regional or district IRS offices.
b. Investigations that did not entail a detailed audit.
c. Investigations requested by stabilization agencies for purposes of gathering information on pending requests for exceptional exemptions. Covers period until June 30, 1972.

Finally, it became apparent that the wage aspects of Phase II did not require a great deal of compliance activity. Table 8-1 shows that less than 3 percent of the complaints received during Phase II involved wages. Many of the complaints involved publicized raises scheduled for government officials. Unless the Pay Board or the CLC wished to push the IRS to seek out violations, wage cases obviously would not occupy more than a small fraction of the total man-hours devoted to compliance.

In fact, the Pay Board was not anxious to push the IRS into a widespread compliance effort. Less than 10 percent of the compliance checks shown in table 8-1 were for wage matters. Basically, the board accepted the attitude that most violators needed education concerning Pay Board rules rather than penalties. This attitude, although accepted by the national level of the IRS, caused some chagrin on the part of IRS personnel at the local level. From one source or other, violations would be identified. But upon hearing about a case, the Pay Board often would decide that the increase merited an exception, even if the reporting requirements had been violated. In such cases the board would not approve litigation. It further resisted IRS efforts to force a refund of monies paid in violation of the rules if there was reason to suppose that the increase would eventually be approved. Instead, the board preferred to order payment above 5.5 percent stopped prospectively until the case had been heard. If the increase was found to be unjustified, a prospective rollback from 5.5 percent would be ordered until the excess payment had been refunded. Although this approach was justified as a sensible method for handling apparent violations, it also averted complaints from organized labor that the Pay Board was loosing bureaucratic oppressors on hapless workers.

Aside from conscious Pay Board policy, IRS wage compliance activities were limited by bureaucratic deficiencies. IRS agents were accustomed to dealing with the types of data the Price Commission used for regulatory purposes. The tax-auditing skills learned from the normal functions of the IRS could be easily transferred to price compliance. The same was not true on the wage side. A firm's normal accounting data would not tell an agent whether a wage violation was present. For example, the appropriate employee unit used for Pay Board regulations often was different from that of the firm. A unit might be a part of a firm, or a firm might be a part of a multi-employer unit. Such features as the period of the firm's control year, the presence of a preexisting productivity incentive plan, or the number of "working poor" do not fall out of a corporate balance sheet. Moreover, IRS investigators would find themselves dealing with union officials and personnel directors, persons normally not involved in tax matters. From the Pay Board's perception, the IRS staff was inclined to work on price matters if given a choice, since these assignments were more closely related to career patterns in the service. In any case, lack of enthusiasm for compliance work was complemented by pressure from the Price Commission on the IRS to conduct a vigorous price program.

To some degree, the fact that the IRS was brought into the stabilization program when its major concern was tax collection was bound to limit its dedication to the assignment. Moreover, in the early days of the Pay Board the IRS found itself splattered by some of the criticism that was generated by the tripartite nature of the board. The board would delegate functions to the IRS, but without policy guidance, so that the IRS was forced to administer a program whose rules were unclear or imprecise. The tripartite Pay Board made decisions in the context of a bargaining process, a slow and painful process. News leaks about upcoming decisions were common—and often inaccurate—and the IRS complained that it was always the last to know about major decisions. The well-publicized exceptions to the standards granted in the board's early period appeared inconsistent with the rules the IRS was struggling to learn and apply.

The Pay Board took the responsibility for training IRS personnel. This was done through a series of seminars held in various regions. As a result, the board's staff became concerned about an apparent high turnover rate at the IRS. This turnover led to increased training needs, since new faces kept appearing at the local level. Pay Board staff who dealt with the IRS also complained about the high degree of autonomy exercised by the IRS district and local offices.

In the compliance area, direct contact between the Pay Board and the IRS was relatively limited. Compliance investigations came about in several ways. First, although complaints for wage violations were comparatively rare, some were received. Second, both the Pay Board and the IRS received reporting forms from units as part of the normal case-processing system. A form with inconsistent or unreasonable data might lead to an investigation. If such a form appeared at the Pay Board, the staff would forward it to the CLC, whose operations unit would direct it to the IRS. Third, local IRS directors could initiate compliance investigations on their own initiative. Fourth, the Pay Board, the CLC, and the IRS might organize "sweeps" of particular industries. Three such sweeps occurred during Phase II, all aimed at executive compensation. Firms were selected on the basis of size and location in the financial, professional service (management consulting), and machinery manufacturing industries. The first two were selected because of their widespread contacts with firms in other industries. It was hoped that word of the investigations would spread and create an impression of a tough program of compliance. Although the act of conducting the audits may have created the desired aura of diligence, relatively few violations were found.

There were also secondary routes for the discovery of wage violations. The IRS maintained an active program of price compliance, and price investigators sometimes identified alleged wage violations as part of the same process. Tax audits might serve the same purpose. Sometimes newspaper reports of large wage increases would stimulate a local inquiry. At the CLC publicly available calendars of union contract expirations were used for compliance purposes. Units whose contracts were believed to have expired would be telephoned and asked if they had sent in the appropriate reporting form.

The IRS insisted on controlling the investigative process and the initial recommendation for court action if violations were identified. Before a case could go to the Justice Department for litigation, however, it had to be approved by the CLC and the Pay Board. This requirement was something of a disappointment to the IRS staff, since decisions were made to send cases to Justice only in a small number of cases. The heavy filtering was the result of the Pay Board's attitude on compliance and the aversion of the Justice Department for cases that did not have a high probability of success.[2]

2. The rationing of Justice Department litigation resources would make an interesting dissertation topic for an enterprising graduate student. No price is charged to a regulatory agency for litigation services in its behalf. Consequently an excess demand for such services is created. As a result the Justice Department has considerable discretion in deciding which cases it wishes to pursue.

Table 8-2. *Internal Revenue Service Wage Investigations as of September 13, 1972, by Cause*

Cause of investigation	Number	Percent of total
Audit	80	39.4
Complaint	51	25.1
IRS initiated	48	23.6
Fact-finding[a]	7	3.4
Prenotification[b]	1	0.5
Alleged violation[c]	1	0.5
Other	15	7.4
Total cases listed	203	100.0

Source: Economic Stabilization Program, Cost of Living Council, "Compliance Investigation Status Report and Watch List" (September 13, 1972; processed). Percentages are rounded.

a. Initiated to gather information for policymaking purposes and not generally intended to turn up violations.

b. Investigation of possible failure to prenotify wage-price increase as required.

c. IRS investigation of alleged violation directed by Pay Board, Price Commission, or CLC.

A Statistical Picture of IRS Investigations

Because of the sensitive nature of IRS investigations, detailed summaries of their results are not publicly available. A summary of IRS operations did survive in the Pay Board's files, however. This summary breaks down IRS investigations that were either active or recently closed as of September 13, 1972. As such, it does not represent a complete tabulation of Phase II, but it does give some insight into the processes involved. Tables 8-2, 8-3, and 8-4 are taken from the investigation list provided in the summary.[3]

A total of 203 IRS wage investigations were listed in the CLC computer records as of September 13, 1972. As table 8-2 shows, about 39 percent of these investigations were begun as audits. These were the general investigations mentioned earlier. It is possible that some of these audits were originally price investigations. About one-fourth of the investigations resulted from complaints received. Another 24 percent were initiated by the IRS at various levels. Only one directed investigation of an alleged violation was listed.

Of the 203 investigations, 70 were already closed, and of these (see table 8-3), about three-fourths were closed because no violations were found. The remaining investigations were closed by the Pay Board, the

3. The case listing was used to compile the various aggregates shown in the tables. In some instances these differ slightly from aggregates shown in the summary.

Table 8-3. *Internal Revenue Service Wage Investigations as of September 13, 1972, by Status*

Status of investigation	Number
Closed, no violation found	53
Closed by Justice Department	5
Closed by Pay Board or CLC	12
Total closed	70
Pay Board or CLC recommended no litigation	4
Violation notice (served by IRS)	5
Pay Board or CLC recommended litigation	7
Filed in court	1
Referred to local U.S. attorney	27
Awaiting national IRS office review	1
Awaiting interpretation, ruling, or clarification	3
Other investigation status	85
Total investigations	203

Source: Economic Stabilization Program, Cost of Living Council, "Compliance Investigation Status Report and Watch List" (September 13, 1972; processed).

Table 8-4. *Internal Revenue Service Wage Investigations as of September 13, 1972, by Industry*

Industry	Number of investigations
Food	40
Retail	22
Wholesale	3
Food manufacturing	14
Eating and drinking places	1
Services and finance	38
Government	28
Metals, metal products, machinery (except electric)	26
Electrical equipment	12
Transportation equipment	8
Textiles and apparel	7
Health services	6
Transportation	6
Construction	6
Printing and publishing	5
Entertainment and recreation	4
Utilities	3
All other investigations for which industry was identified	4
Unknown or unclassified	10
Total cases listed	203

Source: Economic Stabilization Program, Cost of Living Council, "Compliance Investigation Status Report and Watch List" (September 13, 1972; processed).

CLC, or the Justice Department because of lack of a basis for litigation. Four of the open cases had received negative recommendations for litigation from the Pay Board or the CLC but had not yet been officially closed. Only one case was actually in court at the time.

Table 8-4 presents an industry breakdown of the 203 investigations.[4] Almost one-fifth of the investigations took place in a sector of the food industry. This concentration probably reflects both the wage and price pressures that occurred in food. There were almost as many investigations in services and finance as in food. But this concentration was a consequence of the sweep of the professional service and finance industries discussed earlier. Twenty-eight investigations were reported in the government sector. Pay raises for government employees were the one area in which numerous wage complaints from the public did occur. Twenty-six investigations were reported in the metals, metal products, and machinery sector. The remainder were broadly scattered throughout other industries.

Litigation Activities

Although very few cases actually involved judicial proceedings, the few that did are significant in the enforcement process because of the functions they served and will be summarized below. When cases were taken to court, specialized publications dealing with labor matters gave prominence to them. Daily newspapers picked up stories about major cases, particularly those involving parties in their local areas.

The Baltimore Meatcutters

On September 4, 1971, in the midst of the Phase I freeze a contract expired between Local 117 of the Amalgamated Meat Cutters and Butcher Workmen of North America and the Baltimore-area A&P chain. The unit consisted of about seventy-seven workers employed in ware-

4. Some adjustments were needed to compile the industry data for table 8-4. For example, when the title of an investigation was a union name, the industry was originally recorded as "nonprofit membership." This is the industry category for unions as organizations, but not for the industry in which the workers involved are employed. Union names were used to determine the industry of the workers; for example, Teamsters were assumed to be working in transportation.

house operations. While negotiations were under way, the Pay Board was established, and it announced its 5.5 percent standard on November 8, 1971. At that point the employer informed the union that it could not pay an increase in excess of 5.5 percent. Whether the employer acknowledged that it could *negotiate* a higher increase with implementation contingent on a Pay Board exception is not clear. In any case a strike began on November 13, 1971, and lasted until November 21, when a new agreement was concluded that was subsequently estimated to cost 15.5 percent by the Pay Board staff. Since the agreement was concluded during Phase II, it was subject to the 5.5 percent standard (and exceptions) applicable to all such contracts. Nevertheless, the negotiated increment was placed into effect immediately. No exception request was filed until January 10, 1972. Pursuant to the request, the Pay Board determined that the unit was eligible for 7 percent, considerably less than the amount already being paid.

The Justice Department filed suit in the local U.S. district court (Maryland) requesting fines of $2,500 for both the employer and the union and a rollback to the permissible increase. In their client's behalf, the defense questioned the constitutionality of the controls program, asserted that the 5.5 percent standard had no rational basis, and charged that the Pay Board's distinction between new and deferred agreements was arbitrary. It was also argued that the base wage against which the standard should be applied was not that of the unit in question but the prevailing wage on the East Coast or in the Baltimore area for comparable union workers. All these contentions were dismissed by the court, and an order was issued on April 19, 1972, requiring a rollback and imposing fines. This action was later upheld by the Temporary Emergency Court of Appeals, the special court established to deal with stabilization matters. The case therefore established the power under the Economic Stabilization Act to order rollbacks and inflict penalties for wage violations.

Crescent Warehouse

The Crescent Warehouse Company operated several warehouses in the port of Los Angeles area, employed eighteen permanent employees, and had an agreement with Local 13 of the International Longshoremen's and Warehousemen's Union. This obscure enterprise came to national attention when a strike ensued after the employees refused to accept an agreement that contained a clause stating the company would honor the contract to the extent permissible by the stabilization program.[5] The case was the first in which an injunction was issued halting a strike against the stabilization program.

In fact, the employer had made some illegal payments before the strike. The employer's contract expired along with the other West Coast longshore agreements on June 30, 1971, but the company apparently was not a signatory to the basic agreement. Negotiations for a new contract continued until early September 1972. Pending agreement on a new contract, the employer raised wage rates a reported 19 percent as of July 1, an adjustment not permitted under Pay Board regulations without an exception. (An exception probably would have been granted on the basis of tandem with the basic West Coast agreement.)

The strike began in early September and initially was intended to force a settlement on the terms of a new agreement. When Crescent agreed to those terms the strike continued because the employer insisted on a clause indicating that it would not exceed the increment permissible under the stabilization program. At the request of the Pay Board, the Justice Department requested a temporary restraining order from the local U.S. district court (Central District of California). The government's request was granted, and the union members returned to work.

Los Angeles Bus Drivers

The Southern California Rapid Transit District (RTD) operates a publicly owned bus system in the Los Angeles area. A contract between the RTD and Division 1277 of the Amalgamated Transit Union, covering about 650 workers, expired on September 1, 1971. A new agreement was negotiated on March 3, 1972, providing for a 5.5 percent wage increase to be applied retroactively to September 1, 1971, a violation of the Pay Board's rules on Phase I retroactivity. In general, Pay Board rules did not permit retroactivity under successor contracts for agreements expiring during the freeze.

The Justice Department originally requested a $2,500 fine from the employer and the union and restitution of the retroactive payments by the employees. But a compromise settlement was reached. Fines of $1,000 were imposed on the employer and the union. In addition, restitution of 50 percent of the retroactive payments was required from the employees. This amounted to about $50 per worker.

5. *Wall Street Journal,* October 18, 1972.

Meredith Printers

The Meredith case was the first in which an injunction was sought to roll back a wage increase that was not in conformity with Pay Board rules. Meredith was a large company that published nationally distributed magazines. It maintained a printing plant in West Haven, Connecticut, that employed thirty-nine workers who were represented by Local 47 of the International Typographical Union.

An agreement between the company and the union expired on August 23, 1971. Negotiations continued until early December 1971 when a strike began. After a few days, a new two-year agreement was implemented providing a first-year wage adjustment of about 7.5 percent plus additional fringe benefits. This increment was in excess of the Pay Board's standards, but no exception request was filed.

The Justice Department asked for fines of $2,500 from both the company and the union and full restitution of excess wages. Despite the publicity the case originally received, a mutual agreement was eventually reached whereby the court proceedings were "dismissed with prejudice." A stipulation was obtained noting that if the first- and second-year increments were combined, the total amount would not exceed the Pay Board's guideline for two-years' worth of increase. This limited remedy was agreed to because the printing plant involved was scheduled to be closed by Meredith, and there was no desire to inflict further hardship on the employees.

Los Angeles Electricians

Local 11 of the International Brotherhood of Electrical Workers negotiated an agreement with Los Angeles area contractors in 1969 slated to run for three years. In 1970 the agreement was reopened for negotiations by mutual consent of the parties. The new agreement was extended to 1973. Among its terms was a $1.71 increase scheduled for June 1, 1972. Under Phase II regulations, this increment was subject to the review of the Construction Industry Stabilization Committee.

During 1972 the CISC was faced with a significant number of deferred adjustments in union construction providing for large increments. The Bureau of Labor Statistics reported a scheduled deferred increase averaging 11.6 percent for construction contracts involving 1,000 or more workers in that year.[6] Hence the ability of the CISC to review adjustments such as that provided in the Los Angeles electricians' contract was an important issue in itself. In addition, the issue involved with the $1.71 increment—the use of escrow accounts—reflected a question of greater importance to both the CISC and the Pay Board.

The CISC reviewed the proposed increment in April 1972 and found $1.71 (on a wage and fringe base of $9.79) to be unacceptable. It indicated that it would accept an increment of $1. At a subsequent review in July, the CISC reaffirmed its original determination, and the chairman defended this determination as being in accord with the general CISC policy of restoring previously distorted wage relationships. The chairman cited related wage rates prevailing in the Los Angeles area and the state of California. To permit more than a $1 increase, he said, would upset local differentials and have a destabilizing effect on other crafts.

In response to the adverse CISC ruling, Local 11 requested that the employers pay the disputed 71 cents into an escrow fund. The union's proposed Memorandum of Understanding concerning the escrow account specified only that the funds would be paid to the employees (with interest) when the parties could "legally do so." Some contractors apparently made payments to the fund until August 2, 1972, when the employers' association took the position that the payments were unlawful under the regulations of the Pay Board.

Both the Pay Board and the CISC considered the no-escrow principle to be vital to their programs. The intent of the wage side of the stabilization program was to control costs. If disallowed wage increases could be paid into escrow funds until controls ended, there would be no effect on costs. A dollar paid into a bank account costs as much as one placed directly in a pay envelope.[7]

The arguments raised by the union were (1) that the Economic Stabilization Act represented an unconstitutional delegation of authority by Congress to the executive branch of government, (2) that windfall profits

6. See Michael E. Sparrough and Lena W. Bolton, "Calendar of Wage Increases and Negotiations for 1972," *Monthly Labor Review,* vol. 95 (January 1972), p. 6.

7. It was sometimes argued in connection with certain fringe benefits that their inflationary effect was lessened because the money would not be immediately spent. For example, money paid into a pension fund is a form of saving. This view assumes that (1) the money would not have been saved if it had been paid as cash wages, and (2) that workers do not reduce voluntary saving to offset forced saving. In any case most American economists would argue that aggregate demand should be regulated by governmental monetary and fiscal policy and not by attempting to force saving.

would result for employers, and (3) that the CISC ruling was arbitrary.[8] These assertions were rejected by the U.S. district court (Central District of California). The position of the Pay Board and the CISC—that the escrow arrangement was unlawful—was upheld by the court. The decision was later affirmed by the Temporary Emergency Court of Appeals.

Litigation Testing the Validity of Wage Stabilization Decisions

Not all litigation involving Phase II wage controls revolved around alleged misdeeds by particular employee units. In some instances units that had received adverse decisions complied with Pay Board or CLC rulings but tested those decisions in the courts—for example, the successful challenge of the CLC's definition of the working poor as those earning $1.90 an hour or less. Two other challenges, one successful and the other not, are also noteworthy.

An important difference between the stabilization program of 1971–74 and previous wartime control efforts was that the former included state and local employees within its coverage. One of the early cutbacks made by the Pay Board involved civil service employees of the state of Ohio.[9] After Phase II began, the Ohio legislature adopted a new pay schedule for state employees providing an average pay adjustment of 10.6 percent. The Pay Board cut the allowable increase to 7 percent, although it permitted a special time-weighting procedure whereby the 10.6 percent was simply delayed sufficiently to make it equivalent in dollar compensation to a 7 percent increase.

In response the state of Ohio challenged the constitutional right of the federal government to regulate wage practices of state governments. The Ohio Supreme Court accepted this argument and ordered that the entire

8. The windfall profit argument was based on the assertion that bids and contracts were already made on the basis of the $1.71 increase at the time of the CISC cutback. Price Commission rules in effect required a renegotiation of the contract to the extent that a cutback was ordered by the CISC. But the rule originally applied only to contracts negotiated after the establishment of the CISC. This rule was revised later to cover all contracts retroactively. Curiously, the plaintiffs never pursued the windfall further than the contractors. Presumably if the contractors had followed the Price Commission regulations, the windfall would simply have been passed to the contractors' customers.

9. See appendix D.

10.6 percent wage increase be paid, a decision that would have granted state employees an additional $10.5 million. The Justic Department requested a local federal district court to enjoin the increase. The district court in turn certified the case to the Temporary Emergency Court of Appeals, which upheld the right of the federal government to regulate state wages under the terms of the Economic Stabilization Act.

The U.S. Supreme Court rendered a final decision in 1975, over a year after the Economic Stabilization Act had expired.[10] The Supreme Court—with one dissent and one "separate statement"—ruled that constitutional authority for the regulation of state employees' wages did exist. Although the wage payments were intrastate in themselves, they had the potential of influencing interstate commerce. Congress did not explicitly include state employees within the coverage of the Economic Stabilization Act, the Court noted, but the legislative history showed that Congress had explicitly rejected an amendment exempting state and local workers.

Unlike the other cases cited, the Ohio decision has obvious importance outside the context of Phase II controls. The Supreme Court ruling suggests that a future wage control program could, if authorized, extend coverage to government workers at all levels. As the Court noted, the government sector employs a substantial fraction of the work force. Above-standard increases in that sector could have led to demands for comparable wage hikes in private employment.

The State of Ohio case was the second in which a Pay Board cutback was made. The first cutback, involving the major aerospace firms, also precipitated litigation, this time resulting in a reversal of the Pay Board's decision. With hindsight it appears that the board probably could have averted the reversal with a few minor word changes in its decision. But at the time the board was inexperienced in legal matters, and its regulations were fuzzy.

The key issue in the aerospace case was whether a portion of the proposed wage increase was to be treated as a deferred adjustment.[11] Under the previous contract, a cost-of-living escalator clause had been included. As was often the case in the late 1960s, the clause included a "cap" limiting the maximum amount the escalator could pay. About 34 cents would have been paid under the escalator were it not for the cap. Before

10. The decision is reprinted in Bureau of National Affairs, Inc., *Daily Labor Report,* May 27, 1975, pp. D-1–D-6.
11. See chapter 5.

Phase I the parties had informally agreed that the 34 cents would be included in whatever new adjustment might be negotiated.[12]

As expected, the new settlements reached after Phase II began amounted to more than 34 cents. A total increase of 51 cents for the first year was the central feature of the new settlements. The Pay Board viewed the entire 51 cent increment as a "new" adjustment. But the unions argued that the 34 cents was really old money, and that the 5.5 percent standard should be applied *above* it, a position that would have prevented any cutback.

The litigation surrounding the aerospace cases revolved around the technical point of whether an obligation regarding the 34 cents had or had not been established before Phase II. A federal district court found that the 34 cents was indeed old money under Pay Board regulations. The Justice Department appealed to the Temporary Emergency Court of Appeals for a reversal of the lower court's ruling but was unsuccessful.[13] By the time the emergency court finished with the case, the Pay Board had been terminated, and Phase III was well into its death throes. The Cost of Living Council, which had charge of both the wage and price sides of the program after Phase II, oversaw the repayment of the cutback (17 cents) to the workers involved. Ironically, with more careful drafting of its decision, the board could probably have avoided the old-new issue. Later regulations of the board—included mainly to support CISC policy—permitted cuts below 5.5 percent under special circumstances.

Concluding Notes on Compliance

Like many other aspects of the program, the Pay Board's approach to compliance was conditioned by the temporary nature of the Phase II effort. If the Pay Board had believed that it would become a permanent fixture of economic policy, it would have been forced to devote more

12. From an economic viewpoint this agreement had little meaning, since economic conditions (and the cap) ensured that the new settlement would be more than 34 cents anyway. However, it probably had some face-saving value for the leaders of the unions involved—the Auto Workers and the Machinists—who had been embarrassed with the experience under the cap.

13. The decision (*Boldt* v. *UAW and IAM*) is reprinted in BNA, *Daily Labor Report,* June 22, 1973, pp. D-1–D-4.

attention to compliance than it actually did. Phase II took place in a period when the labor market was not especially tight. Thus widespread pressure for evasion of the regulations was not expected. The wage data available for the period (reviewed in chapter 10) did not indicate that any widespread evasion took place. By mid-1972, however, it was widely believed by the economists in the program that 1973 would see a substantial expansion of economic activity and that demand pressures would increase. In any event, a permanent Pay Board would have had to deal with labor markets in varying degrees of tension. Hence the activities during the early phase of the program would have been important for setting the future tone of the enforcement effort. In addition, litigated cases would have had the value of setting precedents for future cases.

Without the need to worry about the distant future, the Pay Board could limit the attention it gave compliance matters. Moreover, apart from economic conditions, any short-run program enjoys a period of grace before the limits of compliance are tested. No one could be certain how intense the enforcement effort would be. The risk of violating the rules may have appeared greater than was actually the case, at least for a while.

It was often said that the employer was the Pay Board's compliance enforcement mechanism. Of course, buyers of goods and services had the same incentive to act as enforcers on the price side. But where wages were concerned, the employer was in a stronger position. Under Price Commission rules the legal price increase for an item depended on the economic condition of the *seller*. The buyer generally would not know if a price was raised illegally. But on the wage side the legal wage increase was based on the economic condition of the *buyer* (employer). Accordingly the employer could determine whether a wage increase he was being asked to grant was within the Pay Board's rules from data he had at hand. If a period of general labor shortage had developed, however, the employer and the employee would have had a mutual interest in evading the regulations. A tighter enforcement effort (or a looser program) would have been required.

In short, the timing of Phase II and the understanding that it would be a temporary program led to the relatively relaxed wage enforcement program. What litigation occurred amounted to only a handful of cases, some of which seemed to peter out rather than resolve themselves. Only a small fraction of the time spent by the IRS on enforcement and compliance went to the wage side of the program.

IX

Tripartitism and the Politics of Wage Stabilization

The Pay Board carried out its duties in a fragile organizational environment. As a tripartite body, the board was a vehicle for explicit bargaining among the major interest groups in the economy. Adversary issues had to be resolved in a manner that accommodated the objectives of the stabilization program, the political needs of the three factions, and minimal standards of due process. Although the board could survive internal dissatisfaction over specific rulings, it could function effectively only if the net effect of its policies and decisions was a working consensus and acceptance, if not support, of the program's goals. The preservation of such a consensus was intrinsically difficult because of the calculated divergence of interests among the three membership groups. In collective bargaining both labor and management normally have an interest in the continued existence and profitability of a business enterprise; in a program of wage controls, their goals may be best served through the impairment or dissolution of the stabilization agency. Even if the individual board members are sympathetic to the aims of the program, they come to their task with a network of affiliations and external interests whose weight the agency might not be able to support.

The Theory of Tripartitism

The record of the Pay Board and its predecessors reveals that the tripartite approach to wage stabilization is inherently unstable and not readily conducive to rational decisionmaking or efficient administration. But the virtues of tripartitism theoretically reside in other considerations that overbalance these deficiencies.

First, tripartitism affords a device for the representation of the major interest groups in what is appropriately viewed as an exercise in national wage bargaining. While the rulings of the Pay Board were equally applicable to unionized and nonunion workers, the tripartite form recognizes the special status of collective bargaining as a procedure for setting wages and working conditions. Thus collective bargaining has been endorsed and supported by public policy. The Pay Board constituted a higher level for review of the agreements reached through labor-management negotiations. If collective bargaining is the preferred device in the first instance, then a similar arrangement is desirable to incorporate the interests of the parties in the review process. In this manner tripartitism can provide for continuity of representation in governmental processes that evaluate the outcomes of bargaining in the light of a declared public interest.

This principle of the conservation of the rights of representation was supplemented by an additional pragmatic factor. By giving management and labor in particular direct representation on the wage stabilization agency, these groups would become parties to the regulatory process and would have less latitude in criticizing the program or in alleging that the process was unjust. In the event that either labor or management did attack the program or cease to participate, these challenges would be unlikely to elicit widespread public support and sympathy.

The role of the public members on a tripartite wage board is somewhat more subtle than that of labor or management. In the metaphysics of tripartitism, "the government" generally is viewed as a party who has narrow political interests that detract from, rather than enhance, the summum bonum. In this context the public members are considered to represent interests other than the government. They are expected to advance not only the stated objectives of the program but some abstract notion of fairness and impartiality as well. For this reason the public members of wage stabilization agencies usually have been drawn from the ranks of labor mediators and arbitrators and have attained a status as independent third parties.[1] This role has been especially important when wage stabilization efforts have been associated with the relinquishment of the right to strike by organized labor.

The singular status of the public members certifies the "independence" of the tripartite wage board. Tripartitism is not a necessary condition for

1. The public members of the National War Labor Board in World War II were William H. Davis, chairman; George W. Taylor; Frank P. Graham; and Wayne L. Morse. (E. Eastman Irvine, ed., *The World Almanac and the Book of Facts for 1943* [New York World-Telegram, 1943], p. 110.) The public members of the Wage Stabilization Board during the Korean war were Cyrus S. Ching, chairman; Clark Kerr; and John T. Dunlop. ("Wage Stabilization Board Lined Up—to Mark Time," *Business Week*, December 2, 1950, pp. 102–06.) In all cases, the public members had well-established reputations as third parties, i.e., professors, arbitrators, and former government officials.

the independent status of a regulatory agency, but in labor-management relations it signifies to the major interest groups, particularly labor, that the board will have wide discretion in its operations. In this respect the concept of independence in the regulation of wages is sharply differentiated from the concept as it is used in other economic areas. Most regulatory agencies, such as the Federal Trade Commission and the Federal Communications Commission, are conceived to be free of the influence of the parties whose activities they regulate. If an advertising executive were nominated for membership on the Federal Trade Commission, he would surely undergo searching scrutiny by Congress before he was annointed with governmental authority. Under a tripartite form of wage regulation, however, "independence" is viewed as a mandate from the government to representatives of special-interest groups to regulate themselves subject only to statutory limits and the restraints that can be exercised by the public members.

Tripartitism also incorporates a dialectical approach to the problem of conflict of interest. If the tripartite form of organization explicitly provides for the representation of parties at interest and lends the sanctions of government to this body's determinations, does not this process constitute a clear conflict of interest? The apparent clash between the desire to afford representation to interest groups and the proscriptions against conflict of interest in the regulatory process ostensibly are resolved by distinguishing between the interests of functional economic blocs and those of specific employers and unions. Under tripartitism the members of the wage stabilization agency presumably represent large blocs and therefore are not sullied by conflicts of interest in individual decisions. This distinction is, of course, extremely tenuous and may lack credibility in individual cases. While the public members can deflect conflicts of interest by casting the swing votes, tripartitism may permit, if not facilitate, an implicit form of collusion when labor and management both perceive their interests to be served by supporting a decision that is inconsistent with public objectives.

Second, it is alleged that tripartitism ensures that a special expertise will be brought to bear in dealing with the problems of wage stabilization. By enlisting practitioners from management and labor, the wage stabilization agency can set policies and render decisions based on a sophisticated understanding of the implications of these determinations for the affected parties. Similarly, expert public members can help identify areas of agreement between labor and management and evaluate conflicting contentions in the light of prevailing industrial relations practices. The desirability of expert knowledge in administering public policy in labor-management relations has been recognized in the activities of the National Labor Relations Board, which is responsible for applying the basic labor statutes in the United States.[2] On a bureaucratic level, the expertise of the wage board members also will guard against undue influence by staff personnel who develop a greater facility in the technical niceties of the regulations than in understanding the practical implications of their interpretations.

Third, the tripartite structure provides a framework for mediation and dispute settlement. The mediation function might be necessary in two situations. On the one hand, the parties to a particular collective bargaining relationship may be unable to reach an agreement that satisfies their goals and the standards of the stabilization program. The wage board members may attempt to work out an agreement that accommodates these conflicting considerations. In this instance the attainment of a mutually acceptable mediation agreement carries with it the de facto approval of the board. In other circumstances management and the union may formally agree to a wage settlement for internal political reasons even though they know it to be inconsistent with the regulatory standards. The agreement is submitted for review with the knowledge that it will be reduced or otherwise modified. The task of the wage board is to determine by administrative ruling the settlement that actually is acceptable to the parties and consistent with the objectives of the program; this type of mediation can be an extremely complex and delicate matter. The labor representatives on the board will bargain with the union officials who are directly involved in the agreement. They will also engage in negotiations with the public and business members. The same process is carried out on the management side.

Tripartitism and the Pay Board

The Pay Board formally adhered to the precepts of tripartitism but deviated from these norms in several significant respects. Its membership

2. The National Labor Relations Board was established by the National Labor Relations Act (Wagner act) in 1935 (49 Stat. 449). This agency was designed to bring special substantive skills to the administration of national labor policy while expediting the disposition of representation elections and unfair labor practice charges. See the National Labor Relations Act and the Labor Management Relations Act, 1947 (Taft-Hartley act), title I (61 Stat. 136), which is an amendment to the former act.

did encompass the usual array of special interests associated with wage stabilization agencies. The labor members were all drawn from the ranks of organized labor. Similarly, the management, or business, representatives came from large firms such as General Electric, Continental Oil, and the Southern Pacific Company. The five public members, however, did not fit into the mold. Judge George Boldt, Arnold Weber, and Neil Jacoby probably departed most from the traditional notion of third-party status associated with public membership on a wage stabilization body. Jacoby in particular came under attack shortly after he had been appointed to the Pay Board when he strongly implied in a speech that excessive wage increases had been a major causal factor in the current inflation.[3] Together, the public members represented an intellectual position explicitly committed to the objectives of stabilization rather than to a posture of impartiality that implied they would serve as a catalyst or balm for the two major interest groups.

Nor could the board boast of a special expertise in labor-management relations. The labor members were, of course, experts in the sense that the conduct of labor-management relations was a central occupational activity. In contrast, only two of the public members, Caples and Weber, had a professional background in this area. On the management side, Virgil Day was the sole industrial relations practitioner. Robert Bassett and Rocco Siciliano had had extensive experience in the past but were no longer involved in labor-management relations.

The mixed background of the public and business members was the target of recurrent scorn on the part of the labor representatives, who frequently characterized the other board members as "a bunch of amateurs." This amateurism was most likely to be revealed in a lack of sensitivity to the niceties of union politics or an unfamiliarity with technical terms rather than the incapacity to understand specific issues. Nonetheless, it is true that the composition of the board did not give exclusive or even predominant weight to industrial relations skills; instead, an understanding of, or commitment to, the economics of the stabilization effort was accepted as an adequate qualification for service.

The Pay Board was also distinguished from previous tripartite groups in that all the members, with the exception of the chairman, served on a part-time basis and continued to perform their regular jobs. This arrangement necessitated the extensive delegation of authority to the staff,

3. *Los Angeles Times,* October 27, 1971.

particularly in routine matters. In general the board members reserved their efforts for broad policy issues and the consideration of major cases. This meant that the staff increasingly asserted responsibility for drafting detailed regulations and handling individual cases. To the extent that this development took place, the board members passively relinquished control over the program, and decisions became less susceptible to the negotiations and flexibility that have been the hallmarks of tripartitism.

The administrative environment of the board was further influenced by the differential commitment of the various members. Some members, such as Day, devoted virtually full time to the board's activities. Other members could not commit large blocks of time to the program but assigned alternates or staff personnel from their home organizations to assume their responsibilities. This was especially true of the labor and business members. Thus there was an "official" board consisting of the presidential appointees and a shadow board made up of full-time alternates or assigned staff from external organizations. This situation put the public members at a relative disadvantage, since they did not command full-time alternates or staff that could be assigned to the board. In any case the nominal part-time status of the board was not calculated to ensure the continued involvement of the members.

The composition of the Pay Board also made it less likely that the agency would become heavily involved in mediation or the settlement of disputes. As indicated in chapter 1, originally the board did contemplate informal efforts at conciliation. As the board evolved, however, these efforts were only sporadic. Indeed the public members increasingly shied away from this activity. The rejection of mediation responsibilities reflected both the experience of the board and a broader intellectual position. First, either through ineptness or the perceived intransigence of the labor members, the early tentative efforts at mediation were unsuccessful and did not inspire optimism that further attempts would be more effective. Second, a distinction was made between the circumstances surrounding Phase II and past stabilization efforts. During World War II and the Korean war considerable emphasis had been placed on maintaining labor peace as well as on economic stabilization. The Phase II venture in controls took place in quite a different context. The requirements of the Vietnam conflict did not necessitate the concerted mobilization of the nation's resources. To the contrary, there was significant slack in the economy in 1971.

Moreover, the board adhered to the view that acceptance of the goal of dispute settlement would be inconsistent with both the economic premises underlying the stabilization program and the standards of equity. The conventional justification for wage and price controls during peacetime is that powerful economic institutions may generate inflationary pressures in the labor and product markets. On the labor side, this power derives from union control over labor supply and the capacity to withhold services from the market. It would be self-defeating to accommodate this power in an administrative process that was designed to restore some balance to economic decisionmaking. An emphasis on dispute settlement as a goal would reward the strong while controlling the weak who had only a limited capacity to inflict their will on the community.

That the Pay Board adopted a policy of economic primacy did not mean that all its decisions exhibited an Olympian detachment. Undoubtedly the board's rulings in the coal and railroad cases reflected management's special anxiety about the impact of possible strikes on production in these essential industries. As noted earlier, during the public hearing on the coal case, Tony Boyle, president of the United Mine Workers, dryly noted that "you can't mine coal with bayonets."[4] The proletarian romanticism of this statement did not detract from its validity, and the contract was ultimately approved by a ten-to-five margin.

The downgrading of the mediation function by the Pay Board did not appear to contribute to the occurrence of labor conflict. None of the major decisions handed down by the Pay Board provoked a work stoppage. As the data in chapter 12 indicate, the incidence of strikes declined sharply during Phase II. To be sure, 1972 was a relatively light year on the bargaining calendar, but the level of industrial conflict was lower than it had been in comparable years in the three-year bargaining cycle. In addition, it is important to recognize that the depreciation of mediation activities did not impair the usual process of bargaining and accommodation in the board's decisionmaking process.

A last difference between the Pay Board and the traditional concept of tripartitism was the actual independence of the agency. Although the Pay Board did enjoy the formal autonomy associated with tripartite efforts at wage stabilization, it was tied to the executive branch by a web of bureaucratic threads. Its autonomy had been a cause célèbre in the events leading to the announcement of Phase II. Ultimately George Meany had been able to brandish the memorandum in which President Nixon

4. Authors' personal records of Pay Board activities.

personally affirmed the board's independence from other agencies of government. While the presidential memorandum did provide a formal declaration of autonomy, the question of the actual independence of the board was more complicated. Under the terms of the memorandum the Cost of Living Council retained the authority to make basic decisions concerning the coverage of wage controls. Because this authority was almost always used to exempt certain sectors of the labor force from controls, the labor members did not protest this encroachment on the board's discretion. In contrast, the board sharply criticized the CLC's determination of the "working poor" under the terms of the amendments to the Economic Stabilization Act. When the CLC stood by its original determination of the working poor as those earning $1.90 an hour or less, the labor members did not seek to shift authority for making this decision to the Pay Board. Instead, they initiated court proceedings that resulted in a vindication of the labor position.[5]

More subtly, the Pay Board occupied the center of the stage but did not control the stagehands or the supporting players. The Pay Board did not have its own field staff; its entire investigative and compliance mechanism was lodged in the Internal Revenue Service and was operated under CLC direction. Similarly, the administrative machinery for handling requests for exceptions was housed in the IRS-CLC structure. All but the major cases had to move through this machinery before they reached the Pay Board. The separation of administration and all but the appellate aspects of case-handling clearly constrained the actual discretion of the board as an independent agency. This arrangement was designed to minimize the size of the bureaucracy involved in the total stabilization program and to permit the CLC to maintain effective administrative control of the program. Both objectives were satisfied to a high degree over the life of Phase II.

The deviations of the Pay Board from the traditional principles of tripartitism were of sufficient magnitude to make playing by the old rules a cause of considerable misunderstanding and controversy. From the outset tripartitism on the Pay Board served to inflame the decisionmaking process at least as much as it facilitated accommodation among the major interest groups. Drawing on their experiences during World War II and the Korean war, the labor members denied the need for a numerical general pay standard. During these prior experiences with controls, indi-

5. *Jennings* vs. *Connally*, 347 F. Supp. 409 (1972).

vidual cases were subject to intensive review and negotiation within a tripartite field structure of regional wage boards.[6] In the absence of a similar structure for the Pay Board, an explicit pay standard was an operational necessity. The controversies arising in the aerospace, railroad, and longshoremen cases also provided dramatic evidence of the sharp differences in expectations and mode of operation with which the different groups approached their responsibilities on the Pay Board.

The Practice of Tripartitism

Because the Pay Board was a confederation of three factions held together by a common statute and shared suspicions, its operation is best understood in terms of the tactics and procedures of each of the three groups. In a very real sense the Pay Board was the sum of its parts.

The Labor Members

Of the three groups on the Pay Board, the labor members were the most homogeneous in interest and the most consistent in behavior. For the labor members, there was a perfect identity of ideology, intellect, and interests in conducting their business on the board. From an ideological point of view they were deeply committed to protecting the economic interests of their members and other wage earners. Intellectually they never had any difficulty in establishing an acceptable basis in "comparability" or "equity" for supporting individual wage claims that came before the board. And clearly they viewed their narrow tactical interests as the protection of labor's position against adversary forces.

During the tripartite stage of the board's existence the labor members voted or acted as a bloc in every instance except when two of them abstained on the vote to approve the wage increase that had been negotiated between the railroads and the United Transportation Union. Their vote reflected the belief that since the board had reduced other agreements, the UTU contract was not sufficiently meritorious to remain untouched. This abstention proved to be an act of temporary pique, however. When the case was brought up for reconsideration, all five labor representatives voted for approval, carrying the day for the contract. Thus when there

6. See Morris A. Horowitz, "Administrative Problems of the Wage Stabilization Board," *Industrial and Labor Relations Review*, vol. 7 (April 1954), pp. 390–403.

were tactical or political differences among the labor members, the discipline of the group was sufficient to restore a common front.

This constancy of behavior was reinforced by the fact that following the promulgation of the basic policies of the Pay Board on November 8, 1971, the official labor members seldom attended meetings. If they did participate in the deliberations of the board, it was on a sporadic basis or when a case involving their particular union was up for consideration. From November 9, 1971, to March 23, 1972, when four of the labor members resigned, the Pay Board held eighty-one official meetings. During this period I. W. Abel attended nine sessions, Frank Fitzsimmons was present at five meetings, Floyd Smith came on eleven occasions, Leonard Woodcock participated once, and George Meany never attended a board meeting after November 8.[7] The participation of the regular labor members virtually ceased by the end of January 1972. For the last two months of the Pay Board's existence as a tripartite body, the task of representing labor's interests was left to alternates.

The alternates generally enjoyed less discretion to modify a position or strike a compromise. If there was any uncertainty concerning the merits of a proposed accommodation with the public and business members, the prudent course of action was to support the position that was objectively consistent with labor's formal interests. This was true even though the Teamsters and the UAW were outside the AFL-CIO. Because they were independent of the labor federation, they were under pressure to demonstrate solidarity so as to avoid the implication that they were pursuing their own interests to the detriment of the labor movement as a whole.

Among the alternates, informal leadership came to be exercised by Pat Greathouse of the UAW and Elliot Bredhoff of the Steelworkers. Greathouse frequently acted as spokesman in presenting the labor position during the Pay Board sessions. He assumed this role as the consequence of his prodigious skills at exposition and debate rather than by any formal action of the labor members. Bredhoff served as the legal technician and protected labor's interests in the drafting of resolutions and regulations. The elaboration of these roles facilitated the business of the board and provided a point of contact for the public and business members. Nonetheless, the leadership was intellectual rather than political and did not afford wide flexibility in negotiations with the other members. When an accommodation was sought in a major case, such as the aero-

7. Attendance figures were derived from the minutes of Pay Board meetings.

space and East Coast longshoremen cases, the direct participation of the regular labor members had to be enlisted.

The Business Members

The business members revealed the widest range of interests and the greatest variation in behavior. Philosophically, all the business members actively supported wage and price controls. In this sense, they mirrored opinion in the business community at large at the end of 1971, when it was widely believed that the current inflation was caused by cost-push factors, especially in the unionized sector. Indeed pressure from the business community was one of the important factors that precipitated the administration's volte-face in economic policy on August 15, 1971. As spokesmen for *class* interests, the business members adhered to the view that a hard line should be taken in wage increases. Their ability to represent these class interests was limited, however, because of the business group's willingness to indulge *specific* interests when they intruded in individual cases. Thus the broad class interests of management might be overbalanced by solicitude for the "uniqueness" of specific cases and concern that a board decision to reduce a wage agreement would result in the disruption of bargaining relationships, a strike, the loss of business, or other hardships. These considerations were important in the coal and railroad cases when business members' votes ensured the approval of contracts that were far above the Pay Board's standards.

The business members' vulnerability to special interests was increased by the absence of a well-defined constituency. The labor members adjusted their behavior to a clearly identifiable constituency, that is, organized labor. In contrast, the business members' constituency was identified amorphously as "the business community." The major business associations, such as the National Association of Manufacturers and the U.S. Chamber of Commerce, do not play a role analogous to that of the AFL-CIO and therefore did not afford an organizational reference group for the business members. At the outset of Phase II an informal "advisory group" to the business members was organized and served as a conduit for broad management opinion. This advisory group was confined to representatives of "big business" and beyond this did not articulate a common strategy or set of values. As a result, each of the business members usually reflected the values and interests of his corner of the business world. For example, Bassett nominally was spokesman for the small-business men and usually took a hard line in controlling wage increases, except when the board considered the general policies concerning merit increases that were widely applied in nonunion situations. On this occasion Bassett reflected the small-business man's interest in flexibility.

The business group attempted to develop a greater sense of consistency and discipline by designating a spokesman who would also provide leadership in its internal deliberations. The selection of the spokesman came about in a casual manner. Following one of the early meetings of the Pay Board at the White House, the business representatives were discussing the situation among themselves as they were leaving the premises. They agreed that the group should have a spokesman and that Virgil Day was the appropriate choice to fill this role. Day was the only business member of the Pay Board with responsibility for labor relations in his home corporation. In addition, he had been made available by the General Electric Company to serve on the board on virtually a full-time basis. As the only management appointee with this freedom, he could give greater continuity to management's participation.

Because Day's mandate was informal and he spoke for an ill-defined constituency, he could not fully assert a leadership role. Although he was an effective spokesman in the oratorical sense and helped to create an orderly process of decisionmaking within the group, this arrangement was not sufficient to override the specific interests that often resulted in a fragmented business position. In the absence of an operational consensus among the business members concerning the specific applications of wage controls, discipline and even consistency in voting behavior proved to be elusive.

This laissez-faire characterization of the business group was not shared by the labor leaders. To the contrary, the labor members imputed to the business group a devious solidarity of purpose orchestrated by Roger Blough, the retired chief executive of the U.S. Steel Corporation who was the guiding figure in the Construction Users Anti-Inflation Roundtable, whimsically dubbed "Roger's Roundtable."[8]

In his excoriation of the Pay Board at the AFL-CIO convention in November 1973, George Meany described the business group in the following terms:

The employer section was run by Mr. Roger Blough. He wasn't the spokesman but he was running the show. I have a suspicion he was running the public

8. For a discussion of the development of this group, see "Business' Most Powerful Lobby in Washington," *Business Week*, December 20, 1976, pp. 60, 63.

group, too. This is the fellow who was Chairman of the Board and President of United States Steel Corporation, who in 1962 was accused of double-crossing the President of the United States, of double-crossing the Steelworkers Union, and of double-crossing the steel industry officials who negotiated with the Steelworkers Union. They signed what was supposed to be a non-inflationary contract. It was sold to the union on the basis of being a non-inflationary contract. As soon as the union ratified it, Mr. Blough went off with his so-called Price Committee of U.S. Steel and he raised prices. So this is the fellow who is now retired.

But he has a labor of love. He has a large staff in Washington and he has been working on this in conjunction with the NAM [National Association of Manufacturers]. He is well supplied with money. He runs an organization that is dedicated to bringing wages down. That is the purpose of his organization, to keep wages down and bring them down. In other words, he has the philosophy that the future of this country can best be served by a low-wage economy, so he is the fellow who was over here running this show. There was a pipsqueak by the name of Day from General Electric who was his mouthpiece, but Blough was the boy.[9]

In fact, Blough scarcely qualified for the role of villainous gray eminence in which he had been cast by Meany. He was active in the deliberations of the business group at the early stages of Phase II when the basic policies were under consideration. It was obvious, however, that he did not exercise a dominant influence. Blough was especially interested in the policy concerning deferred increases because of its relevance to the construction industry. But neither the business proposal nor the policy that was ultimately adopted dealt harshly with this matter. Indeed the policy supported by the business members was broadly permissive. When Blough advised the business group in working out the relationships between the Pay Board and the Construction Industry Stabilization Committee, again there was no evidence of either a Machiavellian influence or an anti-union orientation. As noted in chapter 7, the points of contention between the Pay Board and the CISC were largely procedural rather than substantive. If Roger Blough was "running the show," this fact was lost on both him and the business members.

Overall, the business members on the Pay Board had limited effectiveness. While they were likely to stand together when general issues of principle were involved, there was a strong possibility that individual members would go off in different directions when voting in specific cases where narrow interests or affiliations were involved. In the arithmetic

9. *Proceedings of the Ninth Constitutional Convention of the AFL-CIO, Bal Harbour, Florida, November 18–22, 1971: Daily Proceedings and Executive Council Reports* (AFL-CIO, n.d.), pp. 22–23.

sense, the business members were more likely to cast the swing votes than the public members. But they generally used this leverage in a passive manner that served the tactical needs of either the labor or public blocs rather than the explicit goals of management. Because the business representatives had neither the common interests nor the internal discipline of the other factions, their votes usually were cast for alternatives in whose development they had played only a limited role.

The Public Members

A divergence of viewpoints also existed among the public members. However, because they were not linked to specific interest groups and because their differences were largely normative or intellectual, it was possible to work out some compromise that would permit them to present a united front on the board. This capacity to act as a bloc meant that the public members (along with the labor members) defined the framework within which positions were taken and decisions ultimately reached.

Among the public members, two consistent points of view could be identified. On the one hand, Gordon and Jacoby usually adhered to an economist's approach to the wage stabilization process. They accepted the notion that inflation could be engendered or magnified by cost-push factors arising from wage increases that exceeded national productivity trends. While they recognized that there would have to be deviations from the general pay standard of 5.5 percent, they believed that these variations should be justified by objective factors, such as the need to attract labor and verifiable cost savings for changes in work rules, rather than murky considerations of industrial relations practice or self-defined concepts of equity.

Caples and Weber, on the other hand, were more responsive to industrial relations considerations in adopting positions on general policies and particular cases. They were willing to modify, if not deny, the conclusions from economic analysis in the light of traditional bargaining relationships or their perception of the acceptability of a decision to the union leaders. If the "economists" were more likely to take a uniform and restrictive approach to the task of wage stabilization, the "industrial relations types" showed a disposition to be flexible and particular—although the labor members probably would not have accepted this distinction.

These differences did not mean that the economists always disdained industrial relations practices or that the industrial relations types ignored economic variables. Both groups recognized the significance of a wide range of factors in reaching decisions but assigned different weights to each category. The economists were more interested in program *effectiveness* than *acceptability* and viewed the wage-push phenomenon as a function of pressure directly exerted on the *general level of wages,* rather than through the complexity of *wage structure* that had evolved over decades of collective bargaining.

In the coal and West Coast longshoremen's cases, for example, Gordon and Jacoby were disposed to reduce the settlements to the Pay Board's standard with only limited deviation, while Caples and Weber favored a more generous decision to reflect equity and other factors arising from industrial relations practices within the two industries. Similarly, the economists insisted that fringe benefits should be incorporated in the 5.5 percent general pay standard because they could have a major impact on labor cost.

Judge Boldt occupied an awkward position between, but above, these two approaches. First, Boldt was very sensitive to his dual role as a public member and chairman of the entire board. As a public member, he was disposed to align himself with the other members as part of a solid bloc. As the chairman, Boldt felt responsible for the overall conduct and stability of the board. Therefore, although the judge participated in the public members' caucuses, he remained aloof from the discussion and retained an independent position. Boldt did not vote in Pay Board proceedings unless his ballot was necessary to break a tie. When this occurred, the public members often were unaware how the judge would vote.

Second, by his own admission Boldt was not schooled in the concepts or terminology of either economics or industrial relations. Consequently he usually did not participate in the public members' discussions as an independent source of opinion. Rather, he adopted a judicial posture and gave his views after listening to the various arguments, or he accepted the consensus position after it had been worked out among the other four members. When Boldt was assertive in his own right, he was likely to adopt a stringent position and press for decisions that appeared to be consistent with the suppression of inflation. After all, the attainment of this objective was the reason he had given up a secure, protected position to accept the assignment as chairman of the Pay Board.

Judge Boldt's limitations in industrial relations were compensated for by the personal attributes he brought to the board and the wage stabilization process. Both personally and professionally he was an individual of manifest integrity, and he conducted the business of the board in as even-handed a manner as the circumstances permitted. These qualities afforded an effective shield against criticism of the board by labor spokesmen and other commentators. Although individual public members might be at-tacked, it was difficult to impugn the board as an institution as long as the judge projected a benign, impartial image. Indeed public criticism of the board generally exempted Boldt.

Despite the public members' strong differences of opinion in specific cases, they almost always reached a common position. Although the discussions could proceed in various ways, Jacoby usually would state the alternative that provided a robust expression of the economists' view, while Weber or Caples formulated an approach that gave greater weight to industrial relations factors. In the process Gordon often emerged as the pivotal member. The extent to which Gordon accepted the industrial relations analysis had significant influence on the consensus position that all the members ultimately accepted. If he remained skeptical of the vaga-ries of bargaining structure and equity, then a position closely linked to economic variables was likely to prevail. Thus the public members, like the business group, were constantly engaged in a sequence of internal bargaining coincidental with the negotiations that took place within the full board.

Decisionmaking within the Board

The three groups constituted the cast in a decisionmaking process that was always cumbersome and sometimes raucous. From the outset, the formal sessions played only a limited role in the board's deliberations. Board meetings generally provided a platform for the presentation of familiar arguments leading to predetermined outcomes. But rarely, if ever, was the vote on a particular issue determined by the debate or exchanges in the formal sessions. Only on one occasion, when Pat Greathouse of the UAW argued for the approval of the aerospace contracts, was the dis-course of sufficient eloquence to cause the individual members to re-consider their positions. Even in this case, Greathouse's oration excited considerable admiration but delivered no additional votes.

The meetings of the full board did become working sessions when the members reviewed regulations or orders that implemented earlier deci-sions. If questions were raised concerning the meaning of a rule, they would be reconciled at that time. When the quibbling over terminology masked a more basic issue, the board would adjourn so that the individual blocs could develop their positions. For example, when the board was reviewing the regulations governing fringe benefits, the labor members inquired if the tandem rule would apply to fringe benefits. Under this approach, the level of benefits in different bargaining units could be equalized, even though the cost would be different in the two units and might breach the pay standard. Such a question had significant policy and cost implications and was settled only after the members had reverted to informal discussions outside the meeting room.

The narrow, stylized nature of the formal sessions meant that the main business of the board was conducted in caucuses and through informal negotiations. In most cases, the public members would meet with the business members to determine the areas of agreement or disagreement. Because neither group operated with recognized leadership, the sessions usually included all the public and business members who were present at the time. Meetings with the labor group were less frequent. Some efforts were made to initiate extended discussions, but they were of limited effectiveness because of intrinsic disagreements or misunderstandings.

The decisionmaking process thus was a sequence of separate negotiations within the individual factions and to a lesser extent between the factions. Other than the abortive effort in the aerospace case, the public members did not seriously attempt to mediate differences. A board member acted as an intermediary between a party to a case and the board itself in one instance. This occurred during the consideration of the East Coast longshoremen's dispute. At that time, Frank Fitzsimmons, president of the Teamsters, acted as a go-between for the board and the International Longshoremen's Association in defining a mutually acceptable decision.

Ironically, the absence of ongoing informal communications between the labor members and the other groups on the board permitted labor to enjoy the benefits of mediation without paying the price. That is, because labor representatives usually adopted a predictable fixed approach to issues as they arose, the business and public members frequently adjusted their positions to accommodate the perception of labor's needs and sensitivities. By remaining intransigent the labor group exerted a powerful pull on the other members, and thus the ultimate decision frequently ended up in a middle position without labor making any concessions—or incurring any debts for the accommodation.

This process was, of course, enormously time-consuming. During its first few months, the Pay Board often would stay in session from 9:00 A.M. until midnight. Even when the different groups had defined their positions, one faction might request a recess to explore ways to stave off impending defeat—a practice that was not conducive to administrative efficiency. Consequently a sizable backlog developed that could not be easily reduced through the ponderous process of decisionmaking the board had elaborated for itself. Indeed, because of these procedures and the paucity of staff, the Pay Board never did bring the backlog down to a tolerable level.

If the board's mode of operation was not a cynosure of efficiency, it did provide flexibility and a crude form of due process for the consideration of special interests. Over time, the procedures promoted the development of a common framework and set of understandings, however hostilely these were articulated. Once the board was in business, the procedures generated a momentum that served the goals of the stabilization program. All of this was brought up short, however, with the walkout of four of the five labor members. This withdrawal from the board did not reflect the failures of tripartitism as an internal process of decisionmaking so much as external pressures that undermined the begrudging consensus that had served the board for its first five months.

Conflicts of Interest

While tripartitism represented a traditional approach to balancing special interests in the context of a wage stabilization program, it was not clear when the process of accommodation became a problem of conflict of interest. Throughout Phase II the conflict-of-interest issue was a troublesome one and was never directly confronted or satisfactorily resolved. Although tripartitism had certain political advantages in the conduct of the wage control program, it posed grave questions of the propriety of assigning governmental functions and authority to private parties who had a direct stake in the decisions of the regulatory body of which they were members.

First, as noted earlier, the conflict-of-interest issue is embedded in the concept of tripartitism. Thus if tripartitism was to "work," policies and decisions would have to be the product of compromise between the major groups represented on the board. The determinations of the board would have to be governed as much by their acceptability as by some abstract notion of justice.

Second, the conflict-of-interest issue was sharpened by the fact that nearly all the Pay Board members served on a part-time basis and retained their primary affiliations. Even the public members maintained their regular jobs and extracurricular activities. Three of the public members were also directors of corporations. In the absence of an explicit ban on these affiliations, each public member handled the situation in what he thought was an appropriate manner. One of the public members resigned from his directorship; two retained their seats while serving on the Pay Board. Neil Jacoby, in particular, had been a member of the board of directors of Occidental Petroleum Corporation, a large oil and energy-based company, for many years. Because he was a well-known spokesman for a conservative point of view, Jacoby's association with Occidental was singled out for sharp criticism by organized labor. These attacks became more strident when shortly after the beginning of Phase II Jacoby was elected chairman of the Executive Committee of the Occidental Board of Directors. The Executive Committee was a key management group with responsibility for the continuing review of the policies and operations of the company. When he became the target of union brickbats in the press, Jacoby resigned as chairman of the Executive Committee but kept his seat on the Board of Directors.

Judge Boldt was the only member of the Pay Board who did not come to office entangled by such relationships. In twenty years on the federal bench, he had been subject to well-defined standards of conflict of interest so that he had no affiliations with outside organizations that might dilute his judicial status. When he accepted the position as chairman of the Pay Board, Boldt had stepped down from the active bench and had assumed the role of "senior service" judge, a position of semiretirement within the federal judiciary.

The statutes governing the activities of the Pay Board initially sidestepped and later legitimatized the intrinsic conflicts of interest of the Pay Board members. The original version of the Economic Stabilization Act, which provided the authority for the wage-price freeze and Phase II, did not address the issue at all. Under a strict interpretation of the conflict of interest statutes, the dual status of the Pay Board members was impermissible. Consequently a legal strategy was developed that averted this problem. The regulations governing the operation of the Pay Board specified that all formal authority was lodged in the hands of the chairman, who was the only full-time member of the board. The votes of the full board technically were recommendations to the chairman, who actually rendered the decisions. Since the other members only advised the chairman, they did not exercise authority and therefore were outside the purview of the conflict-of-interest statutes. This tortured line of argument became unnecessary when Congress amended the Economic Stabilization Act in December 1971. At that time, a proviso was placed in the statute that formally exempted the members of the stabilization agencies (both the Pay Board and the Price Commission) from the general standards of conflict of interest.[10]

Given this legal latitude, there was an asymmetry in the expectations concerning the behavior of the labor and business groups. The labor members were expected to be vigorous protagonists for the trade union viewpoint. This expectation was fully realized. In addition, the labor members' advocacy became especially vocal when, as one of them put it, the board started "playing in our pea patch." This reinforcement of general and specific interests was vividly manifested in the aerospace case when Leonard Woodcock, president of the UAW, made a formal appearance as a "witness" during the Pay Board hearing on the merits of the case.

The role of the management representatives was somewhat more delicate than that of labor. Although the business members had explicit corporate affiliations, they were not expected to act with the overt self-interest that characterized the labor members. Presumably they shared the general public interest in promoting wage moderation and the diminution of inflation. This academic attitude was compromised, however, by the obvious implication that business would enjoy the lower costs derived from Pay Board decisions. Whether or not these lower costs would be translated into higher profits would be determined in a large degree by the policies of the board's sister agency, the Price Commission. Certainly the labor members did not believe that the business representatives were motivated by the commonweal.

The business members were most vulnerable to allegations of conflict of interest when they participated in decisions that had a direct effect on their own companies. In these cases, paradoxically, the interests of the business members usually coincided with those of labor. If a business member was associated with a company that was a party to an agreement submitted to the board, he was likely to press for approval rather than for a searching inquiry into the merits. In these cases stability of labor relations was given weight equal to the goal of vanquishing inflation. Prob-

10. Economic Stabilization Act Amendments of 1971, sec. 204.

ably the most egregious case involved the railroads. During the board's consideration of the railroad cases, Benjamin Biaggini, president of Southern Pacific, acted as an outspoken advocate for the approval of the contracts. Undoubtedly Biaggini believed in the virtues of the agreement, and the conflict inherent in his role as a protagonist and a judge was no more severe than that of the UAW and IAM representatives when the board reviewed the aerospace cases. The major difference was that the management representatives were subject to sharp criticism when such conflicts arose, while the labor members were afforded a knowing tolerance. Consequently the business members adopted a more judicial posture over time, and in a few situations individual members disqualified themselves because of their clear interest in the outcome of the case.

The theory of tripartitism contains the inherent belief that the various conflicts of interest will be balanced out and that, overall, the program will serve public objectives. This assumption of compensating biases might be generally true but was tenuous in specific cases. On several occasions the narrow interests of the board members provided the basis for a coalition of convenience in supporting the approval of a wage increase far in excess of the general pay standard. Nor could the situation be rectified by the "pure" stance of the public members who themselves were part of a larger network of relationships. Tripartitism might be an effective method for preserving the consensus necessary to sustain a stabilization program in a democracy, but it was seriously deficient as a framework for a neutral and consistent process of regulation.

Relations with the White House

If the ostensible conflict of interest tainting the labor and business members was their affiliation with specific parties to the board's determinations, then the cross borne by the public members was their relationship with the Nixon administration. From the outset of the stabilization program, the public members had been under a cloud because of allegations that they were the compliant instruments of the administration. According to this line of argument, expressed most vociferously by George Meany, the public members lacked true independence and adjusted their behavior to the administration's bidding.

Except for a brief interlude in the latter part of 1970, relations between organized labor and the Nixon administration could best be characterized as aloof. The circumstances of the freeze and the policies enunciated during the ninety-day period nurtured the belief that the stabilization program was part of a general strategy to limit, if not to repress, labor. These fears were not allayed by the aide-mémoire initialed by President Nixon certifying the Pay Board's independence. Organized labor's apprehensions were magnified by the events surrounding President Nixon's speech at the AFL-CIO convention in Florida in November 1971.

Under these circumstances it was easy for labor to impute bias, if not malevolence, to the public members, especially since Weber had served in the Nixon administration right up to the time of his appointment to the Pay Board and had been the executive director of the Cost of Living Council during the freeze; Caples had had a career in management before becoming a college president; and Jacoby had been a member of the Council of Economic Advisers during the Eisenhower administration. Even Gordon—who was one of the gurus among Democratic economists—was suspect because he had indicated some acceptance of a wage-push theory of inflation. Within this cabal, Judge Boldt's lack of background in industrial relations was perceived as part of a strategy to maintain a weak chairman who would bend to the will of the other public members. In one hyperbolic exchange during a Pay Board meeting, a labor representative stated that he had not previously joined with those who had questioned Boldt's ability but was now persuaded that the judge was both "incompetent and evil."[11]

In fact, there is no evidence that the administration attempted to influence the Pay Board's policies or decisions in even the most indirect manner. No surreptitious contacts were ever made between the White House or high officials of the Cost of Living Council and the public members. The business members consistently disclaimed any White House influence on their deliberations. Except for a few ceremonial meetings with the President and various cabinet officials to review the status of Phase II, communications between the Pay Board and the administration were on a formal, bureaucratic level. A middle-grade civil servant served as liaison from the CLC to the Pay Board and handled communications in both directions. Judge Boldt, along with C. Jackson Grayson, chairman of the Price Commission, met weekly with Donald Rumsfeld, director of the CLC, to discuss administrative matters. Aside from these procedural niceties, there is every indication that the administration maintained a hands-off approach to the Pay Board. Even in the East Coast longshore-

11. Authors' personal records of Pay Board activities.

men's case, when considerations of foreign policy were involved and the Pay Board would have welcomed some guidance from the White House, pressure was not applied.

The formal record of relations between the administration and the Pay Board indicates several significant differences of opinion. For example, the administration rejected the board's majority view that $1.90 an hour was too low a cutoff for defining the working poor. The administration also rejected the board's recommendations that federal employees should be covered by the stabilization program. The only circumstance in which the White House involved itself in internal matters of the Pay Board was when it lent comfort to the CISC's efforts to preserve a loose and ambiguous reporting relationship with the board. Nonetheless, the White House ultimately did step in to mediate the dispute in an evenhanded manner. Furthermore, the construction unions supported John Dunlop, chairman of the CISC, in his effort to keep the Pay Board from closely scrutinizing CISC operations.

Although tripartitism created many problems within the board, domination by the administration was never a real question. To the extent that the board's decisions and policies were consistent with the administration's goals, this outcome reflected the members' view of their role rather than sinister White House intervention.

The Labor Walkout

After five months it appeared that the Pay Board would weather the intrinsic stresses of tripartitism and other strains of its own making. The major policies had been thrashed out and some semblance of administrative organization had painfully taken shape. The flow of requests for the approval of pay increases was steadily increasing, and the staff was shifting its attention from the promulgation of regulations and the design of reporting forms to reducing the backlog. All but one of the "last cows" had been brought through the gate, and the level of acrimony within the board was subsiding. Thus it came as a surprise when George Meany announced that the representatives of the AFL-CIO, the Steelworkers, and the Machinists were withdrawing from the agency. The next day the UAW joined the walkout, leaving the Teamsters as the solitary representative of organized labor.

Verbal Salvos

The resignation of the labor members took place on March 22, 1972. It was accompanied by a broadside criticism of the stabilization program and the Pay Board. The statement of the AFL-CIO Executive Council declared:

Seven months of the Administration's so-called new economic policy—including four months of Phase II controls—have demonstrated that it is nothing more than a device to make the average worker and consumer both the victim and the goat, while the banks and big business pile up increasing profits.[12]

The statement further noted that while there was a "rising tide of price increases," the Pay Board had persisted in holding down workers' wages. Moreover, there were no controls on interest rates, life insurance premiums, and the prices of land and housing. Where price controls nominally were in effect, there was no effective machinery to enforce these curbs. In the judgment of the Executive Council:

The record of flagrant favoritism speaks for itself. The Administration's so-called new economic policy is heavily loaded against the worker and consumer, in favor of the profits of big business and the banks, and is dominated by the view that economic progress begins and ends in the stock market and the corporate financial report.

Slick rhetoric and double-talk cannot hide these self-evident facts from the American people. There is no fairness, no equity, no justice in the Administration's economic program.[13]

The statement had special words of scorn for the Pay Board:

We joined the Board in good faith, desiring—despite our misgivings—to give it a fair chance, and with the hope that we could bring the voice of workers into the decision-making process of an autonomous and genuinely tripartite wage stabilization effort.

. . . the so-called public members are neither neutral nor independent. They are tools of the Administration, and imbued with its viewpoint that all of the Nation's economic ills are caused by high wages.

As a result, the Pay Board has been completely dominated and run, from the very start, by a coalition of the business and so-called public members. All major Board decisions have been concocted by this coalition, with its mechanical majority of the votes. The trade union movement's representatives on the Board have been treated as outsiders—merely as a facade to maintain the pretense of a tripartite body.

The Board's business and so-called public member majority has continuously revealed a contempt for free collective bargaining and freely negotiated labor-

12. Statement adopted by the AFL-CIO Executive Council, March 22, 1972, p. 2.
13. Ibid., p. 2.

management agreements. They have shown an utter lack of understanding of sympathy for workers and the realities of industrial life.

. . . The system of wage control . . . has extended a web of confusion and chaos in labor-management relations across the country. It has been a device to undermine and wreck free collective bargaining.[14]

The labor blast elicited a muted reply from Judge Boldt at a press conference convened with the other public members of the board. Boldt's rejoinder noted that the action of the AFL-CIO came precisely five months after the board had been sworn in. During that period many constructive steps had been taken. The board had enumerated its general standards and policies. It had rendered decisions on major bargaining agreements. And it had formulated the detailed standards necessary to implement the amendments to the Economic Stabilization Act.

The statement took note of the controversy that had been associated with much of the Pay Board's activities.

This progress was not easily or harmoniously achieved. . . . Disagreement can be expected—and indeed is welcomed—in a tripartite body such as the Pay Board, which encompasses the major economic groups in this Nation. Nonetheless, the job has been done and, we believe, with a keen sense of equity. We also feel that these policies are supported by the overwhelming majority of the American public as fair and consistent with the objectives of the stabilization program.[15]

The public members also attempted to refute the accusations that they were "tools of the Administration" and that the board's decisions were dominated by "an unholy alliance" of the public and business members.

"The most cursory examination of the Board's actions reveals that its decisions do not reflect any sinister plot to repress or to deal unfairly with the Nation's wage earners:

—The general wage standard approved by the Board provides for a permissible increase of 5.5%. In other cases, as when employees have not received adequate wage increases in earlier years, increases of 7% are permitted. In addition, the Board's regulations clearly provide for increases above 7% where a justifiable basis can be shown. . . .

—The full Board itself has acted upon eight major wage cases. In five of these, the position of the Labor Members prevailed.

—Since the inception of the Pay Board, the Labor Members have voted with the majority 36 times, in the minority 13 times, split their votes once, and abstained on four occasions. Of the 54 votes taken by the Pay Board on major issues, 28, or over 50%, were unanimous."[16]

14. Ibid., pp. 2–3.
15. Statement of Judge George H. Boldt on behalf of the public members of the Pay Board, March 22, 1972, p. 1.
16. Ibid., pp. 2–3.

The public members' reply concluded with its own peroration:

... we do not subscribe to the view that an effective stabilization program is one which passively acquiesces in every demand of the Labor Members, no matter how stridently they may be expressed. The labor movement in this country is founded on fair play resting on an unemotional review of the facts. We believe that the AFL-CIO action ignores the achievements of the Pay Board and shows little concern for fair play for the American public.[17]

Although the walkout of the labor members was abrupt and unforeseen, the dissolution of a tripartite wage stabilization agency was not a unique occurrence. During the Korean war, the labor members left the Wage Stabilization Board after only two and a half months in protest over the adoption of the so-called Little Steel Formula, which set limits on general wage increases.[18] A second breakup of the War Stabilization Board took place when President Truman overrode its decision to roll back a negotiated wage increase in the bituminous coal industry. On this occasion all the management members and the chairman, Archibald Cox, resigned.[19]

Why the Walkout?

In assessing the withdrawal of the four labor members from the Pay Board, three possible explanations may be considered.

First, the labor members may have been motivated by a sense of cumulative grievance concerning the policies and operation of the board. To be sure, the labor members displayed undisguised suspicion, if not hostility, toward the business and public members. Nor were relations helped by missteps such as that which occurred in the aerospace case. Nonetheless, American labor leaders have a deserved reputation for pragmatism, and personal preferences are invariably subordinated to organized labor's institutional goals. In this respect the record does indicate that the board's policies went a long way to meet specific labor objectives. As indicated in the public members' statement, the labor representatives voted with the majority on thirty-six out of fifty separate ballots. It was also clear in discussions within the board that labor believed it could live with the 5.5 percent standard as long as there was a basis for approving larger increases in the

17. Ibid., p. 3.
18. See Milton Derber, "The Wage Stabilization Program in Historical Perspective," *Labor Law Journal,* vol. 23 (August 1972), pp. 453–61.
19. Ibid., p. 456.

light of "ongoing collective bargaining and pay practices and the equitable position of the employees involved."[20] The board's policy on deferred increases also ensured that existing contracts would continue to operate under their own terms unless subject to a cumbersome challenge and review procedure.

In addition to these accommodations in the Pay Board's policies and regulations, the labor members successfully obtained relief from what they considered to be the most iniquitous actions of the board and the CLC. The board's ban on retroactive wage increases was reversed by congressional action as early as December 1971. Similarly, the AFL-CIO was successful in its suit to modify the CLC's definition of the working poor. Nor did the pattern of wage and price movements during Phase II to the date of the walkout support labor's contention that the stabilization program had been an instrument for the oppression of the working class. Between December 1971 and March 1972 the annual rate of increase in the index of hourly earnings in real terms had been 3.7 percent.[21]

Second, the AFL-CIO representatives may have withdrawn from the board because of indignation over a grievous injustice perpetrated by the board in the West Coast longshoremen's case. The labor walkout came only seven days after the board had decided this case, and publicly at least, the two events appeared to be linked. In the AFL-CIO's parting shot at the board, the only case that was specifically mentioned as evidence of the board's derelictions was the West Coast longshore decision. The statement noted that despite "public lectures [by the Nixon administration] on the urgent importance of increasing productivity . . . the Pay Board has given this issue short shrift so as to leave the major benefits of productivity gains [in the West Coast longshoremen's case] in the pockets of employers."[22]

Again, displeasure over this decision does not seem to be a plausible explanation for labor's actions. The union involved, the International Longshoremen's and Warehousemen's Union, was not even a member of the labor federation. It had been expelled from the CIO for alleged Communist domination and had stayed outside the merged labor federation when the AFL-CIO was established in 1955. For twenty-two years the ILWU had remained a pariah, and considering George Meany's strong opposition to Communism both in foreign affairs and the labor move-

20. See public members' resolution, pp. 50–51.
21. Raw data from *Employment and Earnings*.
22. Statement adopted by the AFL-CIO Executive Council, p. 3.

ment, it is difficult to imagine that the AFL-CIO was especially sensitive to restrictions on this union.

Nor did the economic circumstances surrounding the West Coast long-shore decision justify its elevation to a cause célèbre. Although the total package had been reduced by around 25 percent, from 20.6 percent to 14.9 percent, the amount that was approved was almost three times the general pay standard. In addition, the longshoremen occupied a position near the top of the American industrial wage structure, receiving an average of $8.47 an hour in total compensation.[23] If the AFL-CIO was looking for a situation that would excite public sympathy against the ruthlessness of the Pay Board, the West Coast longshoremen's case seemed miscast for the role. Indeed at the time the Pay Board decided the longshoremen's case none of the regular labor members were present. Instead, they were all represented by alternates.[24] When the board was reviewing the case and meeting in caucuses, the labor alternates offered no response—neither indignation nor a willingness to compromise—when they were informed that a sizable reduction was probable.

Third, the four labor members may have withdrawn from the Pay Board for larger, political reasons. In 1972, a presidential election year, the AFL-CIO had unmistakably indicated its opposition to the reelection of President Nixon. Continued membership on the Pay Board would have identified the labor federation with a major economic initiative of the administration. Consequently it was desirable for the labor members to bolt the Pay Board in order to criticize the administration without the encumbrance of participating in one of its highly visible programs. That Frank Fitzsimmons did not join the walkout adds credence to this political explanation. The Teamsters enjoyed close relations with the Nixon administration and played an important role in the "hard hat" strategy that had been shaped by the Republicans.

If these political considerations were paramount, the timing of the walkout was propitious. The board had completed formulating its major policies, and the loss of future influence would be minimal. In addition, 1972 was a relatively light bargaining round. Once the longshore cases were decided, the board was not scheduled to take up any other cases of national significance. The next round of bargaining would begin in 1973, and the labor federation hoped it could look forward to a more sympathetic occupant in the White House.

23. "Staff Calculation of Percentage Change in First Contract Year," in "Pay Board Staff Submission Papers," PMA-ILWU, March 14, 1972, pp. 12–14.
24. Minutes of the Pay Board, March 16, 1972.

Of the three possible explanations, political factors probably were most important, augmented by a cumulative sense of grievance over the general operation of the program. If labor had been motivated by a sense of outrage or injustice, it is not unreasonable to expect that the walkout would have been followed by some effort to topple the program. No acts of defiance or campaign of noncompliance were initiated, however. After the walkout, the labor representatives maintained active communication with the Pay Board staff in order to expedite consideration of a specific case or to petition for favorable treatment. On one occasion a group of staff representatives from the AFL-CIO met with a subcommittee of the board to discuss improvements in the procedures governing the operation of the Cases and Appeals Panel. This unit considered routine requests for the approval of wage increases in excess of the 5.5 percent pay standard.

If the political explanation for the resignation of the labor members is accepted, tripartitism can be said to have succumbed to factors that were essentially outside the control of the Pay Board. To the extent that tripartitism replicates the divergence of interests in society at large, then the Pay Board was toppled by pressures in this larger arena and not by the inequities produced by its regulations and procedures. As an epilogue, it may be noted that the AFL-CIO ended up adopting a "neutral" stance in the 1972 campaign, abetting the reelection of President Nixon. Although the federation had demonstrated its distaste for the Nixon administration, the prospect of Senator George McGovern in the White House was viewed as a more alarming alternative.

Aftermath: Reconstitution of the Board

When the Nixon administration learned that the labor representatives would leave the board, the response was quick and unequivocal. President Nixon issued a statement attacking the AFL-CIO for its withdrawal. "Fighting inflation must be everybody's job," he said. "Yesterday, George Meany walked off the job." President Nixon also offered a terse, righteous comment on the West Coast longshoremen's decision: "The Pay Board was right. Mr. Meany was wrong."[25]

The President then announced the immediate reconstitution of the Pay Board as an "all-public body" of seven members instead of fifteen.

25. "Economic Stabilization," the President's remarks on the composition of the Pay Board following the resignation of certain labor members, March 23, 1972, *Weekly Compilation of Presidential Documents*, vol. 8, no. 13 (March 27, 1972), p. 670.

The seven members included the five former public members and two new public members with "special interests"—including one from labor and one from business. The "public" member with a special labor interest was Frank Fitzsimmons, the Teamsters president; the one with a special business interest was Rocco Siciliano, one of the former business members. This dialectic—if not bizarre—approach to the reconstitution of the board preserved the fact of tripartitism while rhetorically endorsing the notion that the board was all public in membership and orientation.

The new all-public Pay Board encountered few difficulties in maintaining the agency's continuity. It adjusted its rules and voting procedures to take account of its reduced membership. In addition, the board attempted to preserve the principle of tripartitism in its operations as much as possible. The Cases and Appeals Panel always operated with a business-public member, a labor-public member and one of the former public members. Similarly, whenever a subcommittee was established to examine a new issue, representation was always given to these three varieties of public members. At the same time, the special-interest members served as spokesmen for their outside constituents within the reconstituted board. If an AFL-CIO union wanted to influence the board's deliberations, it generally had to deal with the Teamsters, even though this union had long been excluded from the labor federation.

The most significant change in the operating mode of the new board was the abandonment of the practice of bloc voting. Because the five former public members now held the balance of power, it became unnecessary for them to vote as a group in order to ensure their effectiveness. Hence each public member felt free to vote his intellect or conscience, as the case might be. Caucuses were no longer held, and the formal board meetings became the forum in which decisions were reached. This change improved the board's efficiency and probably the consistency of its decisionmaking as well.

The board operated on this reconstituted, all-public basis from March 24, 1972, until its dissolution by the administration in March 1973. It never faced a direct challenge to its authority nor was there any evidence that its policies had changed significantly. Whatever else it might have achieved, the Pay Board wrote a new chapter in the history of wage stabilization programs in the United States by demonstrating that tripartitism was not necessary for an effective stabilization program and that an all-public membership was not inconsistent with a tripartite structure.

Impact on Wages: The External View

The primary task of the Pay Board—indeed its only legitimate task—was to influence the pattern of wage increases in the economy, although this objective was often obscured by bureaucratic embellishments and the histrionics of the board members. There are two complementary approaches to assessing the extent to which the Pay Board achieved its objective. First, the impact of the controls program on wage movements for the economy as a whole can be analyzed to estimate the board's contribution to the stabilization objective. Second, the wage decisions handled by the board itself—the subject of the next chapter—can be examined to determine how they conformed to the agency's goals and standards. Presumably if the board acted with fidelity to its mandate, this would be revealed in both the external and internal data. It is also possible that the board was ineffective in its own operations, but that the indirect or spillover effects of wage controls per se were so great that they influenced wage behavior for the economy as a whole.

The key question to be asked, of course, is what impact, if any, Phase II controls had on adjustments in wages and fringe benefits and the consequent distribution of income. In addition, it is important to assess the effect of the various exemptions from controls, such as that for the "working poor." Finally, there is the matter of the board's efforts to control executive compensation.

General Measures of Wage Movements

On an economy-wide level, the two most frequently used measures of labor compensation are the hourly earnings index and compensation per man-hour. The hourly earnings index covers nonsupervisory workers in the private nonfarm economy and is based on a monthly survey of establishments. In order to make the index as close to a wage rate index as possible, the Bureau of Labor Statistics adjusts it to remove the effect of shifts between high- and low-paying industries and for overtime in manu-

Table 10-1. *Annual Rate of Change in Earnings and Related Indexes, 1960–73*

Percent

Period	Hourly earnings index		Compensation per man-hour		Output per man-hour	Unit labor costs	Consumer price index
	Nominal	Real[a]	Nominal	Real[a]			
1960–64[b]	n.a.	n.a.	3.7	2.5	3.6	0.1	1.2
1964–65[b]	3.8	2.1	3.8	2.1	2.2	1.6	1.7
1965–66[b]	4.1	1.3	6.1	3.3	4.2	1.8	2.7
1966–67[b]	4.7	2.1	5.5	2.9	1.6	3.8	2.6
1967–68[b]	6.1	1.8	6.9	2.7	3.0	3.8	4.2
1968–69[b]	6.6	1.1	7.2	1.7	0.0	7.2	5.4
1969–70[b]	6.5	0.4	7.2	1.1	0.1	7.1	6.1
1970–71[b]	7.4	2.9	7.5	3.0	3.5	3.9	4.4
1971:2–1971:3	6.3	2.1	5.2	1.1	2.5	2.5	4.0
1971:3–1971:4	5.2	2.8	4.9	2.6	4.7	0.3	2.3
1971:4–1972:1	8.0	4.4	9.1	5.5	5.2	3.8	3.4
1972:1–1972:2	5.6	2.4	4.6	1.5	5.1	−0.5	3.1
1972:2–1972:3	5.0	1.3	6.1	2.4	6.6	−0.4	3.6
1972:3–1972:4	7.6	3.9	7.6	3.9	3.6	3.8	3.6
1972:4–1973:1	4.5	−1.2	10.5	4.4	4.4	5.9	5.8
1972:1–1972:4	6.1	2.5	6.1	2.5	5.1	1.0	3.4
August 1971–November 1971	3.1	1.1	n.a.	n.a.	n.a.	n.a.	2.0
August 1971–January 1973	6.2	2.8	n.a.	n.a.	n.a.	n.a.	3.4
November 1971–January 1973	6.9	3.1	n.a.	n.a.	n.a.	n.a.	3.7
December 1971–January 1973	6.1	2.4	n.a.	n.a.	n.a.	n.a.	3.6

Source: Calculated from U.S. Bureau of Labor Statistics data.
a. Deflated by the consumer price index.
b. Annual changes calculated from second quarter to second quarter.
n.a. Not available.

facturing. This means that the index is still affected by overtime in industries other than manufacturing. (Manufacturing employees represent about 28 percent of the work force in the index.) In addition, the index reflects employment shifts between high- and low-paying occupations.

The hourly earnings index does not cover supervisory workers or fringe benefits. As an alternative, therefore, the index of compensation per manhour is sometimes used. This index includes wages of all occupations and fringe benefits. It is not adjusted for overtime, however, and the series is affected by interindustry employment shifts. Its movements are also affected by changes in social security and other taxes that employers pay for legally required fringe benefits.[1]

Table 10-1 summarizes the movements of the two major wage indexes in the private nonfarm sector during the decade preceding the stabilization program and during the controls period.[2] In the last half of the 1960s the inflationary buildup appears as an acceleration of both wages and prices. As the economy reached a peak in real gross national product in the third quarter of 1969, productivity growth lagged, but compensation accelerated. Consequently unit labor costs rose significantly. In the year just before the freeze, ending in the second quarter of 1971, some deceleration in prices was evident, and productivity resumed its advance. Wage increases continued to accelerate and showed evidence of a catch-up process.

During the controls period the rate of increase of both wages and prices subsided. The quarterly changes shown in table 10-1 do not correspond with the timing of the stabilization program. The most precise picture of developments during Phase II is obtained by omitting the observation that occurred just after the freeze. This approach is appropriate because deferred union wage adjustments blocked by the freeze were allowed to become effective on November 14, 1971, along with adjustments of 5.5 percent or less in categories II and III. On a monthly basis, this created a substantial bulge in November-December 1971. A similar

1. There is evidence that in the long run the incidence of the employer contribution is shifted to labor. In the short run, however, a jump in the contribution rate always causes a jump in the index. Shifting the incidence presumably takes time because of existing union contracts and because prevailing nonunion wage rates cannot be reduced to pay the tax. On tax incidence, see John A. Brittain, *The Payroll Tax for Social Security* (Brookings Institution, 1972), chaps. 2 and 3.

2. The economic data used in constructing many of the tables in this chapter are those that were available during the controls program. Subsequent revisions have usually been minor ones.

Table 10-2. *Monthly and Annual Rates of Increase in the Hourly Earnings Index during Phase II*

Percent

Year and month	All industries	Mining	Construction	Manufacturing	Transportation, communication, and public utilities	Finance, insurance, and real estate	Wholesale and retail trade	Services
				Increase over previous month				
1971 December	1.4	4.9	0.5	1.7	1.9	1.4	1.3	0.9
1972 January	0.8	1.2	0.8	0.6	1.1	1.0	0.5	1.2
February	0.1	-0.2	0.3	0.5	0.4	-0.5	0.0	-0.1
March	0.5	0.4	0.5	0.4	1.3	0.6	0.4	0.3
April	0.9	0.8	0.5	0.5	1.4	1.9	0.8	1.1
May	0.0	-0.4	0.1	0.5	0.1	-0.7	-0.3	-0.3
June	0.3	0.9	0.1	0.4	-0.1	0.3	0.5	-0.1
July	0.6	0.7	0.0	0.2	1.6	0.7	0.7	0.4
August	0.4	0.4	0.8	0.5	0.8	-0.2	0.1	0.0
September	0.7	0.2	0.7	0.5	0.4	0.9	0.6	1.4
October	0.8	-0.4	1.0	0.6	1.9	0.5	0.6	0.7
November	0.1	0.4	0.2	0.2	0.4	-0.3	0.0	0.1
December	0.9	2.3	1.4	0.8	1.0	1.2	1.0	0.8
1973 January	0.3	0.8	1.5	0.4	0.1	0.1	0.0	0.1
				Annual rate of increase				
December 1971–January 1973	6.1	6.7	7.7	5.8	9.8	5.2	4.8	5.3
				Proportion of total				
Sector weights[a]	100.0	1.2	5.9	33.8	8.8	5.5	25.8	19.0
Contribution to increase, December 1971–January 1973[b]	100.0	1	8	33	15	5	21	17

Source: Calculated from U.S. Bureau of Labor Statistics data, seasonally adjusted.

a. Sector weights are the proportion of total payroll covered by the index in each sector. They are affected by distribution of hours and absolute wage level. Thus manufacturing, with relatively high wages and long weekly hours, has a greater weight than its share of employment would suggest.

b. Sector weight times rate of increase as proportion of total increase.

phenomenon shows up on a quarterly basis from the last quarter in 1971 to the first in 1972.

If the analysis is restricted to the four quarters in 1972, wages rose by a little over 6 percent according to the two indexes. In the first quarter of 1973 (coinciding with the beginning of Phase III), the hourly earnings index reveals further deceleration. The index of compensation per man-hour shows a substantial jump during that period, but this appears to be attributable to a combination of a large social security tax hike and inter-industry shifts in employment. From January to May 1973—the five-month period before the price freeze that ended Phase III—the hourly earnings index rose at an annual rate of less than 5 percent. It is reasonable to conclude, therefore, that Phase II did not build up a wage bubble that burst on the economy when controls were relaxed.

The aggregate movements of the hourly earnings index during Phase II were erratic. This pattern is partly explained by the normal problems of data collection, seasonal adjustment, and sampling error that influence most aggregate series. Some of the intra–Phase II movements appear to correspond to the special forces the controls themselves generated. Table 10-2 depicts these movements on a monthly basis.

Four bulges appear in the figures. As indicated earlier, the first bulge occurred in November-December 1971 and resulted largely from the implemented deferred wage increases that had been blocked by the freeze. (The Pay Board's approval of the increase in the soft coal industry is visible in the mining sector. But the overall index was little affected because the mining sector is such a small proportion of all sectors.) Uncertainty about the meaning of the initial Pay Board rules may have extended this bulge into the December-January period. In addition, a deferred increase for 400,000 truck drivers was scheduled for January 1, 1972. The slowing of the index thereafter may reflect the delay in the delegation of authority to the Pay Board's staff and to the Internal Revenue Service to process cases within the basic standards. The next peak in the series (April) probably reflected the initial rush of case-processing that followed the delegation of authority. Deferred railroad increases for 475,000 railroad workers were approved by the Pay Board and became effective April 1. A second deferred increase in trucking contributed to the 0.6 percent increase of the overall index in July.

The index rose rapidly again in September and October. This upsurge may have reflected the decision process of the Construction Industry Stabilization Committee, which delayed the summer construction increases beyond the dates assumed by the seasonal-adjustment factors. (The seasonal factors used in 1972 were largely based on experience before controls.) A number of wage adjustments (railroad, longshore) also came due October 1. Finally, the December bulge is probably a reflection of the Pay Board's control-year concept. Most nonunion workers did not receive short control years and hence became eligible for their second round of increases on November 14, 1972.

In any year, with or without controls, there are always special factors that explain the month-to-month movements in the earnings index. But one point seems clear. The moderate wage movements after January 1973, when the economy was put under the more relaxed Phase III guidelines, indicate that there was no buildup of pressure. The larger rates of increase in the hourly earnings index toward the end of Phase II seemed to be based more on the timing created by the controls system than on a slippage of the system itself.

An Industry Analysis

Table 10-2 also permits some analysis on a broad industry level. Those sectors experiencing above-average wage increases were transportation and public utilities, construction, and mining. Developments in transportation resulted mainly from board approvals of railroad, longshoring, and trucking agreements. The railroad increases were negotiated before Phase II (although there was some question of the actual ratification date in the United Transportation Union case). Both East and West Coast longshore requests were cut, but the amounts involved still were substantial. The wage hikes in trucking were deferred increases negotiated in 1970.

In construction, the Construction Industry Stabilization Committee reduced first-year settlements substantially during Phase II. First-year wage rate adjustments under major construction contracts averaged 6.9 percent in 1972, down from 12.6 percent in 1971. However, there was a major overhang of deferred increases, averaging 11.6 percent, under major contracts scheduled for 1972. Although CISC records indicate that about 1,000 deferred wage increases were cut, the large number of small units in construction meant that many deferred increases were implemented as scheduled. Consequently construction union wage rates in cities of 100,000 population or more rose by 7.1 percent during 1972.[3] (Wages and benefits rose 8.2 percent, but benefits are not included in the hourly earnings index.)

Wage developments in mining shown in table 10-2 reflected the impact of the bituminous coal settlement. In that case the board approved 16.8 percent in wages and benefits over the objection of the public members. The wage increases alone amounted to a little over 10 percent, since much of the economic package was allocated to pensions and other benefits. In addition, a second-year increase scheduled for November 12, 1972, was not challenged by the board, because it equaled 7 percent on a wage and benefit basis. On a wage rate basis alone (relevant for the hourly earnings index), the deferred hike was 8.3 percent. Thus table 10-2 shows a substantial monthly increase in mining for December 1972.

Although the hourly earnings index is the best available measure of wage change on the aggregate level, it is necessary to use average hourly earnings data in reviewing developments at the detailed industry level. Such data are distorted by changes in overtime hours and by shifts between high- and low-paid workers within industries. Nonetheless, they provide a crude measure that suffices for the analysis presented here.[4] Average hourly earnings trends were examined in twenty-nine industries. These were divided into two sectors, depending on whether they were below or above the median gain for all the industries of 6.08 percent between December 1971 and December 1972. Sector A industries were those with earnings gains of less than the median during that period. Industries in Sector B had earnings increases equal to or greater than 6.08 percent. Sector A consisted of ordnance, food, tobacco, apparel, lumber, furniture, printing and publishing, rubber, leather, electrical equipment, miscellaneous manufactures, wholesale and retail trade, finance, insurance and real estate, and services. Sector B consisted of textiles; paper; chemicals; petroleum; stone, clay, and glass; primary metals; fabricated metals; machinery; transportation equipment; professional instruments; mining and quarrying; construction; transportation; telephone and telegraph; and utilities. The earnings gains in these industries stemmed from

3. See U.S. Department of Labor press release, USDL-73-33, February 9, 1973.
4. The technique applied here owes much to an analysis originally developed by the Cost of Living Council and later published. See Marvin Kosters, Kenneth Fedor, and Albert Eckstein, "Collective Bargaining Settlements and the Wage Structure," *Labor Law Journal,* vol. 24 (August 1973), pp. 517–25.

Table 10-3. *Annual Rate of Increase in Average Hourly Earnings,*
by Industry Sector, 1965–72[a]

Percent

Period	Sector A[b]	Sector B[c] Including construction	Sector B[c] Excluding construction	Sectors A and B
1965	4.5	3.4	3.5	4.2
1966	4.6	4.3	3.9	4.5
1967	5.6	4.7	4.2	5.3
1968	7.6	6.8	6.9	7.4
1969	6.1	6.8	5.9	6.3
1970	6.4	6.3	5.8	6.4
1971	6.0	8.4	8.5	6.7
1972	5.6	8.2	8.5	6.4
1965–70	5.8	5.4	5.0	5.7

Source: *Employment and Earnings*, various issues.

a. Calculated on a December-to-December basis. The percentage increase in earnings is weighted by employment in the industries.

b. Includes industries (listed in text) with less than the median gain of 6.08 percent experienced by all twenty-nine of the industries in sectors A and B between December 1971 and December 1972.

c. Includes industries (listed in text) equaling or exceeding the median gain of 6.08 percent experienced by all the twenty-nine industries in sectors A and B between December 1971 and December 1972.

a variety of sources. There were unilateral increases by management, negotiated gains under new union contracts, and deferred increases.

Table 10-3 provides historical data on earnings increases in the two sectors. The striking fact in the table is the reversal of the position of the two sectors around 1970. Those industries that were getting more in Phase II were the ones that were getting less during the latter part of the 1960s. The reversal is even more striking when construction is omitted. During the late 1960s union construction was generating an inflationary momentum beyond levels experienced in other sectors. Without construction, it is clear that many industries that commanded the Pay Board's attention were in the midst of catching up from past moderation. The process was calibrated, not merely with the cost of living, but also with those industries that had moved ahead in a relative sense during the 1960s.

Some of the relative reversal may be explained by cyclical factors. Table 10-4 shows that when construction is excluded, Sector B experienced more rapid employment growth and lower rates of unemployment during 1972 than Sector A. Sector B's rate of profit expansion also was more rapid. These factors would be conducive to above-average wage increases in terms of both labor demand and ability to pay. The labor

Table 10-4. *Economic Characteristics of Industrial Sectors A and B, Various Periods, 1965–72*

Percent

Economic measure and period	Sector A[a]	Sector B[b]		Sectors A and B
		Including construction	Excluding construction	
Annual increase in employment[c]				
1965–70	3.1	1.3	1.3	2.6
1971	1.6	− 0.8	−2.1	0.9
1972	3.9	3.8	4.9	3.9
Unemployment rate, 1972[d]	5.8	5.7	4.5	5.7
Percent increase in after-tax profits, 1971–72[e]	15.7	16.8	16.7	16.4
After-tax return on net worth, 1972[e]	9.6	11.2	11.2	10.6

Sources: Employment data from *Employment and Earnings*, various issues; unemployment rates from unpublished data, U.S. Bureau of Labor Statistics; data on profits and return on net worth from First National City Bank, *Monthly Economic Letter*, April 1973, pp. 6–7.

a. Includes industries (listed in text) with less than the median gain of 6.08 percent experienced by all twenty-nine of the industries in sectors A and B between December 1971 and December 1972.

b. Includes industries (listed in text) equaling or exceeding the median gain of 6.08 percent experienced by all the twenty-nine industries in sectors A and B between December 1971 and December 1972.

c. Calculated on a December-to-December basis, using total payroll employment.

d. Experienced wage and salary workers.

e. Excludes ordnance.

force characteristics of the two sectors (table 10-5) generally suggest that a major difference between the two sectors is the level of unionization. Sector A has more white collar workers, females, and low-wage workers than does Sector B, suggesting that a substantial component of Sector A is nonunion.

In fact, table 10-6 shows that unionization is a feature of Sector B. The unionization rate in this array of industries is over 50 percent; in Sector A it is less than 20 percent. Major unionization—situations involving 1,000 or more workers—is also concentrated in Sector B, as were the contract expirations in large bargaining units scheduled for Phase II. Previous analysis has noted the relatively high unionization of the Pay Board's categories I and II. Thus it is not surprising to find that Sector B has a much larger proportion of its work force in categories I and II than Sector A does. Within categories I and II, Sector B received higher Pay Board approvals during Phase II than did Sector A.

Table 10-5. *Labor Force Characteristics of Industrial Sectors A and B,
1970, and Average Hourly Earnings, December 1971*
Percent

| | | Sector B[b] | | |
Characteristic	Sector A[a]	Including construction	Excluding construction	Sectors A and B
Percent of 1970 total employment				
White collar workers	54.6	30.1	33.7	46.6
Female workers[c]	46.9	16.6	19.9	37.2
Nonwhite workers[d]	7.0	8.4	8.9	7.4
Full-time low-wage				
workers[e]	7.1	4.3	4.4	6.2
Addendum:				
Average hourly earnings,				
December 1971 (dollars)	3.11	4.46	4.11	3.51

Sources: Data on white-collar, female, and nonwhite workers from U.S. Bureau of the Census, *Census of Population, 1970: Occupation by Industry*, Final Report PC(2)-7C (Government Printing Office, 1972), tables 1, 2, 6, 8; low-wage data from ibid., tables 1, 8; and Bureau of the Census, *Census of Population, 1970: Earnings by Occupation and Education*, Final Report PC(2)-8B (GPO, 1973), tables 1, 5, 6, 7, 11; hourly earnings from *Employment and Earnings*, vol. 18 (March 1972).

a. Includes industries (listed in text) with less than the median gain of 6.08 percent experienced by all the twenty-nine industries in sectors A and B between December 1971 and December 1972.

b. Includes industries (listed in text) equaling or exceeding the median gain of 6.08 percent experienced by all the twenty-nine industries in sectors A and B between December 1971 and December 1972.

c. Self-employed proprietors are excluded.

d. In a few cases where appropriate disaggregation was not possible, unpublished ratios of nonwhite workers for March 1971 from the Equal Employment Opportunity Commission were applied to 1970 Census employment data. The commission's data refer to firms of 100 or more workers.

e. Proportion estimated to have earned less than $3,000 in full-time work in 1969.

These data suggest a number of hypotheses to explain the relative performances of the two sectors. The cyclical explanation, noted earlier, has certain attractions. However, the data do not go back far enough to cover several business cycles and to enable a more rigorous test of the hypothesis. Differences in the extent of unionization offer an alternate explanation. Where unions are well entrenched, contracts may prevent rapid adjustment of wages to inflation. More generally, research suggests that union wages are less sensitive than nonunion wages to changes in short-run labor market conditions because they are above market-clearing levels.[5]

5. See Michael L. Wachter, "Cyclical Variations in the Interindustry Wage Structure," *American Economic Review*, vol. 60 (March 1970), pp. 75–84; and Adrian W. Throop, "The Union-Nonunion Wage Differential and Cost-Push Inflation," *American Economic Review*, vol. 58 (March 1968), pp. 79–99.

Table 10-6. *Institutional Characteristics of Industrial Sectors A and B during Phase II*

Percent

| | | Sector B[b] | | |
		Including construction	Excluding construction	Sectors A and B
Item	*Sector A*[a]			
Total unionization rate, 1970	18.6	58.5	54.5	31.6
Unionization rate in major bargaining situations, December 1971[c]	8.2	41.1	39.2	18.1
Expiration rate in major bargaining situations during Phase II[c]	2.7	14.8	12.7	6.2
Proportion of sector's workers in categories I and II, Phase II[d]	12.0	...	52.9	22.5[e]
Average wage increase approved by Pay Board in categories I and II during Phase II[f]	4.8	...	5.6	5.3[e]

Sources: Total unionization rate is the number of union and employee association members, from U.S. Bureau of Labor Statistics, *Directory of National Unions and Employee Associations, 1971*, Bulletin 1750 (GPO, 1972), p. 82, divided by total payroll employment, from *Employment and Earnings.*

The unionization rate in major situations is the number of workers in bargaining situations affecting 1,000 or more workers as of the beginning of 1972, from *Monthly Labor Review*, vol. 95 (January 1972), p. 5, divided by payroll employment in December 1971, from *Employment and Earnings.*

The expiration rate is the number of workers in major union contract expirations from November 1971 to December 1972, from Bureau of Labor Statistics, *Wage Calendar, 1971*, Bulletin 1698 (GPO, 1971), and ibid., *1972*, Bulletin 1724 (GPO, 1972), divided by payroll employment in December 1971, from *Employment and Earnings.*

The percentage of workers in categories I and II is the number of employees in first control year cases from Pay Board computer records of November 14, 1972, divided by total payroll enrollment in December 1971, from *Employment and Earnings;* for construction, the number of nonunion workers in Pay Board Category I and Category II cases was added to the number of workers in major union construction situations, from *Monthly Labor Review*, vol. 95 (January 1972), p. 5.

Approvals are from Pay Board computer records as of March 2, 1973.

a. Includes industries (listed in text) with less than the median gain of 6.08 percent experienced by all the twenty-nine industries in sectors A and B between December 1971 and December 1972.

b. Includes industries (listed in text) equaling or exceeding the median gain of 6.08 percent experienced by all the twenty-nine industries in sectors A and B between December 1971 and December 1972.

c. Major situations are those affecting 1,000 or more workers.

d. Omits postal workers. The estimate excludes workers not required to report to the Pay Board because no wage increase was implemented.

e. Excludes construction.

f. Average approval weighted by the number of employees in each case.

Table 10-7. *Characteristics of Manufacturing Firms in Industrial Sectors A and B, Various Dates, 1965–72*

Percent

Characteristic	Manufacturing firms in Sector A[a]	Manufacturing firms in Sector B[b]	Manufacturing firms in sectors A and B
Annual increase in average hourly earnings[c]			
1965–70	5.2	5.0	5.1
1971	5.8	6.9	6.4
1972	5.6	7.5	6.6
Percent increase in employment, 1972[c]	3.7	5.9	4.9
Unionization rate, 1970	49.5	45.5	47.4
Unionization rate in major bargaining situations during Phase II[d]	24.5	29.3	27.1
Expiration rate in major bargaining situations during Phase II[d]	7.2	7.3	7.3
Unemployment rate, 1972	6.3	4.9	5.6
Average wage increase approved by Pay Board in categories I and II during Phase II	5.2	5.5	5.4
Accession rate per 100 employees, 1972	5.1	3.6	4.4
Addendum:			
Average hourly earnings, December 1971 (dollars)	3.39	4.00	3.71

Sources: Accession rates are averages of monthly data from *Employment and Earnings;* other data, from same sources given for comparable measures in tables 10-3 through 10-6.

a. Those with less than the median gain of 6.08 percent experienced by all the twenty-nine industries (listed in text) in sectors A and B between December 1971 and December 1972.

b. Those equaling or exceeding the median gain of 6.08 percent experienced by all the twenty-nine industries (listed in text) in sectors A and B between December 1971 and December 1972.

c. Calculated on a December-to-December basis.

d. Major situations are those affecting 1,000 or more workers.

On the other hand, when the analysis is confined to manufacturing (table 10-7), the difference in unionization between sectors A and B disappears. In manufacturing, the overall extent of unionization in Sector A is actually somewhat higher than in Sector B, although the reverse is true for the unionization rate for major situations involving 1,000 or more workers. Within this narrower framework, differences in demand still remain, however. Sector B experienced more rapid employment growth than Sector A and had a lower unemployment rate. Accessions ran somewhat higher in Sector A, but this probably reflects the established negative correlation between industry wage levels and turnover. It appears that the high-wage industries pay a premium to keep turnover down and that the catch-up phenomenon was not purely a reflection of the union-nonunion dichotomy of the labor force. Even within the union sector some industries apparently exhibit greater short-term sensitivity in setting wages to demand pressure than others.

Aside from cyclical and institutional factors, there is an alternative, less conventional explanation that might account for the wage lag in Sector B. During the mid-1960s, the Kennedy and Johnson administrations experimented with a voluntary wage-price guideline. Although the question has never been resolved, there is some empirical evidence that the guideposts exerted a restraining effect on wages in visible situations.[6] It is conceivable, although impossible to prove, that the application of the guideposts in the 1960s led to a problem of catch-up in the early 1970s.

The fact that industries with a higher degree of unionization experienced more rapid rates of wage increase does not demonstrate that union workers *in general* experienced more rapid gains than nonunion workers. It is easy to contrive arithmetic examples in which the reverse is true, providing one is willing to assume that nonunion wages within each sector rose at substantially different rates from union wages.[7] On the other hand, if it can be assumed that within industry groups wage adjustments were relatively uniform, then the industry data can be used to generate implicit wage changes for particular groups. It is necessary to know only the number of workers in the group in each industry. These can be used as weights for each industry's increase in earnings. Table 10-8 presents such a tabulation for union workers, union workers in major bargaining situations, and low-wage workers. Not surprisingly, the table indicates that union workers experienced above-average gains in 1971 and 1972 and that union workers in major situations received even more. Low-wage workers—defined as the estimated number of full-time workers earning less than $3,000 annually in 1969—received less than average gains during 1972, despite the low-wage exemption.

6. See George L. Perry, "Wages and the Guideposts," *American Economic Review,* vol. 57 (September 1967), pp. 897–904; and comments on the article and Perry's reply in ibid., vol. 59 (June 1969), pp. 351–70.

7. For example, suppose that Sector I has 100 workers that are 20 percent unionized and that the union workers got 4 percent, while nonunion workers in that sector got 6 percent. Suppose that Sector II has 100 workers—80 percent unionized—and that union workers in that sector got 5 percent, while nonunion workers got 12 percent. In both sectors combined, union workers got an average of 4.8 percent and nonunion workers got 7.2 percent. But the heavily unionized Sector II got 6.4 percent, while the predominantly nonunion Sector I got 5.6 percent.

Table 10-8. *Annual Earnings Growth by Labor Force Group, Assuming Uniformity of Industry Wage Adjustments, 1965–70, 1971, and 1972*

	Annual earnings growth (*percent*)		
Group	1965–70	1971	1972
All workers	5.7	6.7	6.4
Union workers			
Including construction	5.5	7.6	7.3
Excluding construction	5.3	7.5	7.4
Nonunion workers	5.7	6.3	6.0
Union workers in major bargaining situations[a]			
Including construction	5.4	8.5	8.2
Excluding construction	5.1	8.6	8.4
Low-wage workers[b]	5.7	6.5	6.2

Sources: Calculated on a December-to-December basis from data of the U.S. Bureau of Labor Statistics and the U.S. Bureau of the Census. See text for method of calculation.
a. Situations involving 1,000 or more workers.
b. Number of full-time workers earning less than $3,000 annually in 1969.

While these data are suggestive, they only indicate orders of magnitude. First, the assumption of wage uniformity is overly strict. Second, the data are affected by interindustry and occupational shifts within the industries used and by changes in overtime. As an alternative measure, the Bureau of Labor Statistics makes a tabulation for union workers in major situations (involving 1,000 workers or more) of "effective" wage rate changes.[8] The BLS totals all known first-year, deferred, and escalator adjustments, taking account of workers who received no increase. Table 10-9 presents the BLS data on effective adjustments. It shows that such adjustments slowed in 1972 but still seemed to exceed the rise in the hourly earnings index for all workers in major bargaining situations. It also confirms the impression drawn from data presented earlier that the union sector lagged behind the nonunion sector during the period ending in 1969–70.

In manufacturing (where the hourly earnings index is most credible because of the elimination of overtime), the major union sector runs slightly below the hourly earnings index in 1972. This is consistent with earlier data concerning manufacturing, which showed that the correlation between industries that got more and major unionization was slightly negative.

8. The data for 1972 appear in *Current Wage Developments*, vol. 25 (June 1973), p. 48.

Table 10-9. *Comparative Wage Data, 1966–72*

Percent

| | All private nonfarm industries | | Manufacturing | |
Year	Annual increase in hourly earnings index[a]	Mean adjustments in major bargaining situations[b]	Annual increase in hourly earnings index[a]	Mean adjustments in major bargaining situations[b]
1966	4.4	3.7	3.9	3.4
1967	5.3	4.5	5.1	4.3
1968	6.9	6.0	6.6	5.7
1969	6.5	6.5	5.8	5.4
1970	6.8	8.8	6.8	7.1
1971	7.0	9.2	6.3	8.0
1972	6.3	6.6	5.8	5.6

Sources: Hourly earnings index, U.S. Bureau of Labor Statistics data; mean adjustments, *Current Wage Developments*, issues for July 1971, October 1972, and June 1973.

a. Adjusted for overtime in manufacturing and interindustry shift. Calculated on a December-to-December basis.

b. Those affecting 1,000 or more workers.

Table 10-9 shows a drop in effective adjustments from 9.2 percent in 1971 to 6.6 percent in all private nonfarm industries in 1972. About 1 percentage point of this 2.6 percentage point decline was due to the drop in first-year settlements. Because wage controls concentrated on these settlements and deferred cutbacks had only a minor effect of perhaps 0.1 percentage point on the aggregates, this 1 percent drop can be taken as the upper-limit estimate of the control's impact in the major union sector.[9]

In manufacturing, about 0.8 percentage point of the 1971–72 drop of 2.4 percentage points stemmed from the drop in first-year increases. In nonmanufacturing (not shown in table 10-9), effective adjustments dropped from 10.3 percent in 1971 to 7.4 percent in 1972. Of this 2.9 percentage point drop, about 1 percentage point was due to the drop in first-year increases. In this sector the drop in first-year adjustments was affected by combined influences of the Pay Board and Construction Industry Stabilization Committee. Construction first-year adjustments affected about 30 percent of all workers obtaining first-year adjustments in nonmanufacturing.

9. A drop in the magnitude of escalator adjustments accounted for roughly 0.4 percentage point of the 2.6 percentage point drop. Some of this was due to the lower rate of price increase during Phase II. The lower rate of price increase, in turn, may have partially resulted from the *wage* program. But this would be a relatively roundabout effect in a short-run program.

The data also raise significant questions about the effect of the wage controls on the union-nonunion differential. Assume that in the absence of controls, first-year wage adjustments would have continued to run at 1971 rates. In that case the major union sector would have experienced an effective adjustment of about 7.6 percent rather than the actual 6.6 percent. The probable pattern of wage adjustments in the nonunion sector without controls is more difficult to assess. If prices had followed their actual course (that is, a slowdown of 1 percentage point in the rate of inflation), and if real economic performance had followed the upward movement that actually occurred during Phase II, the run-of-the-mill econometric wage equation indicates that what actually occurred was not much different from what would have been predicted. This evidence will be discussed below, but at this point it is sufficient to note that even with a cut of 1 percent in the union sector, the aggregates behaved as predicted. This suggests that the nonunion sector (which dominates the aggregates) was not heavily affected. Consequently the union-nonunion differential was probably narrowed by controls, despite the slanting of Pay Board rules on deferred adjustments, escalators, and short control years toward the union sector, and even though union workers received larger increases than nonunion employees.

The Government Sector

The wage data discussed so far have excluded wages paid in the public sector. The Pay Board's jurisdiction extended over state and local government workers and over federal enterprises (chiefly the 700,000 postal workers). Previous wartime wage controls did not cover state and local governments. This category had greatly increased in significance since the Korean war, however. State and local employment rose 154 percent from 1952 to 1972; total nonfarm payroll employment rose only 49 percent. The unionization of government employees was now an important consideration, particularly because of the militance of public sector unions. About 29 percent of state and local employees belonged to labor organizations in 1972.

The Pay Board trimmed the wage increases of government employees in the states of Pennsylvania, California, Ohio, and Maryland and in the city of New York; of teachers in the state of Georgia; and of postal supervisors. There were other cuts in smaller units. As in the private sector, however, the impact of controls was not measured simply by the cuts made by the wage authorities but also by the voluntary compliance of wage decisionmakers.

The wage levels prevailing in the same localities are a major determinant of state and local wages. The improved budgetary positions of state and local governments in 1972 also would have been a factor in wage movements in the public sector. Under the felicitous influence of the economic recovery and federal revenue sharing, the aggregate surplus of state and local government budgets rose from $4.0 billion in 1971 to $13.1 billion in 1972.[10]

The most comprehensive data on state and local wages are derived from Census Bureau surveys. Average monthly earnings data are collected annually for the month of October. They do not include fringe benefits—often an important element of government employees' compensation—and are affected by shifts between low- and high-paying occupations. Highlights from the Census Bureau surveys are presented in table 10-10.

During the period 1964–70, state and local wages generally increased faster than earnings for nonsupervisory workers in the private sector. This was not true for each year or for each occupational group. But taken as a whole, average hourly earnings in the private nonfarm sector rose at an annual rate of 5.5 percent during the period, while earnings in state and local government rose at a 6.7 percent annual rate. Thus it might be supposed that the pressure for catch-up in the public sector was weaker than in industries that had fallen behind the average. In fact, the state and local aggregates do show a slowdown relative to the private sector during the years affected by controls (1971 and 1972).

The growth in teachers' salaries during October 1970 to October 1971 slowed substantially. Teachers often ran afoul of the freeze rules, since their salaries for the 1971–72 school year did not become effective until September 1971 in many instances. Although the Cost of Living Council had compliance difficulties over the teacher issue, most increases for the 1971–72 school year were not in effect at the time of the October 1971 survey. Under Phase II rules such scheduled increases would generally have been paid retroactively. Hence the increase in teachers' salaries shown for the twelve-month period ending October 1972 is probably exaggerated. In many cases, it may be assumed that the wage increases for

10. See Roger W. Schmenner, "The Determination of Municipal Employee Wages," *Review of Economics and Statistics,* vol. 55 (February 1973), pp. 83–90.

Table 10-10. *Annual Change in Earnings of State and Local Government Employees and Private Nonfarm Employees, 1965–72*

Percent

Sector and occupational group	Year ending in October								October 1965–October 1970
	1965	1966	1967	1968	1969	1970	1971	1972	
Government[a]									
State and local									
All employees	4.2	5.1	8.7	7.8	6.6	7.7	4.7	5.8	6.7
Education	4.2	4.5	7.2	8.2	6.8	7.2	2.9	5.4	6.3
Police protection	4.5	5.3	6.6	11.8	1.8	11.5	6.4	10.5	6.9
Fire protection	4.1	6.1	5.1	7.9	9.9	9.9	6.4	6.6	7.1
All cities									
All employees	3.9	5.2	6.3	8.4	6.4	9.8	7.1	6.5	6.6
Education[b]	2.6	1.7	6.5	5.1	12.0	9.1	4.5	6.2	6.1
Police protection	4.2	5.0	6.5	14.6	–1.0	12.8	6.9	11.7	6.9
Fire protection	4.3	6.1	5.2	7.9	10.1	10.1	6.1	7.1	7.3
Cities with population of 50,000 or more									
All employees	4.1	5.0	6.0	8.8	6.1	10.8	6.5	6.7	6.8
Education[b]	2.8	0.0	6.5	2.4	14.3	11.0	3.2	10.5	6.2
Police protection	4.3	4.9	6.2	18.0	–4.0	14.3	7.4	12.7	7.3
Fire protection	4.8	6.3	5.4	8.6	10.0	10.8	6.9	6.2	7.6
Private									
Total nonfarm nonsupervisory workers[c]	4.6	4.8	4.2	7.0	6.9	5.5	6.7	6.9	5.5

Sources: U.S. Bureau of Labor Statistics, *Employment and Earnings, United States, 1909–75*, Bulletin 1312-10 (GPO, 1976), p. 713; and the following publications of the U.S. Bureau of the Census: *State Distribution of Public Employment in 1964*, G-GE64-No. 1 (Bureau of the Census, 1965), table 3; *City Employment in 1964*, Series G-GE64-No. 2 (GPO, 1965), table 3; *Public Employment in 1965*, GE-No. 2 (GPO, 1965), and issues through 1972, table 2.

a. The annual changes for the government sector are based on monthly earnings.
b. City-operated school and college systems.
c. Calculated from average hourly earnings, seasonally adjusted.

two years are attributed to the one-year period.[11] Other data suggest that teachers' salaries rose more slowly than table 10-10 indicates.[12]

Police salaries rose rapidly during the twelve-month period ending October 1972. Some of this was the result of public concern over law and order and pressure to upgrade the quality of local protective services. Federal aid flowed to state and local governments for this purpose. The Pay Board found itself in a difficult position in one case involving the state of Kentucky, where federal funds were to be used to raise police salaries above the board's guidelines. When Congress provided a large raise to the Washington, D.C., police force, the board reviewed the case, but its decision was only advisory, since any act of Congress superseded the Economic Stabilization Act.[13]

Firemen's earnings rose more slowly than police earnings. Although wage parity between the uniformed services is often a burning local issue, the gross earnings data of table 10-10 are unlikely to show a one-to-one relationship. In any case implicit earnings increases for firemen were being gained in some jurisdictions by weekly hour reductions. Such gains would not appear in data based on monthly earnings.

In summary, state and local earnings do appear to have slowed during the Phase II period. The most outstanding exception is police salaries. The statistical acceleration of teachers' salaries during the year ending October 1972 was attributable, in part, to the freeze and retroactivity rules. Undoubtedly wage administrators in the public sector paid some heed to the Phase II rules, particularly where nonunion jurisdictions were concerned. But other influences were also at work. Some jurisdictions had experienced rapid increases in preceding years. Others were having difficulties with past obligations to expensive pension and health and welfare

11. Nonunion employees in state and local governments were at an advantage under the Phase II retroactivity rules relative to other nonunion workers. Increases in salaries for government workers are generally stated in writing at the beginning of the fiscal year. Hence there would have been no difficulty in demonstrating that an increase was scheduled during the freeze. In the union sector, the public-private distinction was less important.

12. The Office of Education estimates that the average annual salary of an instructional staff member in public elementary and secondary schools rose from $10,100 in the 1971–72 school year to $10,608 the following year, an increase of 5 percent. National Education Association data indicate that in twenty-seven school systems with enrollments of 100,000 or more pupils, minimum salaries for classroom teachers with a bachelor's degree rose 3.2 percent during that period. Maximum salaries rose 4 percent. (Figures provided directly to the authors.)

13. The board raised no objection to the increase.

Table 10-11. *First-Year and Life-of-Contract Wage Adjustments in Major Union Settlements, Annually 1970–72, and Quarterly, 1972*[a]

Percent

Type of settlement and industry	1970	1971	1972	1972:1	1972:2	1972:3	1972:4
First-year change							
All industries	11.9	11.6	7.3	8.7	7.1	7.6	6.4
All industries, excluding construction	10.9	11.6	7.4	7.8	7.3	8.0	6.8
Construction	17.6	12.6	6.9	19.0[b]	6.3	6.4	4.3
Manufacturing	8.1	10.9	6.6	7.2	6.8	6.3	6.4
Nonmanufacturing, excluding construction	14.2	12.2	8.2	8.3	7.8	9.4	7.3
Life of contract							
All industries	8.9	8.1	6.4	7.6	6.5	6.0	5.8
All industries, excluding construction	7.9	7.9	6.5	7.1	6.6	6.1	6.2
Construction	14.9	10.8	6.0	12.7	6.1	5.7	3.6
Contracts with escalators	7.3	7.1	5.7	5.6	6.3	4.8	5.0
Manufacturing	5.0	7.3	5.4	5.6	5.5	5.0	5.0
Nonmanufacturing[c]	11.3	6.8	6.9	6.4	7.7	4.4	5.0
Contracts without escalators	10.1	9.2	6.5	8.7	6.7	6.3	5.9
Manufacturing	7.3	7.3	5.7	5.6	6.4	6.0	6.1
Nonmanufacturing, excluding construction	n.a.	9.9	7.3	9.0	7.1	6.8	6.8

Sources: *Current Wage Developments*, vol. 25 (June 1973), pp. 43–61, and various other issues.
a. Major union settlements are those affecting 1,000 or more workers.
b. Consists of pre–Phase II business handled by the Construction Industry Stabilization Committee during Phase II.
c. There were no construction contracts with escalators among major settlements.
n.a. Not available.

plans. Private-sector wage trends also had an influence, since many jurisdictions use some sort of prevailing wage mechanism in setting salaries.

Collective Bargaining Settlements

The Bureau of Labor Statistics collects data on collective bargaining settlements in situations affecting 1,000 or more workers, but its definition of a "situation" is not necessarily equivalent to the Pay Board's.[14] However, the board's data, when adjusted to BLS concepts, are generally comparable; thus analysis of the BLS data on major settlements provides an alternative view of categories I and II. These data are especially significant, since the earlier discussion of Pay Board procedures in chapter 7 suggests that the impact of the program centered on new settlements.

Table 10-11 reveals a slowdown in first-year wage adjustments in major situations. These adjustments dropped from 11.6 percent in 1971 (which included the Pay Board's soft coal and railroad Signalmen's cases) to 7.3 percent in 1972. In construction—where the Construction Industry Stabilization Committee began operations in March 1971, first-year wage settlements dropped from 17.6 percent in 1970 to 12.6 percent in 1971 and to 6.9 percent in 1972. The large first-quarter increases in construction involved pre–Phase II business handled by the CISC during Phase II. The average drops from 6.9 percent to 5.9 percent when the first quarter data are omitted.

In nonconstruction the average first-year adjustment declined from 11.6 percent in 1971 to 7.4 percent in 1972. These data include increases as approved by the Pay Board during the Phase II period. When adjusted to BLS concepts, the Pay Board records indicate that the 1972 approvals were the end products of requests averaging about 0.9 percent higher. In other words, about one-fifth of the drop in first-year adjustments came from direct Pay Board administrative action. The rest came from the "environment" of controls and other economic conditions that influenced the collective bargaining process. As Pay Board records suggest, nonmanufacturing units (excluding construction) received higher first-year adjustments than manufacturing. The nonmanufacturing data incorporate the Pay Board's approvals in East Coast and West Coast longshoring, the retail food cases, and the United Transportation Union case. The bulge

14. A "situation" represents a group of workers who fall under the same or related negotiations. The group might be covered by several contracts, however. A situation need not coincide with a Pay Board unit.

in nonmanufacturing, excluding construction, probably reflects the East
Coast longshore cases. These cases were initially decided in May, but an
appeal was filed. In early June the Pay Board rejected the appeal. At that
point the parties had to renegotiate to take account of the board's decision.

The nonmanufacturing data for 1972 were heavily affected by situations in which negotiations were under way before Phase II. In manufacturing, aerospace was the main case. Thus after the first quarter the
manufacturing first-year adjustments averaged below 7 percent. At the
time Phase II ended, the BLS reported that cases involving 900,000
workers apparently were still pending at the Pay Board and the CISC.
Those cases remained under the Phase II rules and were processed before
February 28, 1973, when the Pay Board was officially terminated. The
only exceptions were cases in the food and health industries, which remained under mandatory controls. Most remaining Pay Board cases
therefore appeared in the BLS data for the first quarter of 1973. These
data included a few petroleum cases in which tentative settlements had
been reached during Phase II. They were not submitted to the board until
Phase III had begun. The average first-year wage adjustment in manufacturing was 6.5 percent in the first quarter of 1973, basically a continuation of the Phase II trend.[15] In nonmanufacturing the figures were dominated by a railroad settlement negotiated during Phase III. This settlement reduced the nonmanufacturing average (excluding construction) to
4.7 percent primarily because the new contract put most of the additional
money into benefits rather than wages.

The BLS data on annual increases over the life of the agreement are
more difficult to interpret. Two factors boosted the life-of-contract averages. First, escalator clauses seemed to decline in popularity during Phase
II. In general, one would expect bargainers to put more guaranteed money
into deferred adjustments in the absence of an escalator. Since the BLS
does not include an estimate for the cost of an escalator in its calculations,
a drop in the proportion of workers covered by settlements with escalators will often raise the life-of-contract average. Second, the duration of
contracts tended to shorten during Phase II. As a result, the first-year
adjustment had more weight in the calculation of the life-of-contract
averages in 1972 than in previous years. Furthermore, labor contracts are

15. An apparel contract covering 60,000 workers was concluded early in Phase
III and raised wage rates by 8 percent. It is hard to know what the influence of
Phase II was on this contract.

generally front-loaded (bigger increases in the first year than in subsequent years), which also will increase the life-of-contract averages. On the other hand, the fact that the Pay Board concentrated on first-year adjustments during Phase II would be likely to magnify the impact of cuts on life-of-contract averages. A final point is that the board rarely ruled on a second- or third-year adjustment in new contracts negotiated during Phase II. These adjustments would have been subject to "new" case standards had Phase II continued, but there is no way of knowing how the Pay Board would have handled them. The BLS estimated their cost according to their terms.

For contracts with escalators, life-of-contract averages fell from 7.1 percent in 1971 to 5.7 percent in 1972. The reduction in the average was concentrated in manufacturing—heavily influenced by the aerospace industry, which uncapped its escalator. There were very few nonmanufacturing workers covered by escalators. Life-of-contract averages fell for both manufacturing and nonmanufacturing workers without escalators in 1972. Thus the expectation of reduced inflation that occurred during Phase II may have been carried over into later phases of the controls program.

Deferred Adjustments in Major Contracts

In January 1972 the BLS estimated that workers under existing union contracts providing for deferred adjustments would receive mean wage increases of 6.1 percent (ignoring escalators).[16] During 1972 more workers were added to the deferred schedule as the Pay Board decided cases with short initial control years in longshoring, aerospace, and other industries. The final BLS estimate for the mean increase under major contracts that *did* occur in 1972 (ignoring escalators) was 6 percent.

The two estimates are not significantly different and confirm the impression gathered from Pay Board data that no substantial cuts were made in *aggregate* deferred increases. Most Pay Board deferred cuts were concentrated in smaller units, particularly in the retail food industry. The largest deferred case in which the board took action was in the Teamsters master freight agreement involving 400,000 workers. The cut was relatively small (5 cents) and was to be taken as a reduction of the standard

16. See Michael E. Sparrough and Lena W. Bolton, "Calendar of Wage Increases and Negotiations for 1972," *Monthly Labor Review*, vol. 95 (January 1972), p. 6.

applicable to the 1973 negotiations. When Phase III intervened, this nickel was not formally deducted.

Workers under escalator clauses during 1972 also were generally scheduled for guaranteed deferred increases. These workers received wage adjustments averaging 2 percent from their escalator clauses. (Escalators typically give increases less than proportionate to the rise in the cost of living.) The Pay Board's time-weighting procedure for costing escalators substantially reduced the probability that any escalator adjustment would be challenged. None were.

Wage Equation Evidence

Beginning in the late 1950s an extensive literature on econometric wage equations has developed. An initial work that received wide currency was A. W. Phillips's study of wage determination in Britain from the mid-nineteenth century to the mid-twentieth century.[17] The "Phillips curve" described a purported relationship between the rate of change of money wages and the rate of unemployment. The level of unemployment was considered a proxy for the state of excess demand or supply in the labor market. Therefore it was assumed that high unemployment rates should be associated with relatively low rates of wage increase.

Later empirical contributions sought to add more explanatory variables to the model. Most equations added some sort of price change variable on the assumption that wage-setters would give weight to the purchasing power of money wages. Other candidates for wage equations included measures of profits and productivity.[18]

Wage equations have been used to examine such issues as the impact of unionization, the existence of wage rounds, and the impact of the Kennedy-Johnson guideposts.[19] The debate on the guideposts centered

17. A. W. Phillips, "The Relation Between Unemployment and the Rate of Change of Money Wage Rates in the United Kingdom, 1861–1957," *Economica*, n.s. vol. 25 (November 1958), pp. 283–99.

18. See E. Kuh, "A Productivity Theory of Wage Levels—An Alternative to the Phillips Curve," *Review of Economic Studies*, vol. 34 (October 1967), pp. 333–60; and O. Eckstein, "Money Wage Determination Revisited," *Review of Economic Studies*, vol. 35 (April 1968), pp. 133–43.

19. See Perry, "Wages and the Guideposts"; Otto Eckstein and Thomas A. Wilson, "The Determination of Money Wages in American Industry," *Quarterly Journal of Economics*, vol. 76 (August 1962), pp. 379–414; and Gail Pierson, "The Effect of Union Strength on the U.S. 'Phillips Curve,'" *American Economic Review*, vol. 58 (June 1968), pp. 456–67.

on the apparent overprediction of wage equations during the period when the guideposts were in effect. That is, wage equations predicted that wages ought to have been rising faster than they actually were during the guidepost period, suggesting that some other factor was retarding wage growth. Alternatives to the guideposts were suggested as explanations for the overprediction. These included the shift to fringe benefits from wages, a cyclical lag of union wage adjustments, and import competition.

During the mid-1960s economists began to focus on the measurement of the variables that seemed to be important in determining wage movements. A number of researchers experimented with adjusting the official unemployment rate to include an estimate of "discouraged workers." These workers escape official measurement because they do not actively seek work, since they believe that no jobs are available. But their estimated numbers rose during the mid-1960s, and when incorporated into wage equations they "explained" some of the overprediction. That is, the adjusted unemployment rate did not drop as fast as the official rate, so that the wage equations predicted a less rapid wage growth. How people who were not seeking work were able to influence wage determination was not fully explored.

By the late 1960s the overpredictions of wage equations frequently became underpredictions. Economists then shifted from accentuating marginal workers to de-emphasizing them. It was noted that young people and women accounted for a growing portion of unemployment. Therefore it was argued that the unemployment rate should be standardized to remove this demographic trend. The argument was that the labor market was actually tighter than it looked.[20] An alternative method of explaining the underprediction was to incorporate the concept of inflationary expectations.[21] A typical short-run wage equation will indicate that an acceleration of prices is not translated into an equivalent upsurge in wages. It was argued, however, that when inflation reached a critical rate, workers would become more aware of it and that this sensitivity would be reflected in a higher rate of wage increase than otherwise would result. Since the latter part of the 1960s was characterized by relatively rapid price increases, an inflation expectations variable naturally improved the "fit" of a typical wage equation.

20. George L. Perry, "Changing Labor Markets and Inflation," *Brookings Papers on Economic Activity, 1970:3*, pp. 411–41.

21. Otto Eckstein and Roger Brinner, *The Inflation Process in the United States*, A Study Prepared for the Use of the Joint Economic Committee, 92 Cong. 2 sess. (Government Printing Office, 1972).

The behavior of wage equations since the mid-1960s has encouraged a measure of skepticism toward their use in analyzing economic trends. Moreover, the tendency of researchers to invent new variables to explain periods of overprediction or underprediction suggests that the significance of such variables is questionable. A search process will always uncover some new variable or specification that seems to explain the unknown. In the postwar period, although there have been a large number of quarters, there have been relatively few business cycles, periods of rapid inflation, or bargaining rounds. As Robert Solow has noted, "No matter how hard we mine the data—even strip mine the data—there is no way to get results that warrant any faith at all unless and until we get more episodes of persistent inflation or disinflation."[22]

In considering the results of wage equations applied to the Phase II period, it is important to note that the circumstances leading to the establishment of the Pay Board were quite different from those surrounding the Kennedy-Johnson guideposts. Before the experiment with the guideposts, the administration feared that an acceleration of the economy would lead to inflationary consequences. It promulgated the guideposts in the hope of forestalling a predicted event. The Pay Board, on the other hand, was established *after* inflation had failed to subside quickly enough in the face of an economic slowdown. *The hope was to bring prices and wages back to some "normal" rate of increase rather than to hold them below normal. Thus a successful Phase II should have produced a drop in the level of underprediction, not necessarily "significant" overprediction.*

In order to examine the course of wage behavior during the period leading up to and during the economic stabilization program, three relatively simple equations were estimated quarterly over the period 1949:1 to 1969:3. It is hoped that the relatively unrefined character of these equations, plus the rather modest conclusions drawn from them, will allay some of the skepticism described earlier. The final observation is the quarter preceding the economic downturn. All equations predict the quarter-to-quarter percentage change in a measure of wage compensation based on the quarter-to-quarter percentage change in the consumer price index (lagged one quarter) and two measures of economic activity. The estimated equation coefficients appear in appendix E.

Most wage equations typically utilize unemployment as a measure of economic activity on the grounds that it provides information on the

22. See Solow's comments on two papers in *Brookings Papers on Economic Activity, 2: 1972*, p. 425.

state of the labor market. Other measures of economic activity, however, often perform as well as unemployment in wage equations.[23] Accordingly the following sets of economic variables were employed: (1) the ratio of real output in the private nonfarm sector to its trend value, and the quarter-to-quarter percentage change in real private nonfarm output; and (2) the inverse of the unemployment rate for males aged twenty-five to sixty-four and the change in that unemployment rate. The last set was used because of the argument noted earlier that the unemployment of secondary workers, that is, young people, women, and older workers, has less impact on wage determination than the joblessness of males aged twenty-five to sixty-four, the prime working years. Two wage measures were used: the percentage change in average hourly earnings (excluding overtime) in manufacturing (PSTMAN); and the percentage change in private nonfarm compensation per man-hour, excluding legally required employer contributions for social insurance (PCOMP). The former measure is deficient because it omits fringe benefits and is confined to manufacturing; the latter measure is more comprehensive but does not exclude the effect of overtime.[24]

The residuals of the resulting six equations for the period 1969:4 to 1973:1 are shown in table 10-12. Real output-activity measures performed better than the other variables in explaining the proportion of variance and the standard error of the equations. The difficulty of attempting to judge the impact of the wage program from these equations is apparent from the residual pattern. Equations 1 and 4 generally provided positive residuals before the freeze (1971:3). That is, wages appeared to be rising faster than would normally have been expected before controls began. The short period from the beginning of the economic downturn to the freeze, however, is marked by a major automobile strike in 1970:4, which depressed hourly earnings in that quarter, especially in manufacturing. The average residual during the period 1969:4 to 1971:2 was about +0.4 percentage point for PSTMAN and +0.3 percentage point for the period beginning with the freeze. If the Phase II impact is measured beginning 1972:2 to 1973:1 (that is, after the postfreeze bulge), the average residual is +0.1 percentage point. It seems reasonable to include the first quarter of 1973 in calculating this average, since as noted earlier, the

23. Daniel J. B. Mitchell, "Union Wage Policies: The Ross-Dunlop Debate Reopened," *Industrial Relations*, vol. 11 (February 1972), pp. 46–61.

24. To some extent the problem of interindustry shift and overtime is relieved, since cyclical variables will usually explain these effects.

Table 10-12. *Residuals of Six Wage Equations Used to Analyze Phase II*[a]
Percentage points

	Equation[b]					
	1	*2*	*3*	*4*	*5*	*6*
	Percent change in average hourly earnings in manufacturing[c]			*Percent change in private nonfarm compensation per man-hour*[d]		
Year and quarter	*Real output*	*Total unemploy- ment*	*Unemploy- ment of males aged 25 to 64*	*Real output*	*Total unemploy- ment*	*Unemploy- ment of males aged 25 to 64*
1969:4	0.3	0.0	−0.1	0.8	0.5	0.4
1970:1	−0.1	−0.1	−0.2	0.4	0.4	0.3
1970:2	0.3	0.4	0.3	0.3	0.5	0.4
1970:3	0.9	1.0	0.9	0.7	0.9	0.8
1970:4	−0.1	−0.2	−0.3	0.4	0.2	0.1
1971:1	1.4	1.6	1.5	0.3	0.5	0.4
1971:2	0.4	0.4	0.3	0.8	0.8	0.7
1971:3	0.3	0.2	0.2	0.1	0.0	0.1
1971:4	−0.1	0.1	0.0	−0.2	0.0	0.0
1972:1	1.2	1.4	1.0	0.8	0.9	0.7
1972:2	0.1	0.4	0.4	−0.4	−0.1	−0.1
1972:3	−0.1	0.2	0.0	0.0	0.3	0.1
1972:4	0.5	0.8	0.6	0.3	0.5	0.4
1973:1	0.0	0.4	0.3	0.2	0.5	0.4

Source: Appendix table E-1.
a. Residuals equal actual value minus predicted value. The period of estimation is 1949:1–1969:3.
b. See appendix E for actual equations.
c. Dependent variable; overtime and fringe benefits are excluded.
d. Dependent variable; excludes legally required employer contributions for social insurance and includes overtime.

effect of Phase II carried into that quarter as the Pay Board worked off its backlog preliminary to the board's termination.[25] The jump in the residuals in 1972:4, seen in all equations, results from the beginning of the nonunion second control year in November.

Equation 4, based on compensation per man-hour, shows a residual averaging +0.5 percentage point during 1969:4 to 1971:2. For the period beginning with the freeze, the average residual is +0.1 percent. The average residual beginning in 1972:2 is zero. Thus the equations using real

25. The major contract negotiated in 1973:1 that was not directly related to Phase II was the railroad agreement. But this contract did not become effective until July 1973 and thus did not influence PSTMAN or PCOMP before that time.

output as an economic activity measure seem consistent with the notion of a movement from underprediction to normality. The equation using overall unemployment, however, shows no such effect for PSTMAN and only a slight effect for PCOMP. This discrepancy arises because unemployment failed to decline as fast as might have been expected, given the real output increase; therefore the unemployment equations often indicate less pressure on wages during Phase II than the output equations. Since unemployment for males aged twenty-five to sixty-four indicated somewhat tighter conditions during Phase II, equation 6 from PCOMP shows some slowdown.

Part of the explanation for these ambiguous results is that the Pay Board's program was aimed largely at the union sector, and particularly new union contracts. About one-fourth of the workers under major agreements were affected by a contract expiration or reopening in 1972. Even if this ratio applied to both major and minor agreements, only about 30 percent of private nonfarm employment is unionized. Thus only about 7–8 percent of the employees in the private nonfarm sector and perhaps 15 percent of the production workers in manufacturing were in the sections closely scrutinized by the Pay Board.[26] Although proportionately fewer nonunion workers were in manufacturing, more union workers were under deferred contracts and were therefore little affected by controls. So the effect as seen in the equations using PSTMAN must be limited. The heavy concentration of nonunion workers involved in the equations using PCOMP also limits the visible impact.

One way to remedy this deficiency is to estimate an equation for new union adjustments alone. Unfortunately, detailed data on major settlements have become available from the BLS only in recent years. But the BLS does have available a series on *median* collective bargaining first-year adjustments in cents-per-hour terms. This series can be divided by average hourly earnings in manufacturing (excluding overtime) to obtain a rough index of new settlements in percentages.

An annual equation for this variable estimated over the period 1954–

26. The BLS reported 8,920,000 union members in manufacturing in 1972. (*Directory of National Unions and Employee Associations, 1973* [GPO, 1974], p. 80.) It may be assumed that these were mainly nonsupervisory workers. According to Sparrough and Bolton ("Calendar of Wage Increases," p. 5), 22.6 percent of manufacturing workers under major agreements were facing contract expirations or reopeners. If this ratio can be applied to all manufacturing agreements, 2,016,000 workers would have been affected by reopeners or expirations. This is about 15 percent of nonsupervisory employment on manufacturing payrolls in 1972.

69 produces residuals of +1.8 percentage points in 1970 and +6.1 percentage points in 1971. In 1972 the residual drops to +1.0 percent. When dummy variables are used, a dummy for 1970–71 appears significantly positive. A 1972 dummy is not significant.[27] The implication is that union settlements were "abnormally" high before controls but returned to "normal" under Phase II.

These results do not provide strong evidence that controls had a dramatic effect on aggregate wage determination. Of course, some of the impact may escape the equations of table 10-12, since those equations all have a price-inflation variable as an explanatory factor. If wage controls contributed to a slower rate of price inflation, this impact could not be reflected in a wage equation that already incorporates the actual rate of price increase. Even with this qualification, however, the results are not dramatic, since the indirect wage-price-wage effect must surely be moderate over a short period of time.

Two conclusions emerge from these experiments with wage equations. First, at an aggregate level the impact of Phase II on new union wage settlements is generally lost. The effect of controls in bringing new union settlements back toward their earlier relationship with economic factors receives little weight in wage indexes that included nonunion workers and union workers under deferred contracts. Second, when new union settlements are isolated and analyzed separately, the impact of controls does become visible. It would become more prominent if there were some way of measuring directly the change in inflationary expectations of wage determiners in the union sector. But the fact that new union adjustments remained moderate during most of 1973, despite the sudden upward surge in prices, suggests that the Phase II effect continued beyond January 1973.

Additional Studies

Other studies have used econometric techniques to investigate the impact of the wage-price controls program on inflation. In general these

27. The equation estimated was
$$PBLS = -19.89 + 23.48\ RATIO + 0.51\ PCPI,$$
$$(-2.51)\quad (2.90)\quad\quad\quad (2.58)$$
$$R^2 = 0.60;\ \text{standard error} = 1.05;\ \text{Durbin-Watson} = 1.40.$$
where $PBLS$ = annual percentage change of ratio of median manufacturing first-year adjustment to average hourly earnings in manufacturing (excluding overtime); $RATIO$ = ratio of GNP in 1958 dollars to trend (estimated over 1954–72); $PCPI$ = annual percentage change in the consumer price index in percentage points. The numbers in parentheses are t statistics.

studies defined the "effectiveness" of controls as the ability to slow down the rate of wage or price inflation below "normal." That is, the studies follow the earlier Perry technique of examining the degree, if any, of overprediction of wage or price inflation as a sign of program success. As asserted above, this type of test does not appear to be appropriate for the Phase II period. Rather, it seems more relevant to test for above-normal wage change before controls—to see if official concern was warranted—and normal wage determination under controls. The results of such a test cannot be conclusive, since it is always possible to argue that normal relationships might have been restored even without controls.

Table 10-13 provides a summary of seven econometric studies that examined the impact of the economic stabilization program in the more conventional manner.[28] The overall conclusion of these studies is that wage increases at the aggregate level were not held below normal during Phase II. Only the Fortune study suggests subnormal wage adjustments, but this effect does not make itself felt until Phase III. Again, the reader must make his own evaluation of these results based on an initial determination of the appropriate frame of reference for these tests.

The moral of this brief excursion through wage equation evidence is that if one is looking for dramatic and conclusive evidence of a Phase II impact on wages, he will have to look elsewhere. On an a priori basis the

28. These studies were William Niskanen and Robert Berry, "The 1973 Economic Report of the President," *Journal of Money, Credit, and Banking,* vol. 5 (May 1973), pp. 693–703; Peter Fortune, "An Evaluation of Anti-Inflation Policies in the United States," *New England Economic Review,* January-February 1974, pp. 3–27; Robert J. Gordon, "The Responses of Wages and Prices to the First Two Years of Controls," *Brookings Papers on Economic Activity,* 3:1973, pp. 765–78; Robert F. Lanzillotti, Mary T. Hamilton, and R. Blaine Roberts, *Phase II in Review: The Price Commission Experience* (Brookings Institution, 1975), chap. 8; Michael R. Darby, "Price and Wage Controls: The First Two Years," in Karl Brunner and Allan H. Meltzer, eds., *The Economics of Price and Wage Controls,* Carnegie-Rochester Conference Series on Public Policy (Amsterdam: North-Holland, 1976), vol. 2, pp. 235–63; Edgar L. Feige and Douglas K. Pearce, "The Wage-Price Control Experiment—Did It Work?" *Challenge,* vol. 16 (July-August 1973), pp. 40–44; and Michael L. Wachter, "Phase II, Cost-Push Inflation, and Relative Wages," *American Economic Review,* vol. 64 (June 1974), pp. 482–91.

All but two used modified Phillips curves to estimate the wage effect. The two exceptions were the Darby study and the Feige and Pearce study. Darby used a monetarist model to determine the impact of the program on prices. He then interpreted his results—based on an examination of the institutional structure of the program—and concluded that the program had a wage impact. Feige and Pearce used an ARIMA (autoregressive integrated moving average) technique to examine the wage and price impacts separately. (ARIMA techniques explain the movements of a series solely in terms of its own previous behavior, thus sparing the estimator the unpleasant task of specifying an interactive model.)

Table 10-13. *Summary of Seven Econometric Studies of the 1971–74 Wage Control Program*

Study[a]	Description	Final period analyzed	Impact of controls
Niskanen and Berry	Annual reduced form model with monetary and fiscal variables.	1972	No significant effect on wages or prices. Interest rates reduced, suggesting lowered inflationary expectations.
Fortune	Quarterly three-equation model with special consideration of nonfarm sector.	1973:2	Restrictive impact on wages and prices throughout Phases I–III. Price effect exceeds wage effect through Phase II, probably owing to deferred, retroactive, and catch-up wage increases. By Phase III, wage effect exceeds price effect.
Gordon	Variations of a quarterly wage-price model including composition of unemployment and inflation threshold indexes.	1973:3	No significant effect on wages except through price effect. Price inflation significantly reduced. Resulting squeeze in profit margins will come undone when controls expire.
Lanzillotti, Hamilton, Roberts	Reestimate of three quarterly wage-price models (including Gordon). Originally begun at Price Commission.	1972:4	No significant (or perverse) effect on wages except through price effect. Price inflation restricted.
Darby	Quarterly monetarist price model.	1973:3	Significant restraining effect on prices. On institutional grounds, it is concluded that this must have been due to wage impact in union sector and price index distortions.
Feige and Pearce	Monthly autoregressive integrated moving average model using only previous history of wage or price series to develop forecast.	December 1972	Phase I restrained both wages and prices. Thereafter, effect evaporates.
Wachter	Annual model of coefficient of variation of wages among two-digit manufacturing industries.	1972	Wage structure behaved normally before and during controls. Therefore there was no pre-controls cost-push pressure, and controls had no wage effect.

a. For titles of studies, see text note 28.

impact could have been expected to be mild on aggregate measures of wage change because most workers were not involved in new union settlements during Phase II. The impact on the minority in such situations is usually drowned in the "noise" that accompanies any statistical series.

As far as major union settlements are concerned, there are no econometric models that can predict their outcome with enough accuracy to evaluate the impact of a relatively short-lived program with confidence. It is known that first-year major union settlements were running at a rate of approximately 11 percent in 1970 and 1971. There is no assurance that in the absence of controls this momentum would not have continued. And it is known with certainty that the average settlement dropped to 7.4 percent in 1972, despite the improved profit and real output situation.

Those who see virtue in controls will cite this drop as evidence of their efficacy and will suggest that if the major union settlements had not been restrained, they would have eventually created wage pressures on other sectors. Skeptics will assume that the slowdown would have happened anyway. Our own position is somewhat more positive. The evidence suggests reason for concern about wage inflation before controls. Wage pressure would probably have subsided eventually, but no one knew how soon. Controls were implemented as an insurance policy against a prolonged lag and appeared to have reduced this risk.

Shortages and Distortions

One of the major arguments against controls on wages and prices is that interventions in the market place will inevitably cause distortions. Usually economists consider shortages to be the major form of distortion. In a competitive market, for example, if a price is set by law below the level where the market "clears," that is, where demand equals supply, some sort of nonprice rationing must occur, or the quality of the product must deteriorate, or both. Of course, there are other types of distortions that could be considered—for example, the distortions in the industrial relations system that are discussed in chapter 12. But the economist's main concern is generally closely related to the market allocation mechanism.

It is clear from the preceding sections that the overall impact of the Pay Board on average wages was limited. In fact, as has already been argued, the goal of the program was primarily to provide some assurance of a "normal" level of wage inflation, given other economic circumstances. It would have been most surprising if the program had resulted in a *generalized* shortage of labor, one that affected most industries. Shortages can result from distortions in relative wages, however, even if average wages are not below normal. For that reason it is important to consider the shortage issue.

The Pay Board expressed its concern for labor shortages by establishing a special exception for "essential employees." This exception was rarely used, partly because of the difficulty of meeting its evidentiary requirements and partly because of the loose labor market that prevailed in 1972. But infrequent recourse to this exception is not conclusive evidence of a lack of controls-induced shortages. Even where overall demand pressure was moderate, and where aggregate wage indexes moved as expected, controls could have distorted wage differentials. There are several reasons for suspecting that shortages were not a problem.

First, it has been noted that controls were concentrated more heavily on new union settlements than on other types of adjustments. Presumably even if the union sector had fallen behind during the inflation of the late 1960s, wage rates in that sector still would have been above market-clearing levels. That is, wages in union establishments were generally higher than employers would have set them unilaterally to recruit manpower and to keep turnover at optimal levels. Thus assuming that controls did retard wage growth in the union sector, it is unlikely that this would create labor shortages. Indeed it is precisely the differential between market-clearing rates and actual rates that makes controls theoretically feasible without detailed policing and rationing.

If controls did create shortages, they might have been expected to occur in the nonunion sector. But the wage experience immediately after Phase II ended does not suggest that wages in the nonunion sector were greatly repressed. If nonunion wages had been restrained to the point of creating shortages, the lifting of extensive controls in Phase III should have been accompanied by a wage bulge. Nonunion employers, unencumbered by the timing of fixed-term contracts, would have unilaterally raised wages. In fact, the hourly earnings index for February 1973 showed only a slight increase over the January level. And during the period January 1973 to May 1973, the index rose at an annual rate below 5 percent, comparing favorably to the rate of increase during Phase II.

A second piece of evidence on the absence of labor shortages can be obtained from labor turnover data. Available data on unfilled vacancies do not go back far enough for an appraisal of what a "normal" vacancy rate would have been, given the labor market conditions of Phase II.[29] Data on quit rates in manufacturing have been available for a long period, however. If controls were causing distortions in the labor market, quit rates should have been higher than normal. When an annual regression explaining quit rates by the ratio of real goods output to trend was fitted over the period 1950–72, its 1972 predicted value of quit rates was 2.2 quits per 100 workers.[30] This was exactly the level that actually occurred. The implication, therefore, is that at least in manufacturing, employers were not having difficulty retaining labor.[31]

The conclusions from these aggregate data were confirmed by the operational experience of the Pay Board. At one point the board staff attempted to identify occupational labor shortages and was unable to find any significant evidence, anecdotal or otherwise.[32] Moreover, even though the essential-employees exception was a difficult route for an employer with an actual shortage, he had alternatives. It was always possible for an employer to allocate larger increases for shortage occupations in a unit, providing he gave less to other occupations. The Pay Board placed constraints on the average amount granted in a unit, not the specific amount received by an individual, group, or craft within a unit. The Pay Board was concerned about the possibility of shortages in the future if Phase II was continued and if labor markets tightened. At one point the board

29. Since the BLS has discontinued the vacancy series, it is not possible to use postcontrol data to estimate a normal relationship.

30. The equation was

$$Q = -9.19 + 11.14 \, RATIO,$$
$$(-8.53) \quad (10.41)$$
$$R^2 = 0.95; \text{ standard error} = 0.17; \rho = 0.607.$$

where Q is the quit rate per 100 workers, and $RATIO$ is the ratio of actual real goods output to logarithmically fitted trend. The numbers in parentheses are t statistics.

31. Further disaggregation of this test did not produce different results. Equations were estimated explaining monthly quit rates during the precontrol period at the two-digit standard industrial classification level in manufacturing. Explanatory variables included the ratio of industrial production in each industry to its trend value. Alternative tests were also made using the Conference Board help-wanted index as an indicator of labor shortages. Again, evidence of a shortage could not be found. For more details, see Daniel J. B. Mitchell and Ross E. Azevedo, *Wage-Price Controls and Labor Market Distortions* (University of California at Los Angeles, Institute of Industrial Relations, 1976), chap. 4.

32. Pay Board staff paper OCE-103, November 28, 1972.

recommended that the Price Commission permit a labor-cost pass-through of more than 5.5 percent in cases where the increment above 5.5 percent was due to a labor shortage exception. No action was taken on this request by the Commission.

Income Distribution

Incomes policies often politicize questions of income distribution. Even in the United States, where wage-price controls have not been presented as a device to plan incomes, the issue inevitably arose of whether labor was receiving its fair share. During Phase II the charge that wages were frozen while profits soared was frequently leveled by organized labor. This allegation merits examination in its own right and as it relates to the board's objective of maintaining a neutral stance on the question of income distribution.

Undoubtedly profits did rise more rapidly than the total national wage bill during the period of controls. Table 10-14 shows an increase in corporate profits of 24.8 percent during 1972, compared with an 11.1 percent increase in the cost of labor compensation. During economic upturns profits usually rise relative to wages. The issue is whether profits increased relative to labor income more than they usually do at similar stages of recovery.

It might be argued that all income shares were absolutely larger in real terms due to controls. The 1973 *Economic Report of the President* stressed the belief that controls had lessened the risk of accelerating inflation.[33] It is therefore possible that aggregate demand policy was more liberal than it would have been without controls, thus expanding total output. There is no way to quantify this effect, of course, and it leaves the question of the relative shares unanswered.

In general the question of relative shares is closely tied to the issue of the relative impact of controls on wages and prices. Those who believe that wages were less constrained than prices are likely to argue that income was redistributed toward labor. Those who believe the opposite are likely to contend that labor lost some of its relative share. But the view that controls were aimed primarily at returning wage inflation toward

33. *Economic Report of the President, January 1973*, pp. 52–53, 62.

Table 10-14. *Growth in Gross National Income, by Components, Fourth Quarter 1970–Fourth Quarter 1972*

	Annual rate of increase (percent)		
Components	1970:4 to 1972:4	1971:2 to 1972:4	1971:4 to 1972:4
Gross national income[a]	10.4	10.2	11.7
Nonlabor gross national income	12.2	11.4	13.0
Excluding farm proprietors	11.6	10.5	11.8
Labor compensation	9.6	9.7	11.1
Excluding employer contributions to social insurance	9.3	9.5	10.7
Proprietors' income	10.0	11.0	12.8
Farm proprietors	21.7	26.8	31.9
Rental income of persons	4.6	4.2	5.1
Corporate profits and inventory valuation adjustment	23.1	17.2	21.1
Corporate profits	24.5	18.9	24.8
Net interest	10.1	10.1	10.5

Source: *Survey of Current Business*, vol. 54 (July 1974), pp. 15–16.
a. National income plus capital consumption allowances.

normality, and not subnormality, suggests that the relative shares could be expected to remain relatively undisturbed.

Mitchell made a crude attempt to standardize for cyclical effects on income shares and to examine the residual effects, if any, on the shares during Phase II.[34] Taken at face value the results suggested a slight shrinkage in corporate profits relative to the expected share. This result is similar to Gordon's conclusion on profits, although the magnitudes are smaller.[35] A possible interpretation is that the growth in farm incomes, which most economists would probably accept as exogenous to the impact of controls, slowed down the adjustment of wage determination toward normality.[36] This in turn passed the burden of the higher farm share to other components of national income, including profits.

34. Daniel J. B. Mitchell, "Phase II Wage Controls," *Industrial and Labor Relations Review*, vol. 27 (April 1974), pp. 351–75.
35. Gordon, "The Responses of Wages and Prices."
36. Some might argue that prices in the farm sector rose because they were not controlled at a time when other prices were squeezed. The exogenous element of international prices in the farm sector, however, makes this view implausible, particularly in the short run.

Effects of Special Exemptions

Congress mandated special exemptions for qualified fringe benefits, the working poor, and productivity incentive plans. It also encouraged "feasible" exemptions for small businesses. Of these areas of congressional concern, the Pay Board designed the basic regulations for qualified fringe benefits and productivity incentive plans. The Cost of Living Council established the basic requirements for the working-poor and small-business exemptions. Each exemption was intended to encourage more favorable treatment of the target group or type of plan than would otherwise have occurred under the controls program. The extent to which these exceptions actually created opportunities or incentives for differential behavior constitutes an important aspect of the impact of controls on compensation trends and practices.

Qualified Fringe Benefits

Section 203(g) of the Economic Stabilization Act Amendments of 1971 required the exemption of employer contributions to pension, profit-sharing, and savings plans that were qualified under the Internal Revenue Code, plus all contributions to group insurance and disability and health plans. As noted earlier, the amendment effectively raised the Pay Board's compensation standard from 5.5 percent to 6.2 percent through the addition of a basic 0.7 percent standard for qualified benefits. The 0.7 percent standard itself was accompanied by various exceptions that further favored the payment of compensation in the form of fringe benefits. Before Phase II, these benefits already had become an important element of the total compensation package for many workers, and the Phase II rules appeared to have the potential of reinforcing this trend.

The BLS estimates the cost of wage and benefit increases annually for agreements covering 5,000 or more workers. These data are presented in table 10-15 and indicate a slowdown for these contracts between 1971 and 1972 for increases calculated on both a wage rate and on a total compensation (wage and benefit) basis. Thus the wage slowdown was not simply a reflection of offsetting increases in fringe benefits.

The data in table 10-15 can be used to analyze whether or not fringe benefits were stimulated relative to wages. But some caveats are in order.

First, to the extent that the Pay Board made cutbacks, it almost always

Table 10-15. *Wage and Fringe Benefit Adjustments in New Agreements Involving 5,000 or More Workers, 1968–72*

Percent

Year	First-year wage rate adjustment	First-year wage and benefit adjustment	Life-of-contract wage rate adjustment[a]	Life-of-contract wage and benefit adjustment
1968	7.5	8.7	5.8	6.5
1969	9.3	10.9	7.5	8.2
1970	12.0	13.1	8.7	9.1
1971	12.2	13.1	8.2	8.8
1972	8.1	8.5	6.9	7.4

Sources: *Current Wage Developments*, vol. 23 (July 1971), p. 43, and vol. 25 (June 1973), p. 40.
a. Excludes possible escalator adjustments.

permitted an exception for the negotiated qualified benefits and reduced the wage portion of the package. Because the BLS estimated the cost of the contracts in accordance with the final Pay Board action rather than with the original request to the board, the proportion of the settlement that went into qualified benefits is exaggerated.

Second, the BLS did not include an estimate of the effect of the operation of cost-of-living escalators on the life-of-contract data. Since escalators generally have a direct effect only on wages, the proportion of the life-of-contract increment that went to benefits is again exaggerated. That is, some of the wage increase implicit in the escalator contracts is omitted from table 10-15.

Third, some of the benefit money included in the BLS estimates went for fringe benefits that were not qualified. For example, 31 percent of the workers in 1972 union settlements covering 1,000 or more workers received holiday improvements in 1972, 29 percent received improved vacation provisions, 8 percent received improved funeral leave, and 6 percent received improved shift differentials. None of these benefit changes meets the Pay Board's definition of "qualified."

Fourth, a significant portion of benefit improvements comes from "roll-up," the secondary effect of wage increases on fringe benefits. The BLS takes account of this effect (as did the Pay Board) in estimating benefit costs.

Despite these problems of interpretation, the data in table 10-15 suggest that the rate of benefit improvement, taken by itself, did slow in 1972 along with wages. For example, if it is assumed that straight-time wages

Table 10-16. *Percent of Workers and of Situations Involved in Pension and Health and Welfare Adjustments in New Union Agreements, 1962–72*

| | Pension | | | | | Health and welfare | | | | |
| | Workers[a] | | | Situations | | Workers[a] | | | Situations | |
Year	All industries	Manu-facturing	Nonmanu-facturing	All industries[a]	Noncon-struction[b]	All industries	Manu-facturing	Nonmanu-facturing	All industries[a]	Noncon-struction[b]
1962	34.9	...	...	32.8	...	35.1	...	...	44.4	...
1963	37.2	...	...	32.0	...	72.8	...	...	54.1	...
1964	67.8	...	...	46.9	...	62.1	...	...	53.4	...
1965	57.0	...	...	36.3	...	62.7	...	...	47.6	...
1966	50.5	...	...	43.9	...	61.2	...	...	58.2	...
1967	59.5	...	...	52.5	34	69.5	...	...	69.2	60
1968	65.9	74.5	57.4	59.4	39	83.4	85.0	81.9	73.4	68
1969	50.5	46.0	55.4	50.1	40	62.0	60.3	63.8	63.8	69
1970	61.9	80.2	45.8	51.6	44	78.7	84.9	73.2	63.6	67
1971	70.6	82.2	59.8	61.9	51	77.9	87.7	68.8	69.5	71
1972	52.1	66.7	43.2	48.2	53	62.5	69.9	58.0	55.7	68

Sources: *Current Wage Developments*, vol. 25 (June 1973), p. 53; Bureau of National Affairs, Inc., *Collective Bargaining Negotiations and Contracts* (BNA, various years).
a. Bureau of Labor Statistics data for bargaining situations involving 1,000 or more workers.
b. Bureau of National Affairs data for all bargaining situations.

made up about 70 percent of total compensation in the settlements shown on the table, the 1972 first-year wage adjustment of 8.1 percent becomes 5.7 percent on a base of total compensation (0.7 × 8.1). Benefit adjustments then make up the remaining adjustment of 2.8 percent (8.5 − 5.7). This suggests in turn that benefits on a benefit base rose about 9.4 percent (2.8/30). A similar calculation for 1971 suggests a benefit-on-benefit adjustment of 15.2 percent. On a life-of-contract basis the calculation suggests 8.6 percent in 1972 and 10.2 percent in 1971. If a roll-up factor of 25 percent is assumed, 1972 direct benefit improvements in the first year would come to about 4.7 percent ([8.5 − (8.1 × 0.7 × 1.25)]/30) and the 1971 benefit adjustment would be about 8.1 percent.[37] The life-of-contract estimates would be 4.5 percent in 1972 and 5.4 percent in 1971. These figures, especially those involving roll-up adjustments, should be taken as generally illustrative rather than as precise estimates.

In previous years benefits appear to have risen faster than wages. This still seems to have been the case in 1972 after the effect of Pay Board wage cuts. For the larger agreements, however, Pay Board cuts probably reduced the initial request by about 1 percent in the first year and 0.4 percent on a life-of-contract basis. In addition, the life-of-contract wage estimates in table 10-15 do not include escalator adjustments. Thus it appears that without Pay Board cuts, benefits might have slowed to the growth rate of wages or at least might have come closer to it than in previous years. Again, it is important to note that all benefits are included in these estimates, not just qualified benefits.

It is possible that the absence of evidence of a relative shift to fringe benefits reflected the influence of construction. The CISC never took formal account of the congressional mandate for qualified benefits. This indifference increased in importance as the proportion of construction workers to total workers covered by new agreements rose from 1971 to 1972. But other evidence indicated that the phenomenon went beyond the mix of construction and nonconstruction contracts.

Table 10-16 shows the proportion of workers in situations in new settlements receiving pension and health and welfare improvements (including the creation of new plans). The universe of contracts in this table is somewhat larger than in the previous table. Workers under agreements

37. The formula in the text is equivalent to subtracting the sum of the wage increase plus the roll-up effect on fringe benefits from the sum of the wage increase plus roll-up and non-roll-up benefit improvements. The difference is the pure non-roll-up effect that can be divided by base-period fringes.

covering 1,000 or more workers are included. The proportion of workers in major agreements who received pension or health and welfare adjustments appeared to decline in 1972 relative to 1971. When manufacturing is considered alone, the decline is still evident.[38]

The data might also be affected by the industrial mix apart from the influence of construction. The proportion of workers in major agreements with qualified benefit improvements dipped in 1969.[39] This might imply that the contracts expiring in 1972, whose mean duration might be assumed to be about three years, came from units that have some bias against fringe benefit improvements. It is possible to estimate the proportion of major contract expirations in 1972 that stemmed from contracts expiring in 1969 and other years by examining data published each January in the *Monthly Labor Review* on major expirations known to the BLS by year of expiration. These data reveal that in manufacturing about 4 percent of the workers involved in negotiations in major units were covered by contracts that had last been negotiated in 1968, 45 percent were covered by 1969 contracts, 44 percent by 1970 contracts, and about 7 percent by agreements reached in 1971. Only in the apparel and lumber industries were large numbers of workers in manufacturing dominated by contracts negotiated in 1969.

In nonmanufacturing the East Coast longshore cases involved contract expirations in 1969, along with some major broadcasting, retail food, and insurance industry cases. But in the aggregate, BLS data indicate that only about 31 percent of nonmanufacturing expirations in 1972 stemmed from contracts made in 1969. Thus it appears that expirations in 1972, both in manufacturing and nonmanufacturing, were dominated by contracts from years *other than* 1969.

Other variations in the pattern of expirations may explain the modest increases in fringe benefits during Phase II. Both 1972 and 1969 had fewer workers per situation—manufacturing and nonmanufacturing—in their expirations than in 1970 or 1971. The BLS definition of a situation is somewhat arbitrary, but it is possible that the smaller units of 1972 explain the dip in fringe benefits. Nonetheless, because the BLS data relate only to "major" situations, none of these structural explanations are entirely satisfactory. Major union situations typically had established one

38. Looking at manufacturing alone also has the advantage of eliminating railroads, which have the legally required railroad retirement trust fund.

39. Although major tax legislation was passed in 1969, no changes in the law are apparent that would significantly affect the wage-fringe mix.

or more qualified benefit plans before Phase II. In an environment characterized by controls, it would have been a simple matter to allocate some money that might otherwise have gone into wages into these other benefits if that action would have enhanced the chance of obtaining approval of the contract by the authorities.

One further hypothesis should be tested. Since major units were more likely to be limited to the basic 0.7 percent on qualified benefits than other situations, and since roll-up would have encroached on part of that 0.7 percent, negotiators in major cases were more constrained by the standard than an initial impression of the regulations would suggest. An alternative survey from the files of the Bureau of National Affairs, Inc. (BNA) is shown in table 10-16 of situations with pension and health and welfare improvements. The BNA survey is not limited to major units and shows relatively little difference between 1971 and 1972 in the nonconstruction sector. Still, a minor difference is a far cry from a controls-induced upsurge. It is reasonable to conclude that in the union sector no sudden increase in the popularity of qualified fringe benefits occurred because of Pay Board rules.

The national income accounts constituted a more comprehensive source of data on fringe benefits. These accounts provide data on the compensation of employees in all sectors, union and nonunion. Compensation is broken down into various categories, two of which are shown in table 10-17. The table compares the annual change in wages and salaries per full-time equivalent employee with employer contributions to pension and welfare funds per full-time equivalent employee. Quarterly data on the latter series are not available; therefore annual data, which do not capture the exact timing of Phase II, must be used.

The long-term trend toward fringe benefits is evident from the table. In each year shown, private-sector pension and welfare contributions rose relative to wages and salaries. The relation between the relative rates of growth is unstable, however. The fringe benefit dip of 1969, which was noted earlier in the major union sector, appears again in table 10-17, although that table covers a much broader group of workers. Data for 1971 are partially affected by Phase I and the early part of Phase II. During the portion of 1971 affected by controls, no rules were in effect favoring fringe benefits. On the other hand, most of the 1972 compensation adjustments occurred after the Pay Board had adopted its fringe benefit rules.

While the data are inconclusive, again there is no evidence of a con-

Table 10-17. *Trends in Wage and Fringe Benefit Compensation in the Private Sector, 1961–72*

Percent change from previous year

| | Annual change in private sector per full-time equivalent employee | |
Year	Wages and salaries	Employers' contributions to pension and welfare funds
1961	2.7	8.1
1962	3.9	7.2
1963	3.4	5.7
1964	4.8	9.9
1965	3.7	10.2
1966	4.7	5.6
1967	4.3	5.3
1968	6.6	12.2
1969	6.5	8.6
1970	5.6	14.2
1971	6.0	14.0
1972	6.2	12.2

Sources: U.S. Office of Business Economics, *The National Income and Product Accounts of the United States, 1929–65: Statistical Tables* (GPO, 1966), pp. 14, 105, 109; U.S. Bureau of Economic Analysis, *U.S. National Income and Product Accounts, 1964–69* (GPO, 1975), pp. 4, 24; and *Survey of Current Business*, July issues for 1971–74, pp. 16 and 36, 19 and 40, 21 and 42, 16 and 37, respectively.

trols-induced shift to fringe benefits. The differential rate of growth between wages and benefits appears to narrow in 1972 relative to 1971 and 1970. In the absence of a model that predicts year-to-year changes in the relative mix of wages and fringe benefits, it is not possible to estimate what the composition of compensation in 1972 would have been without controls. All that is evident is the absence of an upward "blip" in the fringe benefit series.[40]

Working-Poor and Small-Business Exemptions

Because low-wage employers are often those operating small businesses, it is difficult to segregate the effects of the working-poor and small-business exemptions using available data. The basic small-business exemption came on May 1, 1972. At that time small firms, except those in health and construction, and government units with sixty employees or

40. It might be argued that since 1972 was a year of catch-up pressure, workers would have shown an increased preference for current compensation (wages) over deferred compensation (fringe benefits). In principle this tendency could have offset counterincentives created by the wage control regulations.

less were exempt from all controls. (Later in the program smaller lumber firms were brought back under controls.) The exemption did not apply to small-business men whose employees were blanketed in larger collective bargaining units. The Cost of Living Council originally estimated that about 26 percent of payroll employment was affected by the small-business exemption.[41]

As discussed in chapter 4, the working-poor exemption was based on the CLC's cutoff point of $1.90 an hour. After an adverse court decision the amount was revised upward to $2.75 in July 1972, where it remained for the duration of Phase II. While relatively few workers earned less than $1.90 in 1972, the proportion below $2.75 was considerably greater. Units covered by the working-poor definition were not totally exempt from the program, however. The exemption was administered as an exception to Pay Board standards, so that normal reporting procedures applied. More important, employers with a mixture of higher-wage and working-poor employees in their units would have been reluctant to permit substantial compression of traditional wage differentials.

Shortly after the July decision overturning the definition of the working poor based on $1.90 an hour, the Pay Board staff conducted a survey of closed cases in categories I and II. A recheck of those cases revealed that no cuts had been instituted in any case in which the employees averaged $2.75 an hour or less. There were individual workers in units with higher average earnings who earned less than $2.75, and a few such cases were affected by board actions before July. But overall, the analysis of Category I and Category II units suggests that the small-business and working-poor exemptions did not have a significant aggregate effect. The types of units affected by the exemptions were not the site for wage increases in excess of the board's standards. The only exception was food retailing, where a substantial number of cases involved at least some workers earning less than $2.75. In July 1972 average hourly earnings in retail food were $3.08.

Table 10-18 summarizes the trends in wages during 1972 in the twenty-nine two-digit industries previously used to construct tables 10-3–10-7, broken down by average hourly earnings in December 1971. The table shows the annual rate of increase in average hourly earnings from December 1971 to July 1972 when the definition based on $1.90 was overturned. The rates for July 1972 to December 1972 are also presented.

41. See the CLC press release of May 1, 1972. The CLC estimated that 5 million firms were exempted.

Table 10-18. *Earnings Growth by Range of Hourly Earnings in Twenty-Nine Industries, 1972*[a]

Item	Hourly earnings in December 1971 (dollars)[b]					
	Less than 3	3– 3.99	4 or more	Below 3.50	3.50 or more	All industries
Increase in earnings before and after change in working-poor exemption (percent)[c]						
Before (December 1971–July 1972)	5.6	4.2	4.9	4.7	5.1	4.8
After (July 1972– December 1972)	5.6	8.9	12.6	7.0	11.4	8.7
Ratio, after to before	1.00	2.11	2.58	1.49	2.25	1.79
Unionization rate, 1970 (percent)	16	25	61	14	58	32
Proportion of employment in December 1971 (percent)	33.1	43.7	23.2	62.4	37.6	100.0

Sources: *Employment and Earnings*, various issues; and U.S. Bureau of Labor Statistics, *Directory of National Unions and Employee Associations, 1971*, Bulletin 1750 (GPO, 1972).

a. See p. 289 for list of industries that are included.

b. Earnings before adjustment for overtime or seasonal factors.

c. Percentage changes at compound annual rates for the industries involved, weighted by employment. The exemption change is an increase in July 1972 in average hourly earnings from $1.90 to $2.75, mandated by a court decision.

These data are based on average hourly earnings uncorrected for overtime or seasonal factors. Interindustry employment shifts also affect the rates of change.[42] For these reasons, only a very large acceleration in the earnings of low-wage industries could be taken as significant. Moreover, it has previously been noted that accidents of the timing of particular increases and the beginning of the nonunion control year in November 1972 magnified wage movements toward the end of 1972.

In fact, table 10-18 shows that wage increases accelerated most rapidly in the higher-paying industries after July 1972. Industries with employees earning less than $3 an hour had about the same rates of increase before July as after that month. If the cutoff point is raised to $3.50, some up-

42. Average hourly earnings data are not published in seasonally adjusted form at the detailed industry level. It seemed inappropriate to mix data that exclude the effects of overtime (available only for manufacturing) with data that do not.

surge in the rate of wage increase is shown, notably from the service sector. Nonetheless, one can conclude from the data that low-wage units in general did not show a sufficient change in wage behavior after July to support the attribution of this effect to the working-poor exemption. This does not mean that the effect was zero, only that it was not sufficient to dissipate the ambiguity in the data.[43]

Although the effects of the small-business exemption cannot be isolated in the data in table 10-18, there did not appear to be any wage bulge after the announcement of the exemption on May 1, 1972. At an aggregate level the hourly earnings index showed no abnormal movements in May or June, nor were there any large changes in those sectors of the index where small units are concentrated.

Productivity Incentive Plans

As noted in chapter 3, section 203(f)(3) of the 1971 amendments to the Economic Stabilization Act prohibited the Pay Board from limiting earnings paid as part of new or old employee incentive programs designed "to reflect directly increases in employee productivity." Although the board decided that this so-called Percy amendment referred to plant-wide incentive schemes, such as the Scanlon Plan, it nonetheless followed a similar policy for all types of plans, plant-wide or otherwise.

Pay Board records indicate that thirty-two reports of new plant-wide plans were received. Of these, denials were issued in four cases, and one request was withdrawn. There were 167 reports of new plans limited to less than a single plant. One was withdrawn and 122 were denied. The high denial rate stemmed from unsuccessful attempts to convince the board that plans that did not meet its definitional criteria should nevertheless be considered productivity incentive plans. In particular, applicants in executive units had argued that profits were a form of executive productivity.

Consultants who designed productivity incentive plans did not observe the establishment of large numbers of new plans in response to the controls program during Phase II. Analysis of a sample of the proposed plans, however, suggests that a few may have been created in the hope of

43. The Pay Board staff conducted a survey of Federal Mediation and Conciliation Service personnel in September 1972. It was reported that the $2.75 figure became a negotiations target for some low-paid units in the south. See Pay Board staff paper EAD-77, September 20, 1972.

avoiding the basic standards. In some cases the accompanying documentation stated with surprising frankness that the chief stimulus for the
plan was the wage control regulations.[44] Regardless of the motives, the
number of workers and plans involved in such cases was extremely small,
certainly not sufficient to produce a noticeable aggregate effect.

Executive Compensation

The special rules governing executive compensation also created the
opportunity for wage behavior different from that of the rest of the labor
force. The task of assessing the impact of these special rules is complicated, however, by the paucity of systematic data concerning executive
compensation. The most readily available sources of information on top
executive compensation are scattered surveys in popular magazines.
These surveys, spotty as they are, suggest that Pay Board controls on
executive compensation did not create effective restraint. For example,
two *Business Week* surveys of top executive compensation, summarized
in table 10-19, show that total compensation (including bonuses) rose
13.5 percent in 1972. Salaries alone rose 10.1 percent. Part of this jump
can be explained, if not justified, by the increase in corporate profits, since
bonus plans are often geared to profits. Other reports on executive compensation confirm that large increases occurred in top executive pay,
although they differ in the actual amount. *The Gallagher Presidents' Report* tabulated an 18.3 percent increase in 1972 in "52 leading U.S. manufacturing corporations."[45]

There were two routes by which it was possible for top executives to
obtain generous increases under Pay Board rules. First, they could be
paid more than 5.5 percent if others in their units received less. In large
units this ability to allocate allowable monies provided considerable flexibility. Second, bonus plans were permitted a choice of base year in computing the allowable 5.5 percent increase. The board permitted this choice
because executive pay frequently is volatile on a year-to-year basis. Some
bonus plans geared to profits might have had low or even zero bases had
the standard rules been applied. Hence the Pay Board allowed a choice
of one of the three plan years immediately preceding Phase II. If 1971

44. For more details on productivity-incentive plans under the controls program,
see Mitchell and Azevedo, *Wage-Price Controls*, chap. 5.
45. *The Gallagher Presidents' Report*, vol. 9 (April 24, 1973), p. 1.

Table 10-19. *Percentage Annual Change in Compensation of Top Executives and in Corporate Profits, 1968–72*

	Executive compensation		Corporate profits before tax
Year	Salary	Total	
1968	n.a.	6.0	9.8
1969	n.a.	3.5	−3.1
1970	3.5	2.0	−12.8
1971	7.0	9.3	14.9
1972	10.1	13.5	15.3

Sources: Compensation data from *Business Week*, May 6, 1972, p. 41, and May 5, 1973, p. 42; other data from *Survey of Current Business*, July 1971, July 1972, and July 1973.
n.a. Not available.

was not the highest base, units could pick an earlier year, and the result could be a large increase on a 1971-to-1972 basis.

In an effort to counteract the unfavorable publicity that resulted from the reports of top executive pay, the Cost of Living Council released a survey showing that the average compensation for salaried employees in ninety-four selected companies rose by only 5.1 percent in 1972.[46] As AFL-CIO President George Meany quickly pointed out, however, the survey included only a small proportion of corporate executives.[47]

Although control of executive compensation may be viewed as a purely cosmetic aspect of wage controls, the Pay Board expended a substantial amount of time, both at the board and staff levels, in attempting to regulate this element of the labor force. Had the board known the full extent to which its regulations permitted flexibility, it probably would have enacted tighter regulations. If there was any aspect of the wage stabilization program in which the rules created their own loopholes and legal patterns of evasion, executive compensation seems to merit that dubious distinction.

Overview

Two generalizations can be drawn from the external data on the labor market during Phase II. First, the impact of the wage control program was confined mainly to the union sector. And within the union sector the

46. Cost of Living Council press release CLC-258, May 9, 1973.
47. "Meany Challenges Executive Pay Data," *AFL-CIO News*, May 19, 1973, p. 2.

impact fell largely on units negotiating new contracts during the program. This finding, of course, supports the conclusion of chapter 11, based on the internal records of the Pay Board. Second, the distortions often evoked by economists when controls are imposed did not materialize on a noticeable scale. Labor shortages did not result. Even where exemptions were adopted that seemed to have the potential of causing disruptions, the effect was minimal. Fringe benefits and productivity incentive plans, for example, do not appear to have been artificially stimulated. Thus reasonable exemptions needed to make a wage control program politically acceptable or administratively feasible can be adopted without adverse economic impact if labor markets are not excessively tight.

In terms of its limited goals, the Phase II wage program seemed to be on target at the time it was terminated. Inflationary expectations were reduced. A catch-up round in the labor market was allowed to proceed in an orderly fashion. But catch-up increases for those who merited them were not allowed to set the pattern for other units. Labor market behavior was returning to a more normal, less pressured condition.

XI

Impact on Wages: The Inside View

The impact of Phase II on wage developments in the labor market reflected in part the actual decisions of the Pay Board. While the board's 5.5 percent standard established a general bench mark for unions and wage administrators, the flow of decisions from the regulatory process determined the credibility of the standard. Ideally there should be consistency between the external impact of wage controls and the pattern of regulatory activities.

This chapter is an analysis of internal data concerning wage adjustments that were submitted to the Pay Board for review and disposition. The data were generated by the prenotification and reporting requirements established by the board. As such, they reflected both the operational deficiencies and the peculiar computational rules adopted by the board. In any case, they are the only internal data now available; after Phase II the data files were either lost or deteriorated in quality.[1]

Pay Board data generally included increases in fringe benefits as well as in wages, although a few of the early cases before the benefit rules were announced may not have included qualified benefits. The data also incorporated "roll-up," or the secondary effects of wage increases on fringe benefits. Costing was usually done on the "ice cube" basis, which froze projected hours at the base period level. This approach removed distortions due to changes in employment patterns during the control year. And in general, "time-weighting"—weighting each increase during the year by the proportion of the year in which it was effective—was not permitted, so that the data indicated the percentage increase from the beginning to the end of a control year.

While these rules constituted a sound methodology, there were a number of significant exceptions in practice. For example, escalator increases were in fact time-weighted, thus understating the year-to-year adjustment.

---

1. Even the files maintained during Phase II contain a good deal of "noise." Errors crept in despite the continuous efforts of the economics office to correct inaccuracies. The main problem was that economic data were computerized only as a by-product of case-processing. Case handlers were under great pressure to maintain volume and had few incentives to keep accurate records.

Merit plan increases were calculated using the "double-snapshot" rather than the ice cube approach. This method involved the calculation of average hourly labor costs just before and at the end of the control year. As a result, shifts in the pattern of hours between high- and low-paying jobs were not filtered out of the percentage increase. The demographic trend during Phase II toward a younger labor force, plus the greater discretion in estimation that the double-snapshot method implied, led to the understatement of merit increases. Another source of downward bias in estimates of changes in compensation cost was the decision that fringe benefit increases needed to maintain existing benefits—that is, to correct inadequate past funding—would not be included in the computation. Overall, the tendency was to modify general policies by permitting relaxed computation rules rather than by giving an explicit exception for certain kinds of increases.

The concept of the short control year—a device to ease the transition to a controlled economy—also reduced the size of the average request and approval. Units affected were those with contracts or pay practices with anniversary dates that did not coincide with the first day of Phase II, November 14, 1971. Units without such contracts or pay practices were constrained to calculate their increase over the twelve-month period beginning November 14. But since most union contracts had traditional anniversary dates on other days, the union sector, plus a minority of units in the nonunion sector that had contract-like pay regularities, were permitted to use short control years from November 14, 1971, to the traditional anniversary date. Thereafter, the control year constituted the twelve-month period beginning with that anniversary date.

The short control year concept was most likely to affect old union contracts, that is, those negotiated before Phase II. Consider, for example, a one-year contract signed on July 1, 1971, designating a 6 percent increase on July 1, and another 3 percent on January 1, 1972. From the Pay Board viewpoint, the unit had a short control year running from November 14, 1971, to June 30, 1972. During that time only a 3 percent increase occurred; thus only the 3 percent would be entered on Pay Board records, not the full 9 percent during the contract year. On July 1, 1972, the unit might negotiate another wage increase, say 5.5 percent. This would be entered as a new case for 5.5 percent, producing an average for the first twelve months of Phase II of only 4.25 percent ([3.0 percent + 5.5 percent]/2), even though wages had actually gone up by 8.5 percent (3.0 percent + 5.5 percent) during that period. As a result, the data on old adjustments are affected by small, tail-end wage increases occurring in the latter parts of contract years.[2]

Measured in terms of an absolute standard, Pay Board data were cleanest when confined to new union adjustments, those determined during Phase II. These adjustments were least likely to be affected by escalators, merit plans, or short control years. But even the other types of cases produced useful data. The approvals can still be measured against board standards, since those standards included the computation rules, and they also provide a picture of the size and characteristics of the various categories.

General Characteristics of Categories I and II

Estimates by the Pay Board's staff suggested that categories I and II contained about 15 million to 16 million workers, excluding state and local civil servants.[3] The exclusion was made because under a special certification procedure available to the state and local sector, cases involving increases of no more than the standard might not appear in Pay Board records.[4] However, a rough estimate made by the Bureau of Labor Statistics suggested that the entire Category I and Category II universe consisted of about 19 million workers.[5]

Table 11-1 shows a breakdown of Category I and Category II workers listed on Pay Board computer records as of March 2, 1973.[6] The figures

2. In a few cases, when pre–Phase II negotiations had dragged on into Phase II, new contracts received short control years. The West Coast longshore case was an example. The ultimate increase reported, however, would be a full twelve month's worth in such cases.

3. See statement of George H. Boldt, "The Pay Board After One Year of Operation," in *Price and Wage Control: An Evaluation of Current Policies,* Hearings before the U.S. Joint Economic Committee, 92 Cong. 2 sess. (Government Printing Office, 1973), pt. 1, p. 24.

4. Under the certification procedure state and local units could certify that they would comply with Pay Board standards. This freed them from other reporting requirements. Units wishing exceptions to the standards, however, had to file formal requests.

5. See Victor J. Sheifer, "Reconciling Labor Department and Stabilization Agency Wage Data," *Monthly Labor Review,* vol. 96 (April 1973), pp. 24–30.

6. Although Phase II ended on January 11, 1973, the Pay Board continued terminal operations until February 28, 1973, when its computer system was inherited by the Cost of Living Council. Although almost all Phase II business was concluded by March 2, 1973, some cases had been formally decided but not yet entered into the computer records. About 600 such cases in categories I and II were outstanding as of March 2, 1973, and many of these were simply awaiting computer entry rather than decision.

Table 11-1. *Number of Workers Affected by Category I and Category II Cases Processed by the Pay Board*[a]

Thousands

Category and union status	Workers affected by new cases[b]	Workers affected by old cases[c]	Total workers
Total	12,963	11,539	24,503
Category I	8,486	9,667	18,153
Category II	4,478	1,872	6,350
Union	2,848	9,249	12,097
Category I	1,800	7,954	9,754
Category II	1,048	1,296	2,343
Nonunion	10,115	2,290	12,405
Category I	6,685	1,713	8,398
Category II	3,430	577	4,007

Source: Pay Board computer records as of March 2, 1973. Figures are rounded.

a. Category I includes units of 5,000 or more employees; Category II, of units with 1,000–4,999 employees. Workers are counted for each control year in which their units filed cases. Hence double and triple counting is present in this table.

b. Cases involving labor contracts negotiated after Phase II was initiated on November 14, 1971.

c. Cases involving contracts negotiated before the beginning of Phase II.

shown in this table are not consistent with the estimate of the size of the two categories because some units came in for more than one control year during the program. Under the short control year concept, the figures for workers involved in old cases are especially susceptible to double counting. Thus the problem was most applicable to union workers, since old cases occurred mainly in the union sector. Despite this difficulty, the data on workers in table 11-1 and the corresponding figures on cases processed (table 11-2) can be used to give a general idea of the characteristics of cases in categories I and II.

Table 11-3, based on tables 11-1 and 11-2, shows that categories I and II were 49 percent unionized. Despite the upward bias of the estimate, it is substantially higher than the national unionization rate of approximately 25 percent for all employed workers. The difference in unionization between categories I and II is exclusively a function of the tendency of union workers to be in larger units. About 40 percent of the *cases* in both categories were unionized. Old cases, as one might expect, were mainly union cases. Nonunion units with old cases either had established regularities of timing or had announced increases before Phase II, or—in the government sector—had had their increases specified in pre–Phase II legislation.

Table 11-2. *Number of Category I and Category II Cases Processed by the Pay Board*[a]

Thousands

Category and union status	New cases	Old cases	Total cases
Total	2,569	1,147	3,716
Category I	501	249	750
Category II	2,068	898	2,966
Union	663	807	1,470
Category I	139	155	294
Category II	524	652	1,176
Nonunion	1,906	340	2,246
Category I	362	94	456
Category II	1,544	246	1,790

Source: Pay Board computer records as of March 2, 1973.
a. See notes to table 11-1 for definitions of categories and cases. A case is defined on a control year basis rather than on a submission basis.

Table 11-3. *Characteristics of Category I and Category II Units*

Type of worker and case	Percent unionized	Average unit size[a] (thousands)	Percent in Category I
Workers			
Categories I and II	49	6,594	74
Category I	54	24,204	...
Category II	37	2,141	...
Union	...	8,229	81
Nonunion	...	5,523	68
New cases	22	5,046	65
Old cases	80	10,060	84
Cases			
Categories I and II	40	...	20
Category I	39	...	...
Category II	40	...	...
Union	...	...	20
Nonunion	...	...	20
New cases	26	...	20
Old cases	70	...	22

Sources: Tables 11-1 and 11-2.
a. Workers per unit.

Table 11-4. *Distribution of Wage Rates, by Category, for Union and Nonunion Workers and Cases, Pay Board Closed Cases as of July 1972*
Percent

| Straight-time wage rate (dollars) | Categories I and II[a] | | | | Category III[b] | | |
| | Workers | | Cases | | Workers | Cases | |
	Union	Non-union	Union	Non-union	Union	Union	Non-union
Less than:							
2.35	1	3	2	8	5	3	10
2.85	3	10	14	18	12	12	16
3.35	10	26	26	31	22	24	24
3.85	43	35	40	45	43	44	30
4.35	52	45	62	58	63	67	50
All wage rates	100	100	100	100	100	100	100
Addenda:							
Number of cases	...	...	414	498	...	260	50
Number of workers (thousands)	5,214	2,594	...	...	41	...	...

Source: Data taken from the Pay Board's physical case records by the staff in July 1972.
a. See note a, table 11-1 for definition of categories.
b. Category III (composed of industries with less than 1,000 employees) includes both closed and pending cases. See text note 7.

Although it was hoped that the computer would store information on base wage and fringe benefit rates (and increments) on a disaggregated basis, this aspect of the system did not become operational until the last months of Phase II. Hence useful data on absolute compensation are not available from the Pay Board computer records. Some indication of the straight-time rates prevailing in categories I and II can be ascertained, however, from table 11-4. These data were collected in July 1972 from physical case files as part of a survey associated with the court proceedings overturning the Cost of Living Council's definition of the "working poor."[7] Wage rates in categories I and II, which had a median wage in

7. The survey included all closed cases in categories I and II that were located in the closed-case files. Cases that were not in the files (presumably because adjudicators were using them to process related cases) were not included. The small sample of Category III cases in table 11-4 includes both closed and pending cases where usable data were available. Many Category III cases closed by the Pay Board at that time were received before the delegation of authority to the Internal Revenue Service. Since they often consisted of letters rather than forms, the relevant data, if available at all, were difficult to extract.

excess of $4 an hour, were significantly higher than those generally prevailing in the economy.[8] It is interesting to note that a greater proportion of nonunion workers surveyed were in units that averaged at least $4.35 than were union workers. This anomaly could be the result of sampling error, but the sparse data in the records seem to confirm the finding. It appears that those nonunion workers for whom wages are determined in large units are not typical of nonunion workers generally. Many are in large firms and have their wages determined in some sort of rough tandem to unionized workers in the same firms.

Despite the problems with the data, it is clear that the Category I and Category II workers, who were the center of Pay Board attention, were more heavily unionized and more highly paid than most workers. In addition, the large number of cases and workers under old contracts indicates that many of the adjustments occurring in categories I and II were determined before Phase II.

Pay Board Approvals

Table 11-5 shows a breakdown of Category I and Category II approvals. The overall average approved increase, weighted by the number of employees in each decision, was 5.4 percent. The slightly lower average for Category II is due primarily to the lower rate of unionization in that category, since cases in categories I and II were processed in the same manner by the board. That is, there was no differential treatment between the two categories based on the size of the unit.

The time sequence of new-case approvals reflects the early history of the Pay Board. During the first four months, relatively few cases were processed. The board's negotiations process delayed the assembling of a permanent staff; in any case, the board did not delegate authority to approve cases meeting its standards until late January 1972. Until that time a backlog built up, with only a few large cases (coal mining, railroads, aerospace) plus a handful of others getting through the mill.[9]

After the staff received authorization to handle within-standard cases

8. Average hourly earnings for nonsupervisory workers in the private nonfarm sector during the first half of 1972 were $3.59. In general the mean can be expected to be higher than the median. Further, the $3.59 includes overtime.

9. The coal mining and railroad cases were considered old cases by the board even though they represented first-year adjustments. This is because they had been negotiated before Phase II but could not be implemented without board approval. They were not deferred adjustments in the commonly used meaning of the term; that is, second- or third-year adjustments.

Table 11-5. *Average Wage Increase Approved by the Pay Board,*
Categories I and II, Selected Industries[a]

Percent

Description	New cases	Old cases	Total cases
Category			
I and II	5.4	5.4	5.4
I	5.4	5.4	5.4
II	5.2	5.4	5.3
Processed by board			
First four months	4.6	6.0	5.3
Second four months	5.4	4.6	4.9
Third four months	5.3	6.0	5.6
Last period	5.6	5.5	5.6
Industry			
Durable manufacturing	5.5	5.3	5.3
Nondurable manufacturing	5.3	5.4	5.3
Transportation and warehousing	7.2	6.6	6.7
Communications	5.2	3.8	4.2
Utilities	5.8	5.3	5.6
Wholesale and retail trade	4.3	3.9	4.2
Finance and insurance	4.9	4.1	4.4
Services	5.4	5.7	5.4
State and local government	5.8	6.4	5.8
Extractive	5.8	10.3	8.8
Union	6.9	5.6	5.9
Category I	7.0	5.6	5.8
Category II	6.8	5.9	6.3
Nonunion	4.9	4.6	4.9
Category I	5.0	4.6	4.9
Category II	4.8	4.4	4.7

Source: Pay Board computer records as of March 2, 1973.
a. See notes to table 11-1 for definitions of categories and cases.

and the board established the de facto 7 percent standard for deferred adjustments, the tempo of case-processing increased. At the same time, the board was involved in drafting regulations; thus cases involving requests for above-standard increases stuck in the backlog, while requests for lower increases were approved. Consequently the average pay increase approved for all cases shows a drop during the second four months of operation. It should be noted that under board rules prevailing at that time, deferred adjustment cases that were challenged could still go into operation sixty days after notification. Technically the board could have ordered a rollback when it finally reviewed these cases. In general, however, the board was reluctant to reduce increases that had been paid for a long period of time, even on a prospective basis. The clearing of this backlog helped push up the average percentage increase approved by the board during the third four-month period of operation. Approvals of increases under old contracts declined in the final period of operation—which includes the terminal operations of the board during the early weeks of Phase III. New-case approvals, on the other hand, rose. Included among the new-case approvals toward the end of Phase II was a 6.4 percent increase for 77,000 postal supervisors and some other relatively high increases in airlines and state and local governments.

The industry summaries in table 11-5 show above-average increases approved in transportation (longshoring, railroads, trucking, postal services) and the extractive sector (chiefly coal mining). State and local cases also show approved increases somewhat above the average. Data for that sector are biased upward, since many state and local units took advantage of the special procedure that permitted them to certify that they would not exceed Pay Board standards.

Since the sectors with above-average approved increases are highly unionized, it is not surprising to see that approved union wage adjustments ran higher than nonunion ones. This tendency is evident despite the factors that resulted in a downward bias in the calculation of deferred adjustments (76 percent of union workers during Phase II in categories I and II). The fact that Category II union approvals ran somewhat above Category I for old cases is associated with generous deferred increases in retail food. Most of these deferred increases occurred in small units, owing to the structure of the industry.

Requests versus Approvals

Pay Board request data were entered directly from reporting forms at the time cases arrived. If the applicant miscalculated, the entry was supposed to be corrected at the time of closing. However, probably more discrepancies occur in the request data than in the approval data.[10]

10. When the computer records were cleaned up at various points during the Pay Board's operation, it was easy to spot and correct errors when the recorded wage increase requested was less than the one approved. A requested increase that was erroneously higher than that approved was more difficult to spot if it was above the standards, since it was possible that a cutback had been made. This source of error is relatively slight in the aggregate figures, since in only a small fraction of the case load does the request exceed the grant.

Table 11-6. *Average Wage Increase Requested and Average Approved by Pay Board, Categories I and II, by Union Status*
Percent

Category, union status, and type of contract[a]	Average increase requested	Average increase approved
Categories I and II	5.6	5.4
Category I	5.6	5.4
Category II	5.5	5.3
Union	6.2	5.9
Category I	6.0	5.8
Category II	6.7	6.3
Union, new cases	7.6	6.9
Category I	7.8	7.0
Category II	7.3	6.8
Union, old cases	5.7	5.6
Category I	5.6	5.6
Category II	6.3	5.9
Nonunion	5.0	4.9
Category I	5.0	4.9
Category II	4.8	4.7
Nonunion, new cases	5.0	4.9
Category I	5.1	5.0
Category II	4.8	4.8
Nonunion, old cases	4.6	4.6
Category I	4.7	4.6
Category II	4.5	4.4

Source: Pay Board computer records as of March 2, 1973.
a. See notes to table 11-1 for definitions of categories and cases.

Table 11-6 shows a breakdown of requests and approvals by type of case. Although it is true that the union sector received approvals for higher increases on the average than the nonunion sector, it is evident that the union sector was more heavily affected by cutbacks, especially in new cases. The average new-contract union request was for a 7.6 percent increase, compared with an average approved increase of 6.9 percent. The new-contract union cases included second-year adjustments in contracts negotiated during Phase II. Such contracts were not treated as pre–Phase II deferred adjustments under Pay Board rules. Because second-year adjustments typically were below first-year increases, such adjustments were less likely to be cut back. If Pay Board data are narrowed to Bureau of Labor Statistics definitions, the average increase approved for new cases in 1972 was 7.2 percent, and the average increase requested was 8.1 percent.[11]

Even this gap tends to understate the cutbacks because tandems to the major cases sometimes did not submit their requests until after the board had decided the lead case. They would then request the amount finally approved by the board rather than the original lead request. Thus, for example, the Pay Board cut back the 70 cent wage increase of over 49,000 longshoremen on the East Coast to 55 cents. Thereafter, submissions were received from the ports of Jacksonville, Savannah, and Mobile requesting only the 55 cents, although they had originally agreed to the 70 cent increase in the old contract. Thus the request and grant are recorded as equivalent for these ports, although they were actually part of the rollback.

As might be expected, the liberal treatment of deferred adjustments meant that relatively few workers experienced cutbacks in old cases. In Category II there is a noticeable gap between the average amount requested and approved. This is due to the concentration of deferred cutbacks in the retail food area.

Table 11-7 is a tabulation of those cases in which the recorded request exceeded the grant.[12] This method of attempting to isolate cutbacks is deficient because of the problem and discrepancies discussed above. It

11. The BLS reported first-year major increases in 1972 to have averaged 7.4 percent in the nonconstruction sector. The Pay Board's data indicated 7.2 percent. The average request for the cases in which the 7.2 percent approval was reported was 8.1 percent. The major difference between Pay Board and BLS data for new-contract union cases was that the Pay Board included second-year adjustments in contracts negotiated during Phase II and in government sector cases. In addition, the Pay Board classified the United Transportation Union case as "old" because the contract involved was negotiated before Phase II. For a reconciliation of Pay Board and BLS data, see Pay Board press releases PB-114, July 28, 1972, and PB-135, October 27, 1972.

12. In certain cases the Pay Board delayed the implementation of an increase within a control year. Prominent examples were the state of Ohio and Maryland cases. Such cases would not be picked up by comparing the request and the grant, since according to Pay Board costing rules they were identical. Another case that is missed is the Teamsters deferred increase under the Master Freight Agreement. In this case the board decided to reduce the amount allowed in the next control year by 5 cents but to leave the increase under consideration untouched. Pay Board computer records do not indicate cutbacks explicitly. At the time the system was designed, it was not known whether the board would actually recommend an approvable figure or simply tell the parties to renegotiate and try again. As a result, the system's case designations of "approval" and "denial" did not match eventual Pay Board procedure and were dropped.

Table 11-7. *Pay Board Cases in which Requested Wage Increases Exceeded Grants, Categories I and II*[a]

Category and union status	Number of cases	Number of workers affected (thousands)	Percent increase requested	Percent increase approved
Categories I and II	254	1,488	10.3	7.6
Union	182	799	11.7	8.2
New	105	553	12.1	8.4
Old	77	247	11.0	7.7
Nonunion	72	689	8.6	7.0

Source: Pay Board computer records as of March 2, 1973. Figures are rounded.
a. See text for limitations of this method of isolating cutbacks. See notes, table 11-1, for definitions.

probably exaggerates nonunion cutbacks relative to union ones. Even so, the figures do show that most cutbacks occurred in the union sector and that these cutbacks were more drastic. Three cases in the government sector (California civil servants and two cases involving postal supervisors) account for 39 percent of the nonunion workers in table 11-7. Many other cases in the nonunion sector appear to be tandems to union cases. Thus it appears that private employees in predominantly nonunion firms were virtually untouched by cutbacks. This apparently resulted from a combination of labor market forces and the willingness of nonunion employers to restrain requests to levels within the standards.

The relatively small number of cutbacks does not mean that all other cases fell within Pay Board standards. Some cases exceeded the standards but were granted exceptions. The standard varied considerably for each case. Some units were eligible for exceptions, such as catch-up, and many were eligible for more than the basic 0.7 percent in qualified fringe benefits. Pay Board records do not indicate the maximum amount for which each unit was eligible. It is possible, however, to segregate those cases that involve requests for less than the basic standards (including fringe benefits) of 6.2 percent for new situations and 7.7 percent for old.[13] Table 11-8 shows that 76 percent of Category I and Category II cases fell within the basic standards. As would be expected from previous

13. In some cases units may have exceeded the standards for wages but asked for less than the basic amount for fringe benefits. For example, in a new case an employer requested 5.7 percent for wages and 0.3 percent for qualified fringe benefits but was asking for less than 6.2 percent in total compensation. Nonetheless, this still would have exceeded the standard. It is not known how many such cases are included in the data, but the number can be assumed to be small.

Table 11-8. *Percent of Cases and Workers Making Requests Falling within Pay Board Basic Standards, Categories I and II*[a]

| Description | New requests | | Old requests | | Total |
	Union	Nonunion	Union	Nonunion	
Categories I and II					
Cases	49	81	80	93	76
Workers	44	76	85	93	77

Source: Pay Board computer records as of March 2, 1973.

a. Standards are 6.2 percent for new cases and 7.7 percent for old cases. See notes, table 11-1, for definitions.

analysis, nonunion cases were more likely to fall below the standards than union cases. The high proportion of cases within the standards significantly lessened the staff time needed for case-processing. Cases within the standards could be handled with little more than a cursory check of the costing. Staff time was freed for the remaining cases that requested exceptions.

Table 11-8 also allows an interesting calculation to be made concerning strict enforcement of the Pay Board's standards. The average requested increase submitted to the Pay Board in categories I and II was 5.6 percent. Approvals ran 0.2 percentage point lower on the average. If all new requests had been held to a maximum of 6.2 percent and all old requests to a maximum of 7.7 percent, the average approval would have been 5.0 percent. In other words, strict enforcement would have lopped off another 0.4 percentage point beyond the actual 0.2.[14] This is somewhat of an exaggeration since some of the employers requesting more than the basic standards were eligible for one or another of the board's automatic exceptions.

Table 11-9 presents the most detailed breakdown of average requests and approvals by industry that is available from Pay Board records, but there are significant gaps in the data. Nevertheless, sizable cutbacks can be seen in aircraft and missiles; retail food; health services; lumber; maritime transport; printing and publishing; state and local governments; and the stone, clay and glass industry. Within aircraft and missiles, the major cutbacks came in the aerospace cases involving over 100,000 workers.[15]

Retail food was a continuing problem for the board. About 12 percent

14. This estimate was made by recalculating the average approval on the assumption that all cases that were approved above 6.2 percent or 7.7 percent (as appropriate) had in fact been cut back to those standards.

15. This cutback from 12.2 percent to 8.3 percent was overturned by a court decision after Phase II (see chapter 5).

Table 11-9. *Average Wage Increase Requested and Average Approved by Pay Board, Categories I and II, by Industry*[a]

Percent

Industry	Average increase requested	Average increase approved
Aircraft and missiles	7.3	6.6
Airlines	5.3	5.2
Apparel	5.5	5.5
Chemicals and petroleum	5.4	5.2
Communications	4.2	4.2
Electrical machinery	5.1	5.1
Fabricated metals	6.2	6.1
Finance, insurance, real estate	4.5	4.4
Food products	5.4	5.3
Food, retail	9.1	7.1
Union, new cases	10.7	8.0
Union, old cases	9.2	7.0
Nonunion	5.4	5.4
General merchandise, retail	3.3	3.3
Health services	5.6	5.2
Instruments	4.9	4.8
Lumber, furniture, wood	6.1	5.7
Machinery, except electrical	4.8	4.8
Maritime transport	10.9	9.7
Mining, oil, gas extraction	8.8	8.8
Motor vehicles	4.8	4.8
Paper products	5.3	5.3
Primary metals	6.1	6.1
Printing and publishing	6.1	5.7
Railroads	7.8	7.8
Rubber and plastic	4.9	4.9
State and local government, education	5.7	5.4
State and local government, except education	6.4	6.0
Stone, clay, glass	7.3	6.7
Textiles	5.4	5.4
Trucking and warehousing	6.4	6.2
Utilities	5.8	5.6

Source: Pay Board computer records as of March 2, 1973.
a. See notes, table 11-1, for definitions.

of the recorded union cutbacks came from retail food, although only about 6 percent of the union case load fell in that industry classification. Major wage reductions in new situations occurred in cases involving 13,000 retail clerks in Philadelphia. Here, a 19 percent wage request was pared to 6.7 percent. In Boston's Stop and Shop chain a 14 percent increase for 7,500 workers was cut to 6.6 percent. Significant reductions of deferred increases also were imposed in this industry. The Philadelphia meatcutters' case, in which an 11 percent increase for 3,900 workers was cut to 7.7 percent in June 1972, was the first deferred rollback. A similar cutback was later ordered for 12,700 workers in Washington, D.C., food stores.

In the health services industry cutbacks were made in hospitals in the San Francisco area and in nursing homes in New York City and Nassau County, New York. The major reduction in the lumber industry involved 19,500 workers in the northwestern states represented by the Woodworkers. Their increase was lowered from 9.2 percent to 6.8 percent. The cuts in maritime transport involved the West Coast and East Coast longshoremen's cases. On the West Coast, a 20.6 percent increase was reduced to 14.9 percent. On the East Coast, contracts involving 49,000 workers and three major employer organizations were shaved from an average request for 13 percent to 10.6 percent.

The printing industry experienced two major deferred cutbacks. A wage increase for employees of the *Washington Post* was lowered from 13.6 percent to 9.0 percent. Reductions were also made in deferred increases in the New York City printing industry and New York newspapers. In the state and local government area, significant cutbacks were made in a variety of units involving civil servants of New York City and the state of Pennsylvania, and the Milwaukee police. In education, 55,000 teachers in the state of Georgia were cut from 9.5 percent to 5.5 percent.[16] Finally, the major reduction in stone, clay, and glass occurred in a number of unionized units in the glass industry.

The figures thus far generally refer to the entire Phase II period. Because the Pay Board information system was unreliable until the summer of 1972, it is not possible to look at trends in incoming requests until that point. The Pay Board staff did keep track of new requests beginning in August, especially in unionized situations. Table 11-10 reveals that requests for increases under new union contracts ran at about 7 percent during the fourth quarter of 1972. Although data for previous quarters are not available, the fact that almost all other cases in the Pay Board's records arrived before the fourth quarter allows a computation of the average request in prior periods. Since the average increase requested under new

16. As noted earlier, the cutbacks in the state of Ohio and Maryland cases are not reflected, because the board delayed implementation of the wage increase rather than cut the percentage allowed.

Table 11-10. *Summary of Wage Adjustment Requests Received
by the Pay Board, New Union Contracts, Categories I and II,
August–December 1972*[a]

Period in 1972	Number of cases	Number of workers affected (thousands)	Weighted percent increase requested
August	54	204	5.9
September 1–October 18	63	214	6.4
October 18–31	54	168	6.6
November	69	267	7.5
December	31	120	6.6[b]

Source: Pay Board staff paper OCE-115, January 4, 1973.
a. See notes, table 11-1, for definitions.
b. Requests in December for those cases for which computer records on fringe benefits were available broke down as follows: wages, 4.5 percent; includable fringe benefits, 0.8 percent; qualified fringe benefits, 1.0 percent; total, 6.4 percent.

union contracts during Phase II was 7.6 percent, the average before the fourth quarter of 1972 was approximately 7.8 percent. Thus in very gross terms the trend was downward.

Category III

Because the records of the Category III Panel were not computerized, detailed analysis is not possible. In any case Category III units that reached the panel had to involve requests for more than 5.5 percent. Thus the panel's records do not reflect all adjustments in Category III.[17] Quite the opposite; they reflect the small number of instances in which exceptions were sought. No count is available, but it is known that the Category III Panel's cases were heavily unionized, in contrast to the typical small employee unit. They also appear to have enjoyed average wages roughly in line with units in categories I and II, as the small sample in table 11-4 suggests.

Since Category III units reaching the panel were all asking for exceptions, the rate of cutbacks was higher for Category III than for Category I and Category II cases. Wage reductions in Phase III were somewhat easier to make because relatively few deferred adjustment cases were involved. Category III units did not have to report deferred adjustments,

17. Cases that were processed entirely by the Internal Revenue Service or by the full Pay Board do not appear in the records of the Category III Panel.

Table 11-11. *Percent of Workers Affected by Wage Increase Requests and Approvals Handled by the Category III Panel, by Range of Requested or Approved Increase*[a]

Range of requested or approved increase (*percent*)	Percent of workers affected by request	Percent of workers affected by approval
Under 7	10	23
7–10	38	52
10–15	35	19
15–20	10	4
20 or more	7	2
All cases	100	100
Addenda:		
Number of cases	2,815	336,249
Weighted average increase approved (percent)	...	...
Weighted average increase requested (percent)	11.6	8.8

Source: "Category III Panel—Operation Statistics as of Feb. 28, 1973," tabulation in Pay Board files attached to memorandum from Arnold Strasser to Millard Cass, March 6, 1973.
a. Excludes 183 cases (33,943 workers) involving retroactivity only, and 333 executive compensation, nonunion construction, and "other" cases.

and the only way a deferred increase could come to the attention of the panel was through a challenge made by the employer. Most employers were reluctant to challenge these increases. Although data are not readily available, the cutback rate at the panel was probably in the vicinity of 50 percent.[18]

According to table 11-11, requests reaching the panel were for increases averaging 11.6 percent, and the average increase approved was 8.8 percent. The key feature of the table is the relatively small number of workers involved—336,000. These workers do not include nonunion construction workers or Category III workers whose cases were decided directly by the Pay Board without an initial decision by the panel. If the estimated 19 million private and public sector workers who were in categories I and II are subtracted from nonfarm and nonconstruction payroll employment, about 48 million workers (excluding exempt federal em-

18. A cutback in the case of the Category III Panel is intended to mean any action whereby the unit got less than requested. In some cases this meant that the initial Internal Revenue Service decision was upheld. In other cases, the amount allowed might exceed the amount initially permitted by the IRS but be less than the amount requested. Typically, the Category III Panel permitted the requested increase in qualified fringe benefits to be implemented, even if it exceeded the amount permissible under Pay Board regulations.

ployees) remain. The small-business exemption would reduce this number to perhaps 30 million. Thus roughly 1 percent of the Pay Board's Category III universe filed appeals that reached the Category III Panel, and perhaps half of these experienced setbacks. In categories I and II— again using the estimate of 19 million—the number of workers experiencing cutbacks would have been on the order of 7 to 8 percent.

Nonunion Construction

Nonunion construction units were permitted two choices. They could grant the same cents-per-hour increment that had been approved for union construction workers in the same craft and area by the Construction Industry Stabilization Committee or 5.5 percent, whichever was greater. Although all nonunion contractors were required to comply with Pay Board regulations, it was doubtful that the very small contracting companies were aware of the program. No special compliance drives were launched in nonunion construction. The larger firms did submit cases to the board. In some instances they evidently requested the maximum increment permissible, even if they intended to pay less. The Pay Board's approval provided flexibility in case it proved necessary to pay more than was intended. It should be noted that the cents-per-hour increment approved by the CISC would generally provide a higher percentage increase for nonunion workers than for union workers, because nonunion base wages usually were lower than union wages. Therefore, the Pay Board's standards were quite liberal, and almost all nonunion construction increases that were received could be accommodated.

A special division of the Pay Board handled nonunion construction cases. Cases from that division were not subject to routine accuracy checks by the economics office personnel. Consequently the computer records are even more variable. As of March 16, 1973, the records indicated that 1,227 cases had been processed involving over 79,000 workers. (Some cases did not report the number of employees.) For those cases for which request and approval data are available, about 86 percent of the total, the data indicated an average requested increase of 7.9 percent and an average approved increase of 7.7 percent. A large number of these cases are reported to have requested 5.5 percent or less. These reports were not required by the board but apparently were sent in by mistake. Excluding requests for 5.5 percent or less, the average request was for

11.5 percent, and the average approval was for 11.0 percent. In other words, nonunion construction cases requesting more than 5.5 percent asked for roughly the amount that nonconstruction Category III cases requested from the Category III Panel. But they received larger approvals because of the relative liberality of the standard for nonunion construction.

The average unit size for all nonunion construction cases was approximately 75 employees. Twenty-one Category I and Category II cases were reported containing a combined total of over 50,000 workers. That is, 2 percent of the cases contained over 60 percent of the workers that reported. There appear to have been no cutbacks in this group, probably because the larger firms researched the CISC increment for which they were eligible before applying to the board. Eight of the twenty-one cases are reported to have requested more than 5.5 percent, for a weighted average of 10.8 percent.

Overview

The patterns visible from the Pay Board data files are not surprising in view of labor market conditions prevailing during Phase II. Unionized units, owing largely to catch-up pressure, requested more than nonunion units.[19] Because the Pay Board's exception policy gave weight to catch-up and to equity considerations regarding traditional differentials, many exception requests were approved. On the other hand, since unionized units typically asked for more than nonunion units, they usually experienced a higher rate of cutbacks.

Overall, the relatively high standards for new and old cases, plus the exception criteria used by the board, minimized the number of cutbacks. And once the standards were promulgated, voluntary compliance also reduced the need for reductions in negotiated increases. Relatively few workers—even in categories I and II—experienced direct administrative cutbacks. The vast number of small units in Category III generated a large absolute case load. But only a tiny fraction of the workers in Category III was ever involved in an appeal to the Pay Board, much less a rollback. A larger fraction was involved in some contact with the IRS. However, many appeals submitted to the IRS turned out to have been misfiled (no filing was actually required).

19. Direct evidence on catch-up pressure may be found in chapters 3 and 10.

In categories I and II, the average approval was about 0.2 percentage point below the average request. A rigid policy of denying all exceptions above the basic standards would have increased this gap by another 0.4 percentage point. It could be argued that such a rigid policy would have made possible a comparable reduction in the rate of price inflation and permitted the achievement of the 2–3 percent price target. The Pay Board, however, viewed such a mechanical approach as potentially disruptive. It might have held the line more rigidly during Phase II, but this course of action would have led to distortions in wage structures and ultimately more pressure on wage levels. In addition, using BLS definitions, the average approval for new contracts in categories I and II was 0.9 percentage point below the average request. To the extent that wage pressure was identified with large bargaining units, these units were the focus of the Pay Board's firmest action.

XII

Impact of the Program
on Industrial Relations

The primary purpose of a wage control program is, of course, to bring wage increases to a rate consistent with some price inflation target. But obviously a variety of side effects inevitably flow from controls. In the previous chapter, the economic impact of Phase II wage controls was examined. This chapter deals with the impact on industrial relations. Since the distinction between "economic" and "industrial relations" considerations is not well defined, it is best to simply enumerate the topics to be covered in this chapter: the propensity to unionize, strike activity, contract duration, and the use of escalator clauses. In addition, the question of whether the establishment of a well-publicized wage guideline (for example, 5.5 percent) creates a floor for wage determination will also be discussed.

The Propensity to Unionize

It is possible for a wage control program to stimulate union membership even as it restrains union wage increases. During the program for controlling wages in the World War II period, union security arrangements were sometimes offered as an inducement for restraints on wages and the right to strike. During the period 1940–45, union membership as a proportion of nonfarm payroll employment rose from 26.9 percent to 35.5 percent, a peak never again reached. Obviously several factors (including controls) contributed to this rise. During the Korean war, 1950–53, unionization rose from 31.5 percent to 33.7 percent.[1]

In Phase II the Pay Board attempted to avoid direct involvement in the negotiations process. No rulings were made until the parties had reached an agreement on their own and submitted it to the board. Although the staff was sometimes approached for guidance on what was permissible, it

1. U.S. Bureau of Labor Statistics, *Handbook of Labor Statistics, 1975—Reference Edition* (Government Printing Office, 1975), p. 389.

provided only general information on Pay Board regulations and did not formally offer any opinions concerning whether the board would grant a particular exception. Thus the basic administrative mechanism of the Pay Board did not include dispute-settling machinery. Nor did it include any other mechanism whereby the board might become a party to the negotiations. In following this operating mode, the Pay Board was unlikely to provide any direct encouragement to unionization during Phase II.

Even so, it might be hypothesized that some indirect inducement to unionization could have occurred. For example, the exceptions granted in major unionized situations received considerable publicity, especially at the beginning of the program. In the early months of Phase II even the major cutbacks of the board were well above the standard. Board approvals included an 8.3 percent increase for aerospace workers and 14.9 percent for West Coast longshoremen, and the East Coast longshoremen obtained an average of 10.6 percent in the three employer associations involved. The unions that remained unscathed, such as the United Mine Workers (16.8 percent) and the various railroad crafts (10 percent during 1972), also were widely covered in the press. Although the average worker did not have a detailed knowledge of Pay Board approvals, it is possible that he believed unions received more favorable treatment than nonunion units during Phase II. This could have made unionization seem more attractive as an avenue to favored treatment by the board.

On the other hand, the 5.5 percent standard also received widespread publicity. While the press sometimes noted the additional allowance for fringe benefits and the variety of exceptions, more often than not these accounts simply stated that the guideline was 5.5 percent. It is possible, therefore, that the average worker felt that unionization would *not* prove advantageous. He might have believed that there was little hope of winning more than 5.5 percent.

One source of data does reflect the propensity to unionize on a continuous basis. The National Labor Relations Board (NLRB) conducts elections in "the unit appropriate for the purpose of collective bargaining" when questions of union representation arise.[2] Figures on these elections apply only to the private sector where the NLRB has jurisdiction. Table 12-1 summarizes the outcomes of union elections during fiscal years 1960 to 1971 and during the Phase II period.

The NLRB conducts two types of representation elections. Single-

2. 49 Stat. 453. The election data appear monthly in the "N.L.R.B. Election Report" series. Summaries for fiscal years appear in the NLRB annual report.

Table 12-1. *Percent of Elections Conducted by the National Labor Relations Board that Were Won by All Unions and by Teamsters, 1960–72*

| Fiscal year or period | Percent of union or Teamster wins | | | |
| | Single-union elections | | Single and multi-union elections | |
	All	Involving Teamsters	All	Involving Teamsters
1960	53.7	n.a.	58.6	n.a.
1961	51.3	n.a.	56.1	n.a.
1962	53.6	n.a.	58.5	n.a.
1963	54.9	n.a.	59.0	n.a.
1964	53.7	51.6	57.1	56.8
1965	57.2	54.8	60.2	59.6
1966	57.7	56.8	60.8	60.8
1967	56.2	57.6	59.0	61.4
1968	54.1	55.1	57.2	58.6
1969	51.4	51.2	54.6	55.3
1970	52.4	52.2	55.2	56.1
1971	50.5	49.2	53.2	52.9
Phase II[a]	52.3	52.4	54.5	55.1

Sources: *Annual Report of the National Labor Relations Board*, issues for 1960–71, and data from NLRB, "N.L.R.B. Election Report" (processed), relevant six-month summaries.
a. December 1971–December 1972.
n.a. Not available.

union elections involve cases in which a unit without official union representation considers the option of selecting a bargaining agent. Only one union is in contention in these elections. In multi-union elections, the workers have a choice of more than one union. The latter cases may involve instances where a particular union was previously selected and the real choice is whether or not to shift to another bargaining agent. In all elections, workers are given the choice of having no union, but single-union elections clearly provide a better measure of the propensity to unionize than do multi-union elections. Thus table 12-1 separates the single-union cases from the others, as well as elections involving the Teamsters. This distinction was made because it is conceivable that the Teamsters might have appeared to have an insider's advantage at the Pay Board; the president of that union did not walk out with the other four labor representatives after the decision in the West Coast longshoremen's case.

The table reveals no dramatic change in the rates of total union election victories or wins by the Teamsters between Phase II and earlier years.

This is true whether single-union elections or all elections are considered. It is difficult to disaggregate the NLRB data, since no breakdowns by industry are readily available. The number of elections held during Phase II was relatively high by previous standards, and the average unit size was relatively small. But these factors are not important explanatory variables.[3] It seems most reasonable to assume that the propensity to unionize, at least in the private sector, was not significantly affected by Phase II controls.

The public sector is not included in NLRB data because that agency does not have jurisdiction over governmental units. No comparable comprehensive data series exists for the public sector, so an alternative, more impressionistic source was used. Research directors or their assistants in public-sector unions and employee associations were interviewed by telephone and asked whether they thought Phase II wage controls affected their ability to organize, if they had any membership data that could illustrate their opinion, and if their success rate in representation elections was affected.[4] Many of the unions called did not have or did not provide membership data, but even where they were available, the general observation was that factors other than Phase II explained the movements. That is, most of the representatives did not feel that controls affected the propensity to unionize, although they complained about other aspects of controls. One of the major teacher groups suggested that the controls may have helped in recruiting members by convincing them of the need for effective lobbying in Washington. Two postal unions complained of increased difficulty in recruiting members. When pressed, they attributed

3. A regression of the single-union win rate (1960–71) revealed essentially zero correlation between it and average unit size or number of elections held.

4. The names of the interviewees were taken from U.S. Bureau of Labor Statistics, *Directory of National Unions and Employee Associations, 1971,* Bulletin 1750 (GPO, 1972), and included the National Education Association; International Association of Fire Fighters; Laborers' International Union of North America; National Association of American Letter Carriers; Fraternal Order of Police; National Alliance of Postal and Federal Employees; National Association of Postal Supervisors; American Postal Workers Union; National League of Postmasters; National Rural Letter Carriers' Association; Service Employees' International Union; American Federation of State, County and Municipal Employees; American Federation of Teachers; and the Teamsters. Also included were state employee associations in California, Colorado, Connecticut, Illinois, Indiana, Massachusetts, Michigan, Nevada, New Hampshire, New York, Ohio, Oregon, Utah, Vermont, Washington, West Virginia, and Wyoming. All except the Teamsters ventured some opinion when asked to indicate whether they believed that Phase II controls had no effect on unionization, a negative effect, or a positive effect.

this to hiring limitations in the Post Office rather than to wage controls themselves. A small state employees' association in the West complained that an increase in dues caused a drop in membership during Phase II because wages could not rise sufficiently to pay for it. A large eastern state employees' association stated that workers felt they would get no more than 5.5 percent during Phase II whether or not they organized. This prevented membership from increasing.

Although it is difficult to distill these comments, it is reasonable to conclude that complaints about Phase II were not sufficiently widespread to indicate a negative effect on organization in the public sector. The overall impression obtained from the evidence in the public and private sectors is that controls had a neutral effect on the propensity to unionize.

This conclusion is not surprising. It is true that the union sector often got higher increases during Phase II and that certain aspects of Pay Board regulations favored the union sector. But these regulations dealt primarily with existing union situations (deferred increases, short control years) and provided no advantage to newly formed union units. Pay Board intent, at least in the all-public phase, was to maintain neutrality. For example, late in Phase II the Pay Board explicitly adopted a regulation to ensure that a modification of a control year caused by unionization would not provide any advantage.[5] Moreover, Phase II lasted a relatively short period of time compared with earlier wartime programs. It is reasonable to assume that even if the program did have features that would encourage or discourage unionization, time would be needed before these features could influence observed behavior. The fourteen months of Phase II may not have been a sufficient period.

Strike Activity

In some European countries attempts to impose incomes policies have led to increased strike activity aimed at the controls themselves (and the government) rather than at a particular employer. Presumably whenever a government chooses to exercise wage controls, it risks becoming a target of worker resistance or so distorts the bargaining process that the incidence of strikes increases. During World War II the number of strikes per year was higher than in the years immediately preceding the war, although the average duration fell substantially.[6] The rash of major strikes

5. Pay Board press release PB-146, January 5, 1973.
6. BLS, *Handbook of Labor Statistics, 1975*, p. 390.

Table 12-2. *Strike History, All Industries, 1960–72*

Year	Number of stoppages	Number of workers involved (thousands)	Number of workers involved per stoppage	Man-days idle as percent of estimated total working time
1960	3,333	1,320	396	0.14
1961	3,367	1,450	431	0.11
1962	3,614	1,230	340	0.13
1963	3,362	941	280	0.11
1964	3,655	1,640	449	0.15
1965	3,963	1,550	391	0.15
1966	4,405	1,960	445	0.15
1967	4,595	2,870	625	0.25
1968	5,045	2,649	525	0.28
1969	5,700	2,481	435	0.24
1970	5,716	3,305	578	0.37
1971	5,138	3,280	638	0.26
1972	5,010	1,714	342	0.15

Source: Bureau of Labor Statistics. *Handbook of Labor Statistics, 1975—Reference Edition* (Government Printing Office, 1975), p. 391.

after the National War Labor Board had been terminated suggests that at least some strike activity was deferred to the postcontrol period. Strike activity in the Korean war period appeared to continue postwar trends, although in the period after Korea the number of strikes and workers involved appeared to decline.

Table 12-2 shows a relatively quiet scene with respect to work stoppages in the early 1960s. From 1960 through 1965 the number of stoppages per year recorded by the Bureau of Labor Statistics remained in the 3,000 to 4,000 range. The number of workers involved never reached 1.7 million, and man-days lost, as a percentage of working time, fluctuated around 0.15 percent or less. The economic expansion of the 1960s changed this picture. All measures of strike activity began to climb. The number of strikes, workers involved, and man-days lost as a percentage of working time peaked in 1970. In 1971 the number of stoppages declined, while the number of workers involved leveled off. During 1972, the first full year of controls and a year entirely within Phase II, the number of strikes remained roughly at the 1971 level. At the same time, the number of workers involved and man-days lost as a percentage of working time fell substantially.

During 1972 the mix of strikes between construction and nonconstruction appeared to change—at least for major strikes (those involving 10,000 or more workers).[7] The BLS counted twenty-nine such strikes in 1971, of which eight were in construction. In 1972 there were twenty major strikes, of which ten were in construction. Fifty-eight percent of the workers involved in major strikes in 1972 were in the construction industry, compared with 14 percent in 1971. There were 2.8 million workers under contracts expiring or subject to reopening in 1972 (in agreements involving 1,000 or more workers), compared with 4.8 million in 1971. In construction 770,000 workers were under expiring contracts or reopeners involving 1,000 or more workers in 1972, compared with 532,000 in 1971.[8] These changes in expiration patterns would suggest that the overall number of workers involved in strikes would decline but that a countertrend would occur in construction. These relationships do not explain all of the year-to-year change. The number of workers involved in major expirations and reopeners dropped 41 percent between 1971 and 1972, while the number of workers in major strikes dropped 78 percent. Workers in major construction expirations and reopeners rose 46 percent, while the number of construction workers involved in major strikes dropped 10 percent.[9]

In order to assess more closely the significance of the drop in workers involved in strikes, a simple equation was constructed to explain the year-to-year variations. The explanatory variables were business cycle factors (the ratio of real GNP to trend, and the percentage change in real GNP), the estimated change in workers in major contract expirations, and a dummy variable for 1972. Coefficients and summary statistics of the equation appear in appendix F. The equation indicates that the drop in workers involved in stoppages was significantly greater than would have been predicted based on expirations and economic conditions. A similar equation for changes in man-days lost did not indicate a significant drop. Man-days lost dropped from 48 million in 1971 to 27 million in 1972. As

7. Listings of such strikes appear in annual BLS press releases in the "Work Stoppages" series.

8. Michael E. Sparrough and Lena W. Bolton, "Calendar of Wage Increases and Negotiations for 1972," *Monthly Labor Review*, vol. 95 (January 1972), pp. 3–14; and Leon Bornstein and Lena W. Bolton, "Calendar of Wage Increases and Negotiations for 1971," ibid., vol. 94 (January 1971), pp. 31–44.

9. Note that major strikes are defined as those involving 10,000 or more workers while major expirations are those involving 1,000 or more workers. The two definitions are therefore not synonymous.

might be expected from the slight decline in the number of strikes between 1971 and 1972, the decrease did not appear to be important.

Various explanations may account for the greater-than-expected drop in workers involved in strikes. The number of strikes in a given year can be heavily affected by strikes over work rules, grievances, jurisdictional disputes, and other nonwage issues. During Phase II the Pay Board staff conducted two surveys to gather the impressions of Federal Mediation and Conciliation Service personnel in the field.[10] It was reported that a shift to nonwage issues was taking place, and this was interpreted as a sign that unions were accepting the Pay Board rules and were turning their attention to issues other than wage controls. While the nonwage demands may have been the cause of strikes in some cases, the net result may have been fewer large stoppages.

In other instances a converse factor may have led to the same result. During the controls period a few employers appeared to have decided to rely on Pay Board cutbacks as a substitute for bargaining. This strategy entailed accepting initial union demands with little resistance in the expectation that Pay Board or Internal Revenue Service actions would reduce the actual amount to be paid to a "reasonable" level. Retail food stores seemed to be prone to this tendency. To the extent that employers offered less resistance to union demands, strikes over wage issues would decline. There is no evidence, however, that this "erosion" of bargaining was a major development during Phase II.

Table 12-3 shows the major disputes—those involving 10,000 or more workers—that were in progress during Phase II. The bituminous coal dispute shown on the table began before Phase II, and its settlement was the Pay Board's first case. The dispute involved wages and benefits and also reflected the political difficulties of the incumbent leadership of the United Mine Workers. Both longshore disputes were also pre–Phase II situations that dragged into Phase II. Because of the potential of these strikes for tying up ocean and coastal shipping, they became major board cases. Unlike the coal case, both were cut back.

A brief strike of the Amalgamated Meat Cutters and Butcher Workmen of North America (MCBW) was one of the few instances of a stoppage directed specifically against controls. Members of the MCBW stopped work to hear their union president denounce the Pay Board's policy on retroactivity (later reversed by Congress) at the AFL-CIO

10. Described in Pay Board staff papers EAD-47, July 6, 1972, and EAD-70, August 30, 1972.

Table 12-3. *Work Stoppages in the Nonconstruction Sector Involving 10,000 or More Workers, November 1971–December 1972*

Industry or group and union involved	Date of stoppage	Number of workers involved
Bituminous coal (UMW)	October 1–November 22, 1971	80,000
East Coast and		
Gulf Coast longshore (ILA)	October 1–November 27, 1971[a]	45,000
Meat companies and stockyards (MCBW)	November 22, 1971	55,000
Pacific Maritime Association (ILWU)	July 1, 1971–February 18, 1972[b]	16,500
New York Telephone Company (CWA)	July 14, 1971–February 16, 1972	38,000
Southern Pacific Railroad (UTU)	March 10, 1972	23,500
General Electric Company,		
Louisville, Ky. (IUE)	April 19–21, 1972	13,800
Board of Education,		
Philadelphia, Pa. (AFT)	September 5–27, 1972	22,000
General Motors,		
Georgia, Missouri, Ohio (UAW)	October 13–16, 1972	14,500
General Motors,		
Kansas, Missouri, Texas (UAW)	October 20–22, 1972	12,700
General Motors, Frigidaire Division,		
Dayton, Ohio (IUE)	October 26–27, 1972	12,400
Bakery (BCW)	October 11–December 10, 1972	14,000

Source: U.S. Bureau of Labor Statistics.
a. Terminated by an eighty-day injunction.
b. Interrupted by a Taft-Hartley injunction.

convention. New York Telephone was another case of a pre–Phase II strike that continued into Phase II. In that case, workers in New York had refused to accept the pattern set nationwide for other telephone workers in July 1971. The eventual settlement of 16.8 percent was accepted by the Pay Board on the basis of comparability to the national pattern.

In the Southern Pacific Railroad case the issue was not wages but a jurisdictional clash between railroad switchmen and brakemen. The strike was brought to a quick halt by a court order. General Electric's strike in Louisville also was not a wage dispute. A short walkout resulted when a grievance arose over an employee who allegedly had been laid off improperly. The Philadelphia teachers' case involved both wages and working conditions and was one of a series of teacher walkouts during 1972. A strike resulted after the financially pressed Board of Education offered only a modest wage increase and demanded an increase in the hours of work for the teachers.

The three General Motors strikes were nonwage disputes that centered

Table 12-4. *Percent Distribution of Issues in Work Stoppages in Disputes over New and Renegotiated Agreements, All Industries, 1961–72*

		Issues		
Year	Wages[a]	Job security and work rules[b]	Union organization and job security	Miscellaneous[c]
1961	68.5	6.5	22.1	2.9
1962	70.4	6.0	21.0	2.5
1963	68.2	7.0	21.4	3.3
1964	67.4	7.7	21.0	4.0
1965	68.7	6.7	20.3	4.2
1966	73.1	5.0	19.2	2.6
1967	73.8	5.7	18.2	2.2
1968	78.1	4.4	13.9	3.5
1969	79.4	2.9	14.9	2.9
1970	78.7	3.0	14.7	3.6
1971	79.5	3.8	13.3	3.5
1972	72.4	7.8	16.3	3.5

Source: U.S. Bureau of Labor Statistics, *Analysis of Work Stoppages*, various issues. Figures are rounded.
a. Includes general wage changes, supplementary benefits, and wage adjustments.
b. Includes job security, plant administration, and other working conditions.
c. Includes hours of work, interunion or intraunion matters, other contractual matters, and issues not reported for certain stoppages.

on production standards and alleged attempts by management to force a speedup.[11] Finally, the bakery cases involved a dispute, following a contract reopening, that concerned the workweek. The union demanded a Monday-to-Friday week instead of the split-week schedule under which the workers had been operating.

Although there is little evidence that the controls program contributed to labor unrest, there is support for the contention that controls would cause a shift from wage to nonwage issues in bargaining. The Bureau of Labor Statistics classifies disputes by the major issue involved. Disputes arising during the life of existing contracts are usually based on worker grievances over administrative procedures, that is, nonwage issues. The relatively light bargaining calendar in 1972 boosted the proportion of such disputes and could bias the figures on wage versus nonwage issues. Fortunately BLS figures can be used to isolate disputes arising from con-

11. The Frigidaire unit had agreed to forgo a deferred increase early in Phase II in return for employment guarantees and had received a commendation from the chairman of the Pay Board. The economic difficulties of the plant may have contributed to the unrest over production standards.

tract negotiations (either contract terminations or reopeners). Table 12-4 provides a breakdown of disputes arising out of negotiations, by major causes.

It is clear that 1972 did mark a break from the past in terms of the major causes of disputes. Disputes involving union security, work rules, and similar matters rose in importance. Typically, such issues would not have been considered by the Pay Board. Wage issues—defined broadly to include fringe benefits—declined as a proportion of major causes for disputes.[12] To some extent, then, there appears to have been some displacement of union-management conflict to noneconomic issues, although this process was not of sufficient magnitude to create a significant decline in work stoppages.

Contract Duration and Related Impacts

One of the salutary developments in the American industrial relations system is the multiyear contract. Such contracts permit an extended period of labor peace, usually in exchange for a schedule of deferred or escalator wage adjustments in the later years of the agreement. According to BLS records on major nonconstruction agreements (covering 1,000 or more workers), only 3.7 percent of the contracts on file as of July 1, 1972, were of less than two years' duration.[13] These agreements often involved smaller bargaining units covering an average of 2,263 workers each, compared with 5,072 per agreement in the entire file. In the construction industry 7.7 percent of the major agreements were of less than two years' duration. In the nonconstruction sector relatively few of the agreements in the file would have been negotiated during controls. In construction, however, a larger proportion would have been negotiated during controls, since controls in that sector began in March 1971, several months before the freeze.

12. Supporting data are available from the Federal Mediation and Conciliation Service (FMCS) concerning the type of issues that arose in the course of its interventions. Unlike disputes recorded by the BLS, however, those recorded by the FMCS can be listed as having more than one issue. Wage issues occurring in FMCS cases averaged 48.1 percent of the total issues during the ten years ending with fiscal 1971. During fiscal 1972 and fiscal 1973 the proportion fell still further to 44.9 percent. See Daniel J. B. Mitchell and Ross E. Azevedo, *Wage-Price Controls and Labor Market Distortions* (University of California at Los Angeles, Institute of Industrial Relations, 1976), p. 126.

13. U.S. Bureau of Labor Statistics, *Characteristics of Agreements Covering 1,000 Workers or More, July 1, 1972,* Bulletin 1784 (GPO, 1973), p. 5.

Table 12-5. *Percent Distribution of New Contracts Negotiated in 1970, 1971, and 1972, by Duration of Contract*[a]

		Duration of contract		
Year	One year	Two years	Three years	Four years or more
		All industries		
1970	8	39	52	1
1971	24	32	44	0
1972	n.a.	n.a.	n.a.	n.a.
		Nonconstruction		
1970	8	38	53	1
1971	6	35	58	1
1972	15	34	51	0
		Construction		
1970	7	43	48	2
1971	63	24	13	0
1972	84	12	4	0

Source: Bureau of National Affairs, Inc., *Collective Bargaining Negotiations and Contracts*, various years, "Wages and Fringes" sections.
a. Contracts surveyed numbered 2,819 in 1970, 3,042 in 1971, and 2,790 in 1972.
n.a. Not available.

The Bureau of National Affairs, Inc., tabulates various data on contracts negotiated during each calendar year.[14] These contracts cover agreements of all sizes that come to the attention of the BNA. Table 12-5 presents a summary of these contracts, classified by contract duration. For construction, the pattern is most striking. In 1970, before controls, 7 percent of the contracts were of one year's duration. Since controls were instituted in late March 1971, some of the contracts tabulated for 1971 were negotiated before the Construction Industry Stabilization Committee was created. But the seasonal pattern of construction bargaining suggests that most contracts came under controls in 1971. In that year 63 percent of all contracts were of one year's duration. By 1972 the proportion had risen to 84 percent. For nonconstruction, the pattern is not as sharp. Eight percent of the contracts surveyed were of one year's duration in 1970, 6 percent in 1971, and 15 percent in 1972.

14. Summary tabulations appear in Bureau of National Affairs, Inc., *Collective Bargaining Negotiations and Contracts* (BNA, 1973). The data for 1972 appear on pages 18:935–18:938.

The timing of the move to one-year contracts makes the effect unmistakably the result of controls. It appears that unions found short-term contracts to be a prudent response to controls, since the program was expected to be a short-term phenomenon. The favored tactic, therefore, was to write contracts that would expire as soon as possible after controls ended. At that point it might be possible to "recover" wage increases lost, either because of actual cutbacks, or because of restraint exercised to avoid cuts. Naturally employers would resist a move to shorter contracts, ceteris paribus, because of the reduction of the duration of labor peace. In the construction industry, where the employer is typically a group of small contractors, it is not surprising that the resistance was weaker.

There was an alternative response. Pay Board policy generally focused only on the first year of new contracts. (In a few cases where negotiations had dragged on well into the first year, the board ruled on the second year as well.) A union might have chosen to negotiate as if no controls were in effect. Should a cutback occur, wage payments would be made in the amount allowed by the Pay Board. But if the contract itself were not changed, the old contractual rates would spring back into effect on a prospective basis if controls ended.[15] In fact, this spring effect did become a problem in some cases when Phase III began. It was estimated that a maximum of about $200 million was involved, based on a study of Pay Board records.[16] Employers could be expected to offer resistance to this strategy, however, since they would prefer not to make large increases when controls ended, and they could not be sure that a cutback in the first year of the contract would necessarily occur. There was always a chance that the Pay Board would grant an exception permitting the contract to be implemented without change.

A related strategy would be to maintain traditional contract length but "back load" contracts. Normally, union contracts are "front-loaded." This means that there is more of an increase in the first year of the contract than in later years. For example, a contract might provide increases of 7 percent in the first year and 6 percent in each of the two following years. Since Pay Board scrutiny was concentrated on the first year, some negotiators might have thought it wise to put more money in later years than in the early period. But no instances of back-loading

15. In lieu of government policy to the contrary, the employer would be obligated to pay the wage rates to which he had agreed.

16. Internal Cost of Living Council memorandum to Marvin Kosters and Jeffrey Berlin from Dan Mitchell, February 7, 1973.

Table 12-6. *Mean Annual Wage Rate Increases in Major Collective Bargaining Agreements in Manufacturing, 1971 and 1972*[a]

	Monetary increase			Percent increase		
	Cents per hour		Ratio, first year to life of contract			Ratio, first year to life of contract
Year	First year	Life of contract		First year	Life of contract	
Agreements without escalators						
1971	27.1	25.6	1.06	8.2	7.4	1.11
1972	21.1	20.3	1.04	6.2	5.8	1.07
Agreements with escalators[b]						
1971	48.9	31.0	1.58	12.5	7.3	1.71
1972	31.0	23.1	1.34	7.6	5.4	1.41

Source: U.S. Bureau of Labor Statistics.
a. Major agreements are those involving 1,000 or more workers.
b. Life-of-contract rates exclude estimates for escalator adjustments.

came to the attention of the Pay Board staff, although some may have occurred.

Table 12-6 compares first-year and life-of-contract annual rates of wage increase in major agreements during 1971 and 1972. It focuses on the manufacturing sector to avoid the distortion that would result from incorporating construction, where second and third contract years were becoming rare.[17] Agreements are broken down into those with escalator clauses—which gear wage increases to price increases—and those without them to avoid problems of changes in the mix between the two types of contracts. Contracts without escalators showed little difference between 1971 and 1972 in the degree of front-loading. The ratio of first-year wage adjustments to life-of-contract changes reveals little difference between the two years. (Although some 1971 contracts were approved in the early days of Phase II, their structure can be assumed to be unaffected by controls.) In fact, front-loading as measured by these data probably increased, since the first-year changes were affected to a greater degree by Pay Board actions than were the life-of-contract changes. The agreements with escalator clauses show a decrease in the degree of front-loading, but the sample of escalator agreements in 1972 is quite small. In addition, the cutbacks in aerospace contributed significantly to the reduction in the front-loading of contracts with escalators, as recorded by the BLS.

17. It was not possible to separate construction from other nonmanufacturing industries.

For situations in which short-term contracts were not negotiated—and since back-loading was not manifested—a reopener clause of some type could have been used. Under this arrangement, designated provisions of a labor agreement—usually wages—can be reviewed or renegotiated after some fixed time period. In January 1972 the BLS reported that it knew of 21 major situations involving 60,000 workers that had reopeners scheduled for 1973. In January 1973 it reported 62 situations involving 170,000 workers that were scheduled for reopeners in 1973, a net addition of 41 situations and 110,000 workers.[18] Some of these additions may have been due to late information reaching the BLS about pre-1972 contracts, but it does appear that several of the contracts with reopener clauses were negotiated during 1972.

Reopeners reported by the BLS had fixed dates for commencing negotiations. In some situations, however, clauses were negotiated that called for contract reopening when controls ended. For example, when the West Coast longshore contract was renegotiated in response to the Pay Board cutback, a reopener of this nature was included in the new agreement. The parties were advised by the Pay Board staff that the provision was legal, since no board regulations forbade it. But like other similar clauses, the longshore clause was rendered void by a Phase III policy forbidding the operation of any contractual arrangement (wage or price) geared to the end of controls.[19] It is not known how many contingent reopener clauses in union contracts were affected. The BNA had identified fifty-nine such agreements negotiated in the third quarter of 1972.[20]

It is clear that any controls program creates new uncertainties and that the parties to collective bargaining contracts will adapt their behavior accordingly. During Phase II a major element of uncertainty was the duration of the program itself, which led to adjustments in the length of labor agreements. These adaptations may be viewed as an undesirable side effect of controls. In the American context, however, the industrial relations system has demonstrated strong resilience, and it would be difficult to argue that this pattern of adjustment during Phase II created permanent damage.

18. Sparrough and Bolton, "Calendar of Wage Increases and Negotiations for 1972," p. 5; and David Larson and Lena W. Bolton, "Calendar of Wage Increases and Negotiations for 1973," *Monthly Labor Review*, vol. 96 (January 1973), p. 5.

19. In 1974 when controls ended, a one-day strike "restored" the 1972 cutback.

20. Written submission of George H. Boldt, chairman of the Pay Board, appearing in *Price and Wage Control: An Evaluation of Current Policies*, Hearings before the Joint Economic Committee, 92 Cong. 2 sess. (GPO, 1973), pt. 1, p. 30, note 7.

Escalator Clauses

Escalator clauses are devices in union contracts by which wages are adjusted automatically as prices rise. (Arrangements of this type are sometimes found in the nonunion sector, but no contractual obligation is involved.) Usually the national consumer price index (CPI) is used as a basis for measuring price changes. Some local contracts use the CPI for their city if it is available on a regular basis. By permitting wages to be protected from an erosion of purchasing power due to inflation, escalator clauses help make possible long-term contracts.

The attractiveness of escalator clauses seems to depend on the inflation outlook. When reasonable price stability can be expected, their popularity declines. For example, in 1962 when the economy was characterized by relative price stability, escalators were discontinued in union contracts in steel, aluminum, and cans. In 1971, before the freeze, escalators were re-instituted in these industries and introduced for the first time in communications. During Phase II, cost-of-living reviews took place in these industries, as well as in meat-packing, electrical machinery, motor vehicles, aerospace, and others. Of 10.6 million union workers under major collective bargaining agreements (involving 1,000 or more workers), 4.3 million were known to be covered by escalators in 1972. The BLS estimated that an additional 425,000 workers in smaller union and nonunion situations in manufacturing were covered by such agreements. Escalator adjustments also affected a large number of postal employees and a few others in the public sector.[21]

Escalators generally provide less-than-proportionate wage increases relative to price increases. For example, the Auto Workers' contract with General Motors negotiated in late 1970 provided an increase of 1 cent an hour for each 0.4 point rise in the CPI.[22] At the time the contract was negotiated a 0.4 point rise represented slightly more than 0.3 percent price increase. The formula would have provided a proportionate increase at a wage of about $3 an hour. However, the BLS reported that average hourly earnings in motor vehicles were closer to $5 after the new contracts were put into effect in 1971. Moreover, this figure does not include expenditures for benefits such as pensions. As time passed, the 0.4 point rise in the CPI came to mean a slightly smaller percentage increase than it implied at the beginning of the contract.

21. Sparrough and Bolton, "Calendar of Wage Increases and Negotiations for 1972," pp. 3, 7, and 8, including note 5.
22. See *Monthly Labor Review,* vol. 93 (December 1970), p. 51.

The fact that escalators usually provide increases in money wages that are less than proportionate to changes in the price level reflects their origin in a bargaining process. An employer naturally would prefer a formula that provides less money. In addition, escalators create uncertainty about the level of future wage costs. For this reason escalators are rare in construction where contractors must make bids based on estimated labor costs. Devices such as less-than-proportionate increases and "caps" (fixed limits on the amounts that can be paid under the terms of an escalation, regardless of increase in the CPI) help make escalators mutually acceptable. From the union's viewpoint, there is a need to design the escalator so that it provides some benefit, even if prices do not rise rapidly. Hence some escalators include guaranteed increases, which are nothing more than ordinary deferred adjustments, or permit no decreases in wages should prices fall.

Escalators were affected by Pay Board procedures in three ways. Generally they became effective in the second or third years of a contract. This meant that new escalators generally would not have been affected by board determinations, which usually concentrated on the first year. In addition, most escalators that operated in Phase II were included in contracts negotiated before controls were instituted and therefore were subject to especially liberal rules. Lastly, a special time-weighting computation rule was allowed for escalators that might have been expected to stimulate their creation.[23]

The time-weighting rule theoretically provided a stimulus to the negotiation of escalators. In a given year, escalators would count less than other increases when computed by the Pay Board, provided they were in effect only part of the year. In addition, to the extent that escalator adjustments permitted the Pay Board to pass larger increases, the base for

23. Normally the Pay Board computed wage increases by the "sum-of-the-percentages" method. This meant that if a contract with a base of $5 an hour specified a 25 cent increase on the first day of the control year and 5 cents six months later, the sum of the two percentages, 5 percent (0.25/5.00) and 1 percent (0.05/5.00), or 6 percent, would be considered the total increase that had to be judged against the standard. For escalators, however, the Pay Board permitted time-weighting the increment. In the example just cited, if the 5 cents had been due to the operation of an escalator, the percentage would have been computed as 5 percent plus 0.5 percent (1 percent × 6 months/12 months), or 5.5 percent. Time-weighting, therefore, reflects the amount of money that will be paid during the year, an amount that is obviously reduced as the proportion of the year during which payment is made is reduced. The sum-of-the-percentages method is basically what the BLS calls "equal timing," while time-weighting is referred to as "actual timing." See Lily Mary David and Victor J. Sheifer, "Estimating the Cost of Collective Bargaining Settlements," *Monthly Labor Review*, vol. 92 (May 1969), pp. 16–26.

computing subsequent years would be higher, and 5.5 percent of the base would go further in those years. In short, to take full advantage of time-weighting, a union should have negotiated a contract with large escalator adjustments scheduled toward the end of a control year.

One union did try to take advantage of time-weighting by negotiating a *more* than proportionate escalator for several small Category III units. The independent Chicago Truck Drivers Union negotiated a clause that appeared to provide roughly a 3 percent wage increase for every 1 percent increase in the CPI. No secret was made of this agreement, and it obviously was floated as a trial balloon. In fact, the union sent a letter to the Pay Board concerning the clause. The special escalator was described as noninflationary, since if prices did not rise, wages would not rise either. (There were no scheduled increases under the contracts, other than the escalator adjustments.)

Toward the end of Phase II the union announced it was considering applying the same technique to its large contract for truck drivers in the Chicago area. This agreement had upset the national Teamsters contract in 1970 and thus was considered a key negotiation for 1973.[24] On January 11, 1973—the last day of Phase II—the Pay Board succeeded in placing an Internal Revenue Service ruling in the *Federal Register* declaring more than proportionate escalators ineligible for time-weighting. Early in Phase III, IRS personnel visited the Chicago Truck Drivers Union and explained the new regulations. Nothing further was heard about the escalator, and it presumably was shelved by the union.

Aside from the Chicago Truck Drivers case, there is no evidence available that escalators were stimulated by Pay Board policies. The tabulation below shows the number of workers (in millions) under major contracts with escalator clauses for January of each year from 1960 to 1973:[25]

1960	4.0	1967	2.2
1961	2.5–2.8	1968	2.5
1962	2.5	1969	2.7
1963	1.9	1970	2.8
1964	2.0	1971	3.0
1965	2.0	1972	4.3
1966	2.0	1973	4.1

24. "Militancy is the Bargaining Tactic for 1973," *Business Week,* January 6, 1973, p. 65.

25. David Larson and Lena W. Bolton, "Calendar of Wage Increases and Negotiations for 1973," *Monthly Labor Review,* vol. 96 (January 1973), p. 8.

The number fell slightly between January 1972 and January 1973. Among the major nonconstruction agreements reached in 1972, 19.5 percent had escalator clauses, down from 39.3 percent in 1971. A BNA survey of new agreements for nonconstruction contracts shows a similar drop, from 11 percent in 1971 of all agreements covered in the survey to 6 percent in 1972. The smaller proportions in the BNA survey, compared with that of the BLS, are probably due to the inclusion of many smaller contracts by the BNA.

In an effort to obtain a more detailed impression of trends in escalator clauses, an analysis was made of the descriptions of seventy-one new contracts appearing in *Current Wage Developments* that appeared to be Phase II agreements and to have escalators.[26] Another four agreements were reported to have discontinued a previous escalator clause. Forty-eight of the seventy-one agreements with escalators were continuations of previous escalators. Nine of them specifically mentioned an improvement in the formula or the raising or removing of a cap. There probably were more such improvements, but one could not easily tell because of the terseness of the references. Eighteen of the seventy-one agreements appeared to represent the introduction of new escalator arrangements.

The earlier analysis of Pay Board rules suggests that unions ought to have moved from their previous practice of putting escalators in the second and third years to putting them toward the end of the first year. Although the descriptions in *Current Wage Developments* are often too brief to permit determining exactly when an escalator was activated, it is significant that only three of the seventy-one agreements were of one year's duration. All of these involved the Amalgamated Transit Union and were continuations of previous escalators.[27] One contract was negotiated so early in Phase II that it is hard to imagine that the Phase II rules could have affected union strategy.

Despite the incentive provided for creating escalators, labor and management negotiations evidenced no perceptible reaction. At a Pay Board

26. Information was drawn from the January 1972–April 1973 editions. Settlements that appeared to predate or postdate Phase II were omitted. It should be noted that the descriptions in *Current Wage Developments* are often quite brief, and a degree of judgment was required to interpret some of the statements.

27. The contracts were with the Chicago Transit Authority (contract effective December 8, 1971), Twin City Lines of Minneapolis (negotiated January 11, 1972), and the Massachusetts Bay Transportation Authority of Boston (negotiated February 2, 1972). References appear in *Current Wage Developments* for February, March, and April 1972.

meeting a Teamsters spokesman suggested that it was difficult to explain time-weighting to the rank and file.[28] This difficulty and the subsidence of inflationary expectations are probably the main factors contributing to this paradoxical behavior. In addition, unions were unlikely to adjust their bargaining goals to the complex rules of the controls program as long as they thought it was a transient impediment.

For those workers with escalators under pre–Phase II contracts, the Pay Board policy limited the likelihood of a challenge. Sixteen percent of the 4.3 million workers under contracts with escalators had no other deferred adjustments.[29] Hence their adjustments could not have been high enough to trigger a challenge even without time-weighting. The average deferred wage adjustment for major contracts with escalators in 1972 was 4.5 percent, excluding fringes. Since escalators generally provide for wage adjustments that are less than proportionate to increases in prices, and since the Pay Board included fringe benefits in its calculation, a majority of the remaining 84 percent would also have escaped a challenge, even if their increases had been computed without time-weighting. Pay Board records suggest that this would have been true of the auto industry and electrical equipment industry contracts.[30] The Teamsters contract, which included a cost-of-living review, was subject to a cutback (although the Pay Board's effort was frustrated by the termination of Phase II). It is probable that the Pay Board would have challenged the Teamsters contract based on the wage increment scheduled during 1972 even without the escalator adjustment.[31]

28. A study for the Joint Economic Committee indicated that it was unlikely that a continuation of Pay Board policy would foster the widespread use of escalators unless it became clear that the policy would continue indefinitely. See Lily Mary David, "Cost-of-Living Escalation in Collective Bargaining," *Price and Wage Control,* Hearings, pt. 2, p. 337.

29. According to Sparrough and Bolton ("Calendar of Wage Increases and Negotiations for 1972," pp. 3 and 7), 3.6 million workers with deferred increases also had escalators, out of a total of 4.3 million workers under escalators in major contracts.

30. The statement is based on deferred increases listed as scheduled for 1972 in ibid., and on data on base wages contained in an internal Pay Board memo from Dan Mitchell to Al Eckstein, August 18, 1972.

31. The escalator was capped at 8 cents, and it came early in the control year so that time-weighting was not advantageous. In addition, the Pay Board noted early in Phase II that its control-year rules would have an impact on the Teamsters contract and that it might have exercised its option to challenge, even if the increase had computed out to something slightly less than 7 percent. As it turned out, however, the increment was costed as 8.4 percent.

The Guideline: A Floor or a Ceiling?

When Phase II commenced, wage controls covered all workers in the private sector and the state and local government sector, as well as the Post Office, Tennessee Valley Authority, and similar federal enterprises. It became immediately evident that general rules had to be issued guiding the many units covered by the program. The heart of the Pay Board's regulations was the 5.5 percent general pay standard. As has been noted in earlier chapters, the 5.5 percent guideline was really a 6.2 percent guideline when qualified fringe benefits were added. In addition, a variety of rules determined the period during which the 5.5 percent was to be calculated, its method of computation, and conditions under which it could be exceeded.

During Phase II there were complaints about the guideline approach. Some experts asserted that a publicized standard would become a floor for union wage adjustments. On the other hand, in the nonunion sector, employers would apply the standard as a ceiling even if their units might have been eligible for some sort of exception. If these reactions did take place, then the impact of the controls program would be attenuated, and indeed controls might actually cause a rise in union wage increases and distort the interindustry wage structure. A key question is what evidence on this issue can be gleaned from the Phase II experience.

Since the Pay Board's 5.5 percent guideline was subject to a variety of exceptions, and since qualified fringe benefits had an additional standard and exceptions, it is not possible to identify a specific number as "the" standard for statistical purposes. The BLS data on major nonconstruction union settlements in 1972 shown in table 12-7 are costed on a wage-on-wage basis and do not include fringe benefits of any kind in the base or the increment. Hence there is no way of telling whether fringe adjustments caused the overall standards to be exceeded.

Aside from costing differences, the data in table 12-7 suffer from another deficiency. They include only Pay Board approvals. To the extent that requests differed from approvals (that is, if there were cutbacks), the BLS data do not show the initial reaction of the parties to controls.[32]

32. To the extent that requests for low increases are the main area of interest, this is not a major problem since these requests generally were approved. Some requests for high increases, however, may have been reduced when approved by the Pay Board.

Table 12-7. *First-Year Changes in Wage Rates in Major Union Settlements, Nonconstruction Sector, by Percent of Workers Involved, 1972*[a]

Wage-rate adjustment (percent)	Percent of workers involved in major agreements				
	1972:1	1972:2	1972:3	1972:4	1972
None	1	1	1	0	2
Less than 5	5	10	18	8	11
5–7	19	43	39	59	41
7–9	37	25	22	18	25
9–11	34	8	7	10	14
11–13	2	1	1	1	1
13–15	0	6	2	0	2
15 and over	0	5	11	2	5
Not specified	1	0	0	1	0
All changes	100	100	100	100	100
Addendum:					
Number of workers (thousands)	406	550	511	501	1,968

Source: *Current Wage Developments,* vol. 25 (June 1973), pp. 57, 60. Figures are rounded.
a. Settlements involving 1,000 or more workers.

In an absolute sense the BLS data clearly show that 5.5 percent was
not an impregnable floor for collective bargaining. During 1972, 13 percent of the workers experiencing new adjustments received less than 5
percent on a wage-on-wage basis. Although the Pay Board and the BLS
costing methods are different, it is evident that some of the 41 percent of
the workers the BLS lists as falling in the range of 5 percent to just under
7 percent were also within Pay Board standards. A simple interpolation
of that range suggests that somewhere between one-fifth and one-fourth of
workers under major nonconstruction union settlements received less
than 5.5 percent on a wage-on-wage basis. The time pattern of approvals
does show some reduction in the less-than-5 percent range in the fourth
quarter of 1972 (after an increase in the third quarter). It is not possible
to know, however, whether this was due to an underlying trend as economic decisionmakers internalized the 5.5 percent figure or whether it
reflects accidents of timing of particular types of settlements. Phase II
was too short to make this judgment.

During Phase II in several cases workers agreed to forgo scheduled
pay raises under existing contracts. Employees at a Frigidaire plant in
Dayton, Ohio, made such a concession in exchange for the company's
assurance that it would continue to manufacture appliances in Dayton

Table 12-8. *First-Year Median Wage Adjustments in Major Union Settlements in Manufacturing, 1966–72*[a]

Year	Median adjustment (percent)	Ratio, lower quartile to median
1966	4.2	0.8
1967	6.4	0.7
1968	6.9	0.9
1969	7.0	0.9
1970	7.5	0.9
1971	10.0	0.7
1972	6.2	0.9

Source: Medians, *Current Wage Developments*, June 1973, p. 46; for the ratios, the quartiles were estimated by interpolation. Intervals in which the interpolations were made were 1 percent in width.
a. Settlements involving 1,000 or more workers.

and would recall some of the 3,400 workers it had laid off, and received congratulations from the chairman of the Pay Board.[33] Similarly, a group of 3,000 brewery workers in Newark, New Jersey, made unspecified "concessions" to reduce the plant's operating deficit.[34] Among new settlements, 2,400 rubber footwear workers in Connecticut agreed to a three-year moratorium on wage increases.[35] And a one-year contract with no improvement in wages or benefits was accepted by the pilots of Alaska Airlines.[36]

The BLS has provided historical data on workers under major manufacturing settlements for several years.[37] It is possible to compute a rough index of lower-level wage dispersion by computing the ratio of the lower quartile adjustment to the median adjustment. (The former must be estimated by interpolating the 1 percent intervals provided by the BLS.) Table 12-8 shows that the ratio that prevailed in 1972 is somewhat higher than that of 1971 or 1966–67 but about the same as that in 1968–70. There appears to be no evidence that the dispersion narrowed abnormally in 1972, although the hypothesis that 5.5 percent became a floor would predict such a development.

33. *Monthly Labor Review*, vol. 95 (January 1972), p. 83; and Pay Board press release PB-8 (December 1, 1971).
34. *Monthly Labor Review*, vol. 95 (March 1972), p. 67.
35. Ibid. (August 1972), p. 62. The agreement was an extension of a previous three-year moratorium.
36. Ibid., vol. 96 (January 1973), p. 73.
37. Data are also available for nonmanufacturing, but it is not possible to remove construction from that series.

Table 12-9. *Summary of Requests for Wage Adjustments during Phase II,
New Cases, Categories I and II, by Range of Adjustment*[a]

Percent

Range of requested wage adjustment (percent)	Nonunion requests		Union requests	
	Cases	Workers	Cases	Workers
0.0–3.0	16.1	18.4	4.4	2.9
3.1–5.0	29.0	23.2	11.2	14.3
5.1–6.2	35.5	33.9	33.0	27.2
Total, 0.1–6.2	80.6	75.6	48.9	44.3
Addenda:				
Number of cases	1,906	...	663	...
Number of workers (thousands)	...	10,115	...	2,848

Source: Pay Board computer records as of March 2, 1973.

a. Category I includes industries of 5,000 or more employees; Category II, of industries with 1,000–4,999 employees. New cases are those negotiated after Phase II was initiated on November 14, 1971.

Pay Board computer records for categories I and II provide an alternative source of data. From the records it is possible to look at requests rather than approvals and to compare the union and nonunion sectors. In addition, the records show all of Phase II rather than just 1972 and include the government sector. A summary tabulation of the records for new cases appears in table 12-9.

Request data from the Pay Board files include fringe benefit adjustments, so it is more appropriate to consider 6.2 percent as the standard. Unfortunately the computer data do not permit a determination of which cases were eligible for more than the basic wage or fringe benefit standard. It should also be noted that if settlements were reached in categories I and II providing for no increases in wages or benefits, they would not appear in Pay Board data. Only positive adjustments had to be reported. Finally, new union adjustments include second- and third-year adjustments (as separate cases) implemented under new contracts during Phase II.[38]

The preceding chapter noted that requests for wage increases under new union contracts in categories I and II averaged 7.6 percent, while new

38. Pay Board rules treated adjustments in subsequent years of contracts first negotiated in Phase II as "new." That is, each year was individually subject to the 5.5 percent standard. Hence the computer records do not distinguish between first and subsequent years of new contracts.

nonunion requests averaged 5.0 percent. Therefore it is not surprising that table 12-9 shows that 80.6 percent of new nonunion cases and 75.6 percent of the workers in this sample requested 6.2 percent or less, compared with corresponding union figures of 48.9 percent and 44.3 percent, respectively. Requests just at or under the standard (5.1 percent to 6.2 percent) are found for 35.5 percent of nonunion cases and 33.0 percent of union cases. Below that range the proportions of union cases and workers drop off much faster than the proportions for the nonunion sector.

The Pay Board data confirm the earlier impression gained from BLS statistics that in absolute terms a significant proportion of union applicants requested less than the standards would have permitted. In the nonunion sector, on the other hand, the standard was more of a lid. Pay Board computer records indicate that in the upper ranges of requests (not shown on table 12-9), only 2 percent of the nonunion cases requested over 9 percent, in contrast to almost 20 percent of the union cases.

Naturally, Pay Board data do not exist before Phase II, so that no historical comparisons can be made. Chapter 10, however, noted that the union sector could have been expected to request more than the nonunion sector during the Phase II period because of an underlying catch-up pressure. Presumably the distributions of wage adjustments would have had qualitatively the same relationship as the distributions shown in table 12-9. The nonunion distribution that actually resulted is undoubtedly more truncated than it otherwise would have been. Had labor shortages developed during Phase II, nonunion employers would have had a greater propensity to request exceptions than they actually demonstrated. Hence the experience of Phase II can be considered applicable only to control programs applied under similar economic circumstances.

Conclusion

Discussions of wage controls often focus on the consequences of such programs with respect to inflation and resource allocation. But the impact on industrial relations practices is also important. In the long run the costs of distorting the industrial relations system may overwhelm any short-run gains in suppressing inflation. In this respect the Phase II experience was encouraging. Distortions in industrial relations practices, although not totally absent, were minimal. There is no credible evidence that the controls program per se caused strikes; workers were neither encouraged to join labor unions nor discouraged. It is true that the average contract duration appeared to be reduced, reversing a longtime trend in the United States. In a more permanent program the wage authorities might have become sufficiently concerned about such a trend to create inducements to counter this reaction. The Pay Board, however, did not feel sufficiently concerned about this issue to take it into account in designing the regulations.

It is important to note that despite assertions that a publicized wage guideline will become a floor rather than a ceiling, no firm evidence from Phase II supports this contention. Obviously in individual cases 5.5 percent may have been used as a floor instead of a lower figure that would have been negotiated in the absence of controls. On the other hand, there were settlements below 5.5 percent and even a few scattered instances of zero adjustments. One of the few unequivocal lessons of Phase II concerns the stability and resilience of the American industrial relations system. Although high-level union and management spokesmen might have remonstrated that wage controls were undermining collective bargaining institutions, practitioners at the local level appeared to adapt to the new circumstances without undue difficulty or outbursts of conflict. This picture might have changed if controls had remained in place for a long period of time. Over the fourteen months of Phase II, however, the industrial relations system weathered the shock of direct government intervention without losing its balance.

It may be argued that the limited impact of controls on industrial relations practices was commensurate with the effect of the program on wages; since Phase II had a moderate effect on wage movements, it was unlikely that the Pay Board would wreak havoc with the American system of industrial relations. The argument does not appear to be tenable. A basic criticism of controls is that they impose external constraints and complications that will warp the "natural" patterns of collective bargaining. The very necessity of obtaining government approval introduces delays and uncertainty into the bargaining process. The rules create a new set of incentives for certain outcomes. And the right to strike, the sine qua non of collective bargaining, is implicitly limited by the legal authority to enforce the regulatory decisions. These impediments are largely created independently of the impact of the controls program on wages per se.

There was little evidence of a profound disruption or suppression of the bargaining process. The fact that Phase II was conducted with a light administrative touch, was cast as a temporary system, and enjoyed the tacit acceptance of organized labor contributed to this result. Despite the stresses introduced by the Pay Board, the American industrial relations system proved to be more accommodating than the preconceptions of the program's critics.

XIII

The Pay Board:
Epilogue and Implications

Phase II formally terminated on January 11, 1973. After a period of grace to deal with cases that were still in the pipeline, the Pay Board officially went out of business on March 31, 1973. Although wage and price controls continued in effect for another thirteen months until April 30, 1974, the end of Phase II marked an important milestone in the economic stabilization program. In contrast to Phase II, Phase III and Phase IV were characterized by a progressive trimming back of coverage, a relaxation of reporting requirements, and a switch to voluntary compliance in spirit, if not in fact. Both the Pay Board and the Price Commission's functions were assumed by the Cost of Living Council, which now had comprehensive rule-making and administrative responsibilities.

This transformation of the stabilization program was dictated, not by a judgment that it had failed, but by a belief that maintaining the system as it was in Phase II would create mounting distortions, particularly in the product market. On the wage side, 1973 was to be an active year in collective bargaining, and there was some concern that the AFL-CIO would not accept the stringent Phase II restraints as passively as it had in the past. Beyond these factors top administration officials had a strong distaste for controls that was not mitigated by experience during phases I and II.

In any case the history of the Pay Board during Phase II constitutes a discrete and unique episode in American economic policy. For fourteen months direct wage controls were applied in peacetime on a comprehensive basis by a tripartite (and later "all-public") agency. Obviously this limited experience does not provide a basis for a conclusive judgment on the utility of direct wage controls as an anti-inflation device. Within its limitations, however, the record of the Pay Board may offer instructive lessons. This chapter summarizes the evidence on the effectiveness of Phase II wage controls, examines the process of wage regulation, and explores the implications of these observations for the future use and design of incomes policy.

The Effectiveness of Phase II Wage Controls

There are two aspects to examining the effectiveness of Phase II wage restraints. First, the controls program can be reviewed on the basis of its own internal goals. Specifically, did the Pay Board meet its own standards? Second, did the controls program moderate general wage movements and thereby help to reduce the rate of inflation? These questions are not restatements of the same issue. It would be possible for a wage controls agency to meet its internal objectives but fail to influence significantly the course of wage movements throughout the economy. Alternatively, the agency could fall short of its internal goal and still have some impact on changes in the general level of wages through the spillover effects of the controls program per se.

Internal Performance

The centerpiece of the Pay Board's program was the 5.5 percent wage guideline. This guideline was not intended to be an absolute lid on wage adjustments. If the guideline had been used as a rigid limit, the results would have been inconsistent with the 2–3 percent inflation goal established by the President. Wage adjustments would have *averaged* less than 5.5 percent—assuming universal compliance was attained—and would have resulted in an increase in real wages below historical trends. The 5.5 percent guideline had two functions. On the one hand, it articulated the initial goal for average increases in compensation. On the other hand, it served as an administrative trip wire. Settlements that were above the standard automatically were separated for special review by the board. This gave the board a legal basis for examining and modifying the key settlements, since they generally ran about 5.5 percent during Phase II.

Despite the formal exceptions to the 5.5 percent standard, the higher yardstick for deferred increases, and the congressionally mandated allowances for fringe benefits, Pay Board approvals in categories I and II averaged only 5.4 percent. In many instances, especially in the nonunion sector, requests were received for amounts below permissible levels. On the average, Category I and Category II requests were cut by 0.2 percentage point through administrative action. Voluntary compliance, benign or otherwise, was sufficiently widespread so that even if the board had applied its standards as an absolute lid, wage adjustments would have been reduced only by an additional 0.4 percentage point.

From an internal perspective, therefore, the board appeared to meet its own standard. It was not necessary for the board to slash wage agreements like a thresher in a wheat field, nor was this its intent. Relatively few workers subject to controls suffered cutbacks by direct administrative action. This was the consequence of a loose labor market, diminished inflationary expectations, and the public's perception of a gradual firming of the Pay Board's position toward settlements that did exceed the standard.

All was not smooth sailing, however. Wage pressures usually were concentrated in particular sectors. The so-called last-cow cases presented special difficulties, since their terms reflected conditions and expectations that existed in the precontrols period. In addition, the key bargains—including some settled before the freeze—carried an entourage of smaller contracts that traditionally had followed the leaders. For example, the basic steel settlement, reached shortly before Phase I, was followed by a large number of tandem agreements with identical terms. More subtly, some sectors were highly vulnerable to leapfrogging, whereby each union would attempt to exceed the terms most recently negotiated by other unions. The construction industry constituted a prominent example of this phenomenon. A similar problem was identified in the retail food industry. A committee modeled after the Construction Industry Stabilization Committee was established for this industry after the Pay Board was dissolved.

Impact on General Wage Movements

Press releases and public statements by stabilization officials during Phase II pointed with pride to the slowdown in price inflation, the growth in real wages, and the recovery that then suffused the economy. Before-and-after observations by admiring press officials, however, are an insufficient basis for judgment. A more rigorous analysis requires a comparison of what occurred under controls with what would have transpired in their absence.

Determining the course of wage movements in the absence of controls is the central problem of evaluation. The standard econometric methodology involves the estimation of a model predicting wage and price behavior based on data derived from precontrols experience. On the basis of past relationships between variables, projections can be made of the rate of wage or price inflation for the controls period. If the model predicts a higher rate of wage increase or price inflation than actually occurred, the program is deemed a success. Thus success is associated with subnormality, even though the causal relationship between controls and the behavior of wages and prices may be difficult to confirm. If that notion is accepted, it implies that a successful controls effort must also be permanent, since suppressed inflation presumably will reoccur if controls are lifted.

In assessing the impact of wage controls, primary attention is focused on developments in the unionized sector. This emphasis raises a problem of interpretation. Wage developments in the nonunion sector usually are not viewed as an important source of cost-push pressure. Unfortunately the typical econometric analysis of controls uses aggregate data that lump together the union and nonunion sectors. The result is that wage movements in the union sector, which involve a minority of the labor force, are often lost in the general "noise" and imprecision of the common sources of labor market statistics.

Finally, the spotty record of wage equations in predicting wage inflation should be recognized. The assessment of normality depends critically on the predictive ability of the equation used. But wage equations are notoriously unstable over time. Each episode of underprediction or overprediction elicits a flurry of new equations employing different variables and utilizing "adjusted" data. In econometrics, as in politics, normality is an elusive concept.

In any case the policymakers in the Nixon administration would have been pleased with a return to normality under controls—at least as that condition was identified in the 1960s—especially in unionized situations. In 1970 and 1971 restrictive fiscal and monetary policies were applied to brake the inflation that had gained momentum in the late 1960s. The task proved to be more difficult than had been anticipated. In the labor market the rise in unemployment appeared to have little effect on major union agreements. Generous settlements were reached in the auto, trucking, steel, and telephone industries. By mid-1971 it became clear that similar increases could be expected in coal mining, longshoring, railroads, and aerospace. This pattern could be partially explained by efforts of the unions to recoup past losses in real earnings, by attempts to restore traditional wage relationships that had been distorted by early settlements, and by the general inflationary psychology of the period. Regardless of the cause, the 1971 settlements did seem out of line with prevailing labor market conditions, and there was a concern that they would create further expectations of inflation and set the pattern for future negotiations. Ultimately these pressures could be expected to lift wages in the nonunion sector. Under these circumstances controls were designed to restore normality, not to undercut it.

It is possible to view the relative calm that descended on the labor market during Phase II as part of a natural process of adjustment and to assert that what took place would have transpired anyway. As indicated above, however, the conditions that prevailed in 1971 hardly supported this contention. In the first nine months of 1971 first-year wage adjustments in major collective bargaining contracts averaged 11.8 percent, and there was every indication that this plateau would be maintained or raised in the months ahead. As a dynamic process of wage determination, collective bargaining cannot be viewed as the passive exercise of monopoly power with a one-time effect on wages and prices. Instead, it may generate its own institutional compulsions that have an autonomous influence on economic events, at least in the short run. In mid-1971 normality in the labor market was chimerical, so that the subsidence of the rate of wage increase in the union sector to expected levels during Phase II was a source of genuine relief, if not surprise. Only after price inflation had been re-ignited in 1973 and 1974 did wage movements again reveal a high degree of volatility.

Overall, controls appeared to have had several salutary effects on general wage movements. First, they helped to dampen the expectations of inflation that had been transmitted to the bargaining table in 1970 and 1971. The clearest evidence of this change in attitudes was the declining interest in escalator clauses, even though Pay Board regulations actually rewarded their use. Second, the Pay Board vented the pressure for catchup that had been built up by previous price inflation without permitting these out-sized adjustments to serve as the pattern for situations in which there had not been a comparable erosion of real earnings. Third, by regulating these pressures, controls helped to restore a stable wage structure and to correct the distortions caused by the inflation of the late 1960s.[1] By analogy, the Pay Board did not immediately restrain every union or employer that was exceeding the 5.5 percent speed limit. Rather, it helped to gradually slow the entire traffic flow by permitting some units that had fallen behind in previous laps to regain their former position in the flow. The fact that the end of Phase II did not see a rapid magnification of wage

1. A similar conclusion concerning the effect of wage controls in this period is reached by Robert J. Flanagan in "Wage Interdependence in Unionized Labor Markets," *Brookings Papers on Economic Activity, 3:1976*, pp. 656–62.

increases indicates that wittingly or otherwise the Pay Board carried out its task as traffic policeman with some skill.

Consequences for the Labor Market and Industrial Relations

Consideration of the impact of controls on wage changes records only one side of the ledger. Like other policy instruments, controls incur costs that must be weighted against the benefits of reducing inflation.[2] The findings discussed earlier in chapters 10, 11, and 12 suggest that the costs of wage controls during Phase II were limited both from an economic and an industrial relations point of view. Indeed while critics constantly unearthed distortions created by price controls in the product market, there was little evidence directly linking disruptions in the labor market to the program of wage restraints.[3] To be sure, the Pay Board's determinations were less likely to be unstabilizing than those of the Price Commission, because of labor market conditions and because 1972 was a light year on the bargaining calendar. Nonetheless, the absence of deleterious side effects is striking.

Economic Distortions

When economists consider controls, a major concern is that such a program will create shortages. The definition of a shortage involves subtle distinctions. Under normal circumstances, there is waiting time for certain products after orders have been placed. And employers with job vacancies do not always find new employees immediately, even in the absence of controls.[4] If the discussion is confined to severe shortages during which buyers are unable to satisfy their demands for extended periods of time, it is apparent that this pattern did not emerge in the labor market during

2. This study has been based on the assumption that limiting inflation is a desirable goal. Actually, economists have long wrestled with the question of the "cost" of inflation. A pure textbook inflation would presumably raise all wages, prices, and incomes more or less at the same rate, harming no one, especially if it came to be anticipated. An attempt to determine a specific welfare loss due to inflation may be found in Arthur M. Okun, "Inflation: Its Mechanics and Welfare Costs," ibid., *2:1975*, pp. 351–90.

3. Daniel J. B. Mitchell and Ross E. Azevedo, *Wage-Price Controls and Labor Market Distortions* (Institute of Industrial Relations, University of California at Los Angeles, 1976), chap. 4.

4. Ibid., chap. 3.

Phase II. Employers generally were able to recruit the labor they needed. No evidence indicates that black markets or systematic methods for evasion developed.

There are three probable reasons for the apparent absence of shortages. First, unemployment averaged over 5.5 percent during Phase II. Thus the possibility of a general labor shortage was negligible. Second, the controls program focused on key union contracts. Presumably union wages are higher than those the employer would pay if his wage decisions were based purely on considerations of recruitment and retention. Hence a reduction in the *rate of increase* of wages in the union sector was unlikely to hold the absolute level of wages below market-clearing rates. Moreover, the unionized industries are largely coextensive with what has been called the primary labor market.[5] This sector is characterized by a variety of fringe benefits, which helps reduce labor mobility. It seems unlikely that large numbers of workers in the unionized establishments would quit or that potential new hires would refuse jobs because of the short-term wage effects of the controls program. Third, Pay Board decisions enumerated average wage increases for entire units rather than adjustments for particular occupations or individuals. Because short-term shortages are most likely to arise in specific occupations, the employer could adapt to this exigency by providing more than 5.5 percent to the affected class of workers as long as the average for the entire unit was within the guideline. Under most circumstances this approach provided the employer with sufficient flexibility to handle particular problems of recruitment or retention.

Impact on Industrial Relations

When Phase II was initiated some feared that the new controls system would precipitate industrial disputes; that organized labor might resist the program, or that controls would interfere with the normal procedures for resolving contract disputes. These fears may have been justified on the basis of earlier experiences in the United States and abroad, but the ex post evidence suggests that direct controls can operate for a substantial period of time without creating major disruptions of the industrial relations system. Indeed the 1972 strike record constituted an improvement over the previous four years. This amelioration does not prove that con-

5. See Peter B. Doeringer and Michael J. Piore, *Internal Labor Markets and Manpower Analysis* (Heath, 1971), pp. 163–83.

trols actually reduced strikes. The data are ambiguous on that point. It is apparent, however, that the stabilization program did not increase the propensity to strike. Practically no strikes were aimed against the program itself. Even after four of the five labor members walked off the Pay Board, organized labor maintained tacit cooperation.

Other aspects of the industrial relations system were equally unaffected by controls. There is no indication that the program either abetted or impeded union organization. The direct incentives built into the Pay Board's regulations that might have stimulated an increased interest in fringe benefits, productivity plans, and escalator clauses did not have the expected effects. Undoubtedly individual units did respond to the special incentives created by board regulations, but in the aggregate the impact was minimal.

The only modification of industrial relations practice that could be clearly linked to the controls was a tendency to shorten the average duration of labor agreements. This effect was most pronounced in construction but could be detected in other sectors as well. It apparently resulted from the uncertainty concerning the life expectancy of Phase II. In view of the temporary nature of the program, some negotiators preferred to keep their options open rather than to enter into long-term contracts. If controls were abolished suddenly, negotiators could quickly return to the bargaining table to seek reparation for the real or imagined injuries imposed by Pay Board regulations.

A venerable issue in the controversy over wage controls was the contention that the imposition of rules governing the outcome of collective bargaining would undermine the bargaining process itself. It was argued that employers would no longer resist union demands, since they could rely on the Pay Board to cut back excessive wage adjustments. An appearance before the board would be preferable to a strike. A related argument was that controls would inhibit settlements below the 5.5 percent standard and that the guideline would become a de facto floor in negotiations.

This concern that controls would erode the bargaining process appears to have been exaggerated. There was some indication that employers in the retail food industry agreed to generous wage hikes in the expectation that they would be reduced by the Pay Board. No evidence suggests that the problem was widespread, however. In addition, the parties settled for less than 5.5 percent in many negotiations. Apparently the inertia of established approaches was such that employers did not succumb to the temptation to let the Pay Board do their work. Moreover, the fact that Pay Board policies provided for a wide range of exceptions made it risky for employers to take the path of least resistance and depend on a cutback by the board. Employers were reluctant to bet on a skittish horse.

Equity and Inequity

A controls program should be assessed in terms of equity or fairness as well as economic effectiveness and the impact on industrial relations practices. The concept of fairness, of course, has global implications and may involve broad ethical and social considerations. As a regulatory and administrative process, however, Phase II can be evaluated in a more limited frame of reference. In this respect, three issues of equity may be identified. First, the evenhandedness of the program's administration can be evaluated—that is, did all petitioners to the Pay Board receive equal treatment? This question can be asked independently of any regarding the nature of the rules themselves. A second aspect of equity involves an assessment of the apparent fairness of the policies and regulations. Did the rules provide for an appropriate balance between the union and nonunion sectors, or between the working poor and the higher paid? A third measure of equity is derived from a comparison of the actual consequences of controls with the intent of the regulations. If the rules themselves were fair and if they were applied in a uniform manner, their consequences might still be different from the original intent, generating apparent inequities.

Administration

During Phase II the treatment of smaller units was inherently unfair as a consequence of the category system adopted by the Pay Board. This system was designed to cope with the conflicting goals of extensive coverage and to avoid a large bureaucracy. Little differentiation was made in the attention given to units in Category I (involving 5,000 or more employees) and Category II (involving 1,000–4,999 employees). Both types of units reported directly to the Pay Board and were processed by the same staff. But in Category III—cases involving less than 1,000 workers—applications for review were submitted initially to the Internal Revenue Service and reached the Pay Board primarily on appeal from the IRS. This indirect access to the board created substantial delays in receiving final decisions. A Category III unit that appealed to the board experienced a delay averaging over 200 days. The measures adopted by the board to deal with the backlog of Category III cases were improvised and almost casual; these cases frequently were decided in haste by a special administrative group, the Category III Panel. This procedure resulted in a standard "7 percent approach" whereby individual units might get significantly less—or more—than would have been approved had the case been subject to closer scrutiny.

Rule-making by the Pay Board also was responsive to the more vocal interest groups. The consulting firms that designed and vended executive compensation plans received more than their share of the Pay Board's attention. Issues raised by wage practices in the unionized sector, such as deferred contracts and escalator clauses, commanded exhaustive review, especially during the tripartite period of the board's operations. Other areas of decisionmaking also were subject to external influences. The insurance industry joined in an alliance with organized labor to obtain preferential treatment from Congress for qualified fringe benefits. And the Cost of Living Council clearly was responsive to the administration's policy regarding the federal minimum wage in interpreting the exemption for the working poor.

Obviously these forms of influence and pressure are not unique to wage controls. They occur to some degree in all government regulatory programs. In the case of Phase II, however, the broad coverage of controls and the intensive publicity given to the vicissitudes of the Pay Board gave these influences a notorious quality that was not helpful to a program that relied heavily on public support.

Fairness of the Rules

There was never general agreement that particular Pay Board rules were fair in any normative sense. Each group whose discretion was crimped by the board's regulations believed that it was the hapless victim of inequity. While the board attempted to be fair in formulating policies, its primary method to attain equity was the uniform application of its rules. At an early stage the Pay Board adopted an across-the-board, rather than a case-by-case, approach. Most units were governed by the same rules, the same standards, and the same exceptions. Within the Pay Board's jurisdiction, broad distinctions were made only for executive pay plans and nonunion construction workers.

This approach did not avert criticisms that Phase II was inequitable *in principle*. Indeed it was precisely the formulation of across-the-board rules that the labor representatives and many outside observers criticized as unfair. An alternative model was that used by the Construction Industry Stabilization Committee whereby each case was considered according to its own history and merits. The conflict between the two approaches is not easily resolved. Is it more equitable to be subject to general rules, even if they sometimes lead to arbitrary results, or to wholly idiosyncratic determinations? There is no clear answer. An individual evaluation has the advantage of being responsive to special needs and merits. A lack of general rules, however, can lead to abuse. If an injustice is perpetrated and no formal rules exist, it is difficult to fashion an appeal. How many people, for example, would prefer to have their income tax bill established by a government board on the basis of vague standards of "fairness" set by the board, rather than by the existing—albeit imperfect—system of general rules? In addition to these obvious considerations, each approach should meet the test of effectiveness in the light of the program's goals. Even if the Pay Board had accepted the intellectual merits of the case-by-case approach, it was not a feasible alternative in view of the coverage and objectives of the program. Consequently equity was defined in operational rather than substantive terms.

Intent and Consequences

In developing its rules and policies, the Pay Board adopted a stance of distributional neutrality. That is, it rejected the notion that controls should explicitly influence the distribution of income shares among the various groups in the economy and the labor force. At the broadest level the question of income distribution focuses on the relative shares of wages and profits. Organized labor charged repeatedly that wages were frozen while prices rose freely, implying that controls artificially enhanced profits. In fact, profits did expand during Phase II, but this pattern would have been expected in the recovery stage of the business cycle. Indeed there is some economic evidence that profits rose by less than would have been expected in the absence of controls, although questions could be raised about these results. The one income share that increased more than had been anticipated was that of the farm sector. Food prices, whose sharp rise later was the undoing of Phase III, were already flashing warning signals during Phase II.

In a basic sense the results of controls could not be neutral. To the extent that controls were designed to limit the exercise of power or dissipate invidious pressures in the labor market, they clearly would have some effect on income distribution. This effect, however, should reflect the uniform application of general rules rather than conscious policy. As an analytical and substantive matter, the issue is easier to state than to answer.

Within the labor force Phase II was marked by larger wage adjustments in the union sector than in the nonunion sector. This differential cannot be attributed to controls; rather, it reflected pressures for catch-up in real wages, especially in units covered by multiyear labor agreements. If anything, controls narrowed the union-nonunion differential by focusing attention on settlements significantly above the standard and by limiting the precontrols momentum of union wage increases. Paradoxically, union workers both got more and lost more during Phase II.

Union workers typically are found in higher-paying industries. This association between higher wages and unionization reflects the direct impact of unions, the composition of the labor force, and the market position of the employers. During a period in which union workers receive higher adjustments than nonunion workers, higher-paid workers would therefore be expected to receive more than the lower paid. Despite the working-poor exception, this appears to have happened during Phase II. The regulations gave preferential treatment to applications for wage increases on behalf of the working poor. But the exception was permissive; it did not require wage increases above the standard. Since labor-market conditions did not provide strong incentives for employers to raise the wages of the lower paid, these additional increases did not materialize.

The treatment of executive compensation was a controversial issue throughout Phase II. In one sense the attention given to executive pay was largely symbolic, since the total portion of the national wage bill involved was small. But the revelation of cases in which highly paid executives received increases significantly above 5.5 percent continued to crop up and was a source of embarrassment to the board. The formal explanation was that the increases in question were in compliance with the rules, which permitted variable bonuses for six-figure top executives and $12,000-a-year accountants alike. Obviously this answer did not satisfy the critics and heightened the suspicion that the rules were biased in favor of the well-to-do.

The structure of Pay Board controls also contributed to the executive compensation problem. These controls were based on the unit, not the individual. Any attempt to deal with individuals—whether the working poor or top executives—would be both complex and cumbersome. Executives in large units could grant themselves outsized pay increases at the expense of others in their units and still hold the average increase to 5.5 percent. In other respects as well the Pay Board rules for executives probably were applied more liberally than the board would have wished had it been possible to review the results in advance.

The question of designing and administering rules governing executive pay is intertwined with the more basic issues of the fairness of the pre-existing income distribution. It might be argued that it is inequitable to apply the same 5.5 percent to a person earning $6,000 a year and to one earning $150,000. In the latter case 5.5 percent equals more than the entire annual income of the $6,000 wage earner. There have been attempts in other countries to adopt variable wage guidelines providing for more restrictive limits for higher-paid employees. The Pay Board, however, did not regard the overall reform of existing income distribution as part of its mission.

Why Wage Controls Can Work but Cannot Endure

The impact of direct controls on wages and other aspects of industrial relations constitutes the objective bottom line of a wage stabilization program. This emphasis on outcomes slights the relationship between results and the nature of the regulatory process. Many observers, particularly economists, view controls as a "black box" that mechanically transmits policies to decisionmakers in the labor market and at the bargaining table. In fact, the checkered history of Phase II indicates that there are important relationships between the structure and process of a wage controls program and the ultimate effectiveness of the effort. In a very real sense most of the difficulties and the sometimes erratic course of the Pay Board were not the consequence of inexorable economic forces but of pressures generated by the controls system itself.

Complexity and Administration

Phase II dramatically illustrated the progressive complexity of a program of wage controls. It was launched in a spirit that approached innocence concerning the sheer complexity of the administrative task at hand. The enunciation of the 5.5 percent standard gave only the broadest definition to the program. Even the preliminary step of measuring wage increases involved numerous policy choices and the proliferation of calculating routines. The standard itself engendered a variety of exceptions including catch-up, tandems, qualified benefits, and merit increases, among others. If the controls were to be taken seriously, the process of elaboration had to be pursued so that the rules gave meaningful guidance to executives, professors, and commission drivers. Certainly the Phase II experience demonstrated that a comprehensive system of direct controls cannot be carried out on a "cafeteria" basis whereby the regulators rely on the capacity of those regulated to serve themselves.

It became apparent during Phase II that the bureaucratic burdens of the program necessitated an increase in administrative resources. However, because President Nixon had cast "massive bureaucracies" in the role of villains whose clutches the program would avoid, the hiring of additional personnel was an unacceptable alternative. For this reason the establishment of regional offices, which would have permitted the decentralization of decisionmaking, was never given serious consideration. Caught between a growing case load and a threadbare bureaucracy, the Pay Board created special units with extraordinary powers. These units acted to reduce the backlog but at the price of due process.

To a large degree the Pay Board was the victim of the involuted logic of the economic stabilization program. Wage controls were given the most comprehensive scope, not because there were compelling economic reasons to do so, but as an expression of the political euphoria generated by Phase I and the misconceived notion that equity required all economic units to be covered by the regulatory net. To the contrary, it can be argued that when comprehensive coverage is combined with lean administration, gross inequities will arise from the uneven treatment afforded different units. Although the large units believed that they received excessive scrutiny, at least this review gave the opportunity for detailed consideration of the merits of the case. The smaller units generally had to rely on the vagaries of the Category III Panel.

A preferable approach would have been to limit coverage explicitly to those units where there was some expectation that wage developments would be inflationary in their own right or have serious spillover effects for other situations. If these key units could not be identified by reference to a single criterion, such as size, the controls agency could retain the authority to impose restraints selectively in individual cases. Since the main problem for the regulators during Phase II was the restabilization of the national wage structure, the optimal system would have involved the articulation of a general pay standard but also would have permitted selectivity in the application of the standard. The Cost of Living Council did not implement the authority to exempt small businesses until the end of March 1972, however, when it excluded units with sixty or less employees. This step was too little too late, and the flood of cases continued to engulf the board.

The Tripartitism Trap

The raw problem of administrative efficiency posed by the complexity of Phase II wage controls was compounded by the structure of the Pay Board. As a tripartite body, the board was organized in order to give full sway to bargaining between the regulators and those regulated. Any regulatory process, of course, involves substantial elements of negotiation. In Phase II this attribute was transformed into a lofty principle and a political tactic.

On the one hand, both the policymakers and the interested groups believed that tripartitism was a desirable, if not necessary, approach to wage regulation. Previous direct wage-control efforts had taken place during wartime. Although the history of tripartitism during World War II and the Korean war was not as equanimous in fact as in memory, it fostered the belief—almost an article of faith—that a union-management-public structure was necessary to ensure the success of a wage stabilization program. Certainly this opinion was ardently expressed by the leaders of the AFL-CIO and endorsed by top management officials.

On the other hand, the administration viewed tripartitism as a device to protect its political flank against attack from organized labor. Because of its direct involvement in the administration of the controls program, organized labor would be hard pressed to mount an effective public attack on the perfidies of the board. Even though some labor representatives assailed the integrity (and competence) of the board members, they could hardly occupy the high ground as long as they enjoyed full rights of participation in the regulatory process.

As Phase II progressed, a pattern of compensating cooptation took shape. That is, organized labor did not use its representation on the Pay Board to advance the national interest, as defined by a commitment to vanquish inflation, but to bargain aggressively for what it perceived to be labor's interests. Without a firm consensus concerning the form and desirability of controls, tripartitism was not so much an expression of economic corporatism as it was a basis for leverage within an ill-defined regulatory process. During wartime the consensus for controls is shaped and maintained by the need for national solidarity in the face of an external threat; in time of peace, any consensus is fragile and easily upset. The consumer price index was a less compelling enemy in Phase II than the Wehrmacht was in World War II.

Despite the conventional wisdom that tripartitism is essential to a wage stabilization program, the Pay Board's effectiveness was not undermined by the departure of the four labor members. More to the point, the regulatory process was simplified and stabilized because the board was no longer an arena for nonstop bargaining. In addition, the agency could be more evenhanded in its decisions because it did not have to cope with the political considerations created by the interests of the representatives of particular unions that served on the board.

One of the instructive lessons of Phase II, therefore, is that a formal tripartite structure is not necessary for the conduct of an effective wage controls program.[6] Indeed tripartitism is likely to create obstacles to efficient administration that counterbalance its virtues in the process of policy formulation. The emphasis on tripartitism in discussions of direct wage controls confuses form with outcome. Thus the discussions of tripartitism reflect the proper concern about the need for creating and sustaining a consensus among the major interest groups. In an industrial democracy, controls cannot be maintained for an extended period through coercion, legal or otherwise. In this respect the record in the United States and abroad is clear. If organized labor or, for that matter, management staunchly resist controls because they are perceived to be inequitable, the program will be undermined by systematic evasion or direct confrontation with the regulatory agency. Incarceration has long been discarded as a desirable or effective instrument of industrial relations policy.

To declare that a peacetime program of wage controls must be founded on a consensus does not mean, however, that tripartitism is the exclusive form for the expression of the consensus or, further, that it should be used as the governing principle of administration. The creation and pres-

6. For the opposite view, see John T. Dunlop, "Wage and Price Controls as Seen by a Controller," in Industrial Relations Research Association, *Proceedings of the 1975 Annual Spring Meeting* (Madison, Wisc.: IRRA, 1975).

ervation of a consensus essentially is a *political* problem that is best handled through political mechanisms rather than through administrative structures. Under the Pay Board the commingling of political and administrative functions in a single agency worked to the detriment of both. Tripartitism clearly impaired the administrative efficiency of the board, and the intense intramural bargaining over administrative procedures and rules was an impediment to the shaping of a durable consensus.

Thus an important lesson of Phase II is that it is possible—and probably desirable—to separate the mechanisms for consensus formation from the mechanisms of administration when wage controls are initiated during peacetime. As a political matter, the question of establishing a consensus can best be left to political instrumentalities. If, for example, organized labor believes that the wage stabilization program should also promote income redistribution by exempting low-income workers, then this issue is best resolved by Congress (more carefully, it is hoped, than in Phase II) rather than by the Pay Board. Ultimately the issue of the working poor was disposed of by Congress, with an assist from the courts. But the acrimony arising from efforts to resolve the controversy within an administrative structure was still another blow to the stability of the program.

Extragovernmental arrangements may also be instituted to handle the problem of consensus formation. Although the representatives of the AFL-CIO left the Pay Board, they were able to influence policy through the Labor-Management Advisory Committee, which was established at the outset of Phase III in January 1973. In the interim they were consulted frequently on an informal basis by Secretary of the Treasury George P. Shultz, who also served as chairman of the Cost of Living Council. The refinement of separate but parallel mechanisms for shaping a consensus among the major interest groups while supporting objective, efficient administration constitutes one of the most subtle and challenging questions in the future development of incomes policy in the United States.

The Erosion of Controls

Regardless of how well the problem of consensus is handled, the Phase II experience indicates that comprehensive wage controls give rise to forces that ultimately will cause the dissolution of the program. In a real sense the "black box" carries its own self-destruct mechanisms. First, the progressive complexity of wage controls discussed above results in an intricate set of rules that deflects the program from the objectives that set it in motion. In contrast to those regulatory programs that are concerned with a single industry or limited set of commodities, wage controls encompass a complex array of phenomena that extends to every corner of the economy. Rules are heaped on rules and general principles are warped by exceptions. For example, the Pay Board initially adopted a policy governing merit increases whereby such wage adjustments would be counted toward the 5.5 percent standard in nonunion situations but would be excluded from calculations in unionized establishments. Although there was a crude theory to this approach, the differential treatment of union and nonunion situations provoked an outcry from management and caused the board to revise its regulations. The new regulation provided for a 7 percent limit for all cases in which there was a bona fide merit plan. The assumption was that the exception would not undermine the general pay standard. When a review of the operation of the merit exception revealed that it was used to circumvent the 5.5 percent norm, the exception was rescinded. The point is not that the merit rule was good or bad but that it was encumbered by so many conflicting factors that its relationship to the objectives of the program became tenuous. From the parties' point of view, the revisions of the regulation was a source of frustration and uncertainty. The cumulative effect of a series of such episodes was to raise the transaction costs and reduce the willingness of the parties to cooperate with the stabilization effort. This sensitivity is especially acute in the labor market where wage decisions are closely linked to considerations of individual freedom or social justice.

Second, wage controls, more than any other form of economic regulation, are likely to run afoul of considerations of equity. As discussed earlier, the board attempted to be responsive to factors that would ensure equity in devising its rules and administrative procedures. Although it may have enjoyed some success in *objective* terms, the *perceptions* of employees, union leaders, and employers were a different matter. Inevitably a comprehensive system of wage controls gives rise to mounting feelings of inequity.

One of the virtues of the free market and free collective bargaining is that these processes of decisionmaking are essentially amoral in nature. When a nonunion employer sets a wage, he does not review the writings of St. Thomas Aquinas. Rather, he examines the applicable market rate, the available labor supply, the need for any special skills in the firm, and related factors. Similarly, when union and management representatives sit down at the bargaining table they may engage in homiletics, but they know that the agreement will be determined by the prevailing bargaining pattern, the economic status of the firm, labor market conditions, and the capacity of each party to inflict harm on the other. Some observers may rue the absence of more elegant principles, but in the day-to-day activities of the labor market these decisions are dominated by technical or tactical considerations.

With the launching of the stabilization program, new considerations are introduced. The administrative procedures inherent in the system of controls make explicit and expand the framework for equitable comparisons. Normally a wage agreement reached in the railroad industry would have had virtually no effect on wage determination in the aerospace industry. But under the system of controls, where decisions concerning the public acceptability of these agreements are made by the same group of frail mortals, the relationship between the two decisions has to be kept clearly in mind. Moreover, each individual case may have its own calculus of equity. In the longshore cases, for example, increases significantly above the general pay standard were approved because the unions had agreed to changes that would greatly increase productivity. In the coal industry case, even the public members voted for the approval of a 12 percent wage increase, a substantial part of which was necessary to replenish a pension fund on the edge of insolvency.

The intrusion of considerations of equity into the stabilization program meant that each Pay Board decision left a residue of resentment. Although its regulations necessarily were cast in general terms, each case was different, and equity became an ambiguous standard. At the Pay Board it was sometimes stated that each decision produced one ingrate and two enemies. Hence to the extent that the regulatory process makes considerations of equity explicit, but the supporting administrative procedures have a limited capacity to sustain equitable comparisons, the consensus underlying the program gradually will be eroded.

Third, wage controls are vulnerable to broad political pressures. Although the Pay Board attempted to develop a self-contained system, Phase II became enmeshed in wider controversies. The attitude of organized labor toward the Pay Board was strongly colored by the philosophy and political goals of the labor movement. The AFL-CIO generally was hostile to the Nixon administration, while the Teamsters promoted a labor-Republican alliance. This difference in attitude helped to explain why the AFL-CIO representatives left the board, while the president of the Teamsters remained as a public member.

On a different level the decision on the East Coast longshore case was made in the shadow of a portentous development in foreign affairs. To the extent that the wage control program is part of a broader political process, it is called on to absorb pressures that it is not designed to withstand. Although the political perils that beset the Pay Board were unique in detail, they were generic in implication. A controls system cannot insulate itself from the broad political and social environment in which it operates, and ultimately it will have to bend to these external forces.

Last, to the extent that wage controls involve the substitution of administrative judgment for market decisions, there must be a cumulation of economic inefficiencies. As a consequence, the real cost of the program to the public will rise, creating incentives for evasion or resistance. During Phase II the labor market conditions were favorable to controls, and there was little evidence of distortions. Moreover, distortions are more likely to be a much greater problem for price controls relative to wage controls. In the area of executive compensation, however, where there is a close immediate relationship between performance and compensation, a pattern of "playing the system," if not outright evasion, did develop. With the tightening of the labor market and the passage of time, the gap between market-directed outcomes and the administrative decisions of the wage controls agency will eventually increase, no matter how sagacious the controllers might be. Simple errors of judgment combine with bureaucratic complexity to multiply inefficiency and to reduce the public's enthusiasm for the program.

The enumeration of these factors contributing to the dissolution of a program of wage restraints does not mean that controls lack utility as a defense against inflation. Rather, this analysis indicates that it is unreasonable to expect *comprehensive* wage controls to serve as a continuous policy instrument. Instead, they should be used as a short-term, intermittent device for dealing with special transitional pressures in the labor market. Obviously it is impossible to predict with precision what the half-life of a wage controls program will be under any particular set of circumstances. It is certain, though, that the growth of bureaucratic complexity, the cumulation of perceived inequities, random shocks from the external environment, and the rising economic inefficiencies introduced by administrative decision will raise the costs and the level of conflict associated with controls so that they will be toppled or more quietly laid to rest. In assessing or prescribing the future of wage controls, this pattern of erosion should be recognized both in designing the program and in setting expectations for its achievements.

The Future of Wage Controls

It is more difficult to predict the future of wage controls than to state that controls have a future. Inflation appears to have joined death and taxes as one of modern life's inevitabilities. The simultaneous attainment of stable prices and a high level of economic activity continues to be an elusive goal. As long as this dilemma remains, wage controls will have recurrent appeal as one option in an array of incomes policies.

The history of the Pay Board is, of course, only one chapter in a series of experiments with direct wage controls in the United States and other democratic societies. As a single episode, Phase II cannot be viewed as a literal model for emulation. Both the successes and shortcomings of the Pay Board reflected the special conditions surrounding the founding and operation of the agency. Nonetheless, this uniqueness does afford a basis for exploring the prospects for wage controls as an instrument of economic policy. As the first peacetime venture in direct wage controls in the United States, the Phase II experience tempered both the strictures of ideology and the nostalgia of wartime programs. Recognizing the exceptional qualities of Phase II, what hints does this account offer concerning the future shape of wage controls?

Comprehensive Controls

Phase II points to alternative approaches to wage controls that differ in timing, scope, and structure. One approach parallels that of the Pay Board. Under this model, wage controls are applied *after* inflation has beset the economy. In this circumstance controls serve two purposes. On the one hand, they help to dampen the expectation of inflation that influences wage decisions, particularly at the bargaining table. On the other hand, controls are a tool for managing the catch-up process by which workers whose real earnings have been eroded by past inflation regain their former economic position. The goal of controls is not to suppress the general level of wage increases as such but to minimize distortions in wage structure that otherwise might create cost-push pressures at the bargaining table and in related sectors of the labor market. In focusing on both objectives, the controls are intended to facilitate the adjustment from a more to a less inflationary economy. They will be used as a transitional device in a broad anti-inflationary program emphasizing fiscal and monetary policy. It is expected that inflation will subside, but that the adjustment process may be retarded or undermined by wage developments reflecting *past* inflationary events that may generate their own momentum. In this sense wage controls constitute a smoothing mechanism to reduce the institutional friction in returning to a more stable economic path.

Under this approach the controls system will be formally applied to almost all sectors of the labor force and labor market. This comprehensive coverage is necessary to condition expectations and to establish a framework for equity that will facilitate the public's acceptance of the program. As an operational matter, however, controls will be administered on a more restrictive basis, with exemptions for sectors where controls are redundant. Thus the controllers should have the capacity to identify those sectors of the labor market where significant structural problems might exercise leverage on wages across broad sectors of the labor market. These structural problems might be the consequence of the exercise of market power by individual unions or of the demands of particular groups of workers to catch up for past inflation. Comprehensive coverage helps to anesthetize expectations of inflation while permitting the surgical treatment of specific cases that may set a pattern for oversized increases in other instances.

Within this strategy the comprehensive model of wage controls will be associated with an explicit pay standard or guideline. The standard combines a realistic assessment of current market conditions and a target that is feasible within a designated time period. In applying the standard, various exceptions will be specified to permit the program administrators to discriminate in their treatment of individual cases. The extent of the exceptions will vary with the nature of the general pay standard. If a high standard is adopted, few exceptions will be made; if a low standard is specified, numerous categories for special treatment will be established.

As a transitional program, such a system of controls will be short-lived. If it is not trimmed back or dismantled at the initiative of the controllers, it is likely to be undermined by administrative burdens, the cumulation of inequities, and the rising cost of inefficiencies introduced by errors in judgment.

Alternative Mechanisms

The delineation of this comprehensive ex post model points the way to a consideration of alternative policies that may obviate the need for a controls program. That is, if direct wage controls are a device to bring wage behavior into closer conformity with the immediate economic environment, other policies may achieve the same end. Thus the pressures to catch up with past inflation generally are most acute in the unionized sector. As a general matter, employers do not adjust money wages instantaneously to changes in the general price level. Rather, wage changes usually are initiated on some periodic basis, for example, every six or twelve months, so that they lag economic events. In unionized situations, however, the lags frequently are extended by the negotiation of multiyear contracts. One of the singular achievements of the American industrial relations system has been the development of the multiyear, fixed-term contract. These contracts include scheduled wage increases of a specified amount, and many of them last three years. This arrangement introduces stability into union-management relationships, affords the employer considerable predictability of labor costs, and helps to avert industrial conflict.

The terms incorporated in a multiyear contract represent the parties' best guess concerning the future course of economic events. If there is an unexpected change in economic conditions, either management or the union will have to bear the losses for the life of the contract. Thus a firm that agrees to generous wage increases, assuming a strong expansion of sales, will suffer financial pressure if market demand deteriorates. Similarly, the union that negotiates fixed wage increases based on the expectation of stable consumer prices will experience a significant drop in the real earnings of its members if inflation rises sharply during the contract period.

In both cases the parties will seek compensatory adjustments when the contract expires. The employer may seek an agreement with increases below the current pattern, while the union generally will demand a wage hike larger than would be justified by long-term productivity or labor market conditions. The latter reaction took place in the period 1969–71 and resulted in large union wage settlements despite a rising level of unemployment.[7] A similar sequence of events took place in 1975–76. The unions engaged in this bargaining round were those that had last negotiated contracts in 1972–73 when inflation had moderated (and controls were in effect). In the intervening period the economy was enveloped by

7. Marvin Kosters, Kenneth Fedor, and Albert Eckstein, "Collective Bargaining Settlements and the Wage Structure," *Labor Law Journal*, vol. 24 (August 1973), pp. 517–25.

a surge of inflation that had sharply diminished the real earnings of many workers covered by fixed-term agreements.

During Phase II, controls were used to regulate the process of adjustment to the lags in wage movements introduced by multiyear contracts. This problem, however, can be attacked on an anticipatory basis through two changes in contract terms. First, the duration of the contract can be shortened. Second, labor agreements can incorporate escalator clauses whereby periodic short-term adjustments in money wages will be made on the basis of changes in the consumer price level. In fact, both adaptations are likely when inflation is expected or there is a high degree of uncertainty concerning the future course of prices. In this manner the incidence of escalator clauses usually fluctuates with changes in the rate of increase in the general level of prices. When prices are relatively stable, fixed wage increases have been more appealing to unions than escalator clauses. Conversely, escalator clauses become more widespread during periods of inflation.[8] Where escalator clauses are strongly resisted by management, the union may press for a shorter contract so that price trends can be more quickly reflected in negotiated wage increases.

Despite this pattern, the adjustment of wages to inflation usually is spotty. In many cases unions have obtained escalator clauses after inflation has taken a heavy toll on its members. In addition, many escalator clauses have a cap, or ceiling, on the absolute amount of additional wages that can be generated by the escalator clause.[9] While this device protects the employer from an unlimited run-up of wage costs, it may result in a significant loss of real income by the employees, especially during periods of high inflation.

For these reasons an alternative to ex post comprehensive controls is the formulation of public policies that mandate, or provide incentives for, escalator clauses or contracts of relatively short duration. For example, a policy may state that when the price level rises 5 percent or more in any twelve-month period, a labor agreement without an escalator clause automatically will be subject to a wage reopener on its next anniversary date, regardless of the actual termination date in the contract. Similarly, public policy may require that whenever a contract has a duration of eighteen months or more, it must have an escalator clause that

8. H. M. Douty, *Cost-of-Living Escalator Clauses and Inflation,* Council on Wage and Price Stability Staff Report (Executive Office of the President, Council on Wage and Price Stability, August 1975), pp. 6–13.

9. Ibid., pp. 24–25.

provides at least partial protection of the real wage position of the covered employees. Such arrangements would reduce the discontinuities in wage movements in the unionized sector that arise from intensive efforts to catch up after periods of unexpected inflation.

These alternatives are unorthodox and may impair union-management relations. Moreover, it is contended that indexing will help to start and to sustain the inflationary pressures that created the problem in the first place. In practice, however, most escalator clauses provided for less than full recovery of the loss of real earnings.[10] In the absence of such clauses, unions will come to the bargaining table during inflationary periods with insistent demands that employers restore their real economic position. Certainly shorter contracts and partial indexing would reduce the likelihood of a wage explosion that could destabilize the economy.

Selective Controls

The desirability of some form of anticipatory intervention leads to consideration of an alternative approach to direct wage controls. This option is distinguished from the comprehensive model by its selectivity and permanence.[11] Under this arrangement a permanent government agency or commission would have continuing authority to review and intervene in wage decisions. The forms of intervention would range from the right to hold public hearings on particular wage developments to the power to delay or modify scheduled wage increases. This authority would be applied selectively to individual industries or wage bargains at the discretion of the commission. The prime candidates for attention would be those situations in which weaknesses in bargaining structure create the imminent prospect of leapfrogging whereby one union seeks to exceed the wage gains obtained by another union even though it operates in a comparable environment. Other areas of intervention would involve cases in which workers—or their unions—enjoy a special advantage in the labor market because of monopoly control of an essential good or service and their wage gains would establish coercive comparisons for other situations.

10. Ibid., pp. 26–32.
11. This discussion of selective controls is an extension of an earlier discussion in Arnold R. Weber, "The Continuing Courtship: Wage-Price Policy through Five Administrations," in Craufurd D. Goodwin, ed., *Exhortation and Controls: The Search for a Wage-Price Policy, 1945–1971* (Brookings Institution, 1975), pp. 380–83.

A system of selective controls does not seek to alter the basic power relations in the labor market. Instead, selective controls aim at rationalizing the use of power so that disruptions to the economy arising from the dynamics of wage determination are minimized. The issue of power must be addressed in other forums and must give consideration to factors other than economic stability alone. Questions of the distribution of income and the role of labor in a democratic society should not be left to controllers.

The selective approach has several operational advantages. It relieves policymakers of the need to fashion a broad consensus to sustain a global program. Because such a system of controls would not be viewed as part of a strategy for the redistribution of power and income in society as a whole, it would be more amenable to administrative processes and less likely to excite political controversy. To be sure, when controls are applied in specific cases, the parties might feel disadvantaged by this intervention, but as a political matter it is easier to deal with special interests than with class interests. Experience with selective wage controls in the retail food and construction industries in 1971–73 indicates that such an approach can be maintained without arousing hostility.

Under a selective approach there would also be less need for a general pay standard. Since the wage commission would focus on specific cases, it could consider a wide range of variables that supplement universal criteria, such as national productivity trends. At its best, a selective system would permit the parties to arrive at outcomes they would prefer but are unable to attain because of structural or political factors. At the same time, weight could be given to the spillover effects of individual bargains that are difficult for negotiators and wage administrators to accommodate in their decisions. This approach would not dissipate wage pressures engendered by stimulative fiscal and monetary policies or exogenous shocks, such as the oil boycott of 1973. But it could reduce the likelihood that labor market developments per se will introduce instabilities into the economy.

A Special-Purpose Tool

The two broad approaches to wage controls—comprehensive and selective—obviously are not mutually exclusive. Together they help to delineate the framework within which further variations will take place. To the extent that inflation is an intermittent phenomenon, there will be a tendency to intervene in wage decisions through a comprehensive system of controls of relatively short duration. On the other hand, if the presence or threat of inflation is perceived as a permanent state of affairs, then policymakers are more likely to adopt a durable selective form of controls.

The record of Phase II demonstrates that wage controls by themselves will not slay the inflationary dragon. They are most effective as a device to deal with some of the reinforcing consequences of inflation, particularly as they impact on the wage structure. At the same time, the record of the Pay Board indicates that a formal system of comprehensive controls does not sound the death knell of collective bargaining or paralyze the free market as a mechanism for the efficient allocation of labor. Even highly critical studies of the 1971–74 stabilization program concede that wage controls did not create serious distortions in the labor market and indeed may have had some constructive consequences.[12] In losing its innocence, the Pay Board did not lose its vigor.

Wage controls are best viewed as a special-purpose tool in a set of stabilization measures. As such, they will assume diverse forms and attain varying success in different circumstances. Government intervention in wage decisions will have recurrent appeal as long as society must confront the problems of growth and stability and equity and efficiency. The appeal of wage controls thus reflects the intractability of economic problems, the political tensions inherent in democratic societies, and the deficiencies of other policy approaches. The most instructive lesson of the Pay Board experience is the need for continued experimentation with new social inventions that supersede existing ideology or preconceptions.

12. Marvin H. Kosters in association with J. Dawson Ahalt, *Controls and Inflation: The Economic Stabilization Program in Retrospect* (American Enterprise Institute for Public Policy Research, 1975), pp. 33–36.

Basic Computation Rules

The formulation of basic policies by the Pay Board represented the first step in an extended and sometimes erratic process of interpretation rather than the delivery of fixed principles. The policies initially were tested on the so-called last-cow cases discussed in chapters 5 and 6. But most Pay Board cases were more routine, and it was in the day-to-day operations of the board that basic policies were refined and the technical details were worked out. Thus determinations in a variety of individual cases were the accepted vehicles for policy implementation. In some instances the cases presented novel issues to the board that had to be resolved. Sometimes they simply arrived at a timely moment when the board wanted to implement a new approach.[1] At any rate both the meaning of the policies and the impact of the program were defined by the accumulation of applications in individual cases.

Before any case analysis could be done, the board had to work out a consistent set of computation rules. The allowable 5.5 percent had little meaning unless a unit could compute its increment in a manner consistent with the board's view on how such calculations should be made. Implementation of the standard, then, was largely a matter of defining these rules.

The Appropriate Employee Unit

In order for a computation of a wage increase to be made, the board had to define the borders of the unit for which the calculation was to be applied. For unionized employees the bargaining unit was available as a definition. The board did not require strict adherence to the legal definitions of the appropriate bargaining unit used by the National Labor Re-

---

1. The Philadelphia meatcutters' case (see appendix B)—the first deferred adjustment cutback—just happened to be available when the board was ready to tackle the deferred adjustment issue. And the New York City printers' case was a convenient vehicle for illustrating the board's concern with windfall profits resulting from deferred cutbacks.

lations Board. Rather, it followed the actual structural boundaries of the unit in which bargaining took place. In some cases where multi-employer bargaining was the norm, the unit might cover many firms. In others the firm, or some part of a firm, might be the unit.[2] Similar procedures were followed for nonunion employees, except that nonunion employers obviously had greater leeway than unionized units in defining the locus of wage determination in the firm. Nonunion employers who had 1,000 or more workers, for example, could escape some of the more burdensome reporting requirements by carving themselves up into Category III units. Government employee units, even if nonunion, usually were fairly well defined on the basis of legislative and budgetary practices.

Questions of the appropriateness of a unit rarely arose at the Pay Board. A problem was created, however, when the wage level defining the working poor was raised to $2.75 in July 1972. The board's approach to wage controls was based on regulating the average wage in a unit, not the wages of individuals. In contrast, the working-poor exemption covered individuals, not units. In many units some workers were covered by the working-poor definition and others were not.

One option the board considered was simply to drop the working poor out of the unit entirely. Some problems would have arisen in the case of individuals who earned less than $2.75 in the base period but more after the proposed increase.[3] This, however, could have been dealt with through technical language. Some members expressed concern that redefining the unit would limit the flow of information to the board. If the working poor were excluded from the units—and therefore from reports to the Pay Board—there would be no way of monitoring the impact of the new definition of $2.75.

Eventually the board decided on a partial disaggregation of the unit for certain purposes. A unit wishing 5.5 percent (plus allowable exceptions) or less included the working poor in its calculations. Those wishing to claim the low-wage exemption filed a form covering everyone in the

2. Section 201.2 of the Pay Board's recodified regulations stated: " 'Appropriate employee unit' means a group composed of all employees in a bargaining unit or in a recognized employee category. Such bargaining unit or employee category may exist in a plant or other establishment or in a department thereof, or in a company, or in an industry, or in a governmental unit or in an agency or instrumentality thereof, and shall be determined so as to preserve, as nearly as possible, contractual or historical wage and salary relationships." See *Federal Register*, November 23, 1972, p. 24961.

3. Tips were not included in the calculation of the $2.75. See Pay Board staff paper EPCA-EAD, Micro 158, October 30, 1972.

unit. A separate form covering those who would end up earning more than $2.75 as a result of the increase had to be filed as an attachment. Workers earning less than $2.75 but who would cross the $2.75 line were charged for the increment above $2.75. To this was added the increment below $2.75 up to 5.5 percent of a low-wage base wage that the employer had to calculate. Thus for statistical purposes the employer had to disaggregate his unit.[4]

The Base Rate

In order to determine the percentage adjustment, the Pay Board had to determine the base hourly compensation rate. This rate consisted of the sum of straight-time wage compensation plus hourly benefits. Units determined their base period straight-time wage by dividing total straight-time payroll by hours for the base period.[5] In the case of straight-time pay the base period was usually the payroll period immediately preceding the control year in which the adjustment was to be effective. Such periods were usually one week, two weeks, or a month in duration. In units in which seasonal or other factors produced abnormal results in the previous payroll period, a more typical period could be selected.

For fringe benefits the base period for calculating the hourly benefit rate was generally the year preceding the control year. The rationale for the one-year period for fringe benefits was that many of the more common types of benefits are highly seasonal (vacations, Christmas bonuses)

4. See U.S. Internal Revenue Service, Economic Stabilization Program, *A Special Rule Benefits Low Wage Earners: The Low Wage Exception for Employees Earning Less than $2.75 per Hour,* Publication S-3052 (IRS, October 5, 1972).

5. The Pay Board insisted on basing its calculations on hours worked rather than hours paid. This was to avoid an artificial incentive for indirect compensation through decreased hours with no reduction in pay (more holidays, vacation time, etc.). However, the various reporting forms the board issued used hours paid to compute the straight-time wage. This seeming inconsistency was apparently included to match employer payroll accounting practices. The employer was asked to cost his payroll for all hours paid on a straight-time basis and then to divide by hours paid. If all worker classifications had the same percentage difference between hours paid and hours worked, no problem would arise. If certain classes had different percentages, however, their weight in the computation of the base wage rate would be on the basis of hours paid. This probably would have given slightly more weight to higher-paid employees who might be expected to receive more holiday and vacation time. Calculation of fringe benefit expenses was on a strict hours-worked basis. Thus in the case described above, the average fringe benefit rate and wage rate would have been calculated on a somewhat inconsistent basis.

or are very much affected by economic conditions (overtime). It was less clear, however, why the annual base was applied to fringe benefits but not wages, since both could be affected by seasonal and economic factors.

The Control Year

Initial Pay Board regulations suggested that the first control year should run from November 14, 1971 (the start of Phase II), to November 13, 1972. It seemed logical to use a twelve-month period as the unit of control, since the 5.5 percent standard was understood to mean 5.5 percent a year. And it seemed reasonable to use the twelve months beginning November 14, 1971, as the beginning of that period, since Phase II controls became effective on that date.

For most nonunion units this twelve-month control year was in fact applied, but a problem arose in the union sector. Only by sheer coincidence would a union contract have an anniversary on November 13, 1971. Most contracts would be scheduled for expiration on other dates. Moreover, the timing of union contract expirations is not arbitrary. Timing can affect the bargaining position and tactics of the parties. For example, workers at a summer resort hotel would find it disadvantageous to have their contract expire in the winter, since a strike threat would impose little hardship on management.

Adherence to a year bound by the November 14 date could have created other awkward circumstances in the union sector. Suppose a union had negotiated a one-year contract beginning July 1, 1971, providing for a 6 percent increase on July 1 and another 6 percent on January 1, 1972. The second 6 percent would have been covered by Pay Board controls. Even though it exceeded 5.5 percent, it would have been allowed to go into effect as a deferred adjustment. But if the union negotiated a new contract on July 1, 1972, it might appear that no increase could take effect, since the 5.5 percent for the first year had already been used up. Or alternatively the Pay Board might be in a position of seeming to approve 11.5 percent (6 percent plus another 5.5 percent).

These considerations led to the concept of a short control year. A short control year began on the first day of Phase II and ended on the anniversary of the pre–Phase II contract expiration date. Thus in the example cited above, the unit—at its option—would have had a short control year running from November 14, 1971, to June 30, 1972. Thereafter, regular twelve-month years were used, coincident with the traditional timing of the contract. Some nonunion units also had short control years, when they could show that before Phase II a traditional timing arrangement had been established (for example, the employer's fiscal year). In both cases, union and nonunion, the short control year was intended as a transitional device to bridge the gap between the start of Phase II and the traditional timing date. Automatically, by November 14, 1972, there were no units left with short control years.

Since the control year issue arose largely in union situations, the Pay Board was forced to consider the problem brought about by a transition from a nonunion to a union status. The simple solution would have been to rule that when a new union contract was negotiated, the start of the contract would establish a new control year. Such a ruling, however, could have given an artificial incentive to unionize. For example, suppose a nonunion unit with a November 14 control year received 5.5 percent on January 1, 1972. That increase would have exhausted the allowable amount until November 14, 1972. If a union came in and negotiated a new contract on May 1, 1972, a Pay Board decision permitting a new control year would have enabled the unit to obtain another 5.5 percent. Thus unionization would have been the only way for a nonunion unit to receive more than 5.5 percent before the expiration of the old control year. For this reason the Pay Board held newly unionized units to their old control years. Of course, the control year could be changed at the discretion of the board on the basis of evidence presented in a gross-inequity appeal.

In certain cases, however, the board's refusal to allow a change in the control year when a unit was organized by a trade union appeared to create an inequity. Industries characterized by multi-employer bargaining often negotiate master contracts signed by the union and a bargaining association designated by the various employers. Individual firms are then bound by the master contract. If a nonunion employer became unionized, he could simply agree to abide by the master contract. A situation in which the nonunion employer could not pay the rate specified in the contract because his 5.5 percent had previously been used up could create a discrepancy in timing. The employer's timing might perpetually lag the timing of the master agreement because of a difference in the control years. The board decided that in the case of a master agreement it would permit a change in the control year. The allowable wage rate increment was to be adjusted to remove any gain to the unit from the change in the control year.[6] This ruling came so late in Phase II that it never appeared officially in the *Federal Register*. Thus there was no opportunity to observe its effect in practice.

Sum-of-the-Percentages Method

From the beginning the Pay Board adopted the sum-of-the-percentages method as its basic rule for measuring wage increases. Under this method all increments during a control year were totaled and measured against the base compensation rate. Thus if a unit with a $3 base received increments of 9 cents on the first day of the new control year (3 percent), 6 cents half way through the year (2 percent), and 1.5 cents beginning on the fourth quarter (0.5 percent), the Pay Board viewed the increase as summing to 5.5 percent (3 percent + 2 percent + 0.5 percent).[7]

Labor members of the board pushed on occasion for time-weighting. It was noted that the amount of money paid out in the hypothetical control year would have been the same if the unit had negotiated a 4.125 percent increment on the first day (3 percent × 1 + 3 percent × 0.5 + 5 percent × 0.25). The board rejected this view on the grounds that it would fail to take account of the higher base that results from a 5.5 percent increase—however timed—for the next control year. The only exception made in board rules was for cost-of-living escalators, which were permitted time-weighting for reasons described in chapter 3.

The Ice Cube Approach

In general the Pay Board prescribed the "ice cube" approach as the proper method of costing. Under this approach increments for the control year were to be costed as if the pattern of hours in the base period were frozen and would remain in effect for the control year. The ice cube approach meant that such factors as changes in overtime hours as a pro-

6. Pay Board press release PB-146, January 5, 1973.

7. It was not clear from the regulations what would have happened if the unit had implemented a "temporary" percentage increase during the year and had repealed it before the base period. A literal reading of the rules would suggest that the temporary increment would not count. No known instances of this type of increase occurred.

portion of total hours or changes in the hours of high-paid employees relative to low-paid workers' hours would not be reflected in the percentage calculation.

The ice cube approach had a solid, pragmatic rationale. If units were allowed to adjust for expected changes in the composition of hours, there might be a temptation to use such adjustments to evade the 5.5 percent standard. It would be difficult for the Pay Board to police the reasonableness of the assumptions underlying such projections.

Despite its simplicity, the ice cube approach had some conceptual problems. Basically a frozen-hour assumption produces conceptual problems analogous to those produced by fixed weights in a price index. An employer might attempt to adjust the composition of his hours in response to changes in their relative price. Thus, for example, if the overtime premium rate is increased, an employer might attempt to cut back on overtime by adding an additional shift. In such a case the ice cube assumption would exaggerate the increase in costs from the increased overtime premium. Substitution effects are being ignored.

In principle the regulations directed the parties to take account of negotiated hours reductions, where pay was not to be reduced proportionately.[8] The forms issued by the board, however, did not provide for the calculation of such adjustments. Thus if a new paid holiday was negotiated, the form asked the employer to estimate the yearly cost and divide by hours worked in the base year. This instruction did not take account of the fact that hours worked in the control year would be reduced by eight. For additional holidays, the error involved was minor. But in cases where hours were a major point in negotiations, the ice cube method had to be modified. For example, as part of a productivity agreement reached on the Long Island Railroad, certain nonproductive hours were ended, and the resulting loss of pay was compensated for through an increase in the hourly rate. In principle such an arrangement would not add to costs. The ice cube method produced a substantial apparent increase, and modified costing had to be applied.[9]

The one area in which the ice cube approach was not used was for merit plans. Since merit budgets are based on expected changes in work force composition, it was felt necessary to permit units to cost their increases on that basis.

8. Section 201.64(b) of the recodified regulations, *Federal Register,* November 23, 1972, p. 24979.
9. See Pay Board staff paper EAD-76, September 20, 1972.

Table A-1. *Roll-up Example*

Item	Base period	New control year	Increment
Straight-time rate	$3.00 an hour	$3.30 an hour	$0.30 an hour
Overtime rate	50% × $3.00 = $1.50	100% × $3.30 = $3.30	100% × $3.30 = $3.30 − 50% × $3.00 = $1.80
Standard workweek	40 hours	40 hours	0
Average overtime hours	5 hours a week	5 hours a week	0
Average hours worked	45 hours a week	45 hours a week	0
Health and welfare contribution	$3.00 a week	$3.00 a week	0
Calculation of percentage increment			
Weekly basis			
Straight-time pay	45 × $3.00 = $135.00	45 × $3.30 = $148.50	$13.50
Overtime pay	5 × $1.50 = $7.50	5 × $3.30 = $16.50	$9.00 direct = $8.25[a] Roll-up = $0.75[b]
Health and welfare contribution	$3.00	$3.00	0
Total	$145.50	$168.00	$22.50
Percent change	...	...	$22.50/$145.50 = 15.5%
Hourly basis (weekly cost/45)			
Straight-time pay	$3.000	$3.300	$0.300
Overtime pay	$0.167	$0.367	$0.200 direct = $0.1833[a] Roll-up = $0.0167[b]
Health and welfare contribution	$0.067	$0.067	0
Total	$3.234	$3.734	$0.500
Percent change	...	...	$0.500/$3.234 = 15.5%

a. (100% − 50%) × $3.30 × 5 = $8.25; $8.25/45 = $0.1833.
b. Roll-up factor = 5.6% = $7.50/$135.00 or $0.167/$3.000; 5.6% × $13.50 = $0.75; 5.6% × $0.300 = $0.0167.

Fringe Benefits: Roll-Up and Creep

For many types of fringe benefits, a change in the hourly wage will produce a proportionate change in benefits. For example, if a worker receives eight hours' pay for a holiday, an increase of 5 percent in the hourly wage will also raise the cost of a holiday by 5 percent. The indirect impact of wage increases on fringe benefits is called roll-up. Since the Pay Board was anxious to measure the total cost of compensation increments, it was important to include roll-up effects in the calculation.

In certain respects the isolation of a roll-up effect caused difficulties for the Pay Board. If the board had simply stuck to the principle that it wanted to compare the new base rate with the old one, roll-up would automatically have been included. An employer asked to estimate what next year's fringe benefits will cost must take account of indirect effects if he is to determine what the total costs will be. But the early Pay Board forms were designed to follow Bureau of Labor Statistics costing methodology, which treated roll-up explicitly. This made roll-up an issue.

The question of roll-up can best be illustrated with a numerical example. Consider a unit in which the average worker earns a straight-time wage of $3. Assume that the standard workweek is set at forty hours, and that the average worker typically works five hours a week overtime at a rate of time-and-a-half for overtime. Finally, assume that the employer contributes a flat $3 a week to a health and welfare fund.

In the base period, then, the total number of hours worked is forty-five. An overtime premium of 50 percent above the straight-time wage ($1.50 = 50 percent $\times$ $3) is paid for five of these hours. Hence on an hourly basis the overtime premium comes to $1.50 $\times$ 5/45 = 16.7 cents. The hourly contribution to the health and welfare fund is $3/45 = 6.7 cents. These figures are summarized in table A-1.[10]

Suppose workers are given an average increase in straight-time wages of 10 percent (or 30 cents), a change to a double-time rate for overtime (an overtime premium of 100 percent or $3), but no change in the flat contribution to the health and welfare fund. The roll-up effect in this

10. The example follows Pay Board concepts but not strict methodology. Table A-1 costs wage and benefit increases as a percentage of a weekly base. Actual Pay Board forms calculated the base wage on the basis of the payroll period immediately preceding the control year and fringe benefits on the basis of the full year before the control year.

example will cover the overtime premium—since overtime pay is based on straight-time pay—but not the health and welfare contribution. One way to look at the result is to say that the 10 percent wage increase caused a roll-up of 1.67 percent in the overtime premium (10 percent × 16.7 cents). To this must be added the direct effect of doubling the overtime premium on a straight-time wage of $3.30, which turns out to be 18.33 cents (100 percent × $3.30 − 50 percent × $3.30 = $1.65 an hour, and $1.65 × 5/45 = 18.33 cents). Thus the total overtime increment on an hourly basis is 20 cents (18.33 cents + 1.67 cents). The total compensation increase is the sum of the straight-time increment (30 cents) plus the fringe increment (20 cents), or 50 cents. The base is $3 + $0.167 + $0.067 = $3.234. Hence the percentage adjustment is 15.5 percent ($0.50/$3.234). If the 1.67 percent of roll-up had been omitted, the measured increment would have come to an underestimated 14.9 percent.

The roll-up effect can be calculated by multiplying the straight-time wage increase by a factor consisting of the ratio of those fringe benefits that vary with straight-time pay to straight-time pay, all at base-period rates. In the example in table A-1 the roll-up factor is 5.56 percent ($0.167/$3).[11] Initially the Pay Board's reporting forms PB-1 and PB-2 required the use of the roll-up factor. To the reader, however, it may well seem more straightforward to have calculated the fringe benefit costs for the new control year directly and to have subtracted the base rate to obtain the increment. In the numerical example the control year cost of overtime was 100 percent × $3.30 − 50 percent × $3, multiplied by 5/45, or 20 cents. When viewed in this way, roll-up is submerged in the overall calculation and does not become an issue. And in fact when the Pay Board issued its revised reporting form PB-3, the direct calculation was used.

As noted earlier, because roll-up was treated explicitly it became an area of negotiation, if not controversy, as in the aerospace cases (see chapter 5). Labor argued that roll-up was not a real part of the increase. Despite the difficulties caused by explicit treatment of the roll-up issue, isolating roll-up had some useful aspects. For example, suppose the board

---

11. The concept of roll-up can be viewed algebraically. Let W_1 be the hourly cost of wages in the base period and W_2 the hourly cost of wages by the end of the control year. Let F_1 and F_2 be the hourly cost of fringe benefits that vary with wages in the base period and end of the control year, respectively. Define $c_1 = F_1/W_1$ and $c_2 = F_2/W_2$. Then $\Delta F = F_2 - F_1 = c_2 W_2 - c_1 W_1 = (c_1 + \Delta c) W_2 - c_1 W_1 = c_1 \Delta W + \Delta c W_2$. The expression $c_1 \Delta W$ is the roll-up effect, and c_1 is the roll-up factor. The direct effect is $\Delta c W_2$.

was attempting to maintain a tandem relationship between the wages of two units, the follower unit being the one shown in the numerical example in table A-1. Suppose further that work in the lead unit happened to involve less overtime, say, two hours a week, than in the follower unit. The result would be a somewhat lower base ($3.134) and roll-up factor (2.38 percent) in the lead unit and therefore a lower percentage adjustment (12.3 percent). Yet if the lead unit were permitted an increase, the board might rule that because of the traditional tandem, the follower unit would be permitted the same adjustment in wages and fringes, despite the higher percentage. Thus separating out roll-up was helpful in analyzing tandem relationships.

The roll-up concept also became useful in the implementation of the working-poor exemption, when the definition of the working poor was raised to $2.75. Under the Pay Board policy the roll-up effect of raising workers to $2.75 was not to be charged against the 5.5 percent wage or 0.7 percent fringe benefit standards. In some cases if roll-up had been charged, the effect might have been sufficient to make employers reluctant to make the adjustment. The indirect effect of raising the wages of the working poor might have exhausted some or all of the money available to higher-paid workers. Thus it was conceivable that the inclusion of a roll-up charge might have invited more litigation on the working-poor issue.

Unlike roll-up, which occurs as the result of a conscious decision of wage setters, "creep" is caused by exogenous factors. Creep refers to the increased cost of maintaining existing benefits. For example, if a hospitalization plan provides specified benefits (such as thirty days in a hospital room) rather than dollar amounts, increased charges for those benefits (such as an increase in the daily cost of a room) will require greater employer contributions.

Under Pay Board rules creep was not to be charged against the allowable increase. Thus in the numerical example in table A-1, if creep required that the health and welfare contribution be raised to $3.50 in the control year, the 50 cent increment would be omitted from the calculation. It would, however, appear in the base for the following control year.

The omission of creep was established as a matter of equity, although creep, of course, is a real cost to employers. With the omission of creep, the board faced the possibility that wage controls might be evaded if creep was deliberately created by underfunding new benefits. (Underfunding would mean that in the next control year, the unit would be in a position to request the money needed to "maintain" existing benefits. Technical language was included in the board's fringe benefit resolution to preclude such underfunding. In principle this should have prevented the use of welfare funds to create artificial creep and blocked the use of such funds for escrow purposes.[12]

Despite the lighter reporting requirements, Category III units did sometimes have to file cases with the Pay Board or the Internal Revenue Service. Indeed most cases received by the wage stabilization authorities were from Category III. In addition, Category III employers in principle needed to be able to fill out a Pay Board reporting form to determine if they were in compliance. It was felt, however, that the board's standard forms might be burdensome on smaller units, which typically had fewer resources to apply to stabilization matters. As a result of this concern, the Pay Board decided to issue a simplified short form (PB-3A) for Category III.

The most complicated aspects of the standard forms were those involving fringe benefits. Smaller units typically put less money in fringe benefits, however, so the obvious shortcut for a simplified form involved approximation of fringe expenditures. Units put at a disadvantage by the short-form approximations could use the standard form. The applicant was required only to estimate the straight-time rate in the base period and then to multiply it by a benefit factor of 1.07. This factor included an allowance for benefits and roll-up for includables. The factor was based on a Bureau of Labor Statistics survey of compensation, but was adjusted upward slightly at the behest of the Teamsters representative.[13] The form did not include a roll-up adjustment for qualified benefits.[14] For QBs the base for calculating the adjustment was multiplied by 1.19, the average ratio of total to straight-time compensation.

12. Attempts were made during Phase II to establish escrow funds for the rolled-back portion of wage increases. Since this would have resulted in identical cost increases to what would have occurred if no rollback had been made, the board refused to permit such funds. The West Cost longshore case led to such an attempt. See also chapter 8 on litigation.

13. Updated staff paper appearing in the "Final Agenda" of the Pay Board, September 27, 1972. Based on national-average data for 1970, the staff calculated a roll-up factor for includable fringe benefits of 11.6 percent. Total fringe benefits (includables and qualified benefits) were 18.8 percent. Hence the benefit factor calculated by the staff was $1.188/1.116 = 1.0645$.

14. It was believed that most Category III units would qualify for the 5 percent rule for QB adjustments. Thus most would be allowed full QBs even if roll-up was included. In any case the PB-3A short form was fairly generous in its assumptions, so that the de facto standards for Category III were somewhat raised.

Unfortunately the short form did not become available until October 1972. This meant that most of the Category III cases filed during Phase II came on the earlier long forms. Hence it is impossible to evaluate the usefulness of the PB-3A form based on extensive experience. But the possibility of simplifying the computation rules for smaller units in a wage control program was demonstrated.

APPENDIX B

Deferred Cases

All adjustments under contracts and pay practices established before Phase II were treated as deferred adjustments under Pay Board regulations. With the exception of a few notable cases, such as bituminous coal, most deferred adjustments considered by the Pay Board were established before Phase I as well. The board moved toward the concept of a 7 percent de facto standard for deferred adjustments. This did not become official until after the labor members' walkout. During its "all-public" stage, the Pay Board challenged only those deferred increases that were above 7 percent. Challenges could be made by two board members, or the chairman, or a "party at interest," which was always the employer.[1] Category III deferred adjustments were challenged only if they were sought out by the board or if the board received a party-at-interest challenge, since Category III did not have to report deferred adjustments. After the board tightened its rules for reporting such adjustments, all deferred increases above 7 percent had to be prereported in categories I and II. Lesser increases could be postreported in Category II but in Category I had to be prereported, as did new increases.

Until June 1972 the Pay Board did not find time to hear any deferred cases. A number of increases had been challenged, but these simply waited in the board's backlog. Increases under most of these contracts had gone into effect, although in a few cases employers refused to pay the scheduled increase until the Pay Board heard the cases.[2] In general when the control year was almost over, the board was reluctant to make a cutback. So it is not surprising that for its first deferred case, the Philadelphia meatcutters, the board chose one in which the increment was fairly recent. In addi-

1. The state of New York attempted to challenge a wage increase of a private nursing home association on the grounds that the increase would affect the fees charged to state-subsidized patients. But the board did not accept the state as a party at interest. The issue was moot since the increase had already been challenged.

2. In the nursing home case cited in note 1, the employer refused to put more than 5.5 percent of the deferred increase into effect before the Pay Board's decision. While this was perfectly legitimate under Pay Board regulations, it may have been a breach of contract. In a similar case a court held that employers were obligated by their contracts unless Pay Board rules specifically enjoined payment. See Bureau of National Affairs, Inc., *Daily Labor Report,* October 3, 1972, pp. A-11–A-13.

tion, retail food was known to be an area of pressure generated by the size of deferred wage increases.

The Philadelphia meatcutters' case involved three Category II units organized by the Amalgamated Meat Cutters and Butcher Workmen of North America. Three major food chains were involved in a contract negotiated in 1971, and smaller units were known to be following the big chains in tandem. The scheduled increases for March 1972 averaged about 11 percent in wages. As in the case of many deferred adjustments, no qualified-benefit improvements were involved. Thus if the board decided there were no grounds for special consideration, the units would be rolled back to a flat 7 percent.[3]

Although the case resulted from a board challenge rather than from one by a party at interest, the employers were not especially anxious to make a case for their scheduled increase. Much of the union's arguments centered on productivity improvements that allegedly had resulted from a change in the handling procedures for bonus cuts of meat. The employers argued that they did not believe that productivity was much improved, and in any case that they had no estimates available. This debate led the Pay Board to request productivity data from the employers. The data were inconclusive (see appendix C), and the board became ensnarled in the question of whether the data had to be kept confidential from the union.[4]

In the end the board found no reason to deviate from the de facto 7 percent standard for deferred wage increases. The meatcutters' increase was appropriately reduced, and the staff was instructed to challenge tandems in the Philadelphia area. Having set a pattern of toughness in dealing with retail food deferred cases, the board continued to pursue similar cases in other cities.

One of the issues raised by the deferred adjustment challenge procedure was the possibility of windfall profits to employers. Price Commission rules permitted the pass-through of deferred adjustment costs. Thus if the Pay Board acted after a deferred increase had already gone into effect, prices might well have been advanced to cover the additional costs. The issue had surfaced before the Pay Board began active consideration of deferred adjustments. The Construction Industry Stabilization Committee had requested the Price Commission to adopt rules requiring the

3. Pay Board staff paper EPCA-EAD, Micro 59, June 2, 1972.
4. The board decided that since the confidential data had not figured in the decision, there was no reason to show it to the union. The union angrily denounced this decision. See BNA, *Daily Labor Report,* July 12, 1972, pp. A-7–A-10.

renegotiation of construction contracts based on wages subject to a roll-back.[5] The degree to which the rules were enforced is questionable, given the structure of the construction industry. In any case the windfall would simply be passed to whoever commissioned the construction project. But as in other aspects of the stabilization program, a symbolic interest was involved.

In order to display its concern with windfall profits, the Pay Board decided to combine the announcement of a deferred cutback in the New York City printers' case with a simultaneous announcement of a price rollback. The Pay Board and the Price Commission issued a joint press release detailing the wage and price adjustments affecting newspaper and commercial printers.[6] In principle the Price Commission received a list of all Pay Board rollbacks in categories I and II and therefore should have been alerted to any potential profit windfalls. But except in major cases, the Price Commission relied on reports that employers would eventually file to ensure compliance rather than seeking out possible violations in advance.

When a deferred increase was cut, the board generally asked the staff to locate potential tandems for challenge. A delicate situation arose in the case of a deferred adjustment under the Teamsters National Master Freight Agreement. From the earliest days of Phase II the Teamsters contract was known to have large adjustments scheduled for 1972. The board's concept of a short control year had the effect of dividing the 1972 adjustments into two parts. In the second control year, it was determined that a reduction of 5 cents in the scheduled adjustment would bring the percentage increment down to 7 percent. The board felt that it had to take action in the Teamsters case to avoid charges of favoritism to the one union whose representative on the board had not walked out in March 1972. But a prolonged process of finding the many Category III tandems would be required, so that those under smaller contracts would continue to receive the errant nickel for some time after the main contract had been cut. To deal with this dilemma, the board decided that the 5 cents would be removed from the base and subtracted from the allowable adjustment for the *next* control year in 1973, when a new contract was to be negotiated. The onset of Phase III, however, rendered moot the Pay Board's judgment on the Teamsters' nickel.[7]

5. Ibid., June 14, 1972, p. A-16.
6. Pay Board press release PB-142, November 14, 1972.
7. BNA, *Daily Labor Report*, December 26, 1972, p. A-12.

Implementation of Exceptions for New Cases

This appendix describes in detail the implementation of the Pay Board's catch-up, tandem, essential-employees, and gross-inequity exceptions to the 5.5 percent standard. A general discussion of the board's motivation in establishing these exceptions appears in chapter 3.

Catch-Up

Catch-up was the major exception under Pay Board rules that could be self-executed.[1] That is, Category II and Category III applicants could apply the formula themselves and implement whatever it implied up to 7 percent without awaiting board approval. (Category I units had to await approval for all new adjustments.) Catch-up was made self-executing because it involved the implementation of a mechanical formula, and therefore no discretion was possible. As in other Pay Board matters, however, it took awhile before the exact nature of the formula was clear.

The basic principle the board wished to implement was that if applicants had received less than 7 percent a year during the previous contract (union cases) or past three years (nonunion cases), they could be made whole for this shortfall up to a 7 percent limit in the current year. This principle can best be illustrated by a formula. Consider a case with a three-year catch-up period. Suppose the current year is denoted by subscript "o" and previous years by subscripts -1, -2, -3. The wage in the base period, w_o, can be expressed as

(1) $$w_o = w_{-3}(1 + r_{-3})(1 + r_{-2})(1 + r_{-1}),$$

where w_{-3} is the wage three years ago and r_{-1}, r_{-2}, and r_{-3} are the percentage increases (expressed as decimal fractions) that occurred over the years denoted by the subscripts. The Pay Board wished applicants to be eligible for the *lesser of* 7 percent, or

(2) $$w_{-3}(1.07)^3 - w_{-3}(1 + r_{-3})(1 + r_{-2})(1 + r_{-1}).$$

1. Section 201.15 of the recodified regulations, *Federal Register*, November 23, 1972, pp. 24963–64.

After substituting equation 1 into expression 2, the latter can be rewritten:

$$(3) \qquad w_o \left[\frac{(1.07)^3}{(1 + r_{-3})(1 + r_{-2})(1 + r_{-1})} - 1 \right].$$

Expression 3 would have been difficult to implement in practice because of its seeming complexity. Moreover, some of the Pay Board case analysts and the reporting public were confused about the use of compound formulas. So a formula was worked out that approximated that expression. Applicants simply multiplied 7 percent by the number of years in their catch-up period and subtracted the simple sum of the annual percentage increases actually received. The resulting percentage was then multiplied by the base period wage, w_o. In a three-year case, the formula would be (21 percent $- r_{-3} - r_{-2} - r_{-1})w_o$. It is easy to verify that the discrepancy between expression 3 and the multiplication factor will be relatively slight. For example, if $r_{-3} = 6.5$ percent, $r_{-2} = 6.7$ percent, and $r_{-1} = 7.0$ percent, the simple formula yields 0.8 percent $\times w_o$, while expression 3 yields 0.75 percent $\times w_o$. If $w_o = \$4$, the difference between the two formulas is two-tenths of a cent.

The percentage increase during the catch-up period was calculated from the increment in the average wage in the unit, with no compensating adjustments for changes in the employment pattern of the unit. That is, the methodology essentially followed the "double-snapshot" approach used for merit increases rather than the more general "ice cube" approach. This deviation was basically an accommodation to employers whose records of earlier compensation expenditures might not permit adjustment to some fixed pattern of hours.

The congressional mandate for special treatment of qualified fringe benefits required some adjustment of the catch-up rule. Qualified benefits were removed from the calculation of eligibility for wage catch-up. This would generally increase eligibility for catch-up, since qualified fringe benefit expenditures generally rose faster than expenditures on wages and other benefits during the period preceding Phase II. The base pay rate by which the catch-up percentage was multiplied included qualified fringe benefits.

A catch-up exception was also permitted separately for qualified fringe benefits, in cases where QBs had not increased by 0.5 percent a year (relative to the total compensation base) during the previous three years (nonunion) or contract (union).[2] The formula was basically the same as that

2. Section 201.59(g), ibid., p. 24976.

used for ordinary catch-up, except that the base rates used for calculating catch-up eligibility included QBs. QB catch-up was capped at 1.5 percent above the basic 0.7 percent QB standard, just as wage catch-up was capped at 1.5 percent above the 5.5 percent wage standard. The application of the identical cap to the two exceptions emphasizes the generous nature of QB catch-up relative to wage catch-up, since QBs were a relatively small proportion of the base compared to wages.

The more generous attitude toward QB catch-up relative to wage catch-up can also be seen in the succession of Pay Board policies in this area. Wage catch-up had a finite deadline that was extended twice but that eventually became effective. Moreover, when the deadline was ultimately extended to November 13, 1972, wage catch-up was limited to units with straight-time wages of $3 an hour or less. QB catch-up was never confined to low-wage units. In addition, unused wage catch-up eligibility could not be passed from control year to control year. It was either used when the opportunity arose or not at all. But QB catch-up could be passed to a second control year if it was not used up in the first.

Tandems

As noted in chapter 3, one of the earliest exceptions to the 5.5 percent standard was for tandem relationships.[3] Related tandem exceptions were provided for certain retroactive situations (increases during the freeze) and for qualified benefits. The basic tandem exception for new adjustments during Phase II contained three key provisions. It had to be shown that (1) a clear leader-follower pattern existed within an industry or a local labor market; (2) that the leader-follower pattern had existed for five years in nonunion situations or two immediately preceding contracts in union situations; and (3) that the follower contract or pay practice (later follower wage increase) lagged the leader by no more than six months.

If these provisions were met, an exception of an additional 1.5 percent was allowed—that is, a total of 7 percent. Unlike catch-up, the tandem exception was not self-executing. The applicant had to file with either the Internal Revenue Service or the Pay Board for permission to implement it. In principle if the applicant requested more than the maximum 7 percent, a gross-inequity claim had to be submitted to the Pay Board. For

3. Section 201.13, ibid., pp. 24962–63.

Table C-1. *Tandem Illustration*

Leader	Follower
Contract dates	
Effective August 1, 1966	December 1, 1966
Expiration, July 31, 1969	November 30, 1969
Effective August 1, 1969	December 1, 1969
Expiration, July 31, 1971	November 30, 1971
Effective August 1, 1971	December 1, 1971[a]
Expiration, July 31, 1973	November 30, 1973[a]
Straight-time wage increase	
1966 15¢ (August 1)	15¢ (December 1)
1967 10¢ (August 1)	10¢ (December 1)
1968 10¢ (August 1)	10¢ (December 1)
1969 30¢ (August 1)	30¢ (December 1)
1970 25¢ (August 1)	25¢ (December 1)
1971 40¢ (August 1)	40¢ (December 1)[a]
1972 30¢ (August 1)	30¢ (December 1)[b]

a. Proposed.
b. Second year.

convenience, this section considers all tandem claims, not just those meeting the 7 percent cap.

A typical staff presentation on tandems is illustrated in table C-1. The example shown is idealized, since the follower and leader units exhibit an exact timing and wage increase relationship. In many actual tandems, small deviations occurred. For example, if the follower unit experienced a long delay in reaching an agreement because of a strike over local issues, it might have set the effective date of one of its contracts somewhat later than the lockstep December 1 shown. If the starting date for the 1969 agreement in the follower unit had been, say, December 15, the board would probably have gone along with the tandem. Similarly if 2 cents of the 30 cent increase in 1969 had been diverted to prop up a financially precarious pension fund, the board would most likely have overlooked the discrepancy. And of course, the board would accept tandems based on percentage wage changes or differentials as well as the cents-per-hour type in the illustration.

The board was initially concerned with tandems of the type in table C-1 that bridged the start of wage controls. In the illustration the leader unit reached agreement before Phase I began. But the follower unit, because of its traditional four-month lag, did not negotiate a new contract until Phase II. A number of cases of this type arose in the steel industry, where the basic steel agreement was signed on August 1, 1971. Pay Board approvals for new union cases in primary metals averaged over 9 percent during Phase II in categories I and II, a reflection of both the steel and nonferrous pre–Phase I agreements. No cutbacks in these cases are recorded, although some of the approvals were well above the 7 percent tandem cap. Thus where the Pay Board saw strict tandems with prefreeze agreements, it almost always approved them, even if more than 7 percent was involved.[4]

A second type of tandem relationship resulted from board decisions during Phase II. In some cases where tandems were based on cents-per-hour increments, the basic 5.5 percent in a high-wage unit would lead to tandem claims by other units. For example, in the case of Northwest lumbermen, the base compensation rate was highest in the key unit. Once the board rolled that unit back to 5.5 percent, it had to grant exceptions to lower-base units, allowing them to implement the same absolute wage adjustment.[5] The same principle, of course, applied when the board granted an exception above 5.5 percent to the lead unit. In the case of East Coast longshoremen, for example, the 55 cent increase plus fringe benefits granted to the northeastern ports translated into a 9.8 percent increase. But the same package for the Texas gulf ports and for the port of New Orleans resulted in 11.4 percent and 12 percent, respectively.[6]

When significant cases came to the board, the staff made an effort to locate potential tandems. Thus in the case of West Coast longshoremen the board knew that it would eventually have to grant comparable increases to dock "walking bosses" (supervisors) who are paid a percentage markup above what the longshoremen receive.[7] Similarly, it was known that smaller employers on the docks who were not members of the Pacific Maritime Association also would eventually be filing cases. In such in-

4. A well-publicized example was the New York Telephone case in which the board approved a 16.8 percent increase covering 38,600 workers on the basis of a tandem with a prefreeze national telephone agreement. The New York workers had held out for many months until finally accepting a contract the board considered comparable to the national settlement. See Pay Board press release PB-67, March 31, 1972. (The release misstated the percentage increase by omitting certain fringe benefits.)

5. Bureau of National Affairs, Inc., *Daily Labor Report,* October 31, 1972, pp. A-8–A-9.

6. Pay Board press release PB-85, May 8, 1972.

7. Pay Board staff papers EPCA-EAD, Micro 12, n.d.; and EPCA-EAD, Micro 47, May 15, 1972.

stances, after the decision for the lead contract, the board would often permit the staff or the Internal Revenue Service to approve tandem claims above 7 percent.[8]

It is common practice in collective bargaining for the parties to point to wages received by allegedly comparable units elsewhere in support of their positions. Thus there is nothing surprising in the remarkable ability some applicants showed in finding what they claimed were tandems. In general all wages rise over time, and if the definition of tandem is stretched sufficiently, all wages might appear to show some interrelationship. The board, however, had its limits. In a group of cases involving New York City public employees, for example, claims were made of a tandem relationship to a social services contract that had been concluded just before the freeze.[9] After careful study, no close relationship could be found in terms of timing or increments between the prefreeze contract and the others.

The board was also concerned about what might be called destabilizing tandems. In some instances if two units watch each other, a leapfrogging mechanism can be set in motion. Thus the board attempted to coordinate its decisions regarding Washington and Baltimore food store employees, a few of whom actually worked side-by-side in common warehouses. The board was mindful of the need to avoid disruption of the wage structure relationship between the two localities.[10] Similar attempts were made in cases involving nursing homes in the New York City metropolitan area.[11]

Essential Employees

As noted in chapter 3, the essential-employees criteria for an exception were rarely met. An employer had to demonstrate that wage increases were necessary for recruiting or retaining essential workers, that there had been an extensive recruiting effort for three months, that nonwage conditions of work had not deteriorated, and that the increases proposed could be reasonably expected to relieve the labor shortage.[12]

While few applicants attempted to track the language exactly, some

8. For example, in the Northwest lumber case, the board delegated authority over tandems to the IRS.

9. Pay Board staff report on the New York City cases, final submission, June 27, 1972, p. 21.

10. Pay Board staff paper OCE-DCEP, Micro 189, December 7, 1972.

11. Ibid., EPCA-EAD, Micro 26, April 20, 1972.

12. Section 201.14, *Federal Register,* November 23, 1972, p. 24963.

did attempt to convince the board that a labor shortage existed. The owner of a small soft drink bottling plant cited the failure of a help-wanted advertising campaign for truck drivers as part of an argument involving many other factors as well. The final decision, however, stressed the other factors.[13] In another case a small New Jersey township was granted a 7 percent increase after producing some evidence on turnover among laborers, even though the applicant did not strictly meet the eligibility criteria.[14] Labor shortages were also cited in a case involving a ladies' underwear manufacturer and in another involving medical personnel. In the latter case the applicant produced letters rejecting offers of employment as evidence of a shortage.[15] In still another case, an employer cited Department of Labor permission to hire aliens as proof of a shortage.[16]

Often, however, it was hard to distinguish between claims made on the basis of alleged prevailing wages in a locality and labor shortage claims. Some cases seized on the labor shortage issue without much concern for cogency. A unit of barbers, for example, said that reduced demand for their services due to long hair styles had driven so many of them out of the field that a shortage had developed. The accompanying Pay Board staff paper noted that, as expected, there were in fact symptoms of a surplus.[17]

Gross Inequities

As already noted, exception requests that had aspects of the formula exceptions but deviated in one way or another from the exact wording of the eligibility qualifications had to file gross-inequity claims.[18] This procedure also applied to units that met the qualifications of the formula exceptions but that wanted more than 7 percent. Thus the formula exceptions played a role in suggesting the type of gross-inequity claims to which the board might be receptive. The Pay Board also could use the

13. Pay Board staff paper EAD-42, June 19, 1972.
14. Ibid.
15. Ibid., EPCA-EAD, Micro 27, April 24, 1972; and EPCA-EAD, Micro 313, September 18, 1972.
16. Ibid., EPCA-EAD, Micro 142, September 27, 1972.
17. Ibid., EPCA-EAD, Micro 158, October 30, 1972.
18. Section 201.30, *Federal Register,* November 23, 1972, p. 24966. Gross-inequity exceptions were often referred to as 201.11(d) exceptions owing to the original numbering of the relevant section of the regulations before recodification.

gross-inequity provision of the regulations to grant exceptions for circumstances not suggested by the formula exceptions.

The gross-inequity section of the regulations stated that the Pay Board would *consider* case-by-case exceptions on grounds of "changes in productivity and cost of living, ongoing collective bargaining and pay practices, the equitable position of the employees involved, and such other factors as are necessary to foster economic growth, to promote improvement in the quality of governmental services, and to prevent gross inequities, hardships, serious market disruptions, domestic shortages of raw materials, localized shortages of labor, and windfall profits."[19] This language was obviously broad. For that reason most applicants' arguments for gross-inequity exceptions were taken seriously by the staff. Even if the board had not acted favorably on similar claims in the past, the staff felt obliged to analyze the submissions received more or less at face value.

Productivity claims were common grounds for exception requests. The Percy amendment (see chapter 3) required the board to grant special treatment to productivity incentive plans. But it was silent on individual instances of work rule bargaining. The board usually looked favorably on work rule bargaining in instances where it had genuinely taken place. Many claims simply pointed to general gains in productivity resulting from new technology and investment. The board felt that its basic 5.5 percent standard had taken account of national productivity trends and that deviations for industry differences would not have been sound policy or labor market theory. Genuine work rule bargaining could occur only when a union had over the past acquired a contractual ability to restrict new technology or to limit the cost savings accruing from technical innovation through such devices as manning requirements, output limitation, or other work practices. In some cases a union would claim to have "let" management install some new machine or technique. But a history of passive acquiescence to management prerogatives was not sufficient justification for an exception.

Sometimes productivity claims were made without supporting data. The Pay Board staff would then attempt to obtain the necessary information, finding that meaningful data were not always available. Productivity was often cited in retail food store claims, but the only measure of output available was dollar sales. The staff would attempt to deflate sales by some type of food price index. But the difference between the weights in the price index and the composition of sales in a given market made the procedure dubious. The board was often skeptical of food store produc-

19. Ibid.

tivity claims. After productivity data turned out to be not very helpful in one precedent-setting case, the Philadelphia meatcutters, the board decided not to consider it.[20] The question then was whether the union would be allowed to see the confidential employer data. Thus the board soon had two reasons to discount productivity arguments in the industry: such arguments embroiled the board in the side issue of confidentiality, and the data were so poor that it was difficult to believe that either side had any basis for serious productivity bargaining other than good intentions.

The buy-out provisions for work rules could sometimes raise conceptual problems for the board. In one case the Long Island Railroad bought out some restrictive work rules from the United Transportation Union and the Locomotive Engineers with a lump-sum payment. If the board had followed normal procedures, the lump-sum payment would have appeared as a large percentage increase in the base compensation rate. The resulting percentage increase, however, would not have reflected the change in marginal labor costs. Moreover, if the Pay Board had put the lump-sum in the base and approved it, the second-year increment relative to the base would have been greatly reduced. In this instance the board decided to look at the lump-sum separately from the rest of the increase.[21]

References to the cost of living in particular locales were sometimes included in case presentations. Usually the argument was that because the cost of living in an area was high in absolute terms, wages ought to be increased.[22] Budget surveys of the Bureau of Labor Statistics were generally cited. Little weight was given to this argument, and the board made no judgment about how high someone's real wage ought to be. Hence absolute differentials in the cost of living had no relevance to a board that dealt with rates of increase in wages. Of course, the board did recognize *changes* in the cost of living through its preferential computation rules regarding escalators, and the parties to a contract could take special note of the local rate of inflation by using the local rather than the national consumer price index in their escalators.

As time passed, the degree to which the board would accept special arguments for exceptions to the 5.5 percent standard became more limited. The primary function of the gross-inequity exception was to serve as a bridge during the transition from an uncontrolled labor market to Phase II. Tandems to contracts negotiated just before the freeze became

20. Pay Board staff paper EPCA-EAD, Micro 59, June 2, 1972.
21. Ibid., EPCA-EAD, Micro 55, August 9, 1972.
22. A cost-of-living claim was made in the New York City cases.

less common as the controls program was extended. Inequities caused by the sudden freeze were corrected. Exceptions to the 5.5 percent standard began to be denied with greater frequency. A number of major supermarket wage increases were cut to 5.5 percent, as was the increase for Northwest lumbermen. QBs, however, generally were treated more liberally than wages throughout the program.

At the Category III level greater leniency was shown in the disposition of exception requests. The handling of the large number of small-unit cases filed with the Internal Revenue Service was a definite weak spot in the Phase II administrative structure. Category III applicants suffered long delays if they wished to appeal IRS decisions to the Pay Board.[23] The Category III Panel attempted to cut the backlog by providing quick but rough justice in considering cases, which frequently were poorly prepared by the applicants. Incomplete and improperly costed submissions were common. Small employers were not always anxious to apply for exceptions; they did so in compliance with obligations under a union agreement. Even where the union prepared the basic case, it was not necessarily equipped to deal with a federal regulatory agency.

In compensation for the limited information accompanying Category III cases, the panel developed an uncanny eye for seeing tandem relationships. In other words, it filled in the gap in the applicants' submissions. But since data were often limited, it was not possible to fashion complex remedies. "Seven percent plus QBs" became the standard reaction to cases that seemed to have some merit. Seven percent was the figure the board used for formula exceptions. QBs were allowed because the board rarely cut them back when it heard cases. Consider, for example, the case of eight rabbis who supervised the kosher slaughtering operations at a meat-packing plant in Iowa. It was argued that they suffered a hardship from having to maintain their families in Chicago and commute on weekends because of the absence of an Orthodox synagogue near the plant. In addition, their equitable position had been disrupted because the national union insisted on merging their local with others in the plant, thus delaying their negotiations from the prefreeze period to Phase II. When the case arrived from the IRS, it did not seem possible to convert their proposed complex piece rates accurately into a percentage adjustment. But the remedy was simple: 7 percent plus QBs.

23. The mean waiting time for a sample of Category III cases processed during Phase II between application to the IRS and a decision by the Pay Board was 204 days. See chapter 7.

The Special Sectors: Government Workers and Nonunion Construction Workers

Two sectors of the labor force were singled out for special treatment by the wage control authorities: government workers and nonunion construction workers. The development of these special policies is described below.

The Special Problems of Government Employees

State and local government workers were exempted from earlier wartime wage control programs. Hence their inclusion under controls in 1971 was a new experience for them as well as for the controllers. Problems in the government sector—especially those relating to teachers—had involved controversy and litigation during Phase I.[1] There was no reason to expect the situation to be different during Phase II. To help deal with the government sector, the Phase II administrative framework included a Committee on State and Local Government Cooperation. The committee was composed of state and local government officials and former officials, plus representatives of employee associations and the public.

As might have been expected, the committee often assumed the role of a pressure group for local government interests rather than that of a stabilization agency, and it originally pushed for a special Pay Board for the government sector.[2] The Pay Board asked the committee to confine its suggestions to specific ways in which regulations should be modified to take account of the special problems of the government sector. The committee's response was forwarded to the board on March 31, 1972.[3] Much

1. See Arnold R. Weber, *In Pursuit of Price Stability: The Wage-Price Freeze of 1971* (Brookings Institution, 1973), pp. 96–97.
2. Bureau of National Affairs, Inc., *Daily Labor Report,* December 9, 1971, pp. AA-5–AA-6. This suggestion was echoed by the National Governor's Conference. See ibid., February 24, 1972, p. A-12.
3. The response appeared in Pay Board, "Agenda and Policy Papers" (April 12, 1972; processed).

of what was recommended was eventually adopted; the most noteworthy suggestions involved the treatment of state-mandated minimum salary increases and of officials whose salaries were frozen during their terms of office by state or local law. But the board was unwilling to permit gross-inequity exceptions for government employees that would let them "reach a reasonable pay level in relation to comparable employee groups in the same market area." This committee recommendation smacked of the wage comparability exception that the labor members had urged earlier and that the board had rejected.

The most obvious characteristic of the state and local sector is the political considerations that play on it. Cases involving government employees often became the concern of members of Congress. In addition, the state and local officials involved had ready access to the public ear. Early in the program, state and local government units were given special status not provided for private-sector units, despite Pay Board reservations. Category I and Category II units in the government sector were exempted from the regular reporting rules, provided they certified compliance with the Pay Board's basic standards.[4]

Aside from exercises in special pleading, government workers did have some unique concerns. First, their wages were often set by legislative bodies. This meant that in case of a rollback, it might be difficult to establish new schedules unless the legislative body happened to be in session. To reduce this problem, the board deviated from its usual posture and agreed to provide advisory opinions on proposed government increases in units with populations in excess of 100,000.[5] Second, different levels of government interacted in establishing pay schedules. Sometimes state governments set minimum scales for local government workers. There were even instances of federal involvement in setting local salaries. In addition, where collective bargaining was involved, dispute-settling procedures were often slow to operate. Of course, this condition was not unique to government employees. Areas in the private sector—especially those having emergency machinery to handle disputes—presented the same difficulties. The railroads are an obvious example. Slow-moving

4. Cost of Living Council press release, December 23, 1971. The CLC asked the board for its opinion on the issue. The board apparently did not take up the question, but its executive secretary sent a letter in reply, stating that no reason could be seen for preferential treatment of the public sector.

5. Pay Board press release PB-108, July 18, 1972.

dispute-settling machinery meant that such cases often became entangled in the complex retroactivity rules of the board (see chapter 2).[6]

Certain issues pertinent to government employees were technical questions affecting a small number of workers. Generally, unique circumstances in the public sector, as in the private, were handled on a case-by-case basis through gross-inequity claims. In one type of situation, however, the board did establish a general rule. Certain government officials were barred from receiving wage increases during their terms of office. Their wages were frozen until a new term began, a period that might run four years. Those whose new terms had begun in Phase II might have suffered an inequity had they been allowed only 5.5 percent. The board permitted such officials to receive 5.5 percent times the number of years their salaries had been frozen.[7]

The first major government workers' case to come before the Pay Board involved 56,000 employees of the state of Ohio. The requested increment was calculated at 10.6 percent by the Pay Board staff.[8] Under Pay Board regulations the employees were eligible for 7 percent under the catch-up exception. When the board decided that only 7 percent should be granted, it was faced with a dilemma. It could not order the Ohio legislature back into session to establish a new pay schedule. To handle this situation, the board relied on a creative use of time-weighting. It calculated the amount of money that would have been paid if Ohio had implemented a 7 percent increase on the first day of its control year. The board then permitted Ohio to implement the scheduled 10.6 percent adjustment but delayed the implementation sufficiently into the control year so that the amount of money paid out would be equivalent to the allowable 7 percent. It forbade the 10.6 percent increase to be cited as a tandem by other units and subtracted the overage above 7 percent from the increment to be allowed for the second control year.[9] The time-weighting solution was later applied to other cases in similar circumstances.

6. For example, in the New York City cases some of the proposed contracts were retroactive to January 1971.

7. Pay Board press release PB-108.

8. The staff experienced considerable difficulty in obtaining data from state officials that was consistent with Pay Board regulations.

9. Pay Board press release PB-57, March 6, 1972. Unfortunately the Pay Board staff had been instructing the Internal Revenue Service on the evils of time-weighting as a costing technique at the time of the Ohio decision. It was difficult to explain the difference between a costing technique and an exceptions technique.

The issue of state-mandated salary minima first arose in another Ohio case, this one involving schoolteachers. At the time Phase II operated, twenty-nine states had laws designating minimum salary scales for employees of local educational systems. Thirty-two states had similar laws for noneducational civil servants.[10] Typically, these laws affected only some low-paying jurisdictions, which were generally nonunion. When the minima were raised, the result was increases in low-paying areas but possibly a zero effect in higher-paying jurisdictions.

One solution would have been for the Pay Board to treat each jurisdiction separately. But problems would have arisen for two main reasons. Smaller jurisdictions would have been exempt from the stabilization program because of the small-business exemption. Hence inequities would have been created between small and large jurisdictions. (A similar problem in the private sector resulted from the operation of state and local minimum wage laws. The minimum wage issue was rendered moot, however, by defining the working poor as those receiving $2.75 an hour or less.) In addition, jurisdictions subject to a rollback from state-mandated levels would have been out of compliance with state law. They therefore might have lost state financial aid.

In the case of the Ohio schoolteachers the board permitted each district a maximum of 5.5 percent or the increment needed to comply with the state mandate, whichever was greater.[11] This solution was not entirely satisfactory. Jurisdictions with some teachers below the new minimum and some above might use up all or most of their 5.5 percent raising the wages of the low paid. This would create compression, since little or nothing would be left for increases to other employees.

On the advice of the Committee on State and Local Government Cooperation, and after its own deliberations, the board asked the Cost of Living Council to require prenotification of changes in state mandates.[12] This would prevent forced implementation of such mandates from affecting small jurisdictions otherwise exempted from the program. At its meeting of August 31, 1972, the CLC complied with the board's request. The board at the time was already in the midst of a case involving a mandated increase averaging 9.5 percent for 55,000 Georgia teachers. The increase was cut back to 5.5 percent.

10. Pay Board staff paper, July 5, 1972, in "Agenda and Policy Papers," July 12–13, 1972.
11. Pay Board press release PB-70, April 7, 1972.
12. Cost of Living Council, "Agenda and Policy Papers," August 31, 1972.

A variation on mandating occurred in the case of local police officers in Kentucky. In 1972 the Kentucky state legislature established a fund for the purpose of upgrading local police salaries. The fund subsidized local salaries in order to bring them up to a mandated level. Fifty percent of the expenses were borne by the federal government under the terms of the Omnibus Crime Control and Safe Streets Act of 1968. Increases in salary of up to 15 percent were proposed, and these would come on top of locally scheduled increases. Thus the Pay Board was faced with above-standard wage hikes under terms of a state mandate resulting from a federal anticrime program.[13] The board decided to hold the individual police units to 5.5 percent for each of the two control years under consideration. Above that amount, those police officers earning less than the median rate of compensation would be entitled to an extra 5.5 percent. Thus the board emphasized the 5.5 percent standard, while still permitting upgrading of the lower paid.[14]

Although most government workers covered by the Pay Board's controls were at the state and local level, some federal employees were also encompassed by the controls program. Ordinary federal civil servants were not covered, but workers in federally chartered enterprises were. A number of Federal Reserve Bank employee units fell into Category II and filed reports with the board. Their increases were all within the basic standard. A slight cutback was ordered for certain employees of the Tennessee Valley Authority. In one instance Congress requested an advisory opinion from the Pay Board on a proposed increase for District of Columbia police, although the police were not subject to controls.[15] The largest single group of federal employees, however, was in the Postal Service. As it happened, the union sector of the post office (600,000 workers) was not scheduled for negotiations during Phase II, and the deferred adjustments reported were within the Pay Board's de facto 7 percent standard. On the other hand, an increase of 15.4 percent covering 77,000 nonunion postal supervisors was cut back to 10.3 percent.

Dealing with Nonunion Construction

The Construction Industry Stabilization Committee, which preceded Phase I by several months, was originally created only for the union sec-

13. Pay Board staff paper OCE-DCEP, Micro 140, December 20, 1972.
14. Minutes of the Pay Board, January 3, 1973.
15. Pay Board staff paper EPCA-EAD, Micro 42, May 3, 1972.

tor of the construction industry. It was natural to assume that wage pressure in construction was a product of collective bargaining. Nonunion construction came under the stabilization program only because the nonunion sector of the rest of the economy was to be covered. The result was a peculiar split in jurisdiction, with the CISC handling union construction and the Pay Board handling the nonunion segment of the industry.

Conflict between the CISC and the Pay Board was inevitable for a variety of reasons. Most of these revolved around the handling of union cases by the CISC and the degree to which the Pay Board monitored those decisions. Nonunion construction policy was not the major issue. But because some coordination between union and nonunion construction policy was obviously necessary, policy concerning nonunion workers provided a forum in which the board and the CISC could establish an uneasy truce.

At first the CISC was uninterested in having jurisdiction over nonunion construction. Later it expressed some interest, but nonunion contractors were adamantly opposed to having their wage adjustments reviewed by a panel representing union interests. This fact, plus the interest of the Pay Board in using the nonunion issue to provide an incentive for CISC cooperation, made it certain that nonunion construction cases would be handled by the Pay Board.

The CISC approach to the union sector was basically structural and consisted of restoring traditional wage differentials between crafts in an effort to avoid competitive leapfrogging. This approach meant that the CISC did not apply a percentage guideline, such as the Pay Board's 5.5 percent. Instead, it concentrated on absolute wage differentials. In some instances, as the CISC pointed out, it had required increases of less than 5.5 percent, even zero. Although the Pay Board stated in its recodified regulations that less than 5.5 percent might be approved in some cases, this was aimed mainly at legitimizing the CISC approach.[16] The board itself took 5.5 percent as the minimum for approval.

The CISC expressed concern that if normal Pay Board regulations were applied to nonunion construction cases, it was possible that nonunion wages might exceed union wages. The possibility of this occurring was remote, since segments of nonunion construction had been expanding

16. Section 201.10(c), *Federal Register,* November 23, 1972, p. 24962. A similar provision was incorporated in the regulations for nonunion construction (sec. 201.84(c), p. 24988).

because of their lower labor costs.[17] Of course, it was conceivable that a nonunion contractor might pay more if facing a local labor shortage or perhaps to avoid unionization. The nonunion contractors could still retain a competitive advantage over union contractors because of the greater flexibility they enjoyed in deploying their work force. Ironically, the CISC expressed some concern that nonunion wages would become too high and lure away union craftsmen.

From the Pay Board's viewpoint it was important to maintain some aspects of the 5.5 percent standard in relation to nonunion construction wages, for work load reasons if nothing else. Nonunion construction was basically a Category III industry by conventional Pay Board definitions. Since union construction units of whatever size had to report their increases to the CISC, a similar reporting rule was applied to nonunion construction. The nonunion cases at the Pay Board initially were treated as if they were in Category I; they went directly to the board, not the Internal Revenue Service. Moreover, the small-business exemption did not apply in construction. Thus a case-by-case approach at the Pay Board would result in a large work load from a sector in which controls were largely redundant.

A variety of resolutions were considered that attempted to combine the Pay Board's 5.5 percent standard with the CISC-approved wage rates in local labor markets. In June 1972 the board announced a new policy, which was later spelled out more fully in Pay Board regulations.[18] A new reporting form for nonunion construction, PB-4, was also created, and a small Construction Division, which was essentially a one-man operation, was established within the board.

The first element of the new policy was that the basic 5.5 percent wage standard and the 0.7 percent qualified benefits standard would apply to nonunion construction employees. Category III units granting increases within the standard did not have to report to the board. An exception was available whereby the unit could adopt the CISC dollars-and-cents increment applicable to a comparable craft in the same local area.[19] Thus if

17. The nonunion sector of industrial construction had been growing rapidly in the South. A nonunion contractor estimated the union wage premium as 17 percent in Columbia, S.C.; 24 percent in Charlotte, N.C.; and 54 percent in Atlanta, Ga. (David M. Driscoll, "Nonunion Construction Report," prepared for Pay Board meeting, October 12, 1972.)

18. Pay Board press release PB-97, June 9, 1972, and subpart G of Pay Board regulations, *Federal Register*, November 23, 1972, pp. 24988–89.

19. Whatever roll-up was involved for included benefits was also permitted.

a nonunion unit had a base compensation rate of $5, it could grant up to 27.5 cents without board approval ($5 × 0.055). If in the same area the CISC had approved an increase from $6 to $6.40 for a comparable craft, the nonunion unit could also add 40 cents to its rate. Since 40 cents was more than the 5.5 percent standard would allow, the unit was required to postnotify the board of the adjustment. (No comparable CISC-related exception was available for qualified benefits.)

Nonunion employers were also required to postnotify the board of the rates they had established upon entering a new labor market. Such rates could not exceed the rates approved by the CISC for comparable crafts in the area. An essential-employees exception to the CISC increment or rates could be requested from the Pay Board. Prior approval was required before implementation.

Once they were established, the nonunion construction rules and the cases they covered were not major concerns of the Pay Board. It is possible that many small nonunion construction contractors were unaware of the board's rules. Probably more reports should have been filed with the board than were actually received, but no one felt that the board should encourage the Internal Revenue Service to drum up a work load by searching for noncompliers. Those contractors who did know of the board's requirements often seemed to misunderstand them. Reports were filed unnecessarily concerning increases of 5.5 percent or less. The nonunion construction aspects of the Pay Board's activities were best viewed as defensive tactics in dealing with the CISC and as a symbolic expression of the board's formal commitment to comprehensive coverage.

Regression Results Relating to the Impact
of Phase II on Wage Change

Chapter 10 describes a series of relatively simple wage equations estimated to analyze the trend in wage change during the period immediately
preceding and during the early stages of controls. Table E-1 presents the
coefficients of the independent variables for these regressions. Residuals
from the regressions are discussed in chapter 10 and are shown in table
10-12.

Table E-1. *Wage Equations Used to Analyze Phase II*

Independent variable and summary statistic	Dependent variable and equation number[a]					
	PSTMAN[b]			PCOMP[c]		
	1	2	3	4	5	6
Independent variable[d]						
Constant	−6.15	0.29	0.69	−5.01	0.43	0.59
	(−4.36)	(1.36)	(4.18)	(−4.19)	(2.35)	(4.58)
X_1	7.24	4.08	1.53	5.83	2.53	1.21
	(5.06)	(4.50)	(3.49)	(4.82)	(3.06)	(3.17)
X_2	0.09	−0.33	−0.41	0.15	−0.48	−0.51
	(2.52)	(−3.07)	(−3.84)	(5.26)	(−4.87)	(−5.43)
X_3	0.29	0.26	0.25	0.37	0.34	0.33
	(3.71)	(3.21)	(2.95)	(5.74)	(4.79)	(4.47)
X_4	0.26	0.25	0.23	...	...	...
	(1.89)	(1.74)	(1.59)			
X_5	−0.51	−0.51	−0.54	...	...	...
	(−3.61)	(−3.55)	(−3.63)			
X_6	−1.03	−1.01	−1.04	...	...	...
	(−7.45)	(−7.15)	(−7.23)			
Summary statistic						
$\bar{R}^2$	0.68	0.66	0.65	0.61	0.51	0.54
Standard error	0.44	0.45	0.46	0.37	0.41	0.40
Durbin-Watson	1.61	1.85	1.58	1.80	1.84	1.70

a. The numbers in parentheses are *t* statistics. The equations are estimated over the period 1949:1 to 1969:3.

b. PSTMAN = quarterly percent change in straight-time earnings in manufacturing, not seasonally adjusted.

c. PCOMP = quarterly percentage change in nonfarm compensation per man-hour, seasonally adjusted, with adjustment to remove effect of legally required fringe benefit payroll taxes such as that for social security.

d. In equations 1 and 4, X_1 = ratio of GNP in the private nonfarm sector in 1958 dollars to trend estimated for 1949: 1 to 1973:1; X_2 = quarterly percentage change in private nonfarm output in 1958 dollars in percentage points. In equations 2 and 5, X_1 = inverse of the unemployment rate expressed in percentage points; X_2 = quarterly first difference in the unemployment rate in percentage points. In equations 3 and 6, X_1 = inverse in the unemployment rate for males aged 25–64 expressed in percentage points; X_2 = quarterly first difference in unemployment rate for males aged 25–64 in percentage points. In all equations X_3 = quarterly percentage change in consumer price index in percentage points, lagged one quarter. In equations 1, 2, and 3, X_4 = dummy for first quarter, X_5 = dummy for second quarter, and X_6 = dummy for third quarter.

Regression Analysis Relating to Work Stoppages during Phase II

In chapter 12 an analysis is made of the impact of Phase II wage controls on various measures of industrial relations practices. A key factor in labor-management relations is the availability of the strike-lockout weapon. Table F-1 presents three regression equations estimated to explain the annual change in the number of workers involved in strikes, the number of strikes, and the number of man-days lost in strikes. Phase II is represented by a dummy variable for 1972.

Table F-1. *Equations Explaining the Number, Workers Involved, and Man-Days Lost in Strikes during Phase II*[a]

Independent variable and summary statistic	Annual change		
	Workers involved (thousands)	Number of strikes	Man-days lost (millions)
Independent variable			
Constant	−9,230.8	−8,134.1	−270.2
	(−2.60)	(−2.16)	(−2.75)
Ratio of real GNP to trend[b]	9,764.6	8,235.4	280.8
	(2.72)	(2.16)	(2.83)
Change in real GNP[c]	−73.6	8.9	−1.7
	(−1.68)	(0.19)	(−1.42)
Change in number of workers under contract expirations[d]	340.8	7.9	7.8
	(3.72)	(0.08)	(3.09)
Dummy 72[e]	−1,095.1	−240.6	−7.8
	(−3.33)	(−0.69)	(−0.85)
Summary statistic			
R^2	0.89	0.52	0.76
Durbin-Watson	2.177	1.991	2.331
Standard error	279.4	295.8	7.7

a. The period of estimation is 1961–72. The numbers in parentheses are *t* statistics.
b. In 1958 dollars. Trend is estimated for 1961–74.
c. Annual percentage point change in GNP in 1958 dollars.
d. Annual change in millions of workers under major contract expirations. Expirations are estimated by subtracting workers under deferred agreements from the 10.6 million workers under all major collective bargaining agreements.
e. Dummy equal to 1 in 1972; zero otherwise.

Index

Aavig, Lar, 86n

Abel, I, W., 23, 147n, 228, 262

Administration of Phase II: case processing, 213–23; complexity of, 392–94; efficiency of, 223–24, 236; equity issues and, 388–89; organizational structure for, 211–13; staff for, 209–10, 223–24

Aerospace case: compared with automobile industry negotiations, 169; cutbacks in, 176–80; escalator clause in, 170, 250–51; negotiations, 169–73; Pay Board and, 168, 170–71, 173–80, 206, 207; residual cost of living adjustment in, 171–72, 173, 174, 175, 179; status of "roll-up" in, 171–72, 178. *See also* United Automobile, Aerospace and Agricultural Implement Workers

AFL-CIO, 263; convention, *1971*, 44, 45, 49; criticism of ban on deferred wage increases, 8, 33; criticism of wage freeze, 6–9, 11; merger, 169; opposition to Nixon administration, 280, 398; reaction to CLC rulings, 279; support for comprehensive coverage, 118. *See also* Labor members of Pay Board

Ahalt, J. Dawson, 139n, 406n

Alinsky, Saul, 140n

Amalgamated Meat Cutters and Butcher Workmen of North America, 8, 244–45, 360

Amalgamated Transit Union, 246

American Federation of Labor (AFL), 169. *See also* AFL-CIO

Appeals procedure, 215, 217–18, 221, 223, 235, 236. *See also* Cases and Appeals Panel

Athletes, professional, 125–27, 135

Autoregressive integrated moving average (ARIMA) technique, 313n

Average hourly earnings, 289–91

Azevedo, Ross E., 68n, 87n, 317n, 330n, 363n, 385n

Baltimore and Ohio Railroad, 156

Bannon, Ken, 177

Bassett, Robert C., 23, 147, 257; resolution, 127n; as small-business representative, 24, 39, 263–64

BCOA. *See* Bituminous Coal Operators Association

Beach, Dale S., 79n

Beck, Dave, 25

Bentsen, Lloyd M., Jr., 94n

Berlin, Jeffrey, 365n

Berry, Robert, 313n

Biaggini, Benjamin F., 23, 147, 273; resolution, 163, 166, 167–68

Bituminous coal case, 56, 62n; negotiations, 141–42; Pay Board hearing on, 145–48; Pay Board ruling on, 149–52, 205–06, 207, 259; terms of contract, 142–45

Bituminous Coal Operators Association (BCOA), 140, 142, 146

Blough, Roger M., 231, 264–65

BLS. *See* Bureau of Labor Statistics

BNA. *See* Bureau of National Affairs

Boeing Company, 169, 170, 173

Boldt, George H., 26, 146n, 176, 179, 235, 257, 335n, 367n; background of, 24–25, 26, 271, 274; CISC and, 228, 229, 231; as Pay Board chairman, 25, 147, 268; response to AFL-CIO criticism, 277; role in establishing Pay Board policy, 44, 45, 48, 51–52; voting, 151, 163, 166, 168

Bolton, Lena W., 32n, 111n, 120n, 227n, 248n, 305n, 311n, 359n, 367n, 368n, 370n, 372n

Bornstein, Leon, 120n, 359n

Boyle, W. A. (Tony), 141, 147–48, 259

Bredhoff, Elliot, 262

Brennan, Joseph, 144n, 148

Bridges, Harry, 183, 186, 200

Brinner, Roger, 307n

Brittain, John A., 55n, 285n

Brotherhood of Locomotive Engineers, 153, 155, 161

Brotherhood of Railroad Signalmen (BRS), 152, 155, 159; Pay Board review of contract, 161, 162–63

Brunner, Karl, 313n

Bureau of the Census, 118n, 132

445